Form Design Menus

File
- New ▸
- Close
- Save — Ctrl+S
- Save As...
- Save As Report...
- Output To...
- Print Setup...
- Print Preview
- Print... — Ctrl+P
- Print Definition...
- Send...
- Run Macro...
- Add-ins ▸
- Exit

Edit
- Can't Undo — Ctrl+Z
- Cut — Ctrl+X
- Copy — Ctrl+C
- Paste — Ctrl+V
- Paste Special...
- Delete — Del
- Duplicate
- Select All — Ctrl+A
- Select Form
- Insert Object...
- Links...
- Object
- Tab Order...

View
- √ Form Design
- Form
- Datasheet
- Field List...
- Properties...
- Code...
- √ Ruler
- √ Grid
- Toolbox
- Palette
- √ Control Wizards
- Toolbars...
- Options...

Format
- Apply Default
- Change Default
- Bring to Front
- Send to Back
- √ Snap to Grid
- Align ▸
- Size ▸
- Horizontal Spacing ▸
- Vertical Spacing ▸
- Page Header/Footer
- √ Form Header/Footer

Report Design Menus

File
- New ▸
- Close
- Save — Ctrl+S
- Save As...
- Output To...
- Print Setup...
- Sample Preview
- Print Preview
- Print... — Ctrl+P
- Print Definition...
- Send...
- Run Macro...
- Add-ins ▸
- Exit

Edit
- Can't Undo — Ctrl+Z
- Cut — Ctrl+X
- Copy — Ctrl+C
- Paste — Ctrl+V
- Paste Special...
- Delete — Del
- Duplicate
- Select All — Ctrl+A
- Select Report
- Insert Object...
- Links...
- Object

View
- Sorting and Grouping...
- Field List...
- Properties...
- Code...
- √ Ruler
- √ Grid
- Toolbox
- Palette
- √ Control Wizards
- Toolbars...
- Options...

Format
- Apply Default
- Change Default
- Bring to Front
- Send to Back
- √ Snap to Grid
- Align ▸
- Size ▸
- Horizontal Spacing ▸
- Vertical Spacing ▸
- √ Page Header/Footer
- √ Report Header/Footer

FOR EVERY KIND OF COMPUTER USER, THERE IS A SYBEX BOOK.

All computer users learn in their own way. Some need straightforward and methodical explanations. Others are just too busy for this approach. But no matter what camp you fall into, SYBEX has a book that can help you get the most out of your computer and computer software while learning at your own pace.

Beginners generally want to start at the beginning. The **ABC's** series, with its step-by-step lessons in plain language, helps you build basic skills quickly. Or you might try our **Quick & Easy** series, the friendly, full-color guide.

The **Mastering** and **Understanding** series will tell you everything you need to know about a subject. They're perfect for intermediate and advanced computer users, yet they don't make the mistake of leaving beginners behind.

If you're a busy person and are already comfortable with computers, you can choose from two SYBEX series—**Up & Running** and **Running Start**. The **Up & Running** series gets you started in just 20 lessons. Or you can get two books in one, a step-by-step tutorial and an alphabetical reference, with our **Running Start** series.

Everyone who uses computer software can also use a computer software reference. SYBEX offers the gamut—from portable **Instant References** to comprehensive **Encyclopedias**, **Desktop References**, and **Bibles**.

SYBEX even offers special titles on subjects that don't neatly fit a category—like **Tips & Tricks**, the **Shareware Treasure Chests**, and a wide range of books for Macintosh computers and software.

SYBEX books are written by authors who are expert in their subjects. In fact, many make their living as professionals, consultants, or teachers in the field of computer software. And their manuscripts are thoroughly reviewed by our technical and editorial staff for accuracy and ease of use.

So when you want answers about computers or any popular software package, just help yourself to SYBEX.

FOR A BROCHURE OF OUR PUBLICATIONS, PLEASE WRITE:

SYBEX Inc.
2021 Challenger Drive
Alameda, CA 94501
Tel: (510) 523-8233/(800) 227-2346 Telex: 336311
Fax: (510) 523-2373

SYBEX is committed to using natural resources wisely to preserve and improve our environment. As a leader in the computer book publishing industry, we are aware that over 40% of America's solid waste is paper. This is why we have been printing the text of books like this one on recycled paper since 1982.

This year our use of recycled paper will result in the saving of more than 15,300 trees. We will lower air pollution effluents by 54,000 pounds, save 6,300,000 gallons of water, and reduce landfill by 2,700 cubic yards.

In choosing a SYBEX book you are not only making a choice for the best in skills and information, you are also choosing to enhance the quality of life for all of us.

Your First Access® Database

Miriam Liskin

San Francisco
Paris
Düsseldorf
Soest

Acquisitions Editor: Joanne Cuthbertson
Developmental Editor: David Peal
Editor: Dusty Bernard
Project Editor: Michelle Khazai
Technical Editor: Frank J. Seidel, Jr.
Book Designer: Helen Bruno
Chapter & Production Artist: Charlotte Carter
Technical Art: Delia Brown-Warren
Screen Graphics: Aldo X. Bermudez
Page Layout and Typesetting: Deborah Maizels and Len Gilbert
Proofreader/Production Coordinator: Janet K. Boone
Indexer: Miriam Liskin
Cover Designer: Design Site
Cover Photographer: David Bishop
SYBEX is a registered trademark of SYBEX Inc.

Library of Congress Card Number: 94-65687
ISBN: 0-7821-1540-3

Manufactured in the United States of America
10 9 8 7 6 5 4 3 2 1

ACKNOWLEDGMENTS

First I'd like to thank the Access team at Microsoft for this new and improved version of the program.

Thanks to my agent, Linda Allen, for giving me wise advice and following it up with hard work.

Thanks to Joanne Cuthbertson and David Peal at SYBEX for not typecasting me.

My thanks to technical editor Frank Seidel for doing such a thorough and careful job and project editor Michelle Khazai for pulling everything together. On the editorial side, thanks to copy editor Dusty Bernard for affirming the precedence of function over form and for improving the quality and clarity of my prose without diluting my style.

On a personal level, thanks to Cliff Krouse and Peter Harrington for vibrant neon and dinner conversation to match. Let's do it again real soon, 975 miles from here.

And to Peter, a toast to future explorations, starting at Nine Mile Rock and ending up who knows where.

CONTENTS AT A GLANCE

TABLE OF CONTENTS

INTRODUCTION

Access is a powerful and flexible database manager that was designed by Microsoft for a broad spectrum of users, ranging from complete beginners to programmers who develop customized database applications. The good news is that you won't "outgrow" Access as your databases increase in size and complexity. The bad news is that any program with as many features and capabilities as Access can be a bit intimidating at first.

This book will get you up and running with Microsoft Access as quickly as possible by leading you through the database design process one step at a time. After you've mastered the basics, you can begin exploring more advanced features and capabilities as the need arises.

Once you've learned a little about how databases work, Access is easy to use. If you've worked with other Windows software you'll feel right at home—all Windows programs share a similar user interface and menu structure. True to form, you'll find the familiar File, Edit, Window, and Help pull-downs on the Access menu bar (although some of the options may be different), and if you've ever opened a document in a Windows word processor, you'll recognize the dialog box Access uses to open a database.

HOW THIS BOOK IS ORGANIZED

Although the Access interface is very user friendly, databases are intrinsically more difficult to conceptualize than the documents you produce with a word processor or desktop publishing program or the worksheets you build using a spreadsheet program. When you set up a database, a lot more planning and preparation go into producing a computerized replica of a single paper form. And even if you're a beginner, your database may not be small or simple. Database programs like Access can be used to model very complex business problems that might present formidable difficulties if you were trying to set up a manual record-keeping system.

That's why this book begins by introducing some fundamental database concepts and terminology and follows up with a chapter on how to plan your database on paper just when you'll probably be most eager to begin working with Access. Even if you've used other database programs, don't skip these all-important planning steps. If you're a complete beginner, Chapter 3 will demystify the database design process and give you a straightforward method for laying out the structure of your database.

Once you've set up your database, you'll learn to use the built-in data forms to enter, edit, delete, and view data. You'll learn to rearrange data into different orders, carry out calculations, and work with various subsets of your data. Finally, you'll learn to build custom data entry forms, graphs, and reports and how to do mailings in Access and with your word processor.

This book guides you through the process of building an Access database using a single example—a simple personal or business organizer—as a case study. This system is small, and you won't have to enter a lot of data to try all the examples. When you finish this book, the sample database can become the core of your own organizer application if you need one. Even if you don't, the basic procedures and techniques you'll learn will serve you in good stead when you set up your first Access database on your own.

GETTING HELP

Access offers some special tools for beginners, chief among them Cue Cards and Wizards, and this book shows how to use them to your advantage. Cue Cards, which are part of an auxiliary help system, can prompt you through a complex task with step-by-step instructions that remain on the screen while you work. With this book in front of you, you won't need Cue Cards, but you might find them a valuable aid later on.

The Wizards are on-line assistants that automate the creation of tables, queries, data entry forms, graphs, and reports. Each Wizard presents a series of dialog boxes that ask you questions about the data and appearance of the object you want to create and then automatically create it for you. Using the Wizards is the ideal way to get started because you'll never find yourself facing a completely blank screen and wondering what steps to take and in what order.

This book makes heavy use of the Wizards provided for creating forms and reports, and you may continue to use them even after you no longer consider yourself a beginner. Using the Wizards doesn't limit your options in any way, because the documents they create are no different from the ones you might build from scratch. If you're not completely satisfied with the Wizards' work (and often, you won't be), you can modify the resulting documents later to fine-tune and enhance them.

WHAT YOU NEED TO KNOW TO USE THIS BOOK

You won't need any knowledge of database theory, concepts, or terminology or any prior experience with other database programs to use this book. However, it does assume that you have a basic familiarity with your computer, keyboard, and mouse and that you can find your way around in Windows. It assumes that Windows and Access are already installed on your computer; if this isn't the case, you'll want to install either or both, following the easy instructions provided with the software.

CONVENTIONS USED IN THIS BOOK

When a term is first defined in this book, it appears in *italics*. Information you are required to enter (either by typing or by making selections from lists) appears in **boldface**. Menu choices are indicated by the symbol ➤. For example, "Choose Open from the File menu" is written as "Choose File ➤ Open."

HOW TO USE THIS BOOK

This book introduces all of the concepts and skills you'll need to build a real-world database application. If your application is simple, you'll learn most of what you need to know right here. If your needs are more complicated, you'll want to follow up by reading a more advanced book, such as Alan Simpson's *Understanding Microsoft Access 2* (SYBEX, 1994). By then you'll be well equipped to understand the vocabulary and concepts in the Access *User's Guide* manual and on-line help screens.

You'll get the most out of this book if you read it seated at your computer and take the time to enter the sample data and work through all the examples. This is a very safe way to experiment with new concepts and new commands, because you won't be risking your own valuable data. And experimentation is the key to solidifying your understanding of what you read. Give yourself the time to get comfortable with Access before you embark on a brand new database project. Relax. Have fun.

Introducing Database Management

This chapter introduces the basic database concepts and terminology you'll need to understand before you can work effectively with Access and presents a brief tour of the methods Access uses to carry out the fundamental database operations. If Access is your first database program, this chapter will clarify just what a database program is, what it can do for you, and when it might be better *not* to use a database. If you've worked with other PC database programs and have some familiarity with the basic concepts, pay special attention to any differences in terminology.

WHAT IS A DATABASE PROGRAM?

As the name suggests, a *database program* allows you store and manipulate data. What kind of data? Well, that's entirely up to you. You could use Access to manage donor and contribution information for a nonprofit organization; keep track of customers, inventory, and invoices for a small business; or store patient medical histories and billing data for a medical office. On a more personal level, you could maintain an address and telephone list or catalog your books, videotapes, or music collection.

NOTE

You may also encounter the terms database manager *and* database management system *(DBMS) to describe programs like Access. Sometimes the term* database *is used informally for the same purpose, but this usage is incorrect and misleading—in Access the word* database *refers to the collection of data and forms you are managing, not to the software itself.*

In this respect Access resembles other general-purpose software like word processors and spreadsheet programs. You can use the same word processing program to produce documents that range in type and complexity from simple one-page letters or memos to two-column newsletters with embedded pictures and graphics, or even to full-length books like this one. Similarly, a spreadsheet program does not dictate the contents of your worksheets, which might calculate budgets, sales forecasts, financial statements, loan amortization schedules, or construction estimates.

You don't have to learn any formal database theory to understand what Access can do for you; the most intuitive way to understand database software is in terms of what it does. Regardless of the type of data you need to manage, a database program lets you carry out these fundamental operations:

- Define the real-world entities your database will track and create a structured format for storing the individual items of information you need to maintain about each entity
- Enter, edit, and delete data

- Retrieve data according to a variety of search criteria
- Design custom screen forms for viewing, entering, and updating data
- Design reports, labels, graphs, and screen displays to present selected information in clear, attractive formats
- Work with subsets of the data that satisfy a variety of selection criteria
- View or print data sorted into different orders
- Perform calculations and display or print the results
- Carry out maintenance activities such as importing, exporting, archiving, and purging data

Later in this chapter you'll see how Access carries out these basic database operations.

NOTE

This book uses the term **entity** ***to describe something in the real world that you need to track in your database. An entity might be a type of person (a patient, customer, vendor, or student), a tangible object (an inventory item, book, or record), or a more abstract concept (a general ledger account, invoice, or payment). For each entity, your database will contain many individual instances (many patients, students, inventory items, or payments). Correctly identifying the entities and deciding how best to represent them are crucial steps in designing an Access application.***

Even if you haven't worked with a general-purpose database program like Access, you may have had some contact with computerized databases. Accounting packages, sales contact managers, personal information managers (PIMs), medical billing programs, and job-costing systems are also database managers. The difference is that these specialized programs give you little or no control over the format of the information they store and the ways you can manipulate this data. If you wanted to add a second telephone number to your customer file or change the layout of your accounts receivable journal, you'd probably be out of luck.

In contrast, Access gives you complete freedom to design a system tailored to your own unique requirements and idiosyncrasies. The price you pay for this flexibility is the time you'll spend mastering the program. If you can find a packaged program that fulfills most of your requirements, you'll be up and running a lot more quickly. If you can't find or can't afford commercial software, or if you just want to build your own system, you'll find there's very little you can't accomplish with Access if you are willing to put the time and effort into learning how to do it.

THE ADVANTAGES OF COMPUTERIZING

If you read the list of fundamental database operations in the previous section and thought, "Wait a minute. These activities don't require a computer," you're absolutely right. If you've ever looked up a name in the telephone book, used the card catalog in a library, kept a paper bookkeeping system, or filled out a personnel form or insurance application, you've worked with a database. Computerized database managers like Access let you carry out the same data management tasks a lot more quickly—so much more quickly that operations you wouldn't have attempted by hand become feasible.

You will benefit the most from using a database program when

- You can enter information once and then display or print it in a variety of different formats or different orders
- You need to search for data according to many different criteria
- The ability to produce more timely reports helps you make better management decisions

- The ability to compile summary statistics enables you to produce reports that would be prohibitively time consuming by hand

If the information you need to manage or the output you need to produce isn't particularly structured—for example, if it consists primarily of long text passages—it might be better to use a word processor or text-indexing program. If you need to do a lot of complex calculations but not much sorting, selecting, or printing of formatted reports, a spreadsheet program might be a better choice.

It's just as important to be realistic about where computerizing can't help you at all. It usually takes just as long to enter data into the computer as it would to write or type the same information on a paper form. If a given data item already exists on paper and all you plan to do with it is display or print it in approximately the same form, you'll usually be better off leaving it out of your database.

DATABASE TERMINOLOGY

Although this book strives to minimize the use of jargon and explain database concepts in plain English, some specialized terminology is unavoidable. For one thing, you'll encounter it in the Access reference manuals and the on-line help screens—resources you'll consult frequently as you learn to use Access. For another, some of these "technical terms" are common English words that are used quite differently in colloquial speech, and not knowing the special meanings might lead you to misinterpret what you read in the Access manuals. Furthermore, a little jargon isn't always a bad thing. In any field—medicine, engineering, construction, and sports, to name just a few—learning the specialized vocabulary lets you express some complex concepts very concisely and unambiguously.

NOTE

If you've used other database programs on your PC, keep in mind that there are significant differences in terminology between Access and programs such as dBASE, FoxPro, and Paradox.

In Access, the term *database* describes the collection of data, forms, and instructions for manipulating the data that makes up a business (or personal) application. All these database components are stored in a single disk file, which has the extension .MDB. You can have as many databases as you wish (or have room for on your hard disk), but you can directly view only one at a time. You'll generally want to create a database for each discrete data management project. Thus, a small business might have a mailing list database, an inventory database, and an accounting database.

NOTE

Although only one database can be open at a time, Access allows you to work with data stored in other databases by **importing** ***or*** **attaching** ***the data.***

The data in an Access database is stored in objects called *tables.* An individual instance of the entity stored in a table is called a *record,* and each of the items of information that describe this entity is called a *field.* Thus, a personnel database might include an Employees table, with a record devoted to each employee. Each record in turn has fields for the name, address, telephone number, date of birth, date hired, social security number, salary, and photograph. The default display mode for Access data is a tabular layout (shown later in this chapter, in Figure 1.2) in which each record occupies one row and each field has its own column. Consequently, the terms *row* and *column* are often used interchangeably with *record* and *field.*

Database programs that let you work with multiple related tables are described as *relational.* Programs that can access only one table at a time are called *flat-file managers,* or simply *file managers.*

Although you might occasionally create a database with just one table, such as a mailing list database, nearly all Access applications need two or more (sometimes many) tables. Some of these tables will be entirely separate, while others are related in obvious ways. For example, in a retail sales application there is no direct connection between customers and vendors. However, customers and orders are related—when you look at a customer, you want to see all of that customer's orders, and when you see an order, you want to know which customer placed it—and vendors and payments are related in much the same way. As you'll see in Chapter 2, defining the relationships between tables is a central aspect of system design.

In addition to the tables, which store the data, an Access database can include five other types of objects:

- *Queries:* Instructions for selecting data subsets, sorting (displaying records in different orders), performing calculations, and carrying out table maintenance operations
- *Forms:* Custom screen layouts used for viewing, entering, and updating data
- *Reports:* Custom layouts for printing lists and labels
- *Macros:* Sequences of commands that you can play back later
- *Modules:* Programs written in Access Basic

NOTE

Chapters 5 through 12 will explore queries, forms, and reports. This book does not cover macros or modules.

HOW ACCESS MANAGES DATA

By now you're probably impatient to see how you can put to work the rather abstract definition of database management presented earlier in this chapter. To satisfy your curiosity and whet your appetite for more, here is a brief guided tour of how Access carries out the essential database operations.

DEFINING THE DATA STORAGE FORMATS

You define the structure of an Access table by naming the fields, describing the type of data each may contain (for example, dates, times, numbers, text, photographs) and, if you wish, specifying other details such as a custom display format, default value, validation rules, and other specialized properties. Access provides a *Wizard* (an on-line assistant) that simplifies and automates the process of creating tables by allowing you to choose from a list of predefined fields. If you want more control, you can use the Table Design screen shown in Figure 1.1 to modify tables created by the Table Wizard or to create tables from scratch. Chapter 4 describes how to use both of these methods to create tables.

ENTERING, VIEWING, AND UPDATING DATA

You can update a table or view the result of running a query without designing a custom form by using a built-in display mode called Datasheet view, which is shown in Figure 1.2. Access provides menu commands and controls in the Datasheet window that you can manipulate directly with the mouse to customize the datasheet layout,

FIGURE 1.1 ▸

When you define a table, you specify a name, a data type, and, if you wish, additional properties for each field.

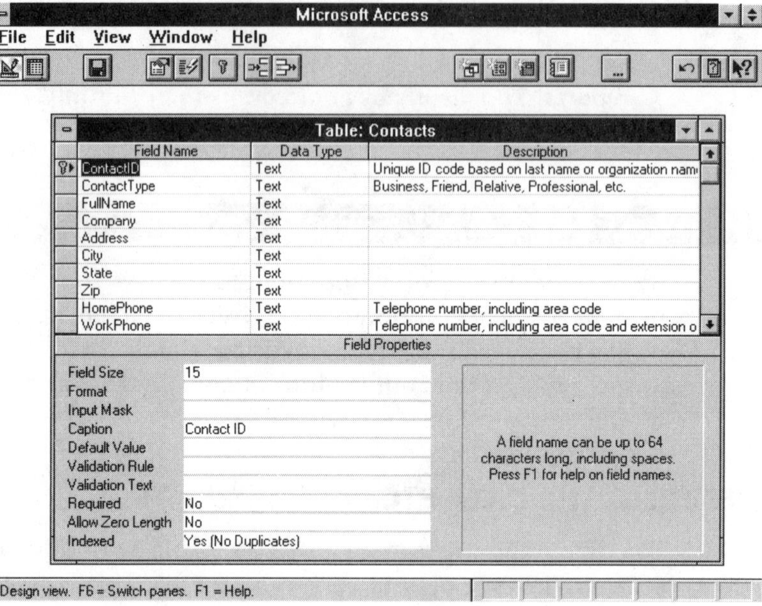

Field Name	Data Type	Description
ContactID	Text	Unique ID code based on last name or organization nam
ContactType	Text	Business, Friend, Relative, Professional, etc.
FullName	Text	
Company	Text	
Address	Text	
City	Text	
State	Text	
Zip	Text	
HomePhone	Text	Telephone number, including area code
WorkPhone	Text	Telephone number, including area code and extension o

Field Properties

Field Size	15
Format	
Input Mask	
Caption	Contact ID
Default Value	
Validation Rule	
Validation Text	
Required	No
Allow Zero Length	No
Indexed	Yes (No Duplicates)

FIGURE 1.2 ▸

In Datasheet view, each record occupies one row, and each column displays the data in one field.

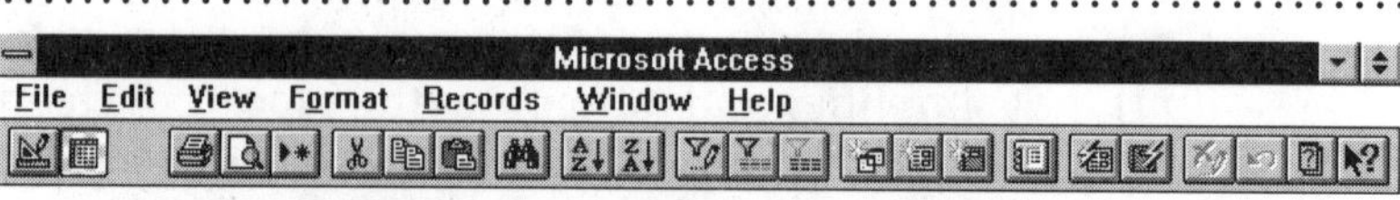

Table: Contacts

Contact ID	Contact Type	Name	Company	Address
ActiveAdventure	Travel	Vera	Active Adventures Travel	940 Solano Ave.
Adams	Graphic Design	Jeffrey Adams		2400 Mariner Squar
Allen	Contractors	Christopher Allen	Allen Electric	825 Kains Ave.
Beverly	Friend	Frank Beverly		8572 Prospect Ave.
Davis	Family	Peter and Laura Davis		215 W 16th St.
Fong	Friend	Melanie Fong		2819 Oak Rd. Apt.
FutureDesigns	Contractors	Marilyn Williams	Future Designs	305 D St.
JacksonOBrien	Contractors	Ann Jackson and Kathe	Gemini Plumbing	2605 Fulton St.
Klein	Friend	Don and Janet Klein		1783 Vallejo St. Apt
MasterBuilders	Contractors	Michael A. Barton	Master Builders	PO Box 5187
Plummer	Friend	Fern Plummer		2910 Ellis St.
QuickPrint	Graphic Design	Barbara Stevenson	Quick Print	362 Grand Ave.
Rainbow	Contractors	George Roth	Rainbow Painters	4610 Doyle St.
RedRock	Travel	Jim McKenna	Red Rock Tours	420 S. Main St.
Rosenberg	Friend	Norman Rosenberg		2218 E. Glenoaks B
Sanders	Family	The Sanders Family		1482 NE 17th St. A
Santorelli	Friend	Linda Santorelli		1738 Sacramento S
TrueType	Graphic Design		True Type Typesetters	1254 Euclid Ave.

Record: 1 of 20

Unique ID code based on last name or organization name

navigate through the table, add new records, and delete existing records. You can update data simply by moving to the appropriate cell in the datasheet and editing or typing over the contents. Each datasheet displays one table, but you can open more than one datasheet at a time. Chapter 5 describes how to update tables in Datasheet view.

DESIGNING CUSTOM INPUT FORMS

If the default Datasheet view doesn't satisfy all your table update requirements, you can design custom screen forms like the one shown in Figure 1.3. Access provides Wizards to help you build several very common form layouts, so it's easy to get started. You can use custom forms to tailor the data entry environment to the specific needs of individual users or different tasks or to expedite data entry by replicating the paper forms you're already using to collect data. Unless your table structures are very large, you can usually fit all the fields on the screen at the same time, so you won't have to scroll back and forth in

FIGURE 1.3 *You can design custom forms that replace the default datasheet for viewing and updating tables.*

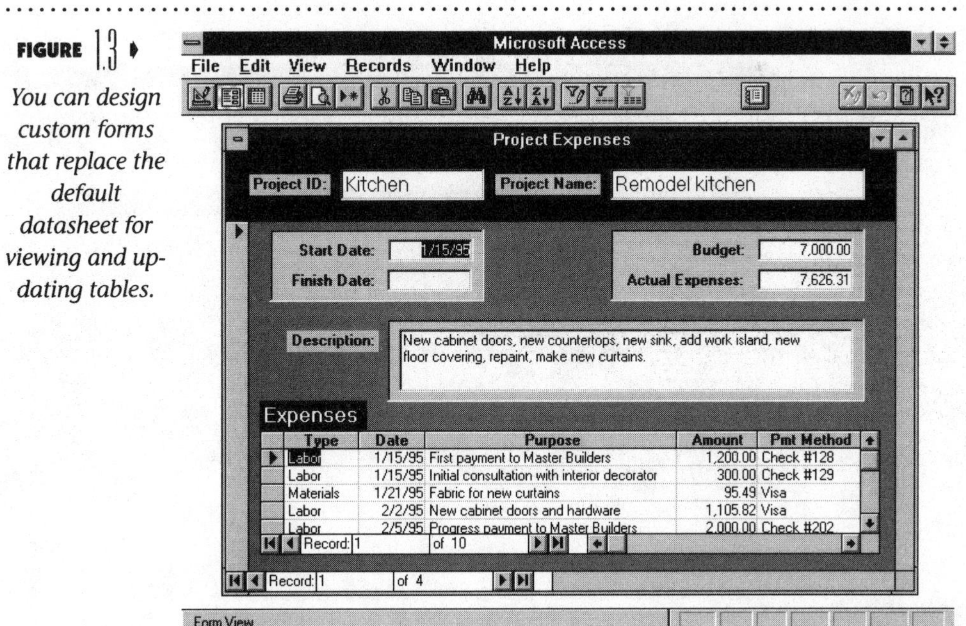

Datasheet view to see a whole record. Unlike datasheets, forms aren't limited to displaying data from a single table or query; you can design complex forms like invoices or customer ledger sheets, which include related records from two (or more) tables.

SORTING AND SELECTING RECORDS

You can use queries and filters (a *filter* is a special type of query used in Datasheet view and with custom forms) to work with specific subsets of data derived from one or more tables and to sort this data into different orders. The result of running a query is functionally equivalent to a table—you can display the data described by a query in Datasheet view or on a custom form, print it on a report, or use it as the data source for a graph. For example, in a project-tracking database, you could use a query to display information from a Project table and an Expense table, sorted into chronological order. Figure 1.4 shows how you'd create this query, and Chapter 6 describes the process in more detail.

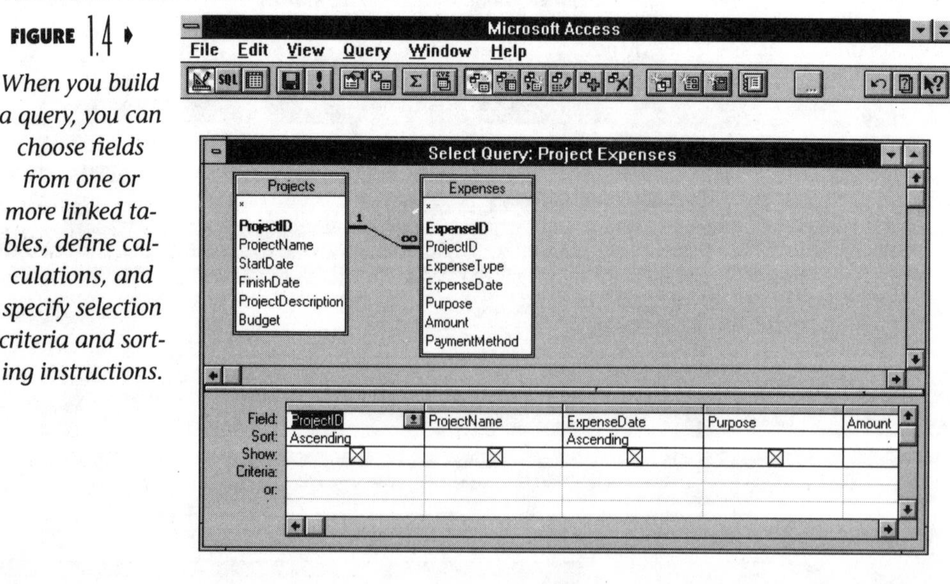

FIGURE 1.4 *When you build a query, you can choose fields from one or more linked tables, define calculations, and specify selection criteria and sorting instructions.*

The power of Access queries goes far beyond these simple examples. You can define queries that perform complex calculations, compute summary statistics, update records en masse, and copy obsolete records to archive tables. Chapter 10 gives you an overview of the possibilities.

DISPLAYING AND PRINTING OUTPUT

Access allows you to print virtually any data you can view on the screen, either in Datasheet view or using a custom form, in approximately the same layout. In most databases, you'll also need to print formatted reports ranging in complexity from simple tabular listings like the example in Figure 1.5 to reports with subtotal groups and

FIGURE 1.5

An Access report can include data from one or more linked tables.

Project Expenses

02-Mar-95

Project: **Remodel kitchen**

New cabinet doors, new countertops, new sink, add work island, new floor covering, repaint, make new curtains.

Started: 1/15/95

Finished:

Date	Exp Type	Purpose	Amount	Pmt Method
1/15/95	Labor	Initial consultation with interior decorator	300.00	Check #129
1/15/95	Labor	First payment to Master Builders	1,200.00	Check #128
1/21/95	Materials	Fabric for new curtains	95.49	Visa
2/2/95	Labor	New cabinet doors and hardware	1,105.82	Visa
2/5/95	Labor	Progress payment to Master Builders	2,000.00	Check #202
2/13/95	Labor	Allen Electric	465.00	Check #231
2/15/95	Labor	Gemini Plumbing	320.00	Check #243
2/16/95	Labor	Final payment to Master Builders	1,100.00	Check #250
2/16/95	Labor	Final payment to interior decorator	400.00	Check #249
2/16/95	Labor	Rainbow Painters	640.00	Check #248
		Total Expenses:	**$7,626.31**	
		Project Budget:	**$7,000.00**	

Page 1

summary statistics, graphs, and multitable forms like invoices or order forms. You can use Wizards to produce several standard report layouts, which you can later modify if they're not perfect, or you can build reports from scratch.

WHAT'S NEXT?

Armed with your new understanding of what a database program can do for you, you're probably impatient to put Access to work. Chapter 2 gives you a hands-on guided tour of Access to prepare you for setting up your first database management project.

Introducing Microsoft Access

This chapter introduces you to Microsoft Access and gives you a brief hands-on guided tour of the working environment, the user interface, and the on-line help system. If you've used other Windows programs, you'll feel right at home, and you can get through this chapter very quickly. If not, you'll be learning about Windows as well as about Access. Don't get discouraged if you feel a bit lost at first—the time you spend mastering the Access user interface will stand you in good stead when you learn your *next* Windows program.

This chapter reviews the essentials of the graphical user interface, or GUI, and tells you everything you'll need to know to use the Access menus, manipulate program and document windows, and find the information you need in the help system. It does assume some familiarity with your keyboard, mouse, and video display and with Windows concepts and terminology. You should know where the special keys (Esc, Ctrl, Alt, Ins, Del, and so on) are on your keyboard and understand how to point, click, and drag with the mouse.

STARTING AND QUITTING ACCESS

You can start up Access from the Windows Program Manager using the same methods you'd use to launch any other Windows program. Here's the easiest way:

1. Make sure the Microsoft Access or Microsoft Office program group window is open.
2. Double-click the Microsoft Access program icon.

TIP

If someone else installed your copy of Access and you're not sure where the Access program icon is, try looking for a group called Microsoft Office (the default group used by the Access Setup program), Access, or Microsoft Access. If you can't see all the icons on the desktop, pull down the Program Manager Window menu and search through the list of program group windows.

TIP

If you use Access often, leave the Access program group window open so it is always visible in the Program Manager window. If you use Access in every work session, add the Access program icon to your Startup group so it starts up automatically each time you load Windows.

To exit from Access, you can use any of the methods that close all Windows programs:

- Press Alt+F4.
- Choose File ➤ Exit.
- Click the close box in the upper-left corner of the Access program window, and then choose Close from the pull-down menu.
- Double-click the close box in the upper-left corner of the Access program window.

Take a moment to start up Access right now so you can follow along with the examples in this chapter.

When you start up Access for the very first time, it displays the startup screen shown in Figure 2.1. If you want more information about any of the topics, you can click the adjacent button. To start right in working with Access, simply double-click the close box to close the window. If you don't want to see this screen again, check the box marked **Don't display this startup card again** before you close the window.

FIGURE 2.1 ▸

The startup screen suggests ways to get started using Access.

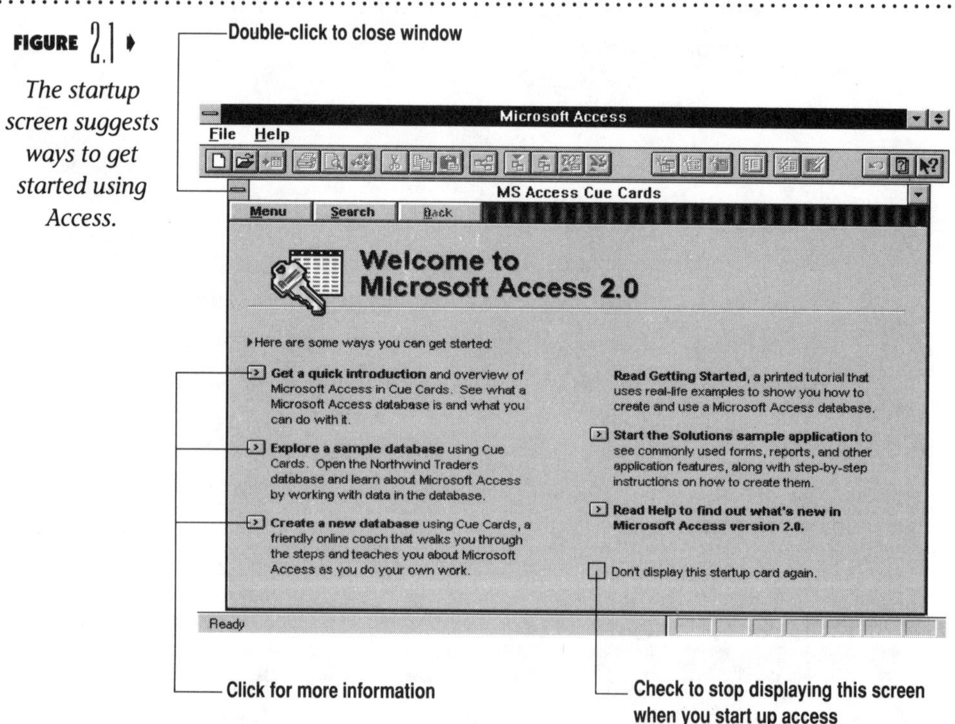

THE ACCESS PROGRAM WINDOW

When you first install Access, the program starts up in a window, which you can move and resize to suit your preferences using the controls labeled in Figure 2.2. Nearly all of the other figures in this book

FIGURE 2.2 ▸

You can use the mouse to move, resize, maximize, or minimize the Access program window.

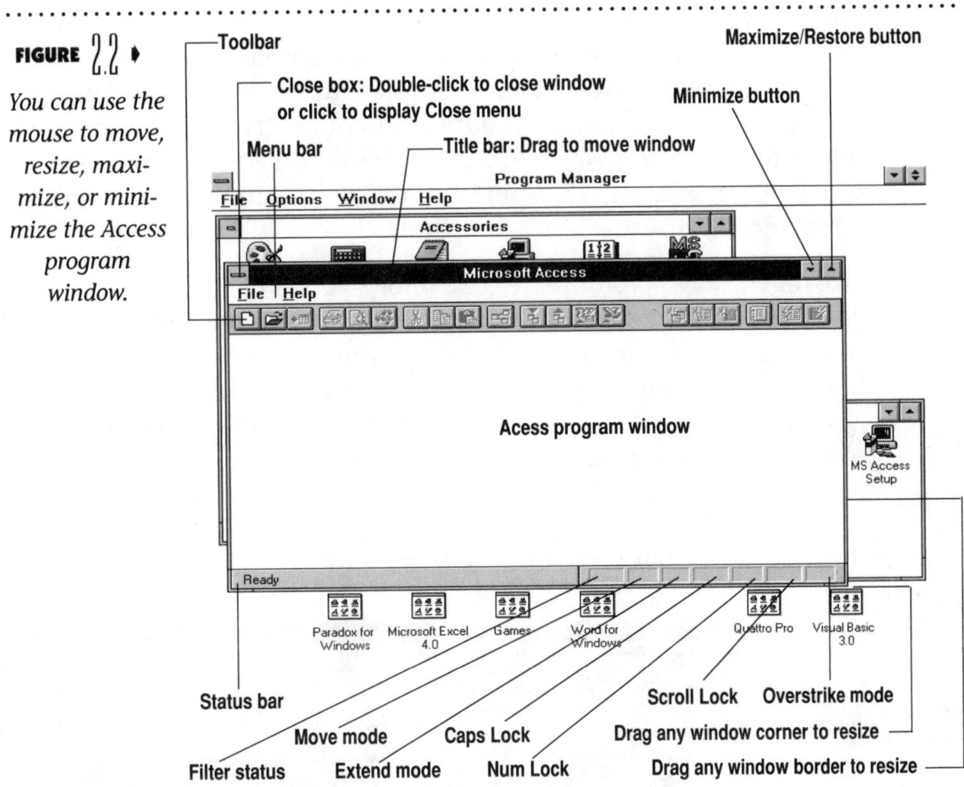

will show the Access program window maximized so it occupies the entire screen. You'll probably want to maximize the Access window most of the time yourself, unless you're moving data between Access and another Windows program.

At the top of the Access program window, below the title bar, is the *menu bar,* and below the menu bar is a *toolbar* consisting of a row of command buttons. Both the menu and the toolbar are dynamic and context sensitive—they change to reflect the demands of the task at hand. Don't try to memorize the structure of the menus or toolbars; you can always browse through the menu options to find the command you need.

The *status bar* at the bottom of the Access program window displays additional information about the working environment. The left side of the status bar is reserved for messages that describe the currently selected menu option, toolbar button, or data entry field. On the right side of the status bar, seven indicators monitor the status of the keyboard toggles (Caps Lock, Num Lock, and so on) and special operational modes.

Like all Windows programs, Access allows you to open more than one document window at a time. In Figure 2.3 you can see four windows: two Datasheet windows, a Form Design window, and a small corner of the Database window. As you can see in Figure 2.3, *scroll bars* appear just inside the bottom and/or right border of any window when the contents won't all fit in the window at once.

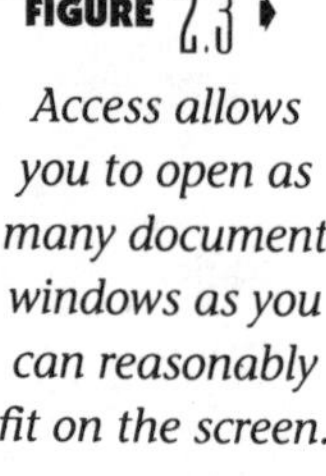

FIGURE 2.3 ▸

Access allows you to open as many document windows as you can reasonably fit on the screen.

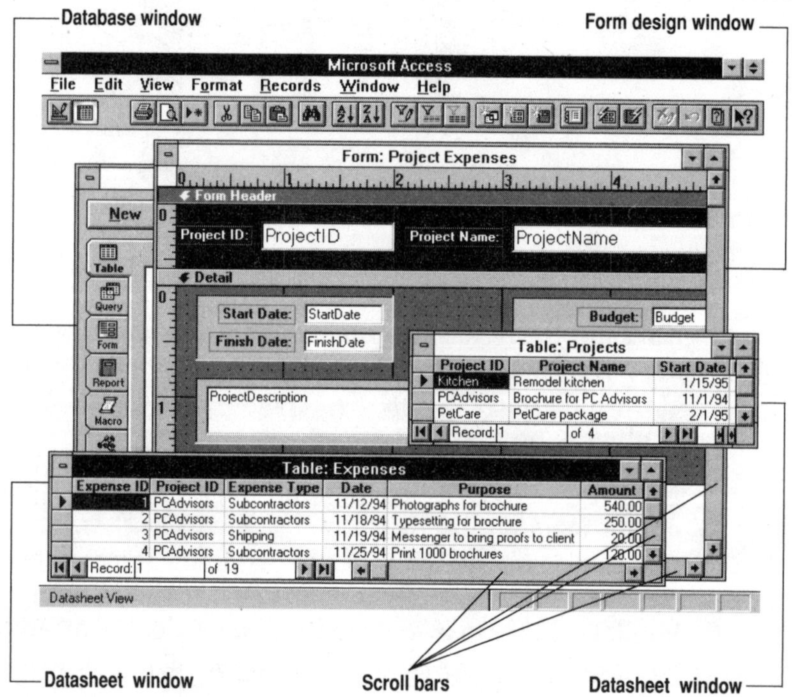

NOTE

In Windows, the term document is used in a broad sense to describe any object whose contents you can control, including tables, queries, screen forms, and reports.

You can use the mouse to rearrange the windows on the Access desktop, just as you might move papers around on your desk. To bring any document window to the top of the "stack" so you can work in it, click in the window or choose its name from the list on the Window menu.

TIP

Try to overlap your document windows so that at least a small portion of each is visible at all times. This way you can switch documents by clicking in the desired window.

USING THE ACCESS MENU BAR

The Access menu bar consists of a series of options, each of which has a pull-down menu attached. Until you open a database you can't do much, and there are only two options on the main menu: File and Help. Figure 2.4 illustrates the Access program window with a database open (you'll learn how to open a database shortly) and the File menu pulled down.

Menu options that are temporarily unavailable are displayed *grayed out* to remind you that you can't select them. A small triangle, which you might visualize as an arrowhead, identifies options that lead to submenus, and menu options that open dialog boxes to collect additional information are followed by *ellipses* (three dots).

You can operate the Access menu bar using any combination of keyboard and mouse commands. Even if you already have a strong preference, make it a point to learn both methods. During an intensive data

FIGURE 2.4 ▸ *When a database is open, the menus include options for working with this database.*

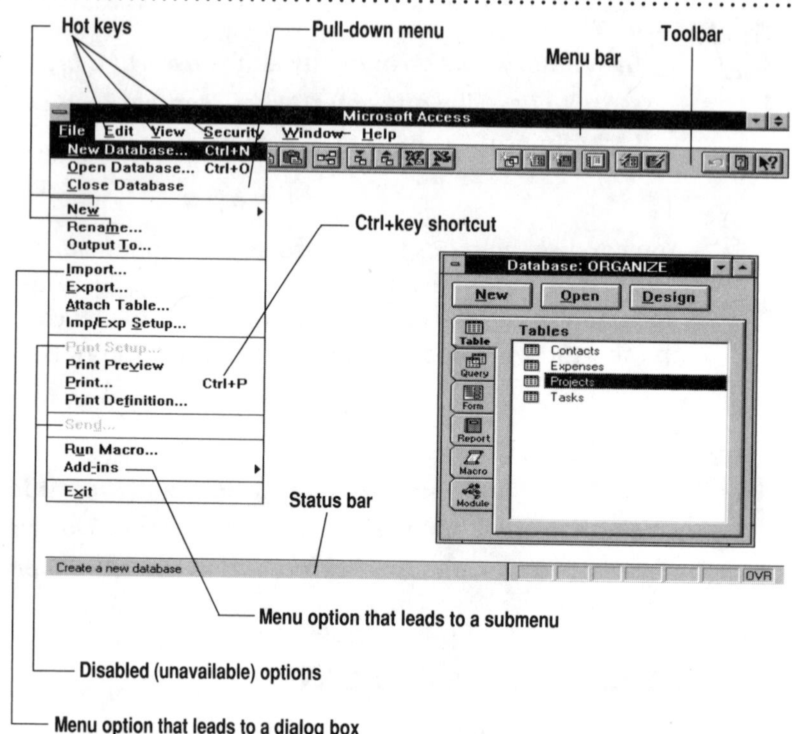

entry session, you may not want to take your hands off the keyboard, but when you are editing forms or reports, the mouse is more convenient—you'll be using it most of the time anyway.

To choose a menu option with the mouse, you simply *point-and-click*—position the mouse pointer over the option and *click* (press and release) the left mouse button. Try using this method to select the File ➤ Open Database option:

1. Click File on the main menu bar to pull down the File menu.
2. Click the File ➤ Open Database option.
3. Click the Cancel button to close the Open Database dialog box without opening a database.

To select a menu option using the arrow keys on the numeric keypad:

1. Press Alt or F10 to activate the menu bar.
2. Use the ← and → keys to highlight a menu bar option.
3. Press ↵ to display the attached pull-down menu.
4. Use the ↑ and ↓ keys to highlight an option on the pull-down menu.
5. Press ↵ to select the option.

If you prefer not to reach for the arrow keys, you can operate the menus by using the underlined *hot keys:*

- To select a menu bar option, hold down the Alt key and press the underlined letter.
- To select a pull-down menu option, press the underlined letter.

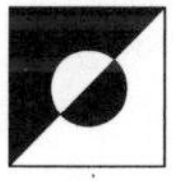

NOTE

You have to press the Alt key to activate the main menu options so that Access does not mistake your keystrokes for data. Once a pull-down menu is displayed, you couldn't possibly be typing anything but a command, so a single letter, without Alt, suffices to activate commands.

If you want to try the keyboard commands, follow these steps:

1. Press Alt+F to pull down the File menu.
2. Press O to select the Open Database option.
3. Click Cancel to get out of the Open Database dialog box.

Finally, there are Ctrl+key shortcuts for the commands you'll use most often. Unlike Alt+key combinations, the Ctrl+key shortcuts issue menu commands without first activating the menu system. You can see in Figure 2.4 that Ctrl+key shortcuts are available for the New Database,

Open Database, and Print options on the File menu. Take a look also at the Edit menu—all of the options have shortcuts, which you'll find particularly useful for editing text.

NOTE

Like the Shift key, the Alt and Ctrl keys don't do anything by themselves—they change the meaning of other keys—and you use them the same way. To type an Alt+key or Ctrl+key combination, hold down the Alt or Ctrl key, tap the letter key once, and then release the Alt or Ctrl key.

NOTE

For the most part, this book won't tell you which method to use to select a given menu command. You're free to use any combination of mouse and keyboard commands.

Access gives you a shortcut for calling up an abbreviated menu of options relevant to an object or region on the screen: *right-click* the object (position the mouse pointer over the object and press the right mouse button). For example, Figure 2.5 shows the result of right-clicking the Database window.

USING THE TOOLBAR

The toolbar gives you another kind of shortcut for executing commands with a single mouse-click. (You can't operate the toolbar buttons with keyboard commands.) At first the meanings of the icons on these buttons may seem no more intuitive than the wording of the corresponding menu options, but they'll soon become second nature. On the inside covers of this book, you'll find a reference guide to the Access toolbars.

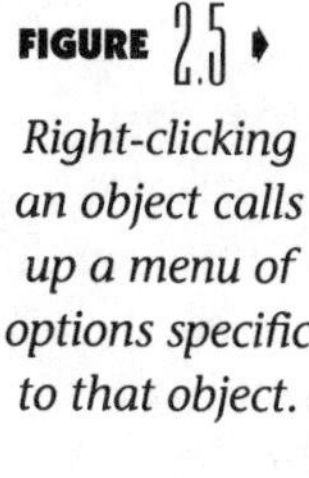

FIGURE 2.5

Right-clicking an object calls up a menu of options specific to that object.

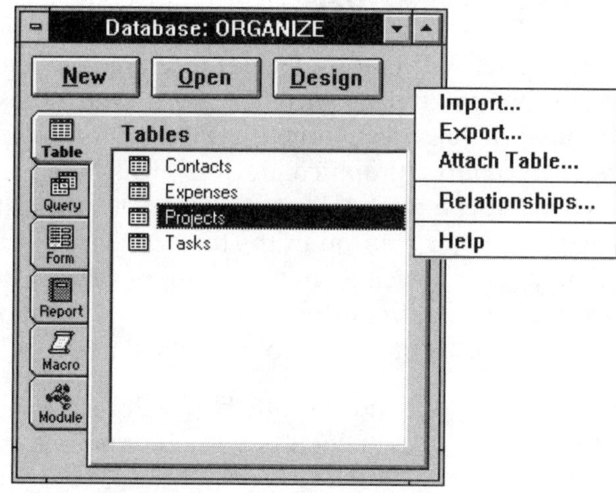

If you need help, watch the status bar as you move the mouse pointer over the command buttons in the toolbar; Access displays a summary of the purpose of the button you're pointing to. If you pause for a few seconds, Access displays a *Tool Tip* below the mouse pointer, like this:

WORKING WITH DIALOG BOXES

When Access needs additional information from you before it can carry out a command, it displays a *dialog box*. Dialog boxes display information and ask questions, sometimes directly and sometimes by displaying various *controls* (graphical devices), which you can use to make selections. If you want to experiment with a typical dialog box, click the Open Database button in the toolbar to invoke the Open Database dialog box, which is shown in Figure 2.6. You may recognize this dialog box, which is very similar to the Open File dialog boxes used by other Windows programs to open documents.

All Windows dialog boxes have a title bar, a close box, and one or more command buttons. The labels on the buttons will vary, but

FIGURE 2.6

Access uses dialog boxes to display messages and collect information it needs to execute a command.

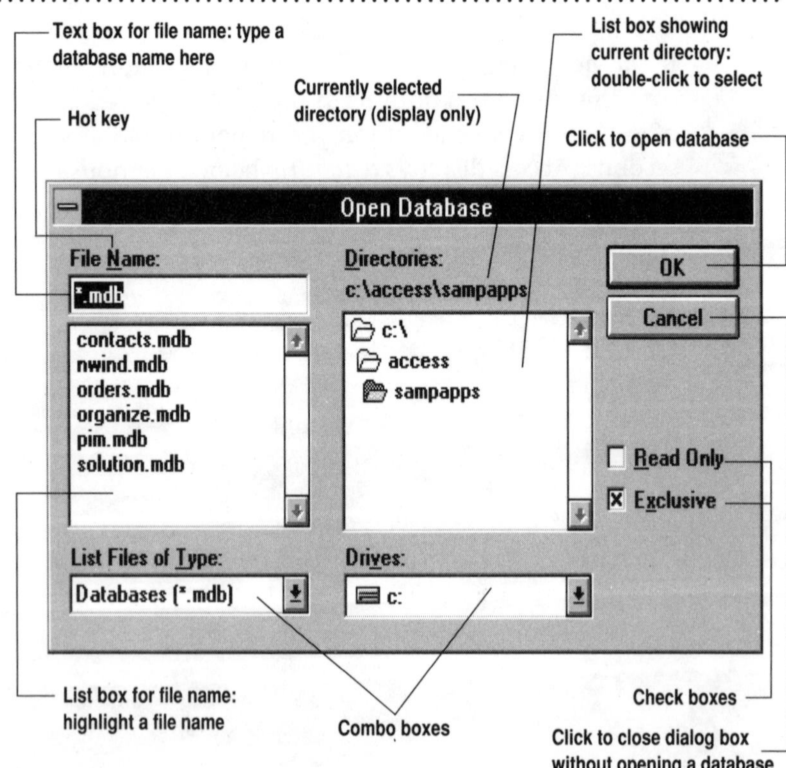

you'll always find one button that closes the dialog box and carries out an action (in this case, opening the database you choose). Another button, usually labeled Cancel, lets you change your mind and close the dialog box without doing anything.

Think of a dialog box as part of your ongoing "conversation" with Access:

> You (by picking Open Database): "I want to open a database."
> Access (by displaying the Open Database dialog box): "Which database?"
> You (by making selections in the dialog box): "The Contacts database, in the C:\ACCESS\SAMPAPPS directory."

Access gives you a variety of controls for answering the questions in the dialog box:

- *Text boxes* let you type an explicit answer to a question.
- *List boxes* display available selections and let you choose one.
- *Combo boxes* let you type text or make a selection from a pull-down list.
- *Check boxes* ask yes-or-no questions and let you turn options on or off.
- *Command buttons* let you call up additional dialog boxes or execute commands.

You can use mouse or keyboard commands to move around a dialog box. If you need to change only one or two entries, it's easiest to use the mouse. For example, in the Open Database dialog box you might only have to choose the database name. If you prefer keyboard commands, use the Tab key to move forward through the options and Shift+Tab to move backward. (Only experience will teach you what *forward* and *backward* mean in a particular dialog box.) You can select an option from a list by pressing ↑ or ↓ to highlight the one you want, and you can check or uncheck a check box by pressing the spacebar. To jump directly to any option, use the Alt+key shortcuts identified by the underlined letters in the prompts. For example, in the Open File dialog, try moving to the Directories list box by pressing Alt+D.

Pressing ↵ in a dialog box is equivalent to clicking the *default button* (usually the OK button)—the one that carries out the menu command that invoked the dialog box—and pressing Esc is equivalent to selecting Cancel. In most dialog boxes, double-clicking the option that provides the answer to the central question Access is asking ("Which database do you want to open?" for the Open Database dialog box) also closes the dialog box and executes your command.

TIP

You can tell which button is the default button because it has a slightly heavier border.

An *alert box* is a special type of dialog box that displays a warning or error message. Some alert boxes have only one button, labeled OK, which you click to acknowledge that you've read the message in the alert box. Others, like the one shown in Figure 2.7, ask for confirmation and give you one last chance to cancel potentially destructive commands.

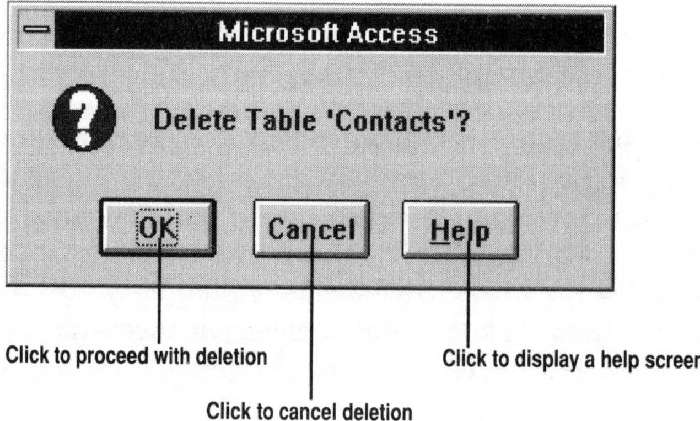

FIGURE 2.7 *Alert boxes warn you and ask for confirmation before carrying out potentially destructive actions.*

There's a fundamental difference between dialog boxes and document windows: once you've opened a dialog box, you must complete the dialog by choosing one of the command buttons before you can do anything else. You can move the dialog box to examine the contents of another window, but you can't move into another window temporarily and then return to the dialog box and pick up where you left off. If you click anywhere outside the dialog box or try to pick another menu option, Access beeps and ignores this action.

To practice using the Open Database dialog box, try opening NWIND.MDB (one of the sample databases supplied with Access):

1. Use the Drives combo box to select the drive on which you've installed Access.
2. Use the Directories list box to select your Access program directory, and then move to the SAMPAPPS subdirectory.
3. Highlight NWIND.MDB in the list of file names.
4. Click the OK button or press ↵.

TIP

To move to any directory displayed in the Directories list box, double-click its name.

NOTE

If you didn't let Access install NWIND.MDB in the SAMPAPPS directory, you may have to search for it. If you can't find this file, open any other .MDB file you wish.

THE DATABASE WINDOW

Whenever a database is open, the Database window, which is shown in Figure 2.8, is your base of operations. The standard location for the Database window is near the upper-left corner of the screen, but you can move it anywhere you want. (In Figure 2.4, the Database window was moved so it wouldn't be partly obscured by the File menu.) The visual metaphor for a database is a stack of six file folders, one each for tables, queries, forms, reports, macros, and modules. When you first open a database, Access shows you the Tables "folder," as you can see in Figure 2.8. The easiest way to switch to another folder is to click its "tab," which functions like a command button.

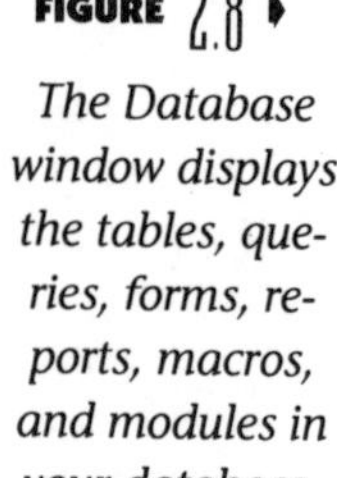

FIGURE 2.8

The Database window displays the tables, queries, forms, reports, macros, and modules in your database.

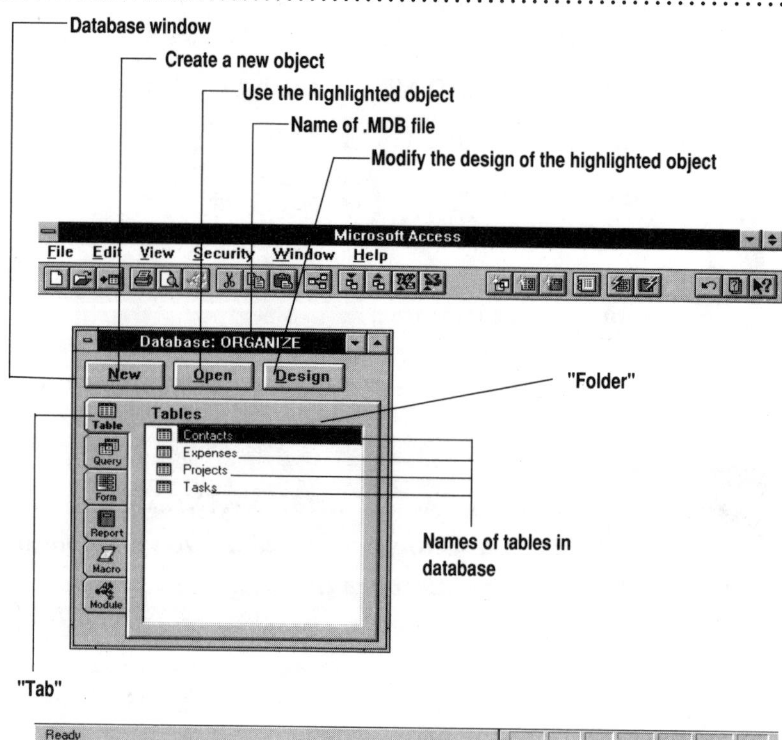

NOTE

Access lists the last four databases you've opened at the bottom of the File menu. You can use these options to bypass the Open Database dialog box and reopen any of these files.

The three command buttons at the top of the Database window enable you to create, use, or modify individual objects of any type. For example, to create a new report you'd switch to the Reports folder and then click the New command button. Access also gives you buttons in the toolbar for creating new queries, forms, and reports.

The meaning of the Open button depends on the type of object, but it always means *use*—this button opens a table in Datasheet view, runs a query, opens a form, or previews a report. For any type of object, double-clicking the name or highlighting the name and pressing ↵ is equivalent to clicking the Open button.

NOTE

The icon to the left of each object name in the Database window identifies the type of object and distinguishes between slightly different types. For example, Access uses different icons for queries that display data, queries that delete records, queries that update records, and so on.

To delete an object, highlight its name in the Database window and then press Del or select Edit ➤ Delete. Think twice before you do this—Access lets you undo a deletion if you discover your mistake immediately, but you won't be able to recover an object after you've done other work in your database. To help prevent you from deleting objects by mistake, Access always displays an alert box like the one shown earlier in Figure 2.7 to request confirmation.

USING THE HELP SYSTEM

When you're learning Access from scratch, your best resources are books like this one and the *Users Guide*. For occasional reference while you're working with Access, the on-line help system is usually more convenient than pulling out the manuals. Figure 2.9 illustrates the Table of Contents screen.

FIGURE 2.9 ▸

The table of contents lets you look up any help topic.

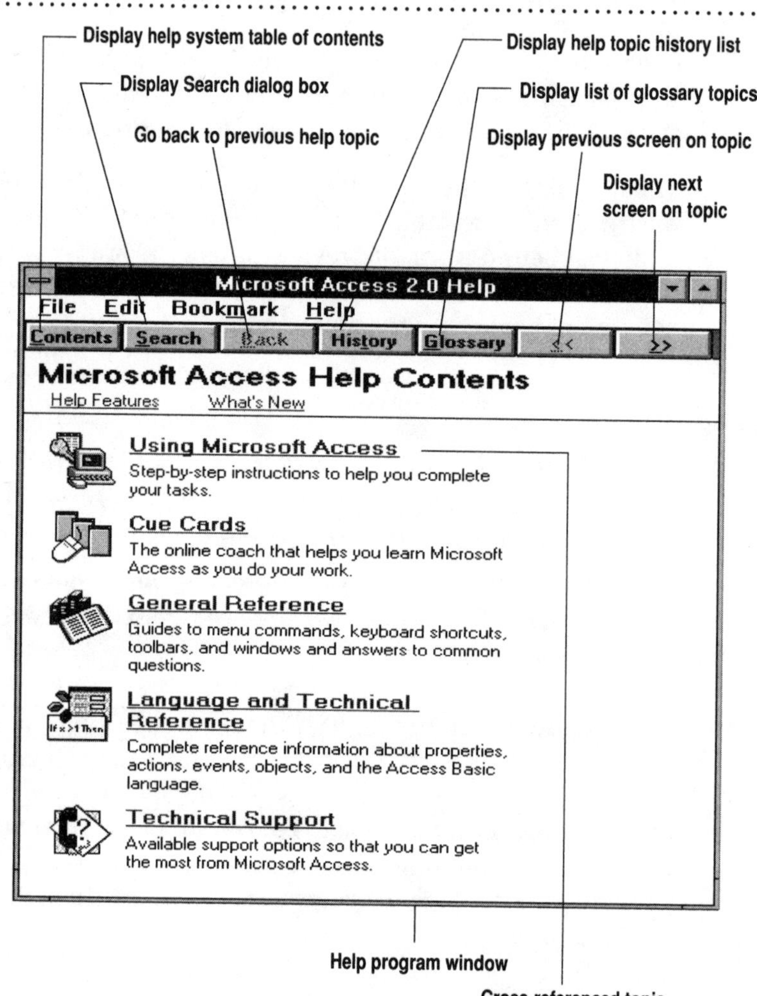

Although the help system looks like part of Access, it's actually a separate Windows application, which is launched in its own window and has its own menu bar and navigation buttons. There's no need to close the help window after reading one topic; if you think you might need more help, leave it open for future reference.

TIP

If the Access program window is maximized, you won't normally be able to see the help window after you return to the Access program window. To keep the help window on top of all the other windows on your desktop, including other application windows, select Help ➤ Always on Top (from the help system's menu, not the Access program menu).

The help system is made up of a network of cross-referenced topics. Like a printed manual, it has a table of contents, a glossary, and an index of keywords, which you can search if you don't know the title of the topic you're looking for. You can open this on-line "manual" to different "pages," depending on how you ask for help:

- To display the table of contents, choose Help ➤ Contents.
- To search for help on a specific topic, choose Help ➤ Search.
- To call up *context-sensitive* help (a description of the currently highlighted menu option or dialog box), press F1.
- To get help on a control or screen region that you can't highlight (such as a toolbar button or window control), click the Help button on the toolbar or press Shift+F1. The mouse pointer changes shape to match the icon on the Help button. Point to any object on the screen and click to get help.

To print a hard copy of a complete help topic, select File ➤ Print Topic in the help system.

NAVIGATING THROUGH THE HELP SYSTEM

No matter how you got into the help system, you can use the menu, navigation buttons, and Search option to move to any available topic. You can use the command buttons at the top of the screen to jump quickly to specific sections of the help system:

BUTTON	DESCRIPTION
Contents	Displays the table of contents
Search	Displays the Search dialog box
Back	Displays the last help screen you read
History	Lets you return to any topic you've read in the current work session
Glossary	Displays the list of terms for which definitions are available
<<	Displays the previous screen in the help system
>>	Displays the next screen in the help system

MOVING TO RELATED TOPICS

One of the virtues of on-line help is the ability to move easily from one topic to a related topic without returning to the table of contents or index. On all the help screens, cross-referenced topics are displayed in green (if you're using the default Windows colors) with initial capital letters and solid underlining. Just click any of these underlined topic names to move directly to the associated help screen. Cross-references that invoke lists of related topics rather than moving directly to a single topic are displayed in green (in the default Windows colors) with broken underlining.

NOTE

If you're not sure where to click, watch the mouse pointer, which looks like a hand with a pointing finger when it is positioned over a cross-referenced topic.

Glossary terms are displayed in lowercase green letters (in the default Windows colors) with broken underlining. When you click a glossary term, the help system pops up a definition (as shown in Figure 2.10), which disappears the next time you press a key or click the mouse.

In addition to the underlined cross-reference topics, many help screens have a list of related topics, which you can view by clicking the words *See Also* at the top of the help window, right below the topic heading. The See Also list may contain references to other help topics, Cue Cards topics (Cue Cards are described later in this chapter), and

FIGURE 2.10

The help system can display definitions of technical terms used in the help topic text.

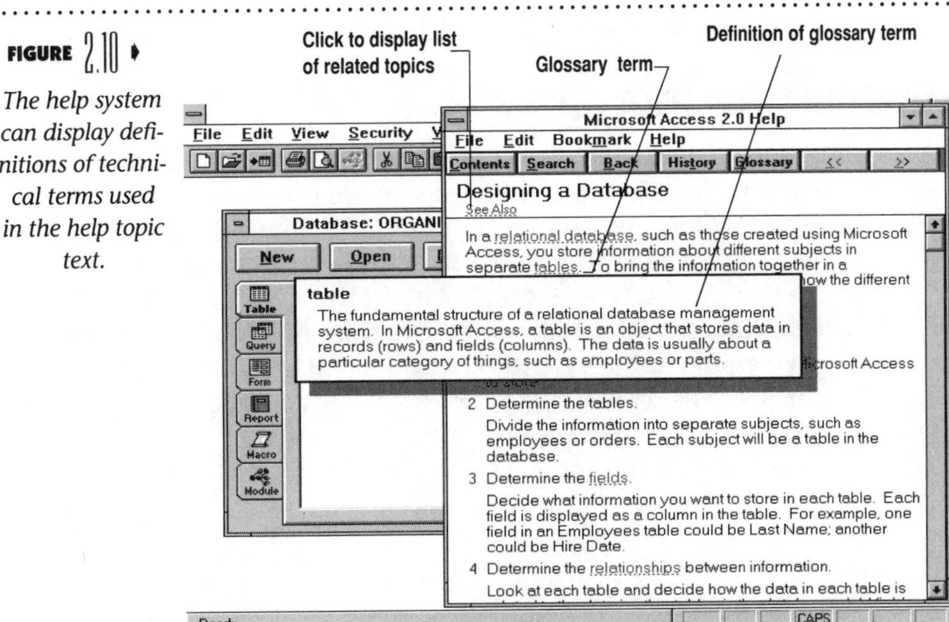

chapters in the printed documentation. You can move directly to any listed help topic or Cue Cards topic by clicking its name in the See Also list.

If you want to explore the help system, try reading some of the screens that describe how to create a table:

1. To launch the help system, choose Help ➤ Contents from the Access program menu.
2. Click the first topic, Using Microsoft Access.
3. In the Using Microsoft Access help screen, click Tables.
4. In the Tables help screen, click Creating a Table with a Wizard.
5. Try clicking some of the glossary terms (table, records, or fields) to display the definitions.
6. Click See Also to display the list of related topics.
7. In the See Also list, click Creating a Table Without a Wizard.
8. Click Back to retrace your steps through the help system until you return to the Table of Contents screen.

SEARCHING FOR HELP ON A SPECIFIC TOPIC

Unless you're looking up a specific command or function, the fastest way to find the help topic you need is to use the Search option, which invokes the dialog box shown in Figure 2.11. Simply begin typing the word or phrase you want to search for in the text box at the top of the dialog box. As you type, the alphabetical list of keywords underneath scrolls to the nearest match, so you can usually zero in on the one you want by typing just a few letters. At any point you can click in the list box and use the scroll bar to browse through the keywords.

FIGURE 2.11 ▸

You can use the Search dialog box to search for a help topic by keyword.

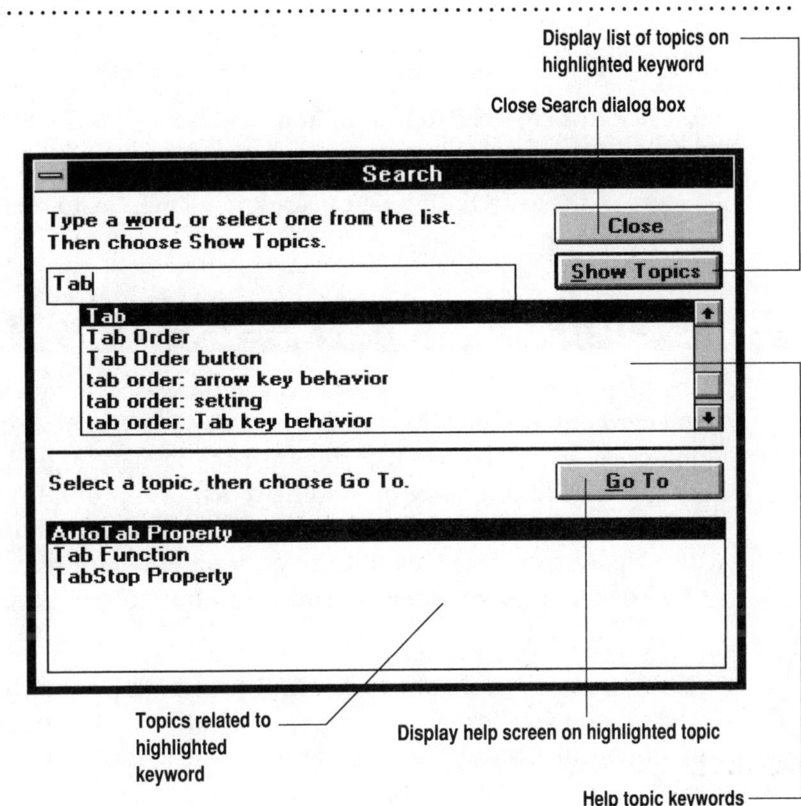

When you see the topic you want, highlight it and then click Show Topics, or double-click the topic. A list of one or more help topic titles will appear in the list box at the bottom of the Search dialog box. To view the help screen describing any of these topics, double-click it, or highlight the one you want and press ↵ or click Go To.

Try using the Search option to find help on creating a table:

1. Click the Search button in the help window.

2. Type the word **tables** slowly, watching the keyword list below.
3. Use the scroll bar to scroll down to tables: creating.
4. Click this keyword to highlight it, and then click Show Topics.
5. Highlight Creating a Table with a Wizard in the list at the bottom of the Search dialog box, and then click Go To to display the help screen.

USING CUE CARDS

The help system is a convenient and comprehensive reference, but when you're first learning Access you may feel you need a little more guidance. To help you get started, Access provides an auxiliary help system called Cue Cards, an on-line coach that prompts you through a task with specific step-by-step instructions. You'll probably outgrow the Cue Cards before long, but they are an excellent resource when you have no idea what steps to take, in what order, to accomplish a particular goal.

The startup screen shown earlier in Figure 2.1 is part of the Cue Cards system, and you can use the command buttons on that screen to call up other Cue Cards screens. Later in a work session, there are four ways to call up Cue Cards:

- Click the Cue Cards command button in the toolbar.
- Choose Help ➤ Cue Cards from the Access program menu.
- Click the Cue Cards topic in the help system table of contents.
- Choose a Cue Cards topic from the See Also list invoked from a help screen.

FIGURE 2.12

Cue Cards can give you step-by-step instructions to prompt you through a task.

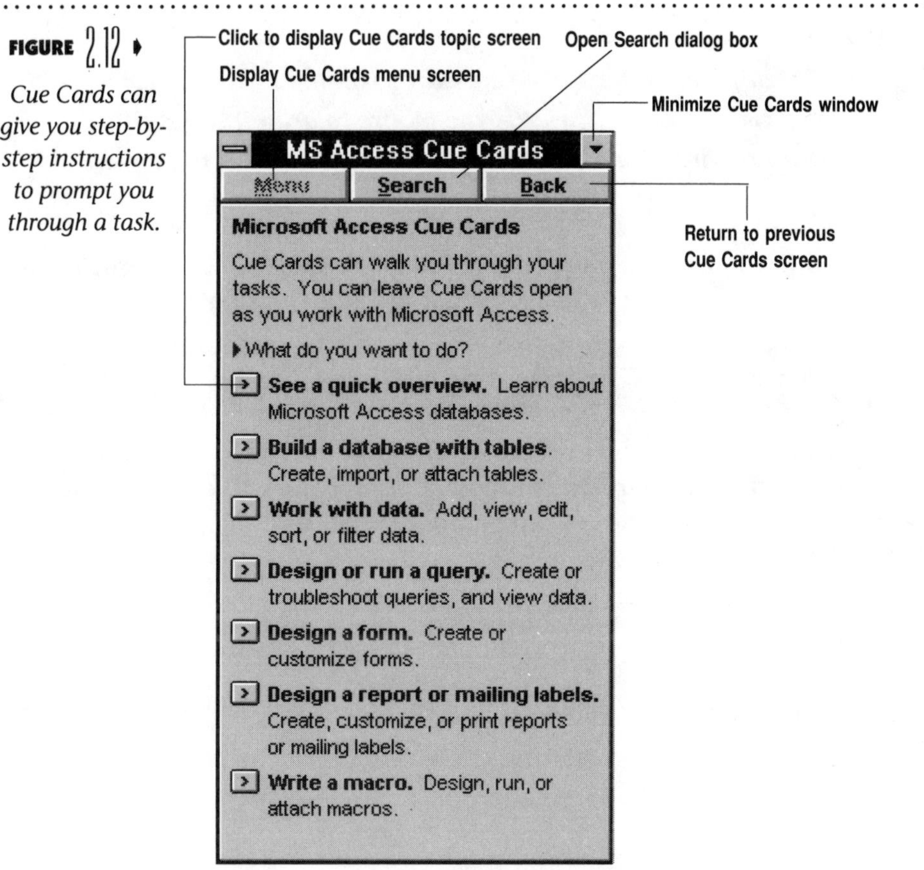
Click to display Cue Cards topic screen
Open Search dialog box
Display Cue Cards menu screen
Minimize Cue Cards window
MS Access Cue Cards
Menu
Search
Back
Return to previous Cue Cards screen
Microsoft Access Cue Cards
Cue Cards can walk you through your tasks. You can leave Cue Cards open as you work with Microsoft Access.
What do you want to do?
See a quick overview. Learn about Microsoft Access databases.
Build a database with tables. Create, import, or attach tables.
Work with data. Add, view, edit, sort, or filter data.
Design or run a query. Create or troubleshoot queries, and view data.
Design a form. Create or customize forms.
Design a report or mailing labels. Create, customize, or print reports or mailing labels.
Write a macro. Design, run, or attach macros.

Figure 2.12 shows the first Cue Cards screen (the Menu screen). Each screen explains one concept or outlines one step in a process and then asks what you want to do next. You can select the next topic you want to read by clicking the corresponding button. When the instructions for completing a task won't fit on one screen, a command button labeled Next appears in the lower-right corner of the Cue Cards window.

The Cue Cards window always stays on top of all other open windows (including other Windows application windows), to ensure that it remains visible while you carry out its instructions. If moving the Cue Cards window doesn't get it out of your way, you can minimize it until you're ready to read the next screen.

TIP

To temporarily move the Cue Cards window or any other window out of the way, use the mouse to grab it by its title bar and drag it most of the way "off the edge" of the screen.

If you want an example of the kind of help Cue Cards can provide, try reading the sequence of screens that describe creating a table.

WHAT'S NEXT?

Now that you know how to move around in Access, you're ready to start setting up your first database. Chapter 3 describes how to plan your application and lay out your table structures.

Designing a Database

The first thing you should do when you think you're ready to set up your first Access database is to turn off the computer. This is probably the last advice you want to hear if you're already impatient to get your application on line, but a little bit of advance planning will save you a lot of time and frustration later on.

Setting up a database does not require any knowledge of relational database theory, and it need not be a formal or lengthy process. If you have set up paper record-keeping systems, you can apply exactly the same analytical skills to laying out your first Access database. Sometimes the process *can* be traumatic, especially if you're designing an application for an established business and are forced to reexamine—and question—procedures that have been in place for a long time. You'll undoubtedly uncover problems in the way the business operates that have lain dormant for years, not all of which can be solved by computerizing.

The most important attributes you can bring to the process are an open mind and a willingness to take a fresh look at familiar data. People with good organizational skills often do better than programmers who have worked only on small pieces of a large project. This chapter outlines a common-sense approach to database design that should serve you in good stead for small to medium-sized applications.

OUTLINING YOUR REQUIREMENTS

The first step in the planning process is to outline the system requirements. At this point don't worry about how you will translate the results of your analysis into an Access database; just concentrate on describing, in the familiar terminology of your business or profession, the information you need to manage and the operations you'll need to carry out. You can classify the information you're compiling into six categories, which you can approach in any order you wish.

IDENTIFY THE FUNDAMENTAL ENTITIES Enumerate the types of people or things your database must track, and list the individual items of information that describe each entity.

SKETCH OUT THE DATA ENTRY FORMS Your sketches should convey the overall layout of each data entry form. Also make a note of any special formatting requirements (for example, fields that must be entered in uppercase and those that require punctuation, such as social security numbers or part numbers) and validation rules (for example, the rules that describe a legitimate zip code).

SKETCH OUT THE PRINTED REPORTS Your sketches should convey the overall layout of each printed report, graph, mailing label, or personalized letter. Also make a note of any calculations, subtotals and grand totals, and summary statistics, and indicate the selection criteria and sort order.

LIST THE SEARCH CRITERIA Enumerate all the ways you'll need to search for data.

OUTLINE THE CALCULATIONS Enumerate all the calculations you'll need to perform, such as computing customer balances, calculating the age of an invoice, or computing discounts and sales tax on invoices.

LIST THE PERIODIC MAINTENANCE PROCEDURES In a typical application, periodic maintenance procedures include options to archive and purge data you no longer need to see every day, to update prices, or to split and combine tables.

During the initial planning phase, you may find that you gravitate toward one aspect of the design. Some people focus on the information they want to enter into the system, while others conceptualize an application primarily in terms of the system's output—the reports it must produce. By all means start wherever you feel most comfortable, but don't neglect any of the essential steps. If you concentrate exclusively on the input, you may omit items from your database that appear on only a few reports. Equally unfortunate, you may include information you are convinced you need but which in fact never appears on any report and is not used in any calculation. Conversely, if you focus on the reports, you may find it harder to figure out the best way to structure the tables.

STUDYING THE MANUAL SYSTEM

If your new Access database will replace an existing manual system, the best way to begin is to study this system. Even if you're already planning major revisions, the existing system can serve as a valuable framework for your analysis.

Start by gathering a set of all the documents you presently use, including both input forms and reports. If possible, these forms should contain matching data. For example, in an accounts receivable system you might collect a customer ledger card, an invoice *for the same customer,* an aging report *that includes the sample invoice,* and the page from your payment register *that records the payment on the invoice.* Paper forms such as order forms, job applications, and medical history questionnaires can serve as models for your data entry forms, and reports you are currently producing by hand can become Access reports. Even more important, these documents will remind you of items of information you might otherwise have overlooked if you simply listed everything you thought you needed to store in your database.

Remember that your manual system is just a starting point; don't feel bound by its specific forms, methods, and procedures. You'll want to improve and enhance your manual system, not just replicate what you are already doing by hand. Mark up your input forms and reports to indicate changes you want to make, sketch any new forms and reports on paper, and make a wish list of other desirable enhancements. It may help to prioritize your wish list items, but be aware that you'll probably end up implementing them in order of difficulty rather than in order of importance.

If you have no manual system, you'll have to simply list the forms, reports, and procedures you think you'll need. Be aware from the outset that your analysis is likely to be less complete, and try to allocate more time later for revisions to your initial design.

When you sketch out a new input form or report, don't waste time making an accurate drawing; it's a lot easier to fine-tune the appearance of a form using the Access design tools. Just make sure you account for

- The fields
- Calculated values, if any
- The record selection criteria
- The sort order (record sequence)
- The subtotal groups, if any (for reports)
- Summary statistics (sums, counts, averages, and so on), if any

Based solely on a study of your manual system, it's all too easy to overlook maintenance operations such as archiving and purging obsolete data or applying global price or rate increases, which in many manual systems are carried out at very irregular intervals, if at all. For example, an inactive customer's ledger card might remain in your manual file for years. In a computerized database, you'll save disk space and speed up processing by deleting customers who haven't placed an order in two years or prospects who have not turned into customers after five years.

LAYING OUT THE TABLES

Once you've identified the entities in your application and listed all the individual items of information you want to maintain, you are ready to lay out the tables. In many databases each entity belongs in a separate table, but you won't always be so lucky. For example, in a *manual* accounts receivable system the main entities are customers, inventory items, invoices, and payments. In an Access database an invoice would include information from four tables—a Customers table (the customer name and address), an Orders table (the order date, number, shipping information, and grand totals), an Order Details table (the product code, quantity ordered, unit price, and line item dollar total), and an Inventory table (the item description).

NOTE

If you want to see an example of a report that looks like a single entity but is in fact derived from several tables, take a look at the NWIND.MDB sample database packaged with Access. The data printed on the Invoice report, which is based on a query called Invoices, comes from the Customers, Orders, Order Details, Products, and Employees tables.

The easiest way to lay out the table structures is to start with a blank sheet of paper for each table and systematically list the fields you'll need. This method lets you spread out all the worksheets on your desk so you can compare the structures and visualize the relationships among the tables. Start with the tables and fields you understand best, and then proceed to the more problematic items. When you think you're finished, make one last pass through all your sample input forms, reports, and wish lists to make sure every item is accounted for.

RULES FOR STRUCTURING YOUR TABLES

You don't need to study relational database theory to figure out how to structure your tables; a few common-sense rules will guide you through the process:

> Rule #1: Each table should represent a different entity, which is described by different fields.

According to Rule #1, an accounts receivable database should use separate tables for customers and orders. As you can see in Figure 3.1, these tables have at least one item in common—the customer account number—but most of the information that describes a customer (name, address, credit terms, and so on) is different from the information that describes an order (order number, date, shipper, subtotal, tax, shipping charges, and so on). On the other hand, you'd probably want to store customers and prospects in the same table, with a field that identifies a particular record as a customer or prospect. In this case most of the information is the same (the Name and Address fields). In a prospect record, you can simply leave blank any fields required only for customers (and vice versa).

Rule #2: Every field in a table should directly describe a single instance of the entity stored in the table.

If you apply this rule to the accounts receivable example, you'll see that the customer's address doesn't belong in the Orders table because the address directly describes a customer, not an order. On the other

FIGURE 3.1

Each table should represent a different entity, which is described by different fields.

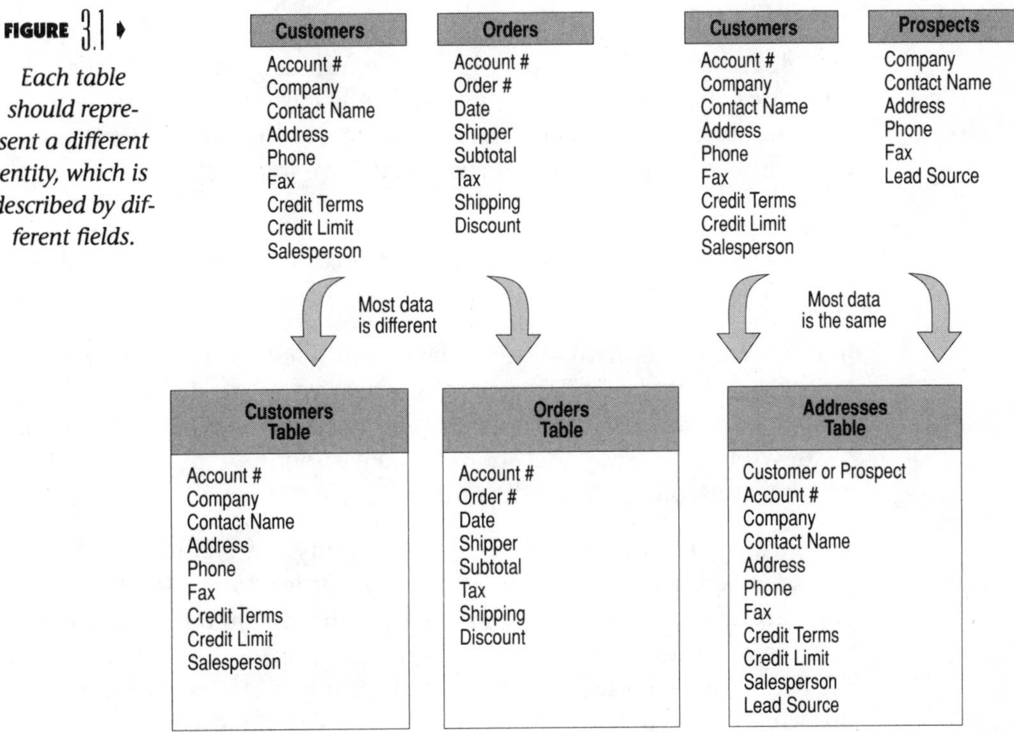

hand, if the billing address is always the same but the shipping address might be different for each order, you should put the shipping address in the Orders table.

If this concept seems abstract, try asking yourself two questions to determine whether a field belongs in a particular table. Does it describe the entity stored in this table at all? If so, could it be different for each record in this table? If the answer to either question is no, the field belongs in a different table.

NOTE

Just because you have to print certain items of information together on a report doesn't mean they belong in the same table. Access makes it easy to display or print fields from two or more tables on the same form or report.

Rule #2 helps you eliminate redundancy and thereby save data entry time and improve accuracy. If you store the customer address in one customer record rather than in many order records, you'll have to enter it only once, and if it changes, you'll have to edit it only in one place.

> Rule #3: Do not define repeating groups of identical fields in one table; create another table instead.

In the accounts receivable example, this rule tells you not to place the order detail lines in the Orders table, where you'd need multiple sets of fields for the part numbers, quantities, prices, and discounts. Instead, as shown in Figure 3.2, you should create a separate table in which each record represents one detail line.

This strategy imparts a great deal of flexibility. For example, suppose you provided six sets of detail fields in the Orders table. The first time you encountered an order with seven line items, you'd have to restructure the order table and edit existing queries, forms, and reports. With the detail lines in a separate table, you simply add a new record to this table for each detail line. Placing the detail lines in a separate

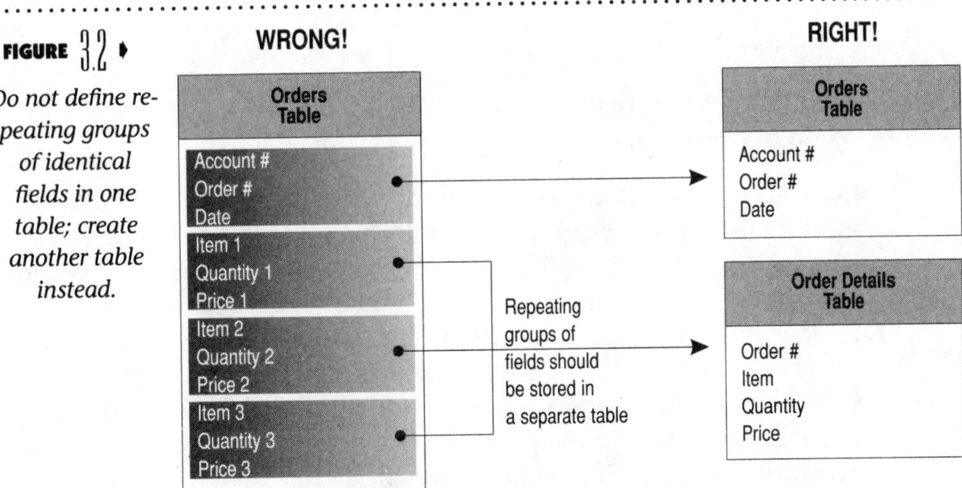

FIGURE 3.2 *Do not define repeating groups of identical fields in one table; create another table instead.*

table also makes it easy to sort them by product code or price and to generate statistical reports on the items ordered (reports that don't include order or customer data).

Rule #4: Don't include fields in a table that can be calculated from data in the same or other tables.

According to Rule #4, you don't need to store the net dollar total for each detail line: you can compute it by multiplying the quantity by the unit price and subtracting the discount. Similarly, you don't need to store the grand total in the order record because you can calculate it by summing the detail lines.

ASSIGNING INDEX KEYS

An *index* is a sorted list of the values in one or more fields in a table, which are called the *keys, key fields,* or *index keys,* together with *pointers* to the original records. Indexes play a crucial role in Access because they

- Determine the default record display order
- Speed up sorts
- Speed up searches for individual records

- Speed up queries that select records
- Support the relationships between tables
- Optionally, ensure that the data entered in a field or combination of fields is unique

Think about the way a book's index can help you find a topic. Without the index, you'd have to start at the beginning of the book and scan each page until you found the topic you wanted. Looking up the topic in the index would be faster even if you had to scan the whole index (the index is much shorter than the book), but of course you don't have to do that. Because the index is in alphabetical order, you can zero in on a given topic very quickly and then go right to the listed page. In much the same way, Access can find data very quickly by searching the index first and then jumping directly to the record referenced in the index.

You can request indexes based on as many individual fields in a table as you wish. For each index you can specify whether or not to allow duplicate values. You'll want to prohibit duplicate values in fields you use as unique record identifiers, such as part numbers or social security numbers. Other indexes, which you need only to speed up sorts or searches—for example, an index based on a zip code or an invoice date—have to permit duplicate values.

You can define up to ten indexes based on more than one field. For example, you might build an index based on the State, City, and ID Code fields in the Contacts table to expedite sorting the table by state, within state by city, and within city by ID code.

NOTE

It's possible to have too much of a good thing. If you build too many indexes, data entry will slow down because each time you add or edit a record, Access has to update all the indexes.

Apart from the indexes required to support the relationships between tables, indexes are entirely optional in Access, and they don't force you to do anything differently. Access automatically uses indexes whenever possible to speed up searches, sorts, and selections. For example, you can sort mailings by zip code without having an index based on the Zip field. If you later build a zip code index, your existing queries and mailing label reports will still work—but performance will be better.

ASSIGNING A PRIMARY KEY

Most tables should have a special index based on a field or combination of fields that uniquely identifies each record. This combination of data is called the *primary key,* and it serves three vital purposes:

- It guarantees that each record has a unique identifier.
- It determines the default display order in Datasheet view.
- It supports relationships among tables.

You don't have to define a primary key for every table, but it's usually a good idea. Most tables already have a unique identifier, carried over in some form from your manual system, such as an account number, a social security number, a part number, a general ledger account number, or a medical record number. If you assign a primary key, Access won't let you enter duplicate values into this field, so you're less likely to generate duplicate records accidentally.

If the primary key isn't particularly convenient for searches, you're not stuck with it. With a social security number or medical record number as the primary key, you could still do most of your searches by name, even if the name isn't guaranteed to be unique. This flexibility isn't possible in a manual record-keeping system—if your medical histories are filed by medical record number, it's not practical to search for a person by name.

DESCRIBING THE TABLE RELATIONSHIPS

After you've laid out the structures of the individual tables in your database, you're ready to diagram the relationships among the tables. Once in a while you'll have a table that stands entirely alone, but most will have some logical connection to at least one other table. For example, in the accounts receivable example, you'd have relationships between customers and orders, between orders and detail lines, and between detail lines and inventory items. When you describe table relationships, it's customary to take the "point of view" of one of the tables, which we'll call the *primary* table.

Each pair of related tables must have a field or combination of fields in common so Access can identify the matching records. For example, to link the line item detail records to the matching order record, you must include the order number in the Order Details table. The common field must be unique (often, it's the primary key) in the primary table—the Orders table in this example—to ensure that for each record in the related table—the Order Details table in this example—Access can find one and only one match in this table.

ONE-TO-ONE RELATIONSHIPS

The simplest type of relationship between two tables is one-to-one: for each record in the primary table there is at most one matching record in the related table. (There may be none.) The field shared by the two tables must be unique in the primary table. Working with two tables that have a one-to-one relationship is a lot like using one large table with all the fields in both structures. Indeed, you might wonder why you can't just put all the fields in one table.

One reason is that Access allows only 255 fields in a table, and this limit (although it may seem astronomical right now) may some day prove constraining. A more common scenario is a database with two or more similar entities that have certain fields in common, together with additional information that is required in only a small percentage of the records. Rather than defining one table, in which you'd end up leaving most of the fields blank in most of the records, you could use two tables with a one-to-one relationship. For example, you could store prospects and customers in the same Name and Address table and use a second table to store the additional data required only for customers.

This relationship is diagrammed in Figure 3.3.

FIGURE 3.3

In a one-to-one relationship, each record in the primary table has at most one matching record in the related table.

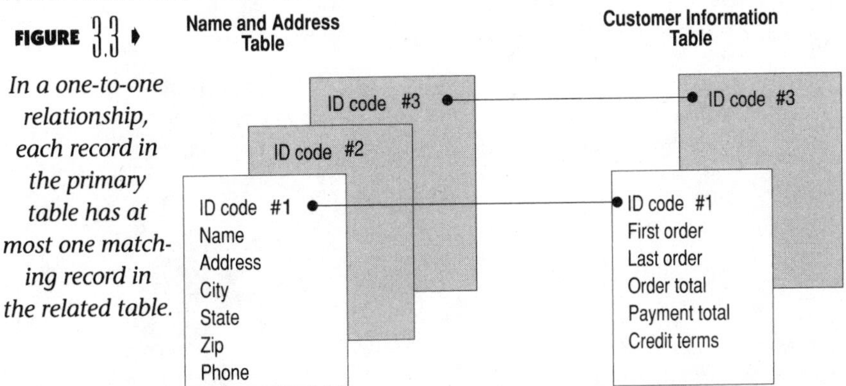

ONE-TO-MANY RELATIONSHIPS

Two tables have a one-to-many relationship if each record in the primary table might have any number of matching records in the related table. For example, in the accounts receivable example, the relationship between the Customers and Orders tables is one-to-many—for each customer, there may be more than one order—as is the relationship between the Orders and Order Details tables. In the context of a one-to-many relationship, the table with one record (the primary table) is sometimes referred to as the *master* or *parent* table, and the table with many records (the related table) may be called the *transaction* or *child* table.

This relationship is diagrammed in Figure 3.4.

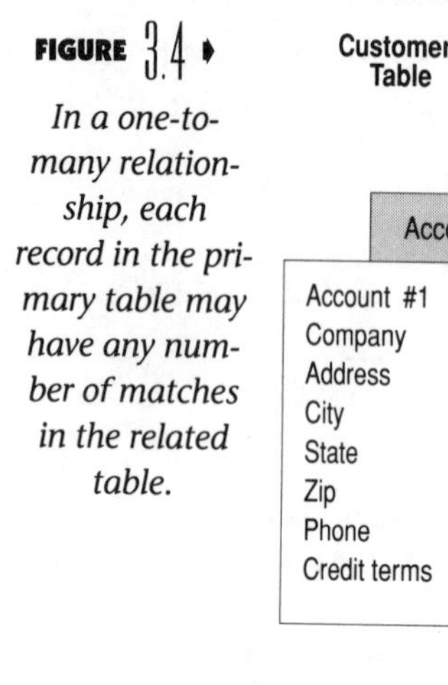

FIGURE 3.4 *In a one-to-many relationship, each record in the primary table may have any number of matches in the related table.*

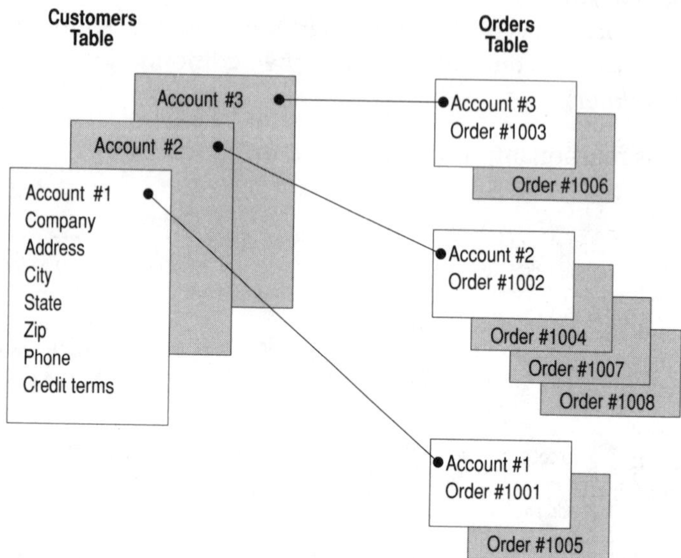

NOTE

It might be more accurate to describe one-to-many relationships as "one-to-any-number" because it doesn't mean that there must be many records in the child table, only that there may be.

In a one-to-many relationship, the common field shared by the tables must be unique in the parent table (it's usually the primary key) to ensure that Access can always find one and only one parent record to match any given record in the child table. In the child table, this field, which is called the *foreign key,* is *not* unique. (If it were, you'd have a one-to-one relationship.)

MANY-TO-MANY RELATIONSHIPS

When two tables have a many-to-many relationship, each record in each table may have many matches in the other. The classic example of a many-to-many relationship is a database for a school, with tables for students and classes; each class has more than one student, and a given student may be in more than one class.

In a many-to-many relationship, the two tables do not have any fields in common, and you have to create a third table to represent the relationship. This table has a one-to-many relationship with each of the two main tables, and it must therefore have fields that correspond to the unique identifiers (the primary keys) from these tables. Often, you don't need any other fields. Thus, to link the Students and Classes tables, you'd create a table with fields for the student ID or name and the class ID. This table will have one record for each valid combination of student and class; four records are required to represent a student who is taking four classes.

This relationship is diagrammed in Figure 3.5.

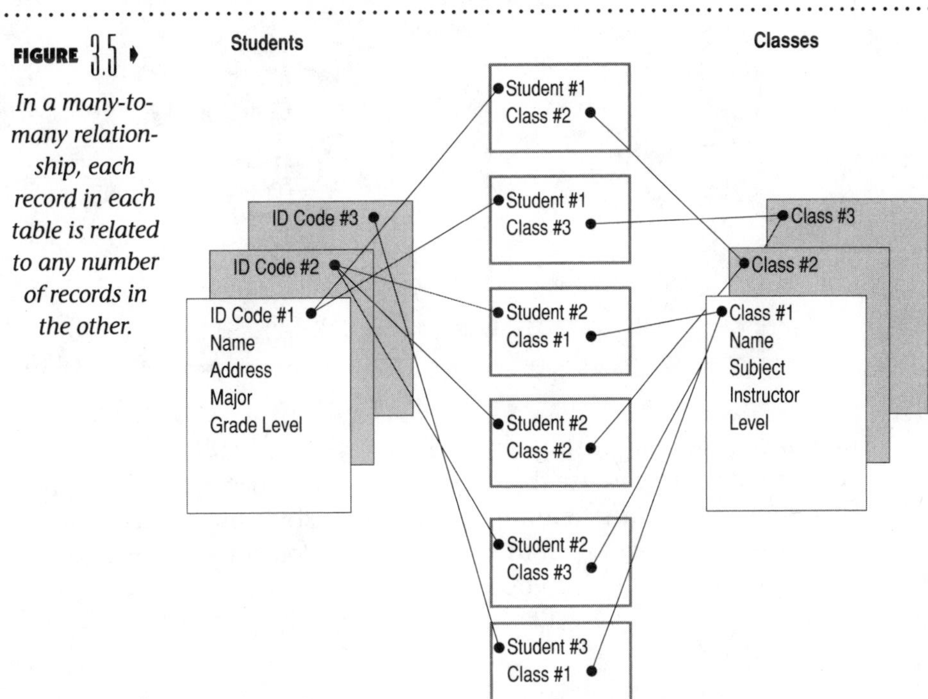

FIGURE 3.5

In a many-to-many relationship, each record in each table is related to any number of records in the other.

FORMALLY DEFINING TABLE RELATIONSHIPS

You don't have to formally define the relationships in your database, but it's to your advantage to do so. First of all, it's easy. Using a screen like the one shown in Figure 3.6, you can build a diagram that displays and defines the relationships between tables. Chapter 4 describes how to do this.

FIGURE 3.6

You can formally define the relationships between the tables in a database.

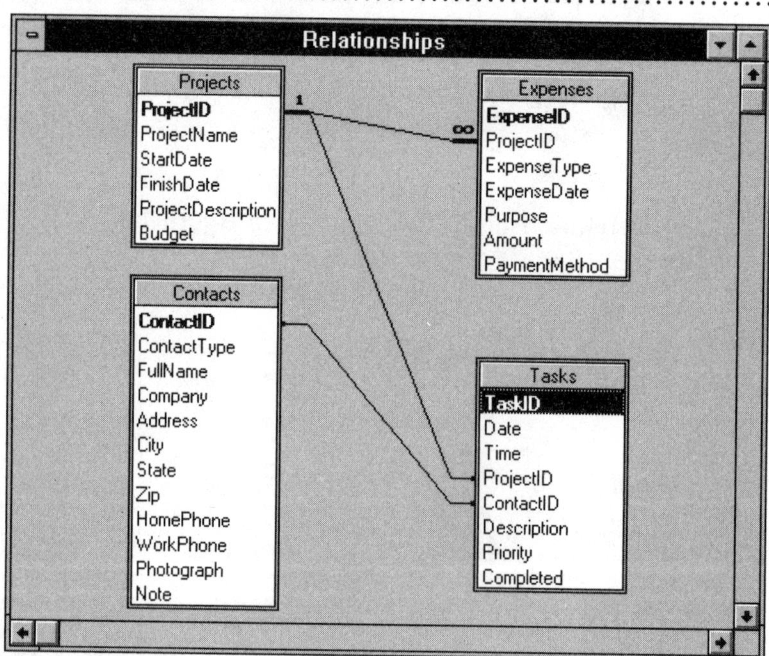

Defining table relationships enables Access to join tables exactly as you intend when you use them together in queries, forms, and reports. Even more important, defining table relationships allows Access to enforce *referential integrity*—that is, preserve the logical relationships between the tables when you add, delete, or change records.

RULES FOR ENFORCING REFERENTIAL INTEGRITY

If you elect to enforce referential integrity between two tables, Access places four global rules in effect:

> Rule #1: You can't add a record to a child table if there is no matching record in the parent table.

This rule ensures that every record in the child table, which is logically subordinate to the parent table, has a match in the parent table. Thus, in the accounts receivable example, you couldn't add an order record for a nonexistent customer.

> Rule #2: You can't delete a record from the parent table if matching records exist in the child table.

This rule prevents you from creating *orphaned* child records—records no longer connected to any parent record. According to this rule, you can't delete a customer who has orders.

> Rule #3: You can't change the primary key in the parent table if matching records exist in the child table.

Like Rule #2, this rule prevents you from creating orphan child records (usually accidentally).

> Rule #4: You can't change the foreign key in the child table so that it matches no record in the parent table.

This rule restates Rule #3 from the point of view of the child table; it too prevents you from inadvertently orphaning child records.

The referential integrity rules apply globally to all your work in Access. You can't violate referential integrity when you add or edit records in Datasheet view, work with a custom form, run a query, or import data.

Most of the time you'll want to enforce referential integrity, but sometimes the rules just enumerated are too restrictive. For example, Rule #3 makes it hard to change a customer's account number once you've entered orders for that customer, and Rule #2 forces you to delete all the order records before you can delete a customer.

You can have it both ways by electing to cascade deletes and/or cascade updates. If you choose to *cascade deletes,* Access automatically deletes all the child records when you delete a parent record. If you cascade updates, Access allows you to change the primary key field in a parent record, and then it automatically changes the corresponding field in the matching child records.

WARNING

The cascade delete and cascade updates options give you more flexibility, but think carefully about whether you're willing to accept the added responsibility. If you request cascading deletes, you run the risk of accidentally deleting not just one record, but many. With cascading updates in effect, you risk accidentally changing a parent record and being unable to find it again.

INTRODUCING THE SAMPLE SYSTEM: A PERSONAL ORGANIZER

The sample system used in this book is a simple personal information manager modeled on a manual organizer. The Organizer application tracks four main entities, each stored in its own table: names and addresses, projects, expenses, and tasks (to-do list items). The sample tables will be small and simple, so you won't have to do a lot of data entry to try all the examples, but it will be complete enough to use as the core of your own personal organizer. Just as you can expand a manual organizer by purchasing new types of pages (mileage records, telephone contact logs, project planning sheets, and so on), you'll be able to add new capabilities to your Access organizer.

THE ORGANIZER TABLES

The Contacts table in the Organizer application can contain names and addresses of many types—personal, business, professional, and even friends and family if you wish. Using just this table you can look up telephone numbers, print an address book, and send mailings (by printing letters, envelopes, or mailing labels) to various subsets of the list. The primary key for the Contacts table is an alphanumeric ID code made up of part of the last name, part of the first name, and, if necessary, a numeric digit as a tiebreaker. This way you can enter the name any way you want (typical entries might include *John Anderson, Thomas and Emily Granger,* and *Dr. Karen Robbins and Bob Rosenberg*) but still use the ID code to view data in alphabetical order.

The Projects table tracks the name and status of current projects. What constitutes a project is completely up to you. If you're a consultant, manager, or professional you may have formal projects you're working on with clients or associates, but a project might also be personal—remodeling the kitchen, organizing a club or study group, or planning a vacation. The primary key for the project table is also an ID code that you assign.

The Tasks table stores action items related to projects, appointments, daily reminders, and, if you wish, long-term goals. (In a more ambitious version of this application, you'd probably want a separate table for appointments.) The system can use this table to print an appointment calendar, a task list by project, and to-do lists in chronological or priority order.

The Expenses table tracks project expenses and prints expense reports by project, by date, or by expense type. A more sophisticated version of this system might also print a summary by general ledger account number (instead of expense type) to aid in preparing financial reports.

Neither the Tasks table nor the Expenses table has an obvious candidate for a primary key. As noted earlier, you don't have to create one, but an easy alternative, which we'll use in the Organizer application, is to use a numeric counter, which Access can enter automatically in each new record, as the primary key.

THE TABLE RELATIONSHIPS

The two central entities in the Organizer application are contacts (people) and projects. The Contacts table has a one-to-many relationship with the Tasks table: you might make many appointments with each person. The system won't enforce referential integrity in this relationship; you'll be *able* to link a task to a contact, but you won't be *forced* to do so.

FIGURE 3.7

The Organizer application consists of four tables, each of which is related to at least one other.

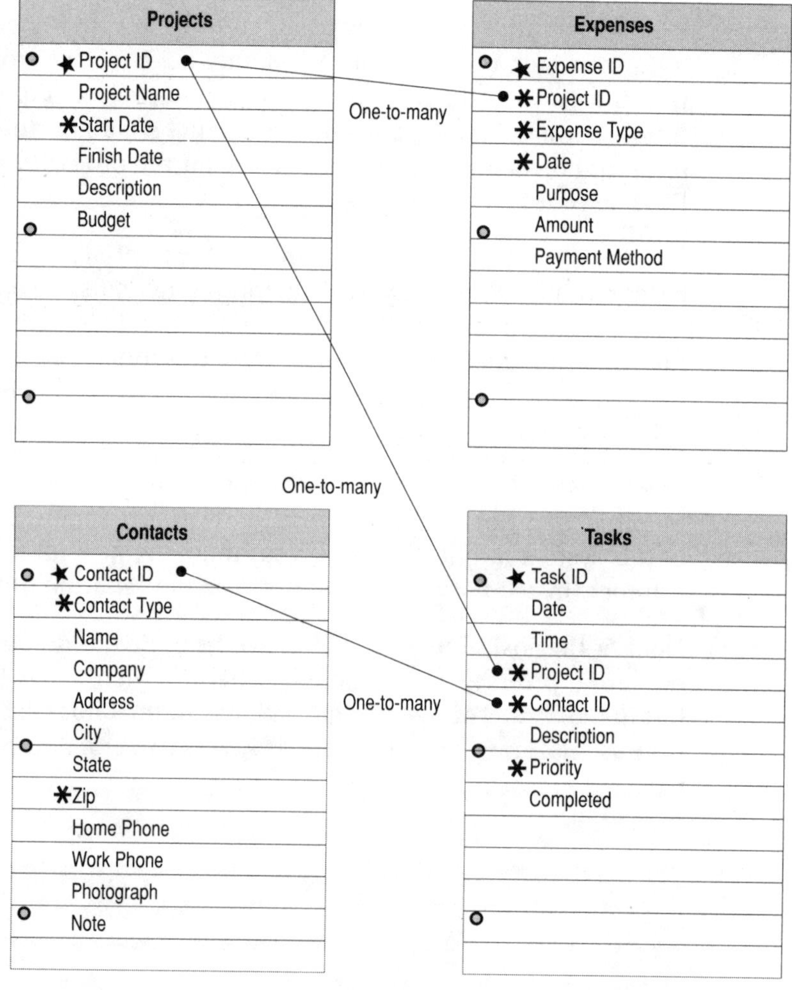

The relationship between projects and expenses is also one-to-many. In this case the Organizer application *will* enforce referential integrity: each expense must be related to an existing project. (If you insist on adding expenses not related to any "real" project, you can create a catch-all project called Personal Budget or Other Expenses.)

The relationship between the Projects and Tasks tables is also one-to-many: for each project, you'll have more than one task. The application won't enforce referential integrity in this relationship; you'll be able to enter a task not related to any existing project.

The Organizer application will print a variety of reports that draw data from two or more tables, including a daily or weekly appointment calendar with contact names and phone numbers and a project summary with both tasks and expenses.

Figure 3.7 diagrams the table structures and relationships in the Organizer application.

WHAT'S NEXT

Now you're ready to turn on the computer, start up Access, and begin constructing the database you've laid out on paper. If you're impatient to get going, take heart—the mechanics of creating a new database and defining your tables are much easier and take a lot less time than the advance planning. Chapter 4 shows you how to do it.

Creating a Database

Once you've sketched out the table structures, creating an Access database and defining the tables is easy. In this chapter you'll create a database for the Organizer application and define the four tables that store the data.

This chapter introduces the first of many Access Wizards—on-line assistants that can help you create tables, queries, forms, and reports. The Wizards interview you by presenting a series of dialog boxes in which you answer questions and make selections, and then, based on your answers, create a database component for you. If you are overcome by anxiety when presented with a completely blank design work surface, the Wizards are a sure cure. And using the Wizards doesn't limit your options—you can always modify the objects they create if you aren't entirely satisfied with the results.

This chapter shows you how to

- Use the Table Wizard to create a table
- Customize the resulting table
- Define a table from scratch

CREATING A NEW DATABASE

The first step in any Access database project is to create the database that serves as a repository for all the data and forms. Each database is stored in a single monolithic disk file, which has the extension .MDB and a first name that you specify. This name must adhere to the standard DOS naming conventions—it can be up to eight characters long and can contain letters, numbers, and certain punctuation marks (but no spaces). You'll see the database name in the title bar of the Database window, so try to choose a name that's clear and descriptive.

NOTE

Only the name of the .MDB file is subject to the eight-character limit. Tables and other objects (database components) are stored inside the .MDB file, not as separate disk files and their names can be up to 64 characters long and can contain spaces and most punctuation marks.

To begin creating a new database, do one of the following:

- Choose File ➤ New Database.
- Click the New Database button in the toolbar.
- Press the hot-key shortcut, Ctrl+N.

NOTE

If you already have a database open, you don't have to close it. Access automatically closes any open database before creating or opening another.

If you want to try the examples in this book, create the database for the Organizer application:

1. Choose File ➤ New Database.
2. If you don't want your database in the drive and directory shown in the New File dialog box, change the drive and/or directory.

3. In the File Name text box, delete the default .MDB file name (DB1.MDB), and enter **ORGANIZE**. (*Organizer* would be a better name, but it is nine characters long.) You can type any mixture of uppercase and lowercase letters, and you don't have to type the .MDB extension. If you're storing ORGANIZE.MDB in the C:\ACCESS\SAMPAPPS directory, your dialog box will look like the one in Figure 4.1.

4. Press ↵ or click the OK button.

In a moment Access displays the Database window with the name of your new, empty database in the title bar. Because you have not yet created any tables, the list in the center of the window will be empty and the Open and Design command buttons will be disabled.

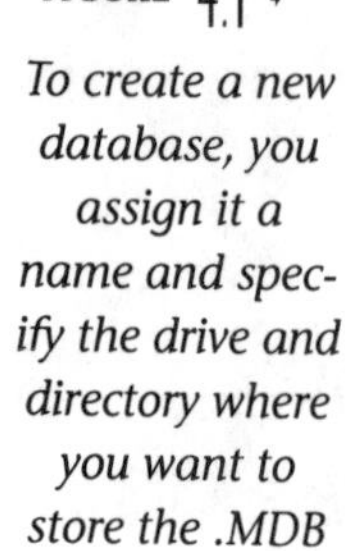

FIGURE 4.1

To create a new database, you assign it a name and specify the drive and directory where you want to store the .MDB file.

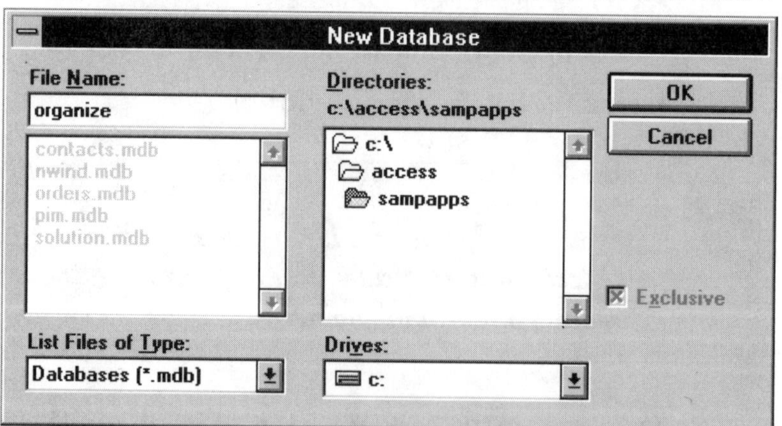

CREATING A TABLE USING THE TABLE WIZARD

You can use the Access Table Wizard to build a new table by choosing fields from a collection of sample tables. Using the Wizard is fast and easy, and the predefined fields will satisfy many simple table requirements. Often, you'll want to refine the structure of the resulting table afterwards, but you don't have to do this right away if you just want to get started entering data.

You'll use the Table Wizard to set up the Projects and Expenses tables and then you'll modify the structures of these tables. You will create the Contacts and Tasks tables in the Organizer application from scratch.

CREATING THE PROJECTS TABLE

To call up the Table Wizard to define the Projects table:

1. Make sure the Organize database is open and the (empty) list of tables is visible.
2. Click the New command button in the Database window or press Alt+N. Access displays the New Table dialog box shown in Figure 4.2.

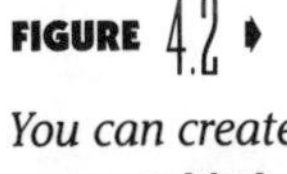

FIGURE 4.2 ▸ *You can create a new table by using the Table Wizard or by defining it from scratch.*

3. Click the Table Wizards button or press Alt+W. The Table Wizard displays the dialog box shown in Figure 4.3.

FIGURE 4.3 ▸

The Table Wizard lets you choose the fields for your new table from a group of sample tables.

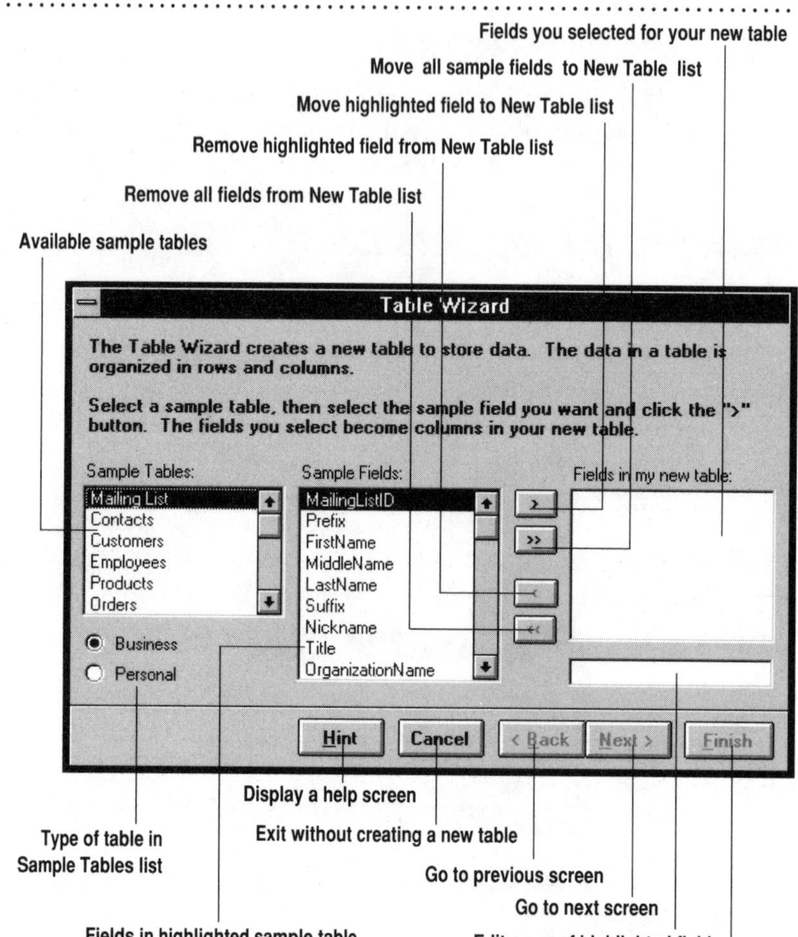

CHOOSING YOUR FIELDS

The Table Wizard displays the names of available tables in the Sample Tables list on the left side of the dialog box. You can choose between two broad categories of sample tables—business or personal—by selecting the appropriate radio button below the list. The Sample Fields list in the center of the dialog box displays the names of the fields in the sample table that is highlighted in the Sample Tables list. Try scrolling through the list of tables and watch the field list change.

On the right side of the Table Wizard dialog box, a list box labeled **Fields in my new table** (we'll call this the New Table list) displays the fields you've already selected for your new table. In Figure 4.3 this list is empty because you haven't yet picked any fields. You can edit field names in the text box below this list. Between the Sample Fields and New Table lists are four command buttons, which you use to add or remove fields. You can also add a field by double-clicking its name in the Sample Fields list or remove a field by double-clicking its name in the New Table list.

TIP

You can choose fields from more than one sample table. To switch to a new source table at any point, simply highlight the one you want in the Sample Tables list.

To choose the fields for the Projects table:

1. Make sure the Business button is highlighted so the Sample Tables list displays business tables.
2. Scroll down the Sample Tables list and highlight Projects.
3. Make sure the ProjectID field is highlighted in the Sample Fields list, and click the > button.
4. Highlight ProjectName in the Sample Fields list, and click the > button.

5. Double-click the ProjectDescription field in the Sample Fields list.
6. Click Next to move on to the next step.

TIP

Pressing ↵ in any of the Table Wizard dialog boxes is equivalent to selecting Next (which is the default button). If you do this inadvertently, simply click the Back button to return to the previous screen and pick up where you left off.

CHANGING THE TABLE NAME AND ASSIGNING THE PRIMARY KEY

After you've chosen your fields, the next Table Wizard dialog box, which is pictured in Figure 4.4, lets you change the table name and decide how the primary key will be assigned. For the Projects table:

7. Retain the default table name, Projects.
8. Click Set the primary key myself.

FIGURE 4.4 ▸

The Table Wizard lets you rename your new table and set the primary key yourself if you wish.

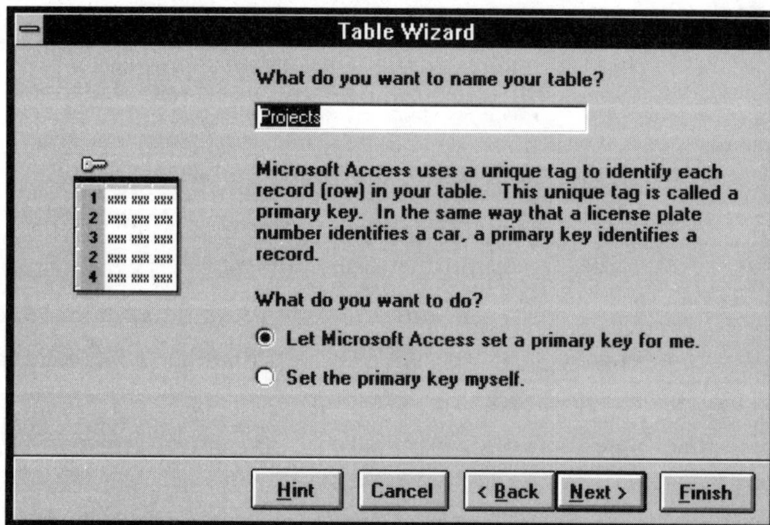

9. Click the Next button to move on to the next step.

If you elect to set the primary key yourself, the Table Wizard displays the dialog box shown in Figure 4.5, which lets you choose the primary key and specify the type of data this field will contain.

Each of the sample tables includes a field intended to serve as the primary key, with a name like ProjectID, EmployeeID, or ProductID. Access guesses that the first such field in your new table should be the primary key, and in most cases this assumption is correct. If you want to pick a different field, use the combo box at the top of the dialog box.

The Table Wizard gives you three choices for the contents of the primary key field, and your selection determines whether the Wizard makes this field a counter, number, or text field. If you don't have an

FIGURE 4.5 ▸

The Table Wizard lets you choose the primary key field and describe its contents.

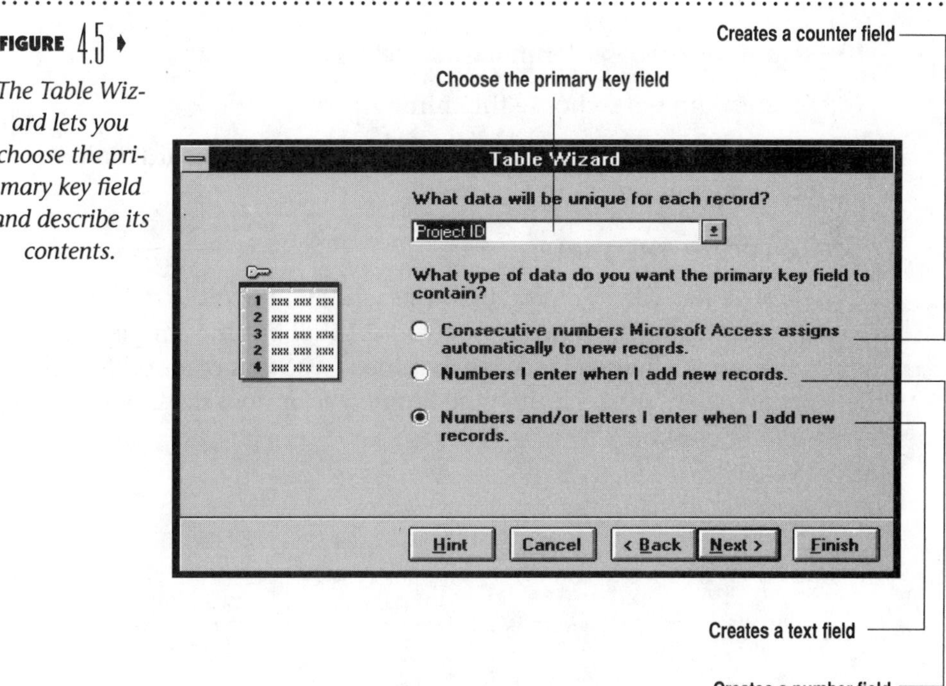

obvious unique identifier in your table, choose the first option to create a counter field, which is guaranteed to be unique (although it's not very convenient for searches).

NOTE

The Table Wizard doesn't allow you to create a primary key consisting of two or more fields. If you need to do this, you must modify the table structure later. You'll learn how to set the primary key later in this chapter, in the section "Defining the Primary Key."

The primary key for the Projects table will be an alphanumeric key, which you'll enter yourself when you add new records. To describe the primary key:

10. Retain the proposed primary key field, ProjectID.

11. For the data type, choose the third option.

12. Click the Next button to move to the final Table Wizard dialog box, which is shown in Figure 4.6.

COMPLETING THE TABLE

The last Table Wizard dialog box asks what you want to do now that you're finished defining your new table. In all but the simplest tables, you'll want to choose **Modify the table design** so you can add fields, rearrange their order, change the data types or field sizes, or create a multifield primary key.

FIGURE 4.6

After the Table Wizard builds your table, you can modify the structure or move directly to data entry.

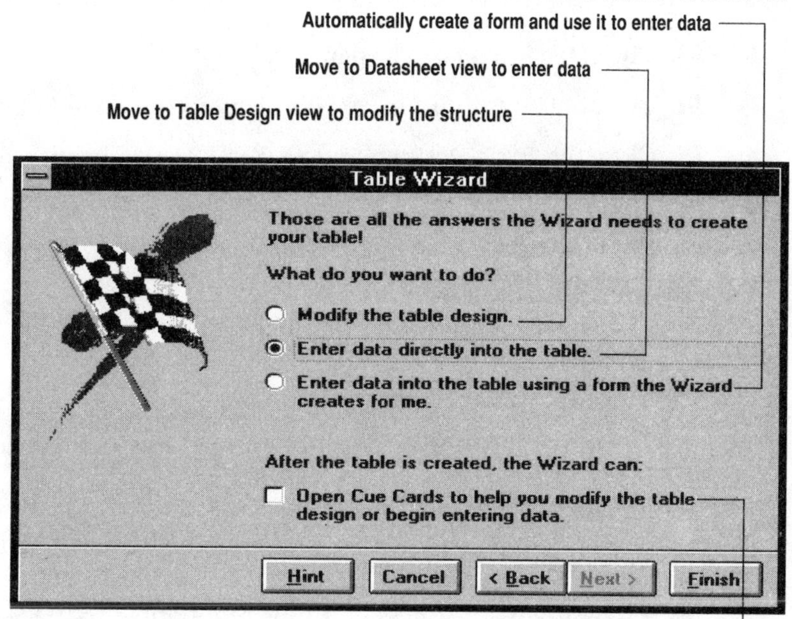

TIP

The Table Wizard doesn't give you the option to just save your new table and return to the Database window. If you want to do this, pick either Modify the table design ***or*** Enter data directly into the table ***and then immediately close the resulting window.***

To complete the Projects table:

13. Click Modify the table design.
14. Click the Finish button. Access displays the table in Design view.
15. Close the Table Design window. You'll return later in this chapter to modify the Projects table structure.

CREATING THE EXPENSES TABLE

Use the Table Wizard to define the Expenses table in the Organizer application:

1. Make sure the Database window displays the list of tables, and click the New command button in the Database window or press Alt+N to open the New Table dialog box.
2. Click the Table Wizards button or press Alt+W to call up the Table Wizard.
3. Make sure the Business button is highlighted so the Sample Tables list displays business tables.
4. Scroll down the Sample Tables list and highlight Expenses.
5. Add the ExpenseID, ExpenseType, and DatePurchased fields to your new table.
6. Click in the text box below the New Table field list, and change the name of the DatePurchased field to ExpenseDate.
7. Add the PurposeofExpense field to your new table, and change its name to Purpose.
8. Add the AmountSpent field to your new table, and change its name to Amount.
9. Add the PaymentMethod field to your new table, and then click the Next button.

10. Retain the default table name, leave Let Microsoft Access set a primary key for me selected, and click the Next button.

DEFINING RELATIONSHIPS BETWEEN YOUR TABLES

Unless you're defining the very first table in a database, the Table Wizard displays the dialog box shown in Figure 4.7, which helps you define the relationships between your new table and existing tables. The Wizard assumes that your new table isn't related to any others, and if this assumption is correct, you can just move on to the next step.

FIGURE 4.7

The Table Wizard reminds you to define the relationships among tables.

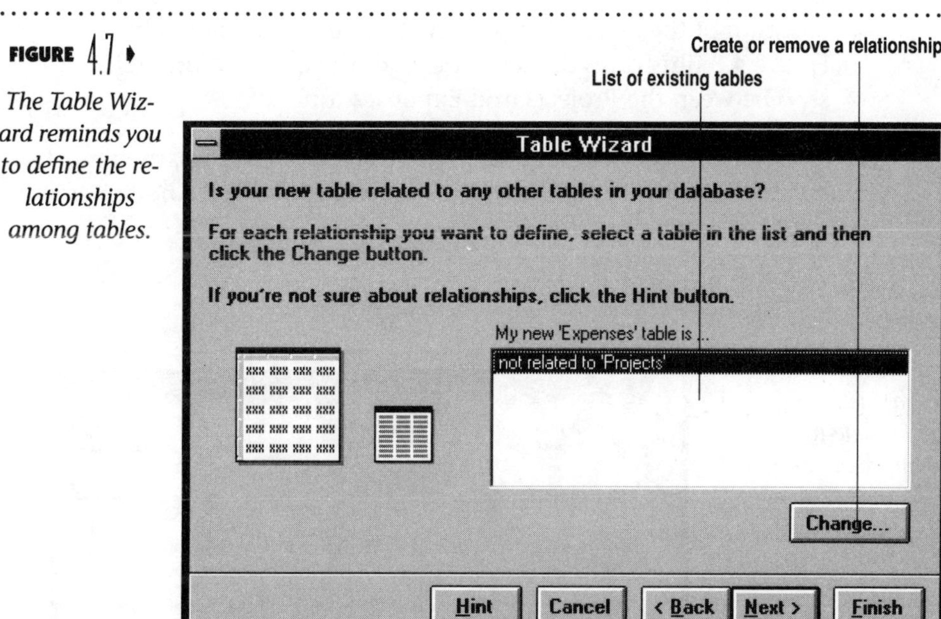

In the Organizer database, the Expenses table should be related to the Projects table. However, if you plan to modify the tables constructed by the Wizard (in particular, if you need to change the size of the primary key field), it's better to defer defining the relationship until afterward. For now, just take a look at how the Wizard helps you set relationships:

11. Click the Change button to move to the Relationships dialog box.

NOTE

When your database contains more than one table, make sure you highlight the right one before you select Change.

12. Click each of the three radio buttons in turn, and look at the diagram of the relationship at the bottom of the dialog box. Figure 4.8 illustrates the description of the one-to-many relationship between the Projects and Expenses tables.

Before you can define a relationship between two tables, they must have a common field that identifies matching records. The Projects

FIGURE 4.8

The Table Wizard lets you define one-to-many relationships between tables.

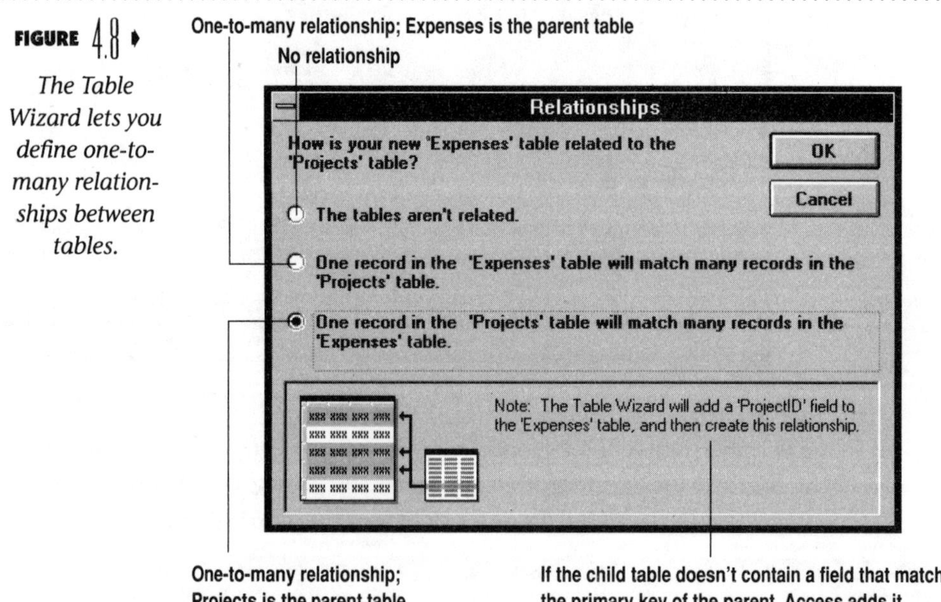

and Expenses tables don't have a common field, but the Table Wizard is smart enough to solve this problem by adding a Project ID field to the child table (Expenses) to match the primary key of the parent table (Projects).

NOTE

The Table Wizard can't define a one-to-one relationship. You must do this yourself afterwards, and you'll learn how later in this chapter, in the section "Defining the Table Relationships." When you create the extra table required to represent a many-to-many relationship between two other tables, you can use the Wizard to define the one-to-many relationships between this table and the two main tables.

COMPLETING THE TABLE

To finish defining the Expenses table:

13. Select The tables aren't related, and then click OK to close the Relationships dialog box.
14. Click Next to move on to the next step.
15. Select Modify the table design, and then click the Finish button.
16. Close the Table Design window.

MODIFYING OR CREATING A TABLE

Using the Table Wizards is very easy, but it gives you little control over the table structure—the only property of the predefined fields you can change is their names. In all but the simplest tables, you'll want to customize other field properties or add fields not provided in the sample tables. You may also find, after working with a table for a while, that you need to add fields, delete fields, or reorder the fields. If you've already begun entering records, don't worry—you won't lose any data (except in fields you intentionally delete or shorten).

If you need a table that isn't even close to any of the Wizard's sample tables, you're better off creating the table from scratch, as described in the next section.

To modify the structure of an existing table, open the table in Table Design view:

1. Make sure the Database window displays the list of tables.
2. Highlight the name of the table you want to modify.
3. Click the Design button or press Alt+D.

To create a new table from scratch:

1. Make sure the Database window displays the list of tables.
2. Click the New command button or press Alt+N. Access displays the New Table dialog box shown earlier in Figure 4.2.
3. Click the New Table button or press Alt+N.

WORKING IN TABLE DESIGN VIEW

Figure 4.9 illustrates the Expenses table created by the Table Wizard in Table Design view. In the upper half of the window, Access lists the field names, data types, and optional descriptions. Additional *properties,* or characteristics, of the currently selected field are displayed in the lower half. In Access, the term *property* is used for a single discrete aspect of an object's appearance or behavior. Properties are often displayed in a list called a *property sheet.* Often, the property sheet appears in its own window on the Access desktop, but the field properties are simply listed at the bottom of the Table Design window.

You can use the arrow keys to move around in either region of the window, and you can switch between the two by pressing F6. You can also use the mouse to move directly to any item visible in the Table Design window. For many properties, you can make a selection from a combo

FIGURE 

You use the Table Design view to modify an existing table or to create a new table from scratch.

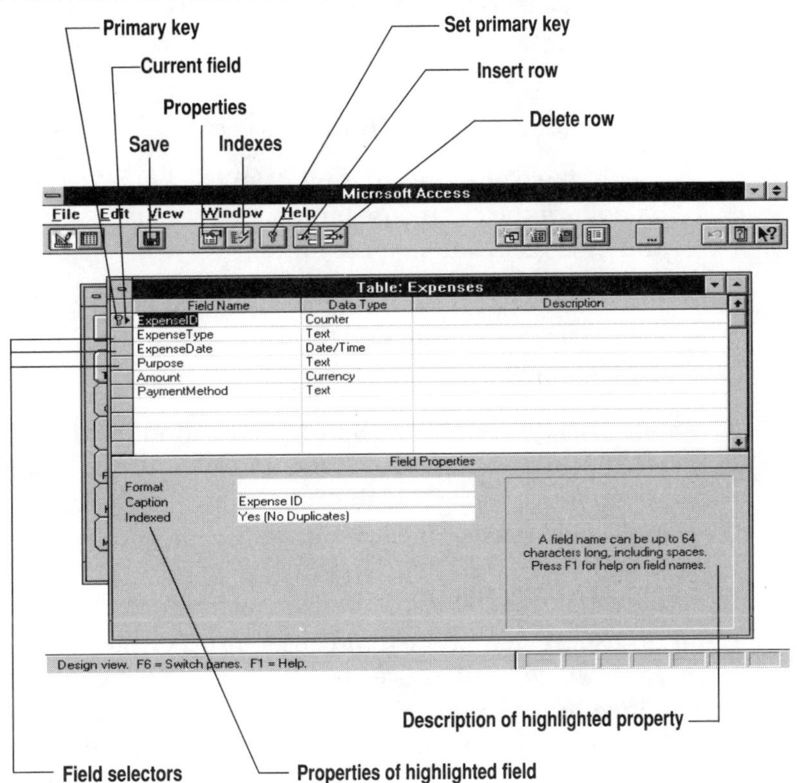

box rather than type it. If a list is available for a property, you'll see the arrow that identifies a combo box when you move into the data entry region. You can also select a list entry by typing the first letter (or two, if the first letter is not unique).

NOTE

If you're working in the Field Properties section of the Table Design window, you must return to the field list in the upper portion of the window to move to another field.

To the left of each field name is a *selector button,* which you use to select entire rows (fields). The easiest way to select rows is to use the mouse:

- To select one field, click the field selector.
- To select two or more adjacent fields, click the first field selector, hold down the left mouse button, drag the mouse to the last field, and then release the mouse button.
- To select nonadjacent fields, click the first field selector, release the left mouse button, and then hold down the Ctrl key while you click additional field selectors.

Access displays a small triangle in this button to indicate the currently selected field and uses a key symbol to identify the field or fields that make up the primary key. You can see both of these symbols in the ExpenseID field selector in Figure 4.9.

REARRANGING FIELDS

In Datasheet view and in data entry forms created by the AutoForm Wizard (which is introduced in Chapter 7), the fields are displayed in the order in which they appear in the table structure. If you find this order inconvenient, you can rearrange the columns in the datasheet, and you can edit any form created by the Form Wizards. Sometimes, though, after you've worked with a table for a while, you'll want to move the fields in the structure itself into a more rational sequence.

To move one or more adjacent fields:

1. Select the row(s).
2. Make sure the mouse pointer is above a selected row, press and hold the left mouse button, and drag the selected row(s) to their new location. Access displays a dark shadow line to monitor the position of the top of the first row you're moving.
3. Release the mouse button to drop the row(s) in the new location.

TIP

After you move rows, they remain selected until you click somewhere else on the screen. It's a good idea to deselect rows as soon as possible after moving them to avoid accidentally deleting them.

DELETING FIELDS

To delete one or more fields, highlight the row(s) and press Del, or select Edit ➤ Delete or Edit ➤ Delete Row. You can also delete one row without first selecting it by moving into the row and then choosing Edit ➤ Delete Row. If you press Del without first selecting a row, Access deletes the highlighted item (for example, a field name or data type), not the whole field. If you're already editing (that is, there's an insertion point visible), pressing Del deletes characters one at a time. If you make a mistake, you can undo your last deletion by using the Undo options on the Edit menu.

ADDING NEW FIELDS

To add a new field at the end of the structure, just move down to the first blank row and type the field name. To add a new field between two existing fields, move down to the row you want to end up *below* the new field and press Ins or select Edit➤Insert Row.

You can get some help in defining your new field by clicking the Builder button in the toolbar, which calls up the same list of sample tables and fields displayed by the Table Wizard. Most of the time, though, you'll be adding fields that you couldn't find in any of the sample tables.

DEFINING FIELDS

For each field in your table, you *must* assign a name. Like other Access names, field names can include spaces and punctuation marks, but as you can see in Figure 4.9, tables created by the Table Wizard have no spaces in the field names.

TIP

As you'll see in Chapter 10, writing the expressions that define calculations is a lot easier if you don't use spaces in your field names.

Assigning a name is the only obligatory step when you define a field, but you'll generally also want to override the Access defaults for at least a few other properties. First and foremost is the *data type,* which determines what type of information you can enter into a field. The Access data types are described in the next section. If you don't choose a data type, Access assumes you want a text field, which can accept any characters.

WARNING

Don't use the field name Name if you plan to use the Mailing Label Wizard (which is described in Chapter 9) to design mailing labels. In the reports created by this Wizard, Access will confuse this field name with the name of the report form itself. Use a field name like FullName or NameOfPerson instead.

You can use the optional description to enter up to 255 characters of notes on a field. When you update the table, either in Datasheet view or using a custom form, Access displays as much of the description as will fit (about 90 characters) in the status bar at the bottom of the screen. The description thus gives you a very easy way to attach a customized message that "tags along" with a field in many different contexts to explain its purpose or usage.

If you move down through the list of fields in the Expenses table, you'll see that the available properties in the lower half of the Table Design window vary, depending on the data type. The following table provides a complete list of properties. You don't have to understand these properties in detail yet; they're listed just to give you a taste of the possibilities, some of which we'll explore in later chapters.

PROPERTY	DESCRIPTION
Field Size	For text fields, the maximum length of any entry; for number fields, the type of number and its length
Format	The overall display format—how the data entered in a field appears on the screen
Input Mask	A character-by-character formatting pattern—for example, to insert the parentheses and hyphens in a phone number such as (408) 555-1272
Caption	A prompt used instead of the field name as a label in forms and reports
Default Value	A value entered automatically into new records—for example, CA for a state field
Validation Rule	A condition that describes valid entries—for example, a rule that zip codes must be exactly 5 or 10 digits long
Validation Text	The error message displayed when the data you enter does not satisfy the validation rule
Required	Specifies whether the field must be filled in
Allow Zero Length	Specifies whether a text or memo field must be filled in or can be left blank
Indexed	Specifies whether the field is indexed and if so, whether duplicate values are permitted

CHOOSING DATA TYPES

Database programs aren't as flexible as human beings, and database programs require a more detailed description of the type of data you want a field to be able to accept. The payoff for this added burden is more consistent and accurate data. For example, on a manual order form, a clerk might write *ASAP* in a box labeled Due Date. In an Access database you can store the due date as a date/time field, which accepts only legitimate dates or times, not letters of the alphabet.

Access recognizes eight data types, which are listed in the following table:

DATA TYPE	DESCRIPTION
Text	Stores up to 255 characters, including letters, numbers, punctuation marks, and graphics symbols
Memo	Stores up to 32,000 characters, including letters, numbers, punctuation marks, and graphics symbols
Number	Accepts only digits, a minus sign, and a decimal point. There are five types of number fields, which vary in the size of the numbers they can store and the number of significant digits
Date/time	Accepts dates and/or times
Currency	Accepts only digits, a minus sign, and a decimal point. Access automatically formats currency fields with a currency symbol, separators every three digits, and a decimal point
Counter	Stores a counter that is automatically incremented (increased by 1) in each new record
Yes/no	Stores only the logical values Yes and No, which can also be displayed as True or False, or On or Off
OLE object	Stores nontext data created by other programs, such as graphics images, spreadsheets, digitized photographs, sound recordings, or video recordings

If you find the data types overwhelming, it's possible to avoid the issue by using the text data type for most fields, but you'll sacrifice the benefits that accrue from choosing a data type that more accurately reflects a field's intended contents. Here are some guidelines for choosing the right data type:

- *Use a memo field* when you need to enter more than 255 characters of text (the maximum length of a text field).
- *Use a number field* whenever you need to carry out calculations or compute summary statistics (sums or averages) on a value. If a field contains only digits but won't be used in calculations, such as a zip code or part number, it's usually better to use a text field. If a field requires embedded punctuation, such as the dashes in a social security number, you *must* use a text field.
- *Use a currency field* if you always want to display a numeric value formatted with a currency symbol, decimal point, and comma separators.
- *Use a date/time field* for a calendar date and/or time to take advantage of the automatic formatting and validation available for this data type. Access won't allow you to enter impossible dates like February 30 or invalid times like 26:30. You can display dates and times in a variety of formats, and regardless of the display format, Access can sort dates and times into correct chronological order. It can also do *date arithmetic*—subtract two dates or times to calculate the elapsed time, or add or subtract a specified time interval to or from a date or to obtain a past or future date or time (for example, to calculate an invoice due date).
- *Use a yes/no field* for storing the answers to a yes-or-no question. You can display a yes/no field as Yes or No, True or False, or On or Off, and you can represent yes/no fields on forms as check boxes.

- Use an OLE object field for data derived from another program, such as a spreadsheet, word processor document, scanned photograph, sound recording, or video clip. To view the data in an OLE object field, the program that created the data must be available.

SETTING THE FIELD SIZE

For text fields the field size establishes the maximum number of characters you can enter. For number fields the field size determines what type of number Access stores in the field. The following table lists the choices:

NUMBER TYPE	DESCRIPTION
Byte	Integers (whole numbers) from 0 to 255
Integer	Integers from –32,768 to 32,767
Long Integer	Integers from approximately –2 billion to 2 billion
Single	Real numbers (numbers that may have a fractional portion) with six significant digits
Double	Real numbers with ten significant digits

NOTE

The term* significant digits *denotes the number of digits used in calculations, not the length or size of the numeric value. Thus, 252,817 and 2.52817 both have six significant digits. If you enter the value 2,252,817 into a Single field (which has six significant digits), it is stored as 2,252,820.

If you don't explicitly set a field size, Access assumes a default value, and this is often larger than you need—for example, 50 characters for text fields. The Table Wizard is even more liberal; it assigns the maximum length, 255, to many text fields and uses the Double size for most number fields.

Retaining the default doesn't waste storage space, because Access stores only as many characters as you actually enter. There are two main reasons for changing the field size:

- The Form and Report Wizards deduce the width of a field from its size.
- You'll often want to limit the length of the value entered into a field (for example, a U.S. state abbreviation, which is always two characters long).

ASSIGNING A CAPTION

The caption serves as an alternative prompt, which is used instead of the field name in Datasheet view and to label the field on forms and reports. As noted earlier, it's a good idea not to include any spaces in your field names. If you don't like the looks of prompts such as ExpenseType and FullName on forms and reports, you can assign friendlier captions, such as Expense Type and Full Name or Name. The Table Wizard uses this strategy, as you'll see shortly when you modify the tables you created earlier in this chapter.

TIP

You can conserve space on forms and in Datasheet view by assigning a short caption to substitute for a long field name. For example, a long field name like ExpenseType makes it clear, when you define calculations based on multiple tables, exactly which field you're talking about. In the Expense table's Datasheet view, the caption Type might be sufficient to identify the field.

CUSTOMIZING THE INPUT MASK

An *input mask* is a pattern of characters that describes the way you want a field formatted. You can use input masks to enforce consistency in the way data is entered. For example, you can insert punctuation in fields such as telephone numbers and social security numbers, and you can restrict date/time fields to a particular format. The Table Wizards create input masks for all date/time fields and for many others, including telephone numbers. If you don't want to be restricted to one format, modify the table structure and delete the input mask.

DEFINING THE PRIMARY KEY

To assign a primary key (or change an existing primary key), select the rows for the field(s) that will make up the primary key, and then click the Set Primary Key button in the toolbar or select Edit ➤ Set Primary Key. Access automatically builds an index based on the primary key and prohibits duplicate values in this index.

SAVING THE TABLE STRUCTURE

To save the table structure at any point, do one of the following:

- Choose File ➤ Save.
- Click the Save button on the toolbar.
- Press the shortcut key Ctrl+S.

To exit from Table Design view and save your changes, use any of the standard methods for closing a Windows document window. (For example, press Ctrl+F4 or double-click the close box.) If you have made any changes since you last saved the structure, Access displays an alert box to notify you and let you decide whether to save or discard your latest modifications.

MODIFYING THE ORGANIZER TABLES

To practice modifying a table structure, you'll add three new fields to the Projects table—for the project starting date, ending date, and budget—and make a few other changes:

1. Open the Projects table in Table Design view.
2. Make sure the ProjectID field is highlighted, and press F6 to edit the field properties.

3. Change the field size to 15, and then press F6 to return to the field list.
4. Move down to the ProjectName field, and note that this field is indexed. Press F6 to edit the field properties, and set the Indexed property to No to remove the index, and then press F6 to return to the field list.
5. Move down to the ProjectDescription field, and press Ins to insert a new row.
6. Type the name of the new field, **StartDate**, and press Tab to move to the Data Type column.
7. Click the arrow to display the combo box drop-down list, and choose Date/Time from the list.
8. Press F6 to edit the field properties.
9. Display the Format drop-down list, and choose Short Date.
10. Enter **Start Date** for the caption.
11. Set the Indexed property to Yes (Duplicates OK), and then press F6 to return to the field list.
12. Insert another row above the ProjectDescription field, and define the FinishDate field (also a date/time field, displayed in Short Date format) with the caption Finish Date.
13. Move down to the first blank row below the ProjectDescription field, and enter the field name, **Budget**. Press Tab to move to the Data Type column.
14. To choose the data type, type **N**, and note that Access fills in the complete data type (number). Press F6 to edit the field properties.
15. Choose Standard for the format, and enter **2** for the Decimal Places property.
16. Press Ctrl+F4 or double-click the close box to close the Table Design window.
17. Choose Yes from the dialog box that asks whether you want to save your changes.

Next, you'll modify the structure of the Expenses table to adjust the field sizes, add indexes, and, most important, add a ProjectID field to support the relationship between this table and the Projects table. Here are the steps:

1. For the ExpenseType field, change the field size to 15 and set the Indexed property to Yes (Duplicates OK).
2. For the ExpenseDate field, enter the caption **Date** and set the Indexed property to Yes (Duplicates OK).
3. For the Purpose field, change the field size to 50.
4. For the Amount field, change the data type to number, the format to Standard, and decimal places to 2.
5. Insert a new row before the ExpenseType field, and define the ProjectID field as a text field with a field size of 15. Enter the caption **Project ID**, and set the Indexed property to Yes (Duplicates OK).
6. Close the Table Design window and save the structure.

CREATING A NEW TABLE FROM SCRATCH

Once you know how to add a new field to an existing table, as described in the preceding section, creating a new table from scratch is easy. When you use any of the methods enumerated earlier in this chapter to begin defining a new table, you'll see the same Table Design window you used to modify an existing table, but the field list will be blank. Simply begin filling in your field specifications in the upper half of the window and entering properties in the lower half.

Access automatically assigns each new table a name—Table1 (for the first table you create), Table2, and so on. The first time you save the table, Access displays a Save As dialog box so you can enter a more descriptive name.

In the Organizer database, you'll create the Contacts and Tasks tables from scratch. The table on the following page lists the structure for the Contacts table.

FIELD NAME	CAPTION	DATA TYPE	SIZE
ContactID	Contact ID	Text	15
ContactType	Contact Type	Text	15
FullName	Name	Text	50
Company		Text	50
Address		Text	50
City		Text	25
State		Text	2
Zip		Text	10
HomePhone	Home Phone	Text	14
WorkPhone	Work Phone	Text	30
Photograph		OLE object	
Note		Memo	

Enter the following descriptions for the ContactID, ContactType, HomePhone, and WorkPhone fields (and others, if you're so inclined):

FIELD	DESCRIPTION
ContactID	Unique ID code based on last name or organization name
ContactType	Business, friend, relative, professional, and so on
HomePhone	Telephone number, including area code
WorkPhone	Telephone number, including area code and extension or message number

The primary key for the Contacts table is the ContactID field. To set the primary key:

1. Click the record selector for the ContactID field.
2. Click the Set Primary Key button in the toolbar.

To speed up sorts and selections, you'll need indexes based on the ContactType and Zip fields, both of which should allow duplicate values.

The following table shows the structure for the Tasks table.

FIELD NAME	CAPTION	DATA TYPE	SIZE	FORMAT
TaskID	Task ID	Counter		
Date		Date/time		Short Date
Time		Date/time		Medium Time
ProjectID	Project ID	Text		15
ContactID	Contact ID	Text		15
Description		Text		50
Priority		Number	Byte	
Completed		Yes/no		Yes/no

The primary key for the Tasks table is the Task ID field, which is guaranteed to be unique because it's a counter field. Like the Expenses table, this table has no logical candidate for a primary key, and the most expedient solution is to allow Access to generate a unique value in each new record. To speed up sorting and selections, you'll need indexes based on the ProjectID, ContactID, and Priority fields, all of which should allow duplicate values.

DEFINING THE TABLE RELATIONSHIPS

You define the relationships between your Access tables by creating a diagram like the one in Figure 4.10, which shows the tables in the Organizer application. To display the Relationships window, do one of the following:

- Click the Relationships button in the toolbar.
- Choose Edit ➤ Relationships.

FIGURE 4.10 ➧ *You can use the graphical Relationships window to define table relationships.*

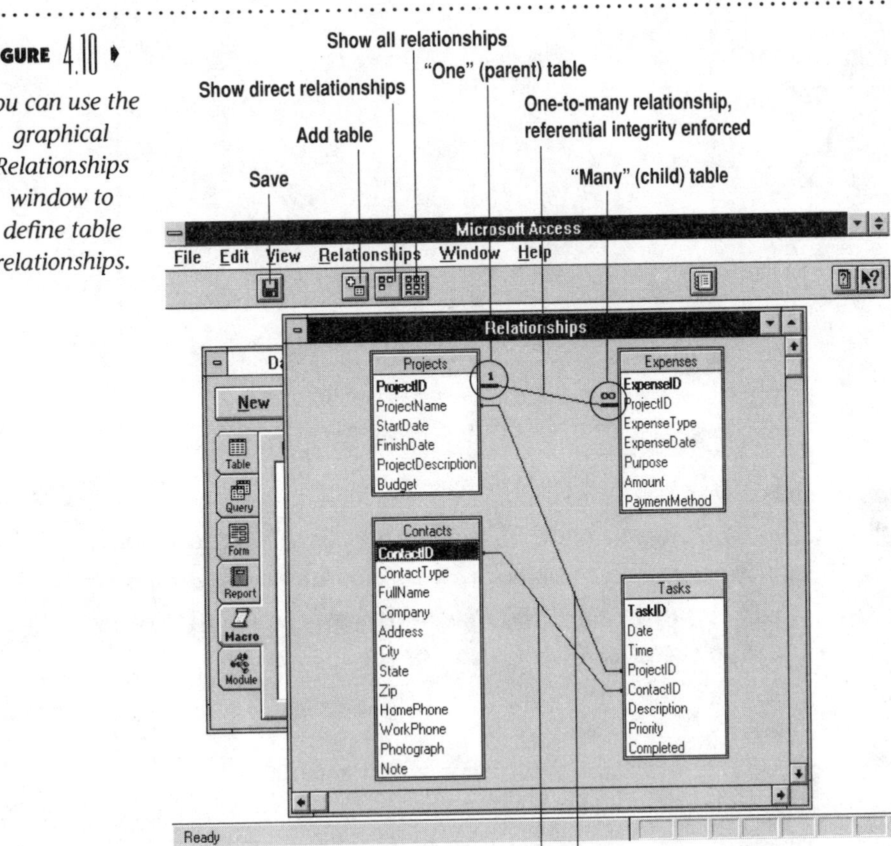

If you haven't defined any relationships yet, Access displays the Add Table dialog box shown in Figure 4.11. To choose a table, you can double-click its name or highlight the name and click the Add button. When you're finished adding tables, click the Close button.

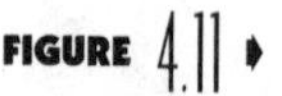

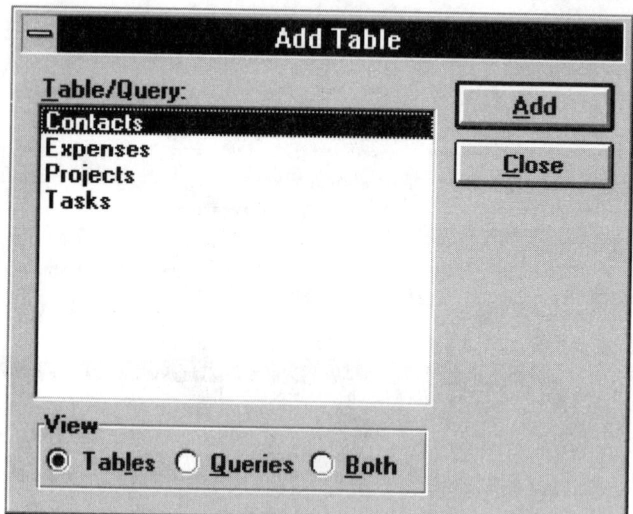

FIGURE 4.11

The Add Table dialog box lets you choose which tables (or queries) you want in the Relationships diagram.

NOTE

You don't have to add all your tables to the Relationships diagram at once. You can call up the Add Table dialog box at any point by selecting Relationships ➤ Add Table or by clicking the Add Table button in the toolbar.

After you've added your tables to the Relationship window, you diagram the relationships by drawing lines between the matching fields with the mouse, and, optionally, defining additional properties of the relationships. If you elect to enforce referential integrity in a one-to-many relationship, Access marks the parent table with a *1* and the child table with ∞ (the infinity symbol).

NOTE

Access doesn't distinguish between a one-to-one and a one-to-many relationship unless you elect to enforce referential integrity. If you don't, a record in the primary table can have one or more corresponding records in the related table, so there's no need to make the distinction.

Each of the field lists in the Relationships window behaves like a little window. You can move a list by using the mouse to drag it by the title bar, and you can resize a list to display more (if not all) of the fields. To indicate a relationship based on one field:

1. Point to the linking field in the primary table.
2. Press and hold the left mouse button.
3. Drag the mouse to the linking field in the related table.
4. Release the mouse button. Access displays the dialog box shown in Figure 4.12.
5. If you wish, select additional options in this dialog box, and then click OK to save your selections.

If you need to define a relationship based on more than one field, use the mouse to indicate the first field and then add the others in the lists at the top of the Relationships dialog box.

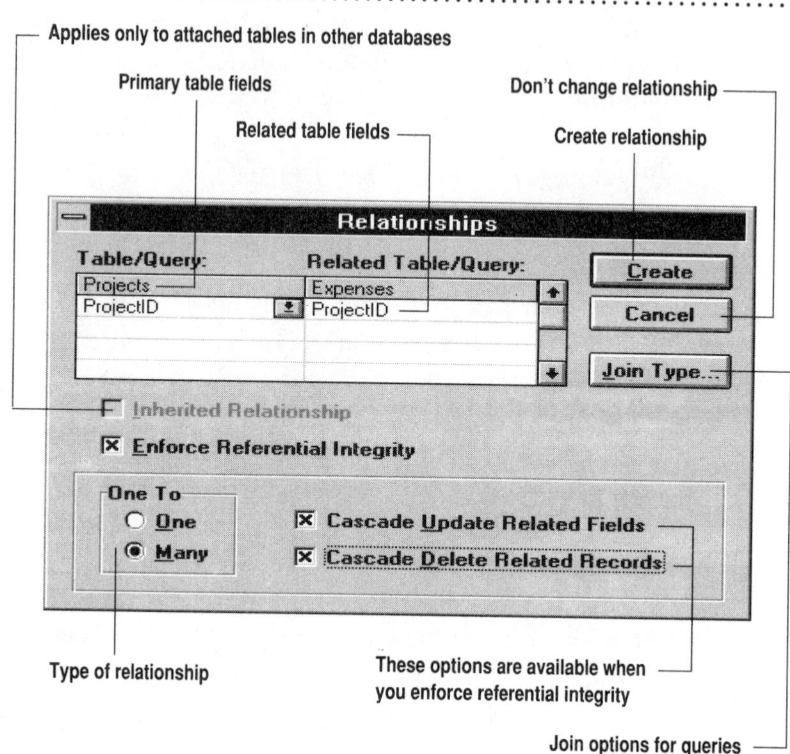

FIGURE 4.12 *You can define relationships based on more than one field and select referential integrity options in the Relationships dialog box.*

To define the relationships in the Organizer database:

1. From the Database window, select Edit ➤ Relationships or click the Relationships button in the toolbar.
2. Add all the Organizer tables to the Relationships window, and then close the Add Table dialog box.
3. Drag the windows into the layout shown in Figure 4.12, and resize the Contacts and Tasks table windows so you can see all the fields.

4. To define the relationship between the Projects and Expenses tables, drag the ProjectID field from the Projects table over to the ProjectID field in the Expenses table. Check the Enforce Referential Integrity, Cascade Update Related Fields, and Cascade Delete Related Fields check boxes, and click the Create button to create the relationship and close the dialog box.

5. To define the relationship between the Projects and Tasks tables, drag the ProjectID field from the Projects table over to the ProjectID field in the Tasks table. Click Create without making any additional selections. (You're not enforcing referential integrity in this relationship.)

6. To define the relationship between the Contacts and Tasks tables, drag the ContactID field from the Contacts table over to the ContactID field in the Tasks table. Click Create without making any additional selections. (You're not enforcing referential integrity in this relationship.)

7. Close the Relationships window, and choose Yes from the dialog box that asks whether you want to save your changes.

DOCUMENTING A DATABASE

You can print a description of any database component by highlighting the object's name in the Database window and choosing File ➤ Print Definition. Access previews the printout on the screen, but you can print it by selecting File ➤ Print or clicking the Print button in the toolbar. You probably won't use this option much for forms and reports because a sample page or two produced by printing the form or report with your data is a clearer, more intuitive way to document its purpose, but it's a good idea to print your table definitions for reference. To print a diagram of the table relationships, open the Relationships window and then choose File ➤ Print Definition.

When you print a table definition, Access displays the dialog box shown in Figure 4.13 to let you specify how much detail you want. For now, try turning off all the table options and selecting Names, Datatypes, and Sizes for fields and Names and Fields for indexes. Figure 4.14 illustrates the printed definition of the Tasks table.

To print a summary of all the table relationships in your database, open the Relationships window and then choose File ➤ Print Definition. Access displays the relationships diagram in Print Preview. To

FIGURE 4.13 ➧

You can print a table definition with various amounts of detail.

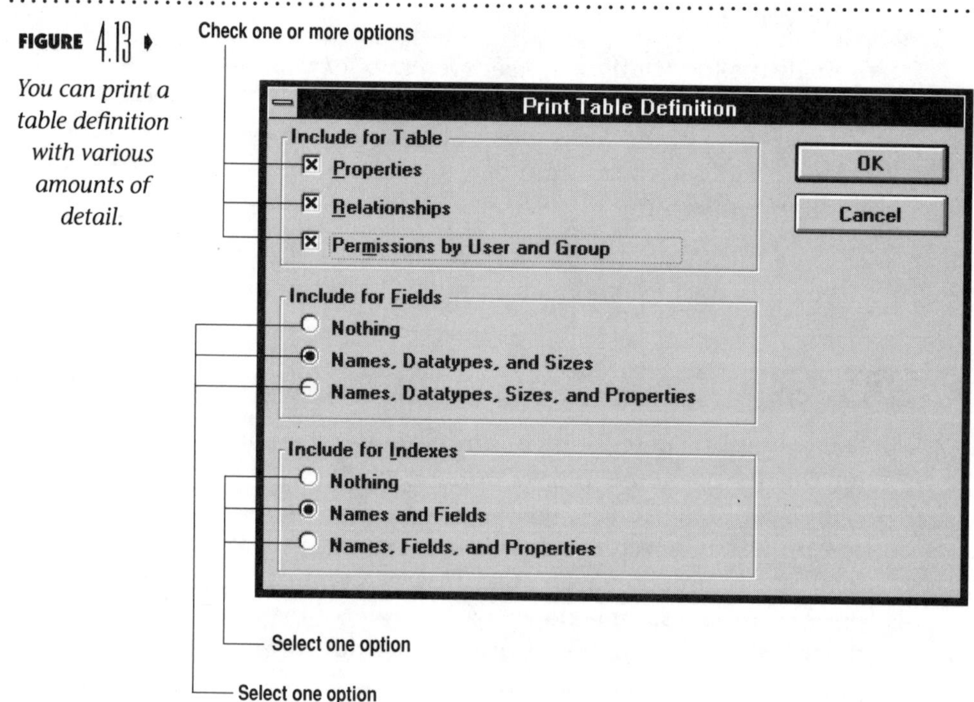

FIGURE 4.14

The printed definition of the Tasks table shows the fields and indexes.

C:\ACCESS\SAMPAPPS\ORGANIZE.MDB — Wednesday, March 02, 1994
Table: Tasks — Page: 1

Columns

Name	Type	Size
TaskID	Number (Long)	4
Date	Date/Time	8
Time	Date/Time	8
ProjectID	Text	15
ContactID	Text	15
Description	Text	50
Priority	Number (Byte)	1
Completed	Yes/No	1

Table Indexes

Name	Number of Fields
ContactID	1
Fields:	ContactID, Ascending
PrimaryKey	1
Fields:	TaskID, Ascending
Priority	1
Fields:	Priority, Ascending
ProjectID	1
Fields:	ProjectID, Ascending

print it, click the Print button in the toolbar. Figure 4.15 shows the printout for the Organizer database.

FIGURE 4.15

Access can print a summary of the relationships displayed in the Relationships window.

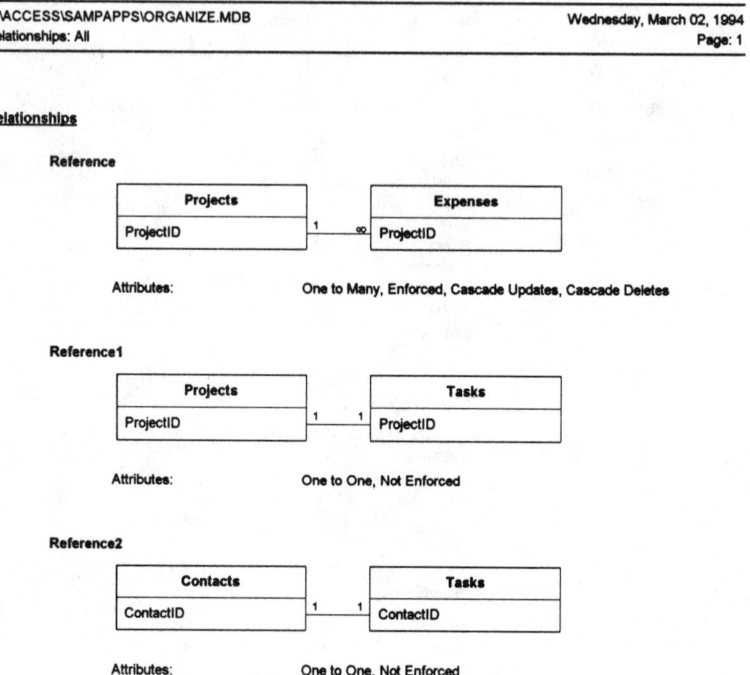

C:\ACCESS\SAMPAPPS\ORGANIZE.MDB
Relationships: All

Wednesday, March 02, 1994
Page: 1

Relationships

Reference

Attributes: One to Many, Enforced, Cascade Updates, Cascade Deletes

Reference1

Attributes: One to One, Not Enforced

Reference2

Attributes: One to One, Not Enforced

WHAT'S NEXT

Now that you've defined the tables in the Organizer database, you're ready to begin entering data. Chapter 5 describes how to update tables in Datasheet view to get you started quickly.

Updating Tables in Datasheet View

If you're anxious to begin using your new Access tables, your patience is about to be rewarded. You don't have to spend any more time on preliminaries before you can start entering data. Access gives you a built-in form called the *datasheet,* which you can use for all the essential table maintenance activities—viewing, editing, adding, and deleting records. (If you've forgotten what the datasheet looks like, take a peek ahead at Figure 5.1.)

Even after you've designed custom forms for specific purposes, you'll find the datasheet useful. The tabular layout is ideal for browsing through a large table to spot trends, making occasional changes, adding a few records, or deleting individual records (or groups of records). For tables that don't have too many fields to fit on the screen at once, it's also a convenient data entry form.

Finally, it's usually a good idea, especially if you haven't had much experience with databases, to enter some sample data into all your tables before you invest a lot of time in designing forms. If this testing reveals problems (missing fields, inappropriate data types, field sizes that are too short or too long)—and it usually does—you can fix them at this stage and avoid having to edit your forms to account for any changes you make in the table structures.

THE DATASHEET WINDOW

When you open a table from the Datasheet window, Access displays it in *Datasheet view,* a tabular layout with a row for each record and a column for each field, arranged in the order the fields occupy in the table structure. If you've used a spreadsheet program, you'll feel right at home in the datasheet. To open a table in Datasheet view, make sure the Database window displays the list of tables, and then do one of the following:

- Highlight the table name and press ↵.
- Highlight the table name and click Open or press Alt+O.
- Double-click the table name.

Since you haven't yet entered any data into the Organizer tables, take a moment to open the Customer table in NWIND.MDB (one of the databases supplied with Access, which is normally installed in the ACCESS\SAMPAPPS subdirectory) so you can experiment. Figure 5.1 shows what the screen looks like when you first open the table.

NOTE

When you work with one table at a time, you'll often want to maximize the Datasheet window to display as much data as possible. To make it easier to discern the window controls, the figures in this chapter do* not *show the Datasheet window maximized.

When you first open a table in Datasheet view, the records are displayed in primary key order (in the NWIND Customers table, the Customer ID field is the primary key), but you'll see in Chapter 6 how easy it is to change the order. The number of rows and columns you can see at once depends on your video display, but even in Super VGA mode you'll only be able to see all the rows and columns in a very small table.

In any Access window, the object or item of data that you're currently working in is said to *have the focus.* In Datasheet view, the field that has the focus is the one you're currently editing.

To the left of each row is a *row selector,* and at the top of each column is a *column selector.* You can use these buttons just as you do the row

FIGURE 5.1 ▸

In addition to the usual window controls, the Datasheet window includes special controls for navigating through the table.

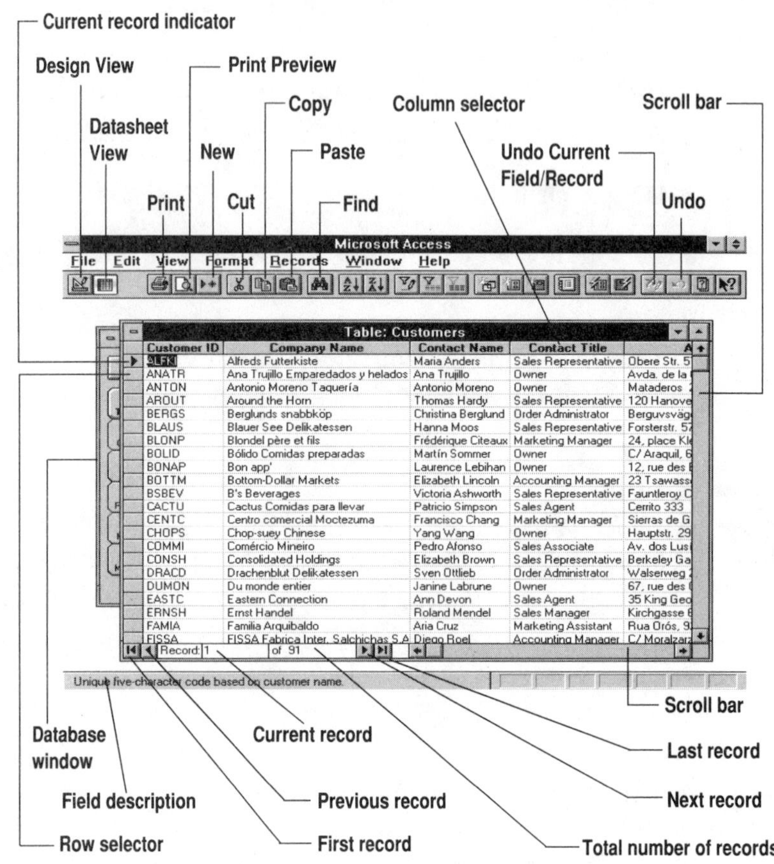

selectors in Table Design view to operate on one or more rows or columns. The triangle symbol in a row selector identifies the *current* record (the one that has the focus). The column selectors serve double duty: they also display the field names (or captions, for fields that have captions) as column titles.

If you entered a field description when you defined the table, Access displays it on the left side of the status bar whenever the field has the focus. Otherwise, you'll see *Datasheet View* in the status bar.

NAVIGATING THROUGH A TABLE

You can visualize the Datasheet window either as a small window onto a much larger chart, which extends in all four directions behind your computer screen, or as the view-finder of a camera, which shows you a small portion of the scene in front of you.

Access gives you a variety of controls for moving this window around to see different groups of rows and columns. If you wish, you can go anywhere in the table just by using the horizontal and vertical scroll bars. The easiest way to move through a table one record at a time is to use the *VCR buttons* at the bottom of the Datasheet window. To move to a specific record, Press F5 or click the box labeled Record, and then type the record number.

TIP

Usually you won't know the number of the record you want to find. The easiest way to move to an approximate location in a large table is to use the vertical scroll bar.

NOTE

If you're new to Windows, note that the scroll bars move the window, **but they don't automatically change the focus.** ***Unless you click somewhere in the window, you'll revert to the cell that last had the focus when you begin typing. In contrast, using the navigation controls*** **does** ***move the focus.***

While you're entering or editing records, you might not want to take your hands off the keyboard to operate the navigation buttons or scroll bars with the mouse. The following table lists some keyboard commands you'll find useful in Datasheet view:

KEY	PURPOSE
→	Move right one column
Tab	Move right one column
←	Move left one column
Shift+Tab	Move left one column
↓	Move down one row
↑	Move up one row
PgDn	Move down one screenful of data
PgUp	Move up one screenful of data
Home	Move to leftmost column in current row
End	Move to rightmost column in current row

EDITING DATA

Editing records in Datasheet view is very direct and immediate: simply use any combination of mouse and keyboard commands to move into any field on the screen and then replace, delete, or edit the contents. When you use keyboard commands to move into a field, Access *selects* the entire contents—it displays the field highlighted (white on black in the default Windows colors). In Figure 5.1 the Customer ID field in the first record is selected. You can select a field with the mouse by clicking the left column border. When the mouse pointer is in the right spot, it looks like this:

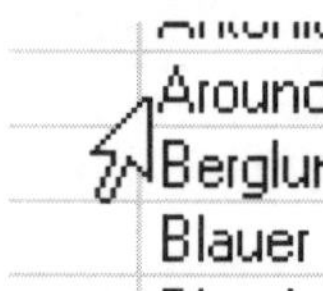

WARNING

It's essential to notice whether a field is selected because in Windows, anything you type* replaces *the selected data. If you press Del with all or part of a field selected, Access deletes the entire selection. Unless this is your intention, don't just move into a field and start typing.

To edit a field, click where you want to begin editing or press F2 while the field is selected. To terminate editing, press F2 again or simply move to another row or column in the datasheet. While you're editing, Access displays an *insertion point* (a vertical line) in the field to indicate your current position, and the arrow keys move the insertion point through the field rather than letting you move around the datasheet. To select *part* of a field so you can delete or replace it, hold down the Shift key as you press the arrow keys, or click the field and drag the mouse to delineate your selection. The most important keys and key combinations are listed in the following table:

KEY	PURPOSE	WITH SHIFT
→	Move right one character	Extend selection right one character
←	Move left one character	Extend selection left one character
Ctrl+→	Move right one word	Extend selection right one word
Ctrl+←	Move left one word	Extend selection left one character
Home	Move to beginning of field	Extend selection to beginning of field

KEY	PURPOSE	WITH SHIFT
End	Move to end of field	Extend selection to end of field
Ins	Switch between insert and overstrike modes	

TIP

When you press F2, Access puts the insertion point at the end of the field. If you know exactly where you want the insertion point, it's easier to initiate editing by clicking with the mouse.

If a column isn't wide enough to display the full contents of a field, Access scrolls the data to follow the insertion point. Later in this chapter, in the section "Changing Column Widths," you'll learn how to adjust the column widths. If you need more space to edit a long text or memo field, you can open a larger editing window like the one in Figure 5.2 by pressing Shift+F2 or by right-clicking within the field and then choosing Zoom from the popup menu. To close the window and return to the datasheet, press ↵ or click OK.

FIGURE 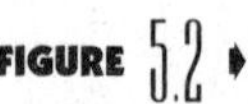

You can use the Zoom command to open an editing window for any field.

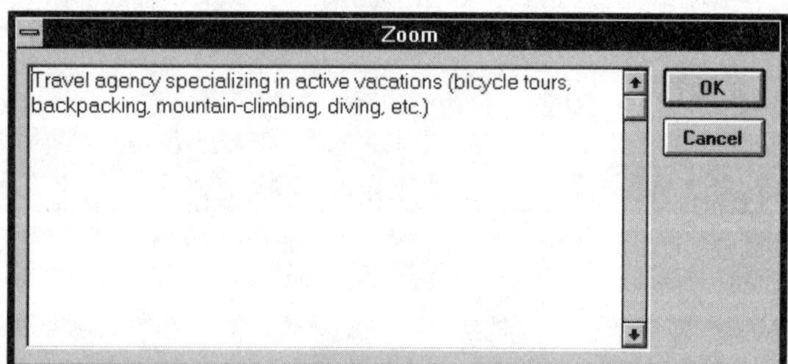

By default, Access edits in *insert mode*—each character you type is *added* to the field to the left of the insertion point. In *overstrike mode*, characters you type *replace* existing characters. You can switch between insert and overstrike modes by pressing the Ins key.

TIP

If you forget which mode you're in, look for the OVR (overstrike) indicator in the status bar. Also, in overstrike mode the insertion point disappears and Access highlights one character (the one that will be replaced by the next character you type).

FORMATTING AND VALIDATION

In most cases you can just type data into your table exactly as you would on paper, but be aware of a few special considerations for fields of various data types:

- To include a *hard return* (a line break) in a text or memo field, press Ctrl+↵. (Pressing ↵ moves you to the next field.)
- Don't enter currency symbols or commas into number fields. Access inserts the punctuation automatically in fields assigned the Currency or Standard format. Otherwise, it discards these characters when you leave the field.
- You don't have to type the decimal point if there are no digits beyond it. Access always displays the number of decimal places defined in the table structure.
- You can enter dates and times in any valid Windows format (for example, 18-Mar-95, 3/18/95, or Saturday, March 18, 1995, for dates, or 3:25 pm or 15:25 for times). The date and time fields are displayed according to the format assigned in the table structure.

- You can enter Yes/No fields as

  Yes, No

  True, False

  On, Off

  –1, 0

  using any mixture of upper- and lowercase letters.

- Don't try to enter a value in a counter field. Access automatically supplies the value.

If you enter prohibited characters (such as letters in a number or date/time field), Access displays an alert box with the warning message The value you entered isn't appropriate for this field when you leave the field.

If you (or the Table Wizard) defined an input mask for a field, Access won't let you enter a value that doesn't conform to the input mask. For example, using the Wizard's input mask, you must enter dates in *mm/dd/yy* format (with or without leading zeros). If you violate these rules, Acess displays an alert box that notifies you, The value you entered isn't appropriate for the input mask specified for this field.

The referential integrity rules you defined in the Relationships window are always in effect—in Datasheet view and while you're using a custom form. For example, if you try to add a record to the Expense table that doesn't match any record in the Projects table, Access displays an alert box with the error message Can't add or change record. Referential integrity rules require a related record in table "Projects".

Access won't let you leave a field blank if it's part of the primary key. If any such fields are blank when you try to leave a record, Acess displays an alert box that warns you Index or primary key can't contain a null value. (*Null* means blank.)

SAVING AND UNDOING CHANGES

Access normally saves your changes one record at a time: it saves the record you're editing when you move to a different row in the datasheet. You can save the current record any time you want with the File ➤ Save Record command or by pressing Shift+↵. These commands are most useful when you need to make extensive changes to lengthy text or memo fields—it's prudent to save the record before you start editing each field in case you later decide to undo subsequent changes.

If you've changed the current record since you last saved it, the symbol in the record selector changes from a triangle to a pencil:

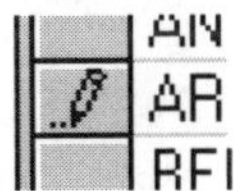

No matter how careful you are, you'll sometimes make changes that you immediately regret. Access lets you undo your mistakes (or simply change your mind) at several stages.

- *To undo all changes to the current field,* do one of the following:
  - Press Esc.
  - Click the Undo Current Field/Record button on the toolbar.
  - Use the Edit ➤ Undo Current Field command.
- *To undo your most recent change (the last characters you deleted or changed),* do one of the following:
  - Click the Undo button in the toolbar.
  - Use the Edit ➤ Undo Typing command.
- *To undo all changes to the current record,* undo the changes to the current field, and then do one of the following:
  - Press Esc.
  - Click the Undo Current Field/Record button on the toolbar.
  - Use the Edit ➤ Undo Current Record command.

- *To undo all changes to the last record you saved,* use the Edit ➤ Undo Saved Record command.

NOTE

If you use File ➤ Save Record and then continue editing the same record, this record will be the one restored by the Edit ➤ Undo Saved Record command, not the previous record you changed.

ENTERING NEW RECORDS

At the bottom of the datasheet Access displays a blank row with an asterisk in the row selector as a placeholder for the next new record you'll add to the table. To enter a new record, do one of the following:

- Move into any field in the blank row and begin typing.
- Click the New command button in the toolbar.
- Use the Records ➤ Go To ➤ New command.
- Use the Records ➤ Data Entry command.
- Press Ctrl++ (hold down the Ctrl key and press +).

The last four methods are just shortcuts to move you to the blank record at the bottom of the table. The Records ➤ Data Entry command works differently: it suppresses the display of all existing records and shows you a blank datasheet. In data entry mode you'll see only the new records you add, and you can easily proofread or print your new entries without being distracted by the rest of the records in a large table. To return to viewing the whole table, do one of the following:

- Close the Datasheet window and reopen it.
- Click the Show All Records button in the toolbar.
- Choose Records ➤ Show All Records.

TIP

To automatically repeat the value you entered into the same field in the previous record, press the "ditto" key, Ctrl+' (hold down the Ctrl key and press the single quote key).

ENTERING THE CONTACTS TABLE SAMPLE DATA

Now you're ready to begin entering the Organizer sample data:

1. If the ORGANIZE database is not already open, open it.
2. Open the Contacts Table in Datasheet view and enter the first ten records:

Contact ID	**Beverly**
Contact Type	**Friend**
Name	**Frank Beverly**
Address	**8572 Prospect Ave.**
City	**Santee**
State	**CA**
Zip	**92071**
Home Phone	**(619) 482-3984**

Contact ID	**WrightMills**
Contact Type	**Friend**
Name	**Carol Wright-Mills**
Address	**2432 9th St.**
City	**Berkeley**
State	**CA**
Zip	**94710**
Home Phone	**(510) 548-1891**

Contact ID	**JacksonOBrien**
Contact Type	**Contractors**
Name	**Ann Jackson and Katherine O'Brien**
Company	**Gemini Plumbing**
Address	**2605 Fulton St.**
City	**Berkeley**
State	**CA**
Zip	**94704**
Work Phone	**(510) 848-2350**

Contact ID	**Klein**
Contact Type	**Friend**
Name	**Don and Janet Klein**
Address	**1783 Vallejo St. Apt. 112**
City	**San Francisco**
State	**CA**
Zip	**94123**
Home Phone	**(415) 861-5498**

Contact ID	**TrueType**
Contact Type	**Graphic Design**
Company	**True Type Typesetters**
Address	**1254 Euclid Ave.**
City	**Berkeley**
State	**CA**
Zip	**94708**
Work Phone	**(510) 821-3540**
Note	**Don't expect fast turnaround.**

Contact ID	**Adams**
Contact Type	**Graphic Design**
Name	**Jeffrey Adams**
Address	**2400 Mariner Square Dr. #138**
City	**Alameda**
State	**CA**
Zip	**94501**
Home Phone	**(510) 845-6783**
Work Phone	**(510) 522-8950**

Contact ID	**ActiveAdventure**
Contact Type	**Travel**
Name	**Vera**
Company	**Active Adventures Travel**
Address	**940 Solano Ave.**
City	**Albany**
State	**CA**
Zip	**94706**
Work Phone	**(510) 524-3801**
Note	**Travel agency specializing in active vacations (bicycle tours, backpacking, mountain-climbing, diving, etc.)**

Contact ID	**Plummer**
Contact Type	**Friend**
Name	**Fern Plummer**
Address	**2910 Ellis St.**
City	**Berkeley**

State	**CA**
Zip	**94703**
Home Phone	**(510) 549-3769**

Contact ID	**QuickPrint**
Contact Type	**Graphic Design**
Name	**Barbara Stevenson**
Company	**Quick Print**
Address	**362 Grand Ave.**
City	**Oakland**
State	**CA**
Zip	**94610**
Work Phone	**(510) 654-8342**

Contact ID	**FutureDesigns**
Contact Type	**Contractors**
Name	**Marilyn Williams**
Company	**Future Designs**
Address	**305 D St.**
City	**San Rafael**
State	**CA**
Zip	**94901**
Work Phone	**(415) 459-2939**
Note	**Interior designer.**

When you add new records to a table, Access displays them in the order in which you entered them, as shown in Figure 5.3. Preserving the original order helps you proofread, especially if you want to compare

FIGURE 5.3 ➧

First ten records in the Contacts table

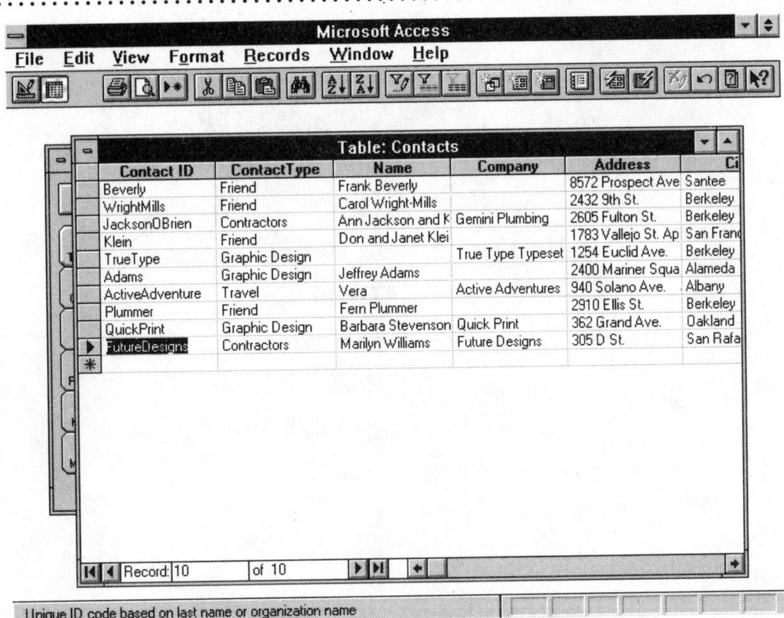

the screen to a paper input document that lists multiple records (like an order form or sign-up sheet). The next time you open the table, all the records will be displayed in primary key order. Verify this in the Contacts table:

3. Close the Contacts table and then reopen it. You'll see your first ten records in alphabetical order by Contact ID.

4. To enter the next ten records, choose Records ➤ Data Entry. Remember to press Ctrl+↵ after the first line of the two-line addresses in the last two records. Here is the data:

Contact ID	**MasterBuilders**
Contact Type	**Contractors**
Name	**Michael A. Barton**
Company	**Master Builders**
Address	**PO Box 5187**

City	**Vallejo**
State	**CA**
Zip	**94590**
Work Phone	**(707) 452-1385**
Note	**Car phone: 651-2398**

Contact ID	**RedRock**
Contact Type	**Travel**
Name	**Jim McKenna**
Company	**Red Rock Tours**
Address	**420 S. Main St.**
City	**Moab**
State	**UT**
Zip	**84532**
Work Phone	**(801) 259-4492**
Note	**Mountain bike tours and guided rides.**

Contact ID	**Sanders**
Contact Type	**Friend**
Name	**The Sanders Family**
Address	**1482 NE 17th St. Apt. 6**
City	**Portland**
State	**OR**
Zip	**97232**
Home Phone	**(503) 652-8938**
Note	**Bob and Leslie, kids are Kimberly (born 1/18/85) and twins Frank and Mark (born 11/8/92).**

Contact ID	**Rainbow**
Contact Type	**Contractors**
Name	**George Roth**
Company	**Rainbow Painters**
Address	**4610 Doyle St.**
City	**Emeryville**
State	**CA**
Zip	**94608**
Work Phone	**(510) 601-8350**
Note	**Architect recommended by Fern Plummer.**

Contact ID	**Davis**
Contact Type	**Friend**
Name	**Peter and Laura Davis**
Address	**215 W 16th St.**
City	**Lawrence**
State	**KS**
Zip	**66044**
Note	**Kids are Jenny (born 8/1/87) and Gary (born 5/25/90).**

Contact ID	**PetCare**
Contact Type	**Client**
Name	**Melanie Fong**
Company	**PetCare Services**
Address	**2819 Oak Rd.**
City	**Walnut Creek**
State	**CA**

Zip	**94596**
Home Phone	**(415) 982-3055**

Contact ID	**Rosenberg**
Contact Type	**Friend**
Name	**Norman Rosenberg**
Address	**2218 E. Glenoaks Blvd.**
City	**Glendale**
State	**CA**
Zip	**91206**
Home Phone	**(818) 528-3899**
Work Phone	**(213) 952-3845 ext. 544**

Contact ID	**Allen**
Contact Type	**Contractors**
Name	**Christopher Allen**
Company	**Allen Electric**
Address	**825 Kains Ave.**
City	**Albany**
State	**CA**
Zip	**94706**
Work Phone	**(510) 525-9221**
Note	**Recommended by Master Builders.**

Contact ID	**Vargas**
Contact Type	**Graphic Design**
Name	**Carmen Vargas**
Address	**242 Stockton St. Suite 208**
City	**San Francisco**

State	**CA**
Zip	**94108**
Work Phone	**(415) 536-0942**
Note	**Works well with both small companies and large corporations.**

Contact ID	**PCAdvisors**
Contact Type	**Client**
Name	**Robert Santorelli**
Company	**PC Advisors**
Address	**1738 Sacramento St.** **Suite 802**
City	**San Francisco**
State	**CA**
Zip	**94109**
Work Phone	**(415) 626-3528**

5. Choose Records ➤ Show All Records to redisplay the whole table in primary key order.

DELETING RECORDS

To delete one or more records, select the record(s) and then press Del or select Edit ➤ Delete. The easiest way to select records is to use the row selectors:

- *To select one record,* click the row selector.
- *To select two or more adjacent records with the mouse,* click the row selector for the first record in the group. Then click the row selector for the last record or drag down the mouse to the last record.
- *To select two or more adjacent records with the keyboard,* move into the first record in the group, press Shift+spacebar to select this row, and hold down the Shift key while you press ↑ or ↓ to reach the last record.

TIP

There's an easy way to delete the current record without first selecting it: press Ctrl+–.

Access always displays an alert box that reminds you how many records you just deleted and gives you a chance to change your mind. Think twice before you select OK to proceed with the deletion; there's no way to recover a record afterward.

CUSTOMIZING THE DATASHEET

You can get a lot of work done using the default datasheet layout, but based on your experience entering the 20 Contacts table records, you undoubtedly already have some improvements in mind. You'll nearly always want to adjust some of the column widths, and increasing the row height makes it easier to enter and edit long text or memo fields. For specific data entry tasks, you might also want to rearrange some columns and hide others.

NOTE

All the customizations described in the next few sections affect only the appearance of the datasheet, not the underlying table structures, so you can't do any damage by experimenting. Also, Access always asks whether to save or discard your modifications when you close the Datasheet window. If you've chosen a particularly ugly font or completely scrambled the column order, the easiest way to start over with a clean slate is to close the datasheet without saving your changes and then reopen it.

MOVING COLUMNS

You won't always want to see the columns in the datasheet in exactly the same order. For example, if you're making phone calls you might want to see the Home Phone, Work Phone, and Note columns next to the Name column in the Contacts table datasheet. To move columns, simply select one or more columns and then use the mouse to drag them where you want them.

- *To select one column,* click the column selector.
- *To select two or more adjacent columns with the mouse,* click the selector for the first column in the group, and then click the selector for the last column or drag the mouse left or right to the last column.
- *To select two or more adjacent columns with the keyboard,* move into the first column in the group, press Ctrl+spacebar to select this column, and hold down the Shift key while you press ← or → to reach the last record.

Once you've selected one or more columns, you can just *click-and-drag* to move them: click any selected column, hold down the left mouse button, drag the highlighted column(s) until the dark line that identifies the left border is where you want them, and then release the left mouse button.

Try setting up the Contacts table datasheet for use as a telephone contact list:

1. Click the Company column selector to select the column, and then release the left mouse button.
2. Use the click-and-drag technique to move the Company column between the Contact Type and Name columns.
3. Scroll the datasheet all the way to the right.

4. Click the Home Phone column selector, hold down the left mouse button, drag the mouse to the right to select the Work Phone column, and then release the left mouse button.
5. Use the click-and-drag technique to move the selected columns between the Name and Address columns.
6. Click anywhere else in the window to deselect the columns. Your screen should look something like the one in Figure 5.4.

FIGURE 5.4

You can rearrange the columns in the datasheet.

Table: Contacts

Contact ID	ContactType	Company	Name	Home Phone	Work
ActiveAdventure	Travel	Active Adventures	Vera	(510) 524-3801	
Adams	Graphic Design		Jeffrey Adams	(510) 845-6783	(510) 522
Allen	Contractors	Allen Electric	Christopher Allen		(510) 525
Beverly	Friend		Frank Beverly	(619) 482-3984	
Davis	Friend		Peter and Laura Da		
FutureDesigns	Contractors	Future Designs	Marilyn Williams		(415) 459
JacksonOBrien	Contractors	Gemini Plumbing	Ann Jackson and K		(510) 848
Klein	Friend		Don and Janet Klei	(415) 861-5498	
MasterBuilders	Contractors	Master Builders	Michael A. Barton		(707) 452
PCAdvisors	Client	PC Advisors	Robert Santorelli		(415) 626
PetCare	Client	PetCare Services	Melanie Fong		(415) 982
Plummer	Friend		Fern Plummer	(510) 549-3769	
QuickPrint	Graphic Design	Quick Print	Barbara Stevenson		(510) 654
Rainbow	Contractors	Rainbow Painters	George Roth		(510) 601
RedRock	Travel	Red Rock Tours	Jim McKenna		(801) 259
Rosenberg	Friend		Norman Rosenberg	(818) 528-3899	(213) 952
Sanders	Friend		The Sanders Famil	(503) 652-8938	
TrueType	Graphic Design	True Type Typeset			(510) 821
Vargas	Graphic Design		Carmen Vargas		(415) 536
WrightMills	Friend		Carol Wright-Mills	(510) 548-1891	

Record: 1 of 20

HIDING COLUMNS

Moving columns is only part of the solution to the problem of creating the optimum datasheet layout for a particular data entry situation. Sometimes you simply don't need to see some (or most) of the columns in a table. For example, it would be easier to work with the contact name and telephone list if you eliminated the Address, City, State, Zip, and Photograph columns entirely.

The easiest way to hide columns is to select them and then choose Format ➤ Hide Columns. Try using this method to hide the Contact ID and Contact Type columns:

1. Click-and-drag the Contact ID column selector to the right to select the Contact Type column, and then release the left mouse button.
2. Choose Format ➤ Hide Columns.
3. Scroll all the way to the left and verify that the Company column really is the first column.

Because you can't select nonadjacent columns, this method can be cumbersome if you have more than a couple of columns to hide. A more general way to hide columns and/or redisplay hidden columns is to use the dialog box shown in Figure 5.5. To call up this dialog box,

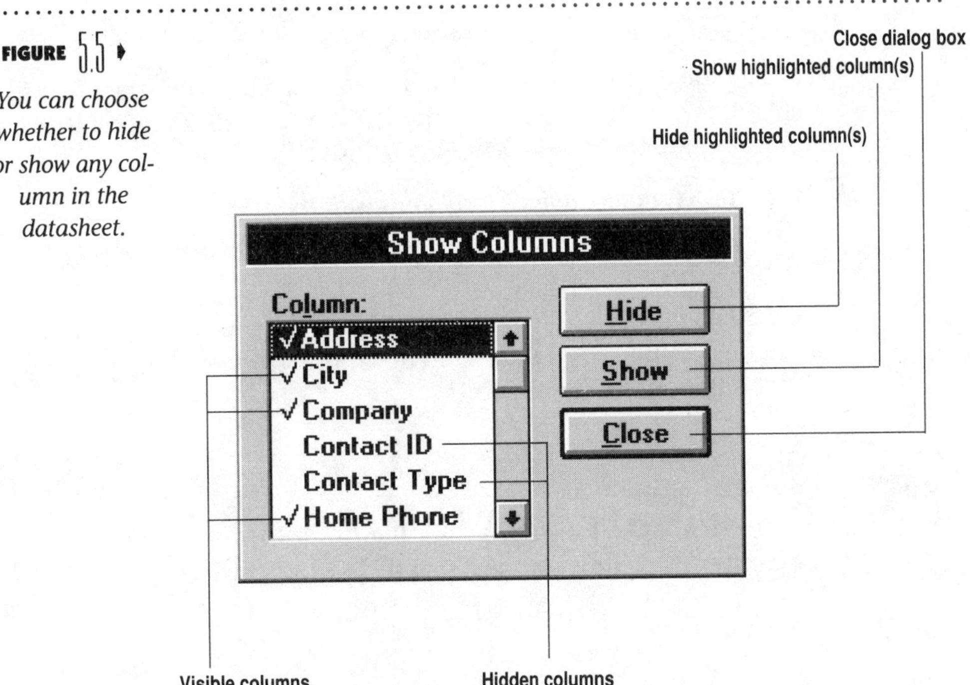

FIGURE 5.5 ➧ *You can choose whether to hide or show any column in the datasheet.*

choose Format ➤ Show Columns or right-click the title bar of the Datasheet window and then choose Show Columns from the popup menu. The wording *Show Columns* is a little misleading, and it's easy to forget that you can use it to hide columns as well as show them. Simply select the columns you want, and then click either Show or Hide. Access displays a check mark next to the name of each column that is currently visible, so it's easy to verify the datasheet setup.

NOTE

The field names (or captions, for fields that have captions) in the Column list are displayed in alphabetical order, not in the order in which they occur in the table structure or in the current datasheet layout.

You can select any number of columns at once, adjacent or not:

- *To select one column,* click its name.
- *To select two or more adjacent columns with the mouse,* click the first field name and then hold down the Shift key and click the last field name, or drag the mouse down to the last field name.
- *To select two or more adjacent columns with the keyboard,* press Shift+spacebar to select the first column, and hold down the Shift key while you press ↑ or ↓ to reach the last column.
- *To select nonadjacent columns,* click the first field name, release the left mouse button, and then hold down the Ctrl key while you click additional field names.

TIP

To quickly check or uncheck any column in the Show Columns dialog box, double-click it.

Use these methods to finish customizing the Contacts table datasheet for use as a telephone list:

1. Choose Format ➤ Show Columns.
2. Click-and-drag until City is also selected. Click Hide and verify that Address and City are no longer checked.
3. Click Contact Type, and then click Show to redisplay this column.
4. Scroll down the list, click Photograph, and then, holding down the Ctrl key, click State and then Zip. Click Hide to hide these three fields.
5. Close the Show Columns dialog box, and verify that only the Contact Type, Company, Name, Home Phone, Work Phone, and Notes columns are visible.

FREEZING COLUMNS

You can freeze one or more columns on the left side of the datasheet so they remain fixed as you scroll to the right. This option enables you to use one or more columns of data as "row titles" that always remain visible, no matter how wide the datasheet is. Typically, you'll want to freeze columns that uniquely identify the data in any row—for example, the Contact ID and/or Name columns in the Contacts table or the Expense ID, Project ID, and Expense Date columns for the Expenses table. To freeze the columns, select one or more columns and then choose Format ➤ Freeze Columns or right-click any selected column and then choose Freeze Columns from the popup menu. To unfreeze the columns, choose Format ➤ Unfreeze All Columns.

SAVING THE DATASHEET LAYOUT

When you close the Datasheet window after making any layout changes, Access displays an alert box that asks whether you want to Save layout changes to Table. Don't automatically choose Yes—sometimes you'll customize the datasheet layout for a specific situation that may never arise again. That's what you just did with the Contacts table, so close the datasheet now without saving the layout.

NOTE

You're not deciding whether to save the data, just the appearance of the Datasheet window. Access always saves the changes you make, one record at a time.

CHANGING COLUMN WIDTHS

The easiest way to adjust the width of a column is to drag the column selector border with the mouse:

1. Position the mouse pointer over the right boundary of the column selector so the mouse pointer looks like this:

2. Click-and-drag the column border to a new position.
3. Release the left mouse button.

To prepare for adding the first three records to the Projects table, open the table and adjust the column widths:

1. Open the empty Projects table in Datasheet view.
2. Move the Datasheet window to the upper-left corner of the Access program window and make it as wide as you can without maximizing it.
3. Narrow the Project ID, Start Date, Finish Date, and Budget columns to just a little wider than the column titles.

4. Widen the Project Name column to about 1½ times its original width.

5. Widen the Description column to take up the remaining space.

CHANGING THE ROW HEIGHT

When most of your fields are short, the default row height usually serves the purpose. If your table has long text fields or memo fields, increasing the row height lets you see more data without making the columns disproportionately wide, because Access word-wraps the text onto multiple rows. It's also much easier to view and enter fields that include hard returns, such as the two-line addresses in the Contacts table.

TIP

Increasing the row height to about 1½ times the default height will make the listing produced by printing the datasheet much more readable.

The easiest way to adjust the row height is to drag the row selector border with the mouse:

1. Position the mouse pointer over the lower boundary of any row selector so the mouse pointer looks like this:

2. Click-and-drag the row border to a new position.

3. Release the left mouse button.

NOTE

You can't change the height of individual rows in the Datasheet window. The height you set applies to all the rows.

Increase the row height in the Projects datasheet, and then enter the first three project records:

1. Set the row height to about three times the standard height.
2. Enter the three records:

Project ID	**Kitchen**
Project Name	**Remodel kitchen**
Start Date	**1/15/95**
Project Description	**New cabinet doors, new countertops, new sink, add work island, new floor covering, repaint, make new curtains.**
Budget	**7000.00**

Project ID	**PCAdvisors**
Project Name	**Brochure for PC Advisors**
Start Date	**11/1/94**
Finish Date	**11/28/94**
Project Description	**Design a brochure for a small company that provides consulting and training services on PC and Macintosh systems, networks, and software.**
Budget	**1800.00**

Project ID	**PetCare**
Project Name	**PetCare package**
Start Date	**2/1/95**
Project Description	**Design a brochure, letterhead, business cards, one-page flyer, and newspaper ad for a new pet care and housesitting business.**
Budget	**3200.00**

At this point your screen should look like the one in Figure 5.6.

FIGURE 5.6

The Projects table datasheet layout makes it easy to read and edit the Description field.

Table: Projects

Project ID	Project Name	Start Date	Finish Date	Project Description	Budget
Kitchen	Remodel kitchen	1/15/95		New cabinet doors, new countertops, new sink, add work island, new floor covering, repaint, make new curtains.	7,000.00
PCAdvisors	Brochure for PC Advisors	11/1/94	11/28/94	Design a brocure for a small company that provides consulting and training services on PC and Macintosh systems, networks, and	1,800.00
PetCare	PetCare package	2/1/95		Design a brochure, letterhead, business cards, one-page flyer, and newspaper ad for a new pet care and housesitting business.	3,200.00
					0.00

Record: 3 of 3

TIP

Once you've entered a few records, it's very easy to set the row height to exactly twice or three times the standard height. Simply drag down the lower boundary of any row selector until it is superimposed on another row border.

CHOOSING THE FONT AND SIZE

The default font in Datasheet view is 8 pt. MS Sans Serif. If you don't like this font or if it's too small to read easily on your monitor, you can change the font by using the dialog box shown in Figure 5.7. To call up this dialog box, choose Format ➤ Font or right-click the title bar of the Datasheet window and then choose Font from the popup menu. If you've used any other Windows software, you've probably seen this dialog box or one like it.

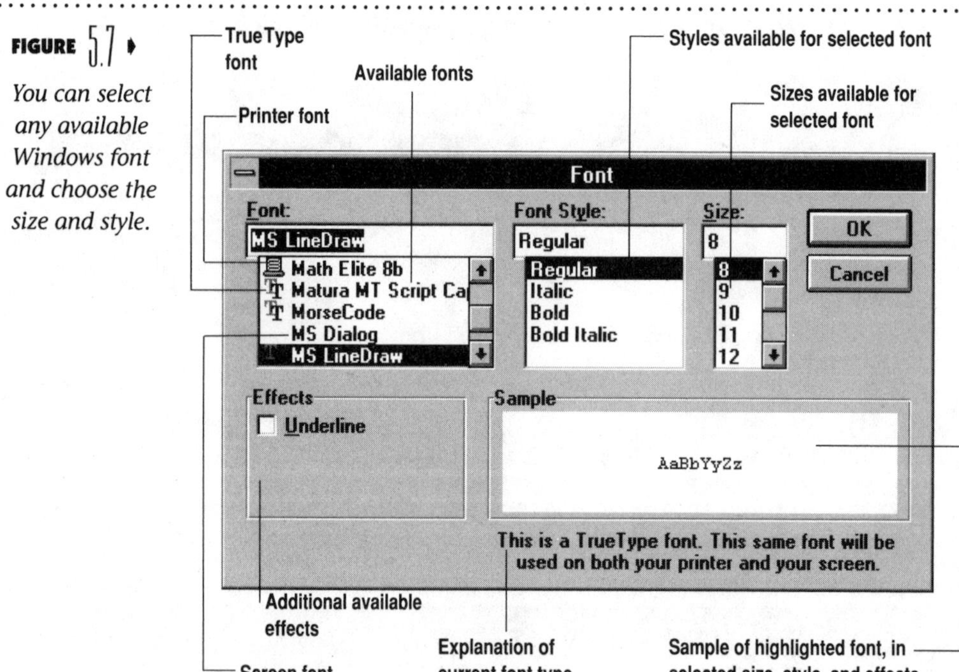

FIGURE 5.7 ➧ *You can select any available Windows font and choose the size and style.*

NOTE

When you try changing the fonts on your own computer, the font names in the Font list box probably won't match Figure 5.7. You'll see only fonts that are actually installed on your machine.

The symbol to the left of the font name identifies each font as belonging to one of four general classes:

- *Screen fonts,* which you can use only in screen displays.
- *Printer fonts,* which you can use only in printed output.
- *TrueType fonts,* which look exactly the same on the screen and in printed output.
- *Adobe Type Manager fonts,* which look exactly the same on the screen and in printed output.

You can choose any available font for the datasheet; Access won't show you an option you can't select. If you choose a printer font, Access uses the closest match for screen displays, and if you choose a screen font, Access uses the closest match when you print the datasheet.

Try scrolling through the list of fonts, and watch how the choices in the Font Style and Size list boxes change to reflect the options available for the highlighted font. The Sample box shows you what this font looks like in the size and style you've chosen. You'll be thankful for this preview when you discover that the font you like best doesn't come in the size you need, and you find yourself searching through a long list of unfamiliar fonts to find the closest match. The screen in Figure 5.8 shows the Projects table datasheet in 9 pt. Courier New, with the row height and column widths adjusted to show all the data.

FIGURE 5.8 ▸

You can customize the font used in Datasheet view.

Table: Projects

Project ID	Project Name	Start Date	Finish Date	Project Description	Budget
Kitchen	Remodel kitchen	1/15/95		New cabinet doors, new countertops, new sink, add work island, new floor covering, repaint, make new curtains.	7,000.00
PCAdvisors	Brochure for PC Advisors	11/1/94	11/28/94	Design a brocure for a small company that provides consulting and training services on PC and Macintosh systems, networks, and software.	1,800.00
PetCare	PetCare package	2/1/95		Design a brochure, letterhead, business cards, one-page flyer, and newspaper ad for a new pet care and housesitting business.	3,200.00
*					0.00

Record: 1 of 3

NOTE

Access doesn't automatically adjust the row height or column widths after you switch fonts or change the font size, so it's best to choose your font first.

ENTERING THE EXPENSE TABLE SAMPLE DATA

Now solidify your understanding of how to customize the datasheet and enter data by entering the first 14 records into the Expenses table. You'll probably want to see the projects while you enter expenses, so leave the Projects table datasheet open. Here are the steps:

1. Adjust the size of the Projects table Datasheet window so it's just large enough for the three records.
2. Return to the Database window by clicking the Database Window button in the toolbar.

3. Open the empty Expenses table. Click anywhere in the Projects table window to bring it in front of the Database window, and then click again in the Expenses table window. Resize and reposition the window so it fills the rest of the Access program window.

4. Adjust the column widths to approximately match those in Figure 5.9, which shows you what the screen will look like after you've finished entering the data.

FIGURE 

You can open more than one table at a time in Datasheet view.

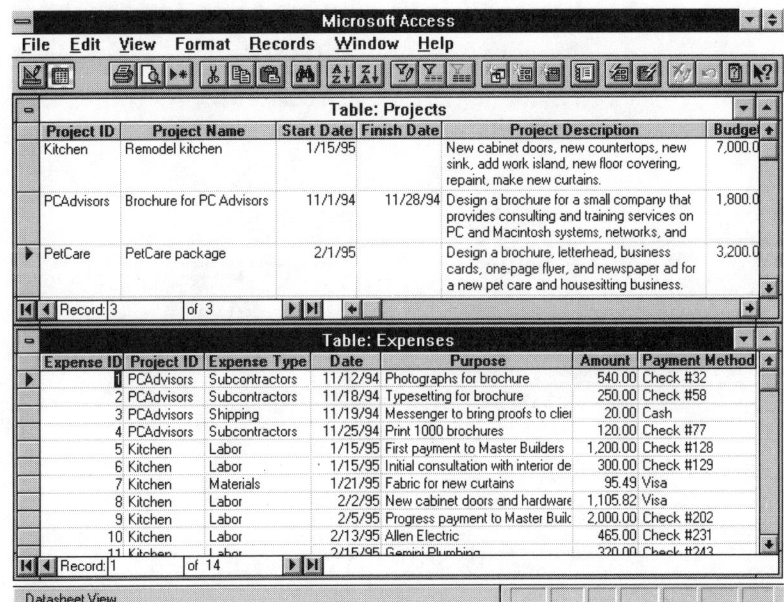

5. Enter the following data:

Project ID	**PCAdvisors**
Expense Type	**Subcontractors**
Date	**11/12/94**

Purpose	**Photographs for brochure**
Amount	**540.00**
Payment Method	**Check #32**

Project ID	**PCAdvisors**
Expense Type	**Subcontractors**
Date	**11/18/94**
Purpose	**Typesetting for brochure**
Amount	**250.00**
Payment Method	**Check #58**

Project ID	**PCAdvisors**
Expense Type	**Shipping**
Date	**11/19/94**
Purpose	**Messenger to bring proofs to client**
Amount	**20.00**
Payment Method	**Cash**

Project ID	**PCAdvisors**
Expense Type	**Subcontractors**
Date	**11/25/94**
Purpose	**Print 1000 brochures**
Amount	**120.00**

Payment Method	**Check #77**

Project ID	**Kitchen**
Expense Type	**Labor**
Date	**1/15/95**
Purpose	**First payment to Master Builders**
Amount	**1200.00**
Payment Method	**Check #128**

Project ID	**Kitchen**
Expense Type	**Labor**
Date	**1/15/95**
Purpose	**Initial consultation with interior decorator**
Amount	**300.00**
Payment Method	**Check #129**

Project ID	**Kitchen**
Expense Type	**Materials**
Date	**1/21/95**
Purpose	**Fabric for new curtains**
Amount	**95.49**
Payment Method	**Visa**

Project ID	**Kitchen**
Expense Type	**Labor**
Date	**2/2/95**
Purpose	**New cabinet doors and hardware**
Amount	**1105.82**
Payment Method	**Visa**

Project ID	**Kitchen**
Expense Type	**Labor**
Date	**2/5/95**
Purpose	**Progress payment to Master Builders**
Amount	**2000.00**
Payment Method	**Check #202**

Project ID	**Kitchen**
Expense Type	**Labor**
Date	**2/13/95**
Purpose	**Allen Electric**
Amount	**465.00**
Payment Method	**Check #231**

Project ID	**Kitchen**
Expense Type	**Labor**
Date	**2/15/95**

Purpose	**Gemini Plumbing**
Amount	**320.00**
Payment Method	**Check #243**

Project ID	**Kitchen**
Expense Type	**Labor**
Date	**2/15/95**
Purpose	**Rainbow Painters**
Amount	**640.00**
Payment Method	**Check #248**

Project ID	**Kitchen**
Expense Type	**Labor**
Date	**2/16/95**
Purpose	**Final payment to interior decorator**
Amount	**400.00**
Payment Method	**Check #249**

Project ID	**Kitchen**
Expense Type	**Labor**
Date	**2/16/95**
Purpose	**Final payment to Master Builders**
Amount	**1100.00**
Payment Method	**Check #250**

SEARCHING FOR RECORDS

If your tables are small and you're intimately familiar with the contents, the scroll bars and record navigation controls may be the only search tools you need. When you have to work with larger tables or with data you didn't enter yourself, you'd waste a lot of time scrolling through hundreds or thousands of records to find the one you want.

It's much more efficient to search for records based on their contents. To carry out a simple search based on the complete contents of one field:

1. Click any row in the column you want to search.
2. Call up the dialog box shown in Figure 5.10 by using any of these methods:
   - Choose Edit ➤ Find.
   - Click the Find button in the toolbar.
   - Press Ctrl+F.

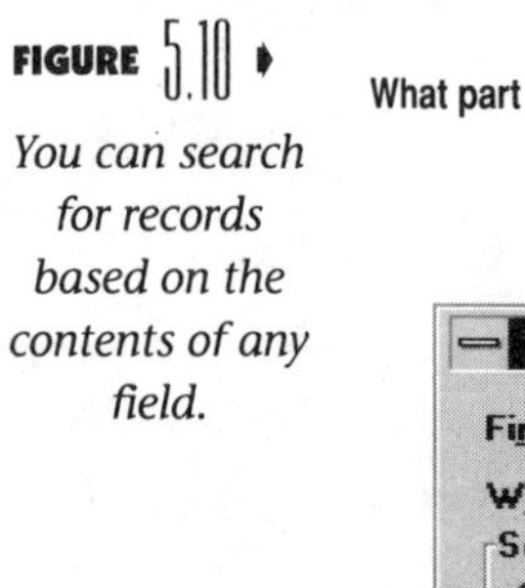

FIGURE 5.10

You can search for records based on the contents of any field.

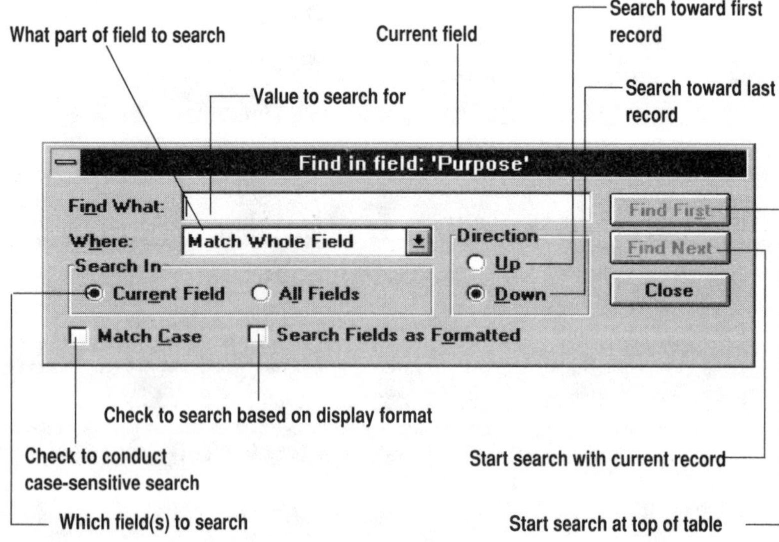

- Right-click the title bar of the Datasheet window and then choose Find from the popup menu.

3. Enter the value you want to search for in the Find What text box.
4. Click Find First to begin the search at the top of the table, or click Find Next to begin searching with the current record.

Access doesn't close the Find dialog box when it finds a matching record; it simply highlights the data that matches your search text. If this isn't the record you want, click Find Next to continue searching. If it is, click Close to close the Find dialog box.

TIP

If you can't see enough of the record Access found to decide whether it's the one you want, move the Find dialog box somewhere else on the screen, out of your way.

CUSTOMIZING THE SEARCH STRATEGY

The fastest way to find one particular record is to search for an exact match on the primary key field. Unfortunately, life isn't always that simple. For example, you might be using a social security number as the primary key but would rather search for a person by name. Furthermore, you might not be sure exactly how you entered the name—as *Michael A. Barton, Mike Barton,* or *Mr. M.A. Barton,* among many other possibilities. Or suppose all you remember about a person is that he lives on Vallejo Street or that either the person's name or the company name has *Allen* in it.

The options in the Find dialog box let you choose where and how you want to search:

- Choose a data-matching strategy in the Where combo box:
  - Choose Match Whole Field to search for an exact match on your search text.

- Choose Start of Field if the field *begins* with your search text.
- Choose Any Part of Field if your search text might be *anywhere* in the field.

- Choose Current Field to limit the search to the current field, or All Fields to search the entire table.
- Check Match Case to make the search case sensitive, or leave it unchecked to treat uppercase and lowercase as equivalent.
- Check Search Fields as Formatted to base the search on the display format rather than on the way the data is stored. (You'll rarely need to use this option.)
- Choose Up to search backward (toward the top of the datasheet) or Down to search forward (toward the end of the datasheet) from the current record.

If Access can't find your search text, it displays an alert box that warns you that Microsoft Access has reached the end of the records and lets you resume the search from the top (if you're searching *down*) or from the bottom (if you're searching *up*). Whenever it has searched the entire table without finding a match, it displays a simple alert box to apprise you of this fact.

You can use *wildcards* (symbols that represent other characters) in your search text to find records that have similar but not identical values in a field. For now, stick with the two simplest wildcard symbols:

? Represents any single character

* Represents any group of characters

Because you can use the Any Part of Field option to search for a partial match on a text or memo field, you'll find the wildcards most useful with date/time fields. For example, you could search for any date in July 1995 by entering **7/*/95** as the search text.

WARNING

Remember that each ? in the search string represents a character position. If you search for 7/??/95, you won't find dates between July 1 and July 9.

Try searching for data in various fields in the Expenses table:

1. Click the Expense Type field in the first record, and then click the Find button in the toolbar.
2. Enter **Labor** in the Find What text box, make sure Match Whole Field is selected in the Where combo box, make sure Current Field is selected, and click Find First. Access highlights the Expense Type field in record 5.
3. Click Find Next to find the next match, and then close the Find dialog box.
4. Move over to the Purpose field, and choose Edit ➤ Find.
5. Enter **Master Builders** in the Find What text box, select Any Part of Field in the Where combo box, and click Find First. Access highlights the search text in record 5.
6. Use Find Next to find the search text in records 9 and 14.
7. Click Find Next again. Click No when Access asks if you want to keep searching from the top of the table, and click OK in the alert box that informs you that Access has searched the whole table.
8. Close the Find dialog box.
9. Click the Date field in the first record, and then click the Find button in the toolbar.
10. Enter **2/*/95** in the Find What text box to find the first expense in February 1995. Click Find First. Access highlights the Date field in record 8.
11. Close the Find dialog box.

REPLACING DATA

The Find options let you search passively for data. Access also gives you a *search-and-replace* capability not unlike that of a word processor. To search for one value and replace it with another:

1. Click any row in the column you want to search.
2. Choose Edit ➤ Replace or press Ctrl+H. Access displays the dialog box shown in Figure 5.11.

FIGURE 5.11 ➧

Access lets you search for one value and replace it with another.

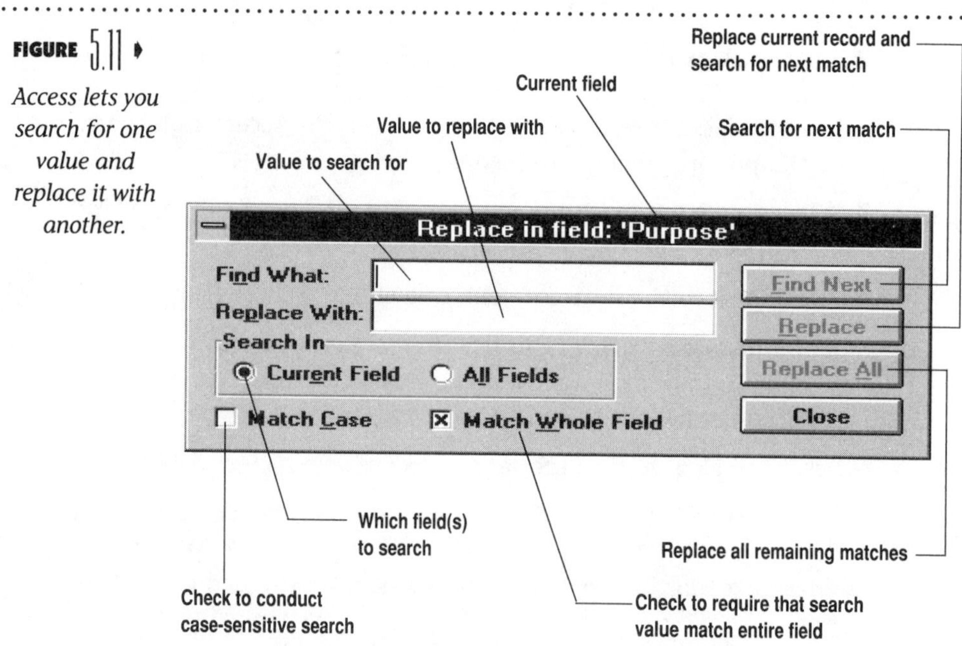

3. Enter the value you want to search for in the Find What text box.
4. Enter the replacement value in the Replace With text box.
5. Click Find Next to begin searching.

Just as when you search, Access doesn't stop after finding the first match, and it doesn't replace data without your permission; it stops and highlights the search text (not necessarily the whole field) so you can decide what to do next:

- Click Replace to carry out the replacement in the current record and search for the next match.
- Click Find Next to leave the current record unchanged and search for the next match.
- Click Replace All to perform a *global* search-and-replace—that is, replace all remaining occurrences.

After completing a global search-and-replace, Access displays an alert box that warns you that You won't be able to undo this replace operation and gives you a chance to cancel your changes. Think twice before you click OK to proceed with this potentially destructive operation. The only way to undo the changes later is to perform another search-and-replace—search for the new value and replace it with the original.

The options in the Replace dialog box let you customize the search strategy:

- Choose Current Field to limit the search to the current field, or All Fields to process the entire table.
- Check Match Case to make the search case sensitive, or leave it unchecked to treat uppercase and lowercase as equivalent.
- Check Match Whole Field to search for an exact match on the whole field, or leave it unchecked to find the search text anywhere in the field.

WARNING

Set the Replace options carefully because the price of an error is higher than in a simple search. For example, if you're trying to replace the name* Mark *with* Marc, *the Match Case option will prevent you from replacing the verb* mark *as well, and the Match Whole Field option will protect words like* marker *and* marking. *Don't do a global replace if you can't use some combination of options to guarantee that you won't find any erroneous matches.

PRINTING THE DATASHEET

You can print a very close replica of the datasheet display by doing one of the following:

- Click the Print button in the toolbar.
- Choose File ➤ Print.
- Press Ctrl+P.
- Right-click a table name in the Database window, and then choose Print from the popup menu.

In Chapters 8, 9, 11, and 12 you'll learn to design formatted reports, but printing the datasheet is a good way to get a quick hard copy for your own use or print just the new records added to a table for proofreading. You can print either from the Database window or from Datasheet view:

- *To print a whole table in the datasheet layout as you last saved it,* highlight the table name in the Database window and then choose one of the print commands.
- *To print a customized datasheet layout,* open the table in Datasheet view, modify the layout as you see fit, and then choose one of the print commands.

TIP

If you need to switch printers or print pages selectively, choose File ➤ Print Setup before you print, or click the Setup button in the Print dialog box. To preview the printout on the screen before you print, click the Preview button in the toolbar or select File ➤ Print Preview instead of File ➤ Print.

Figure 5.12 illustrates the printout of the Expenses table datasheet.

FIGURE 5.12 ➧

Access lets you print a nearly exact replica of the datasheet.

Expenses 3/2/94

Expense ID	ProjectID	Expense Type	Date	Purpose	Amount	Payment Method
1	PCAdvisors	Subcontractors	11/12/94	Photographs for brochure	540.00	Check #32
2	PCAdvisors	Subcontractors	11/18/94	Typesetting for brochure	250.00	Check #58
3	PCAdvisors	Shipping	11/19/94	Messenger to bring proofs to client	20.00	Cash
4	PCAdvisors	Subcontractors	11/25/94	Print 1000 brochures	120.00	Check #77
5	Kitchen	Labor	1/15/95	First payment to Master Builders	1,200.00	Check #128
6	Kitchen	Labor	1/15/95	Initial consultation with inerior decorator	300.00	Check #129
7	Kitchen	Materials	1/21/95	Fabric for new curtains	95.49	Visa
8	Kitchen	Labor	2/2/95	New cabinet doors and hardware	1,105.82	Visa
9	Kitchen	Labor	2/5/95	Progress payment to Master Builders	2,000.00	Check #202
10	Kitchen	Labor	2/13/95	Allen Electric	465.00	Check #231
11	Kitchen	Labor	2/15/95	Gemini Plumbing	320.00	Check #243
12	Kitchen	Labor	2/15/95	Rainbow Painters	640.00	Check #248
13	Kitchen	Labor	2/16/95	Final payment to interior decorator	400.00	Check #249
14	Kitchen	Labor	2/16/95	Final payment to Master Builders	1,100.00	Check #250

Page 1

TIP

If you find the gridlines distracting, choose Format ➤ Gridlines to turn off the grid display before you print the datasheet.

Compared to what you can do with a custom report, the datasheet printout is relatively crude, but it's adequate for many purposes. Access does some minimal formatting; it prints the table name and current date at the top of the page and numbers the pages at the bottom. Most important, it prints enough continuation pages for each group of records to include all the columns, and it never splits a column across a page break.

TIP

To print a portion of a large table, select the columns or rows you want to print, and then click Selection in the Print dialog box. An easy way to print selected columns for a group of records is to hide the columns you don't want to print and select the rows you do want to print. To print any rectangular section of the datasheet, click-and-drag with the mouse to delineate the desired rows and columns, and then choose Selection in the Print dialog box.

WHAT'S NEXT

The techniques described in this chapter give you all the tools you *need* to view, enter, and update data. It won't be long, though, before you'll *want* a more customized view of your data, especially if your tables are large. Chapter 6 describes how to sort records to view them in sequences other than primary key order and how to select which fields and/or records you want to see in a given context. And if you don't think you'll be satisfied forever with the datasheet, Chapter 7 describes how to begin designing custom forms.

Sorting and Selecting Records

Unless your tables are very small, you won't be satisfied for long with viewing all the records in primary key order. You'll want to *sort* your tables—rearrange records into different orders—and *select* various subsets of the fields and records. The ability to view data selectively, and in an order that's relevant to the task at hand, is the key to turning raw data into meaningful information.

If this is your first experience with databases, don't let the terminology mislead you. In colloquial speech, the word *sort* is sometimes used interchangeably with *select*. Thus, you might say, "I need to sort by city for a mailing," meaning, "I need to pick out individual cities for a mailing." In database jargon, *sort* means rearrange into a different order, and *select* means work with a subset of the data that satisfies certain criteria.

It's also time to step beyond working with one table at a time and fulfill the promise made in Chapter 2—that you can view data from related records in two (or more) tables. In this chapter you'll learn how to use queries to join tables based on common fields and display information from the related records in Datasheet view. Once you've defined a query, you can use it as the data source for any form, report, or graph.

USING THE QUICK SORT COMMANDS

You can sort a table based on any field except a memo field or an OLE object field. The easiest way to sort is to use the Quick Sort buttons on the toolbar in Datasheet view or the equivalent menu options, Records ➤ Quick Sort ➤ Ascending and Records ➤ Quick Sort ➤ Descending.

The Quick Sort options are also available on the menu displayed by right-clicking a column selector. The icons on the buttons remind you that an *ascending* sort (the button on the left) will arrange records in order from *A* to *Z* going down the datasheet, and a *descending* sort (the button on the right) will result in *Z* to *A* order:

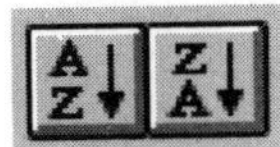

NOTE

***The precise meanings of the terms* ascending *and* descending *depend on the data type—alphabetical order for text fields, numerical order for number fields, and chronological order for date/time fields. When you sort a yes/no field in ascending order, yes comes before no. In a text field, upper- and lowercase are treated as equivalent, and the digits* 0 *through* 9 *sort before the letter* A.**

To sort records based on the contents of any column, click anywhere in the column and then use one of the Quick Sort commands, or right-click a column selector and then choose Quick Sort Ascending or Quick Sort Descending from the popup menu. Try sorting the Contacts table into zip code order:

1. Open the Contacts table in Datasheet view.
2. Click any row in the Zip column.
3. Click the Sort Ascending button in the toolbar.

TIP

You don't need indexes to sort, but sorting on an indexed field is faster because the index is, in effect, a presorted list of the values in the field. If you didn't foresee the need for a certain index when you created a table, you can always open the table in Design view and add the index.

Sometimes a simple sequence based on one field isn't enough. For example, you might want to see the Contacts table arranged in order by state, and within each state by city, and within each city by zip code. You can use the Quick Sort commands to sort by more than one field, but the columns have to be adjacent, and they have to be arranged from left to right in the same order as the sort sequence (with the largest grouping on the left):

1. If necessary, move the sort columns into the right order.
2. Use the column selectors to select all the sort columns.
3. Click one of the Quick Sort buttons in the toolbar or choose one of the Records ➤ Quick Sort commands.

TIP

After you sort, you can move the columns back to their original order without disturbing the record sequence.

Try sorting the Contacts table into state/city/zip code order:

1. Move the State column to the left of the City column.
2. Leaving the State column selected, hold down the Shift key and click the Zip column selector to select all three adjacent columns (State, City, and Zip).

3. Click the Sort Ascending button on the toolbar. Pan the screen to the right so you can see all three sort fields. The datasheet should look like the one in Figure 6.1, with the records arranged in alphabetical order by state; within each state, in alphabetical order by city; and within each city, in order by zip code.

NOTE

Access doesn't give you an "unsort" command. To return to the original order, re-sort the table based on the primary key, or simply close the datasheet and reopen it.

FIGURE 6.1 ▸

You can use the Quick Sort options to sort by more than one field.

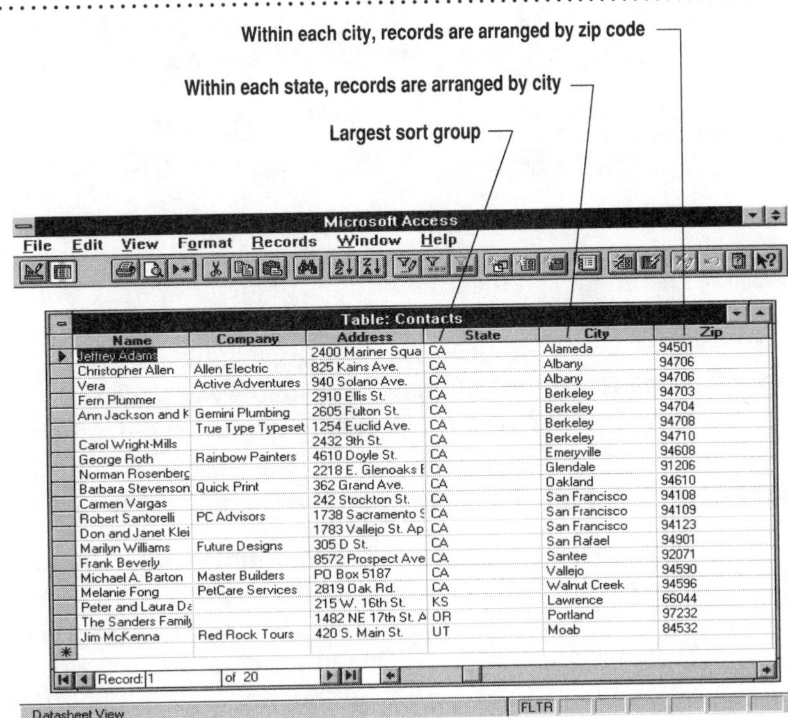

USING FILTERS IN DATASHEET VIEW

You may have noticed that after performing a Quick Sort, Access displays the FLTR indicator in the status bar. (It's visible in Figure 6.1.) In fact, the Quick Sort options are nothing more than shortcuts for creating very simple *filters,* which in turn are simple queries. (Queries are described later in this chapter.) By defining filters, you can go beyond the simple Quick Sort; you can sort by one or more columns, regardless of their position in the datasheet, and you can also define record selection criteria. You can build filters on the fly in Datasheet view and, as you'll see in Chapter 7, while you're using a custom form.

To define and use filters, you can use the three toolbar buttons shown below (from left to right, these execute the Edit Filter/Sort, Apply Filter/Sort, and Show All Records commands) or the identically worded options on the Records menu or the popup menu invoked by right-clicking the title bar of the Datasheet window:

The images on the filter buttons suggest how they work. You can visualize using a filter as pouring your table through a specially designed filter, or sieve, that allows only some of the records to pass through. Don't forget, though, that filters allow you to define sorting instructions as well as record selection criteria.

DEFINING A FILTER

To begin defining a filter, click the Edit Filter/Sort button, choose Records ➤ Edit Filter/Sort, or right-click the title bar of the Datasheet window and then choose Edit Filter/Sort from the popup menu. The Filter Design window, which is shown in Figure 6.2, is divided into two regions. In the upper portion of the window is a list of the fields in the table you're viewing, with the primary key field(s) displayed in bold. In the lower portion is a grid, which you use to describe your sorting

FIGURE 6.2

You can use filters to define sorting and selection instructions for the table you're updating in Datasheet view.

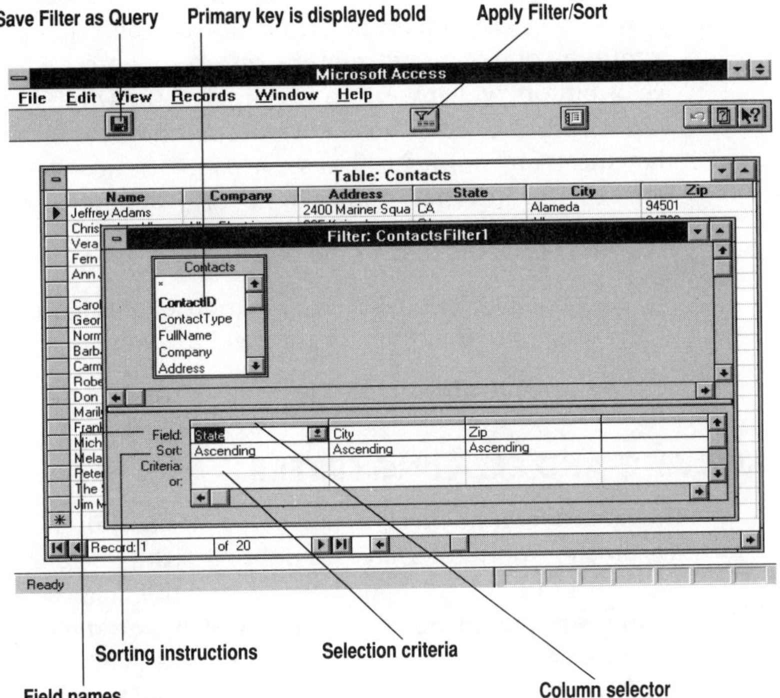

and selection instructions. As in Table Design view, you can switch between the two regions by pressing F6, or you can simply click anywhere in either portion of the window.

NOTE

Because the Quick Sort commands are just shortcuts for creating filters, the instructions for performing the last Quick Sort you used will be visible in the grid when you open the Filter Design window.

Each column in the grid represents a field in the datasheet. You enter your sorting instructions in the row labeled Sort and place selection criteria on one or more Criteria rows. At the top of each column is a selector button, which you can use to select the whole column (to move or delete it). You don't have to create columns for all the fields in the datasheet, only for fields that serve as sort keys or contribute to selection criteria. To add a column to the grid, do one of the following:

- Double-click the field in the field list.
- Select one or more fields, use the mouse to drag the field(s) over the grid, and drop them in the Field row of any column.
- Use the combo box in the Field row of the grid to choose a field.

APPLYING AND CLEARING FILTERS

To place a filter in effect, click Apply Filter/Sort in the toolbar, choose Records ➤ Apply Filter/Sort, or right-click the title bar of the Datasheet window or the Filter Design window and then choose Apply Filter/Sort from the popup menu. To return to viewing all the records in the table in primary key order, click Show All Records, choose Records ➤ Show All Records, or right-click the title bar of the Datasheet window and then choose Show All Records from the popup menu. Access doesn't forget your last filter when you return to displaying all the records in the table; the Apply Filter/Sort command reinstates this filter.

TIP

If you've forgotten whether a filter is currently in effect, look for the FLTR indicator in the status bar.

NOTE

Closing the Filter Design window by double-clicking the close box or by pressing Ctrl+F4 does not place the filter in effect.

Each time you return to the Filter Design window, Access shows you the last filter you created (whether or not it's currently in effect) so you can modify it rather than start from scratch. If you do want to clear the grid and start with a clean slate, select all the columns in the filter grid and press Del or choose the Edit ➤ Clear Grid command.

DEFINING SORTING INSTRUCTIONS

To define your sorting instructions, you create a column in the grid for each field on which you want to sort and then enter **Ascending** or **Descending** in the sort row for each. The order of the columns in the grid determines how Access sorts; it proceeds from left to right, just as it does when you use the Quick Sort options.

NOTE

The order of the columns in the grid has no effect on the display order of the columns in the datasheet. It controls only the sort order.

Each cell in the Sort row is a combo box, and if you're a mouse user, the fastest way to specify the sort order is to choose Ascending or Descending from the drop-down list. If you prefer, you can type **Ascending** or **Descending**, or simply **A** or **D**. If you change your mind about a column, there are three ways to cancel a sort:

- If you don't need the column for selection criteria, delete it from the grid by doing one of the following:
  - Click the column selector, and then press Del.
  - Choose Edit ➤ Delete Column.
- Select (not sorted) from the Sort combo box.
- Delete the word *Ascending* or *Descending* to leave the Sort row blank in the column.

Try sorting the Contacts table in ascending order by ContactType and ContactID:

1. From the Datasheet window, click the Edit Filter/Sort button in the toolbar.
2. If you've used the Quick Sort options, choose Edit ➤ Clear Grid to clear the grid.
3. Double-click ContactType in the field list to move this field to the first column in the grid.
4. Use the mouse to drag the ContactID field to the second column in the grid.
5. Click near the right side of the Sort row of the ContactType column to display the drop-down list, and select Ascending. Press Tab to move to the ContactID column.
6. Type **A**, and notice that Access immediately fills in the rest of the word *Ascending*.
7. Click the Apply Filter/Sort button in the toolbar. Your datasheet should look like the one in Figure 6.3.

DEFINING SELECTION CRITERIA

You enter your selection criteria on one or more rows at the bottom of the grid, starting with the one labeled Criteria and continuing onto as many additional rows as you need. Exactly how many Criteria rows you'll see at once depends on the size of the Filter Design window (two are visible in Figure 6.2), but you can scroll down to reveal additional rows if you need them. You can base selection criteria on fields you're already using for sorting instructions or on any other fields in your table.

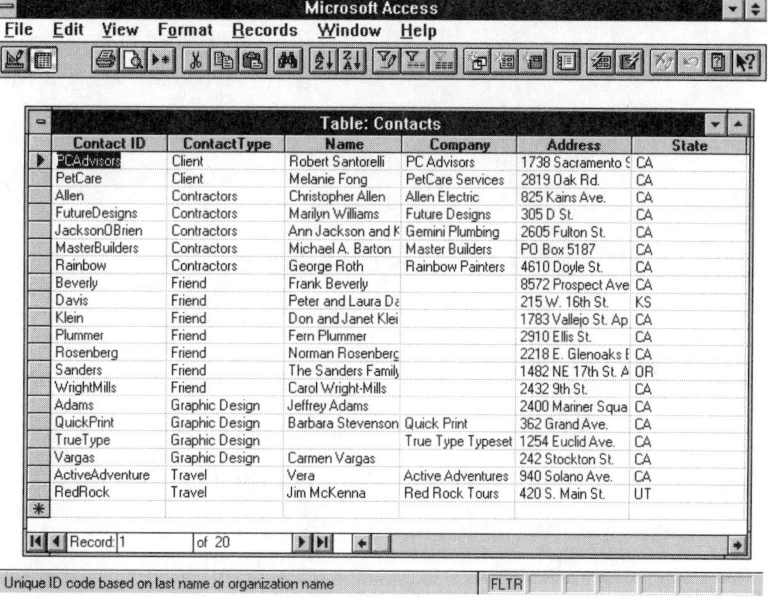

Contact ID	ContactType	Name	Company	Address	State
PCAdvisors	Client	Robert Santorelli	PC Advisors	1738 Sacramento S	CA
PetCare	Client	Melanie Fong	PetCare Services	2819 Oak Rd.	CA
Allen	Contractors	Christopher Allen	Allen Electric	825 Kains Ave.	CA
FutureDesigns	Contractors	Marilyn Williams	Future Designs	305 D St.	CA
JacksonOBrien	Contractors	Ann Jackson and K	Gemini Plumbing	2605 Fulton St.	CA
MasterBuilders	Contractors	Michael A. Barton	Master Builders	PO Box 5187	CA
Rainbow	Contractors	George Roth	Rainbow Painters	4610 Doyle St.	CA
Beverly	Friend	Frank Beverly		8572 Prospect Ave	CA
Davis	Friend	Peter and Laura Da		215 W. 16th St.	KS
Klein	Friend	Don and Janet Klei		1783 Vallejo St. Ap	CA
Plummer	Friend	Fern Plummer		2910 Ellis St.	CA
Rosenberg	Friend	Norman Rosenberg		2218 E. Glenoaks E	CA
Sanders	Friend	The Sanders Family		1482 NE 17th St. A	OR
WrightMills	Friend	Carol Wright-Mills		2432 9th St.	CA
Adams	Graphic Design	Jeffrey Adams		2400 Mariner Squa	CA
QuickPrint	Graphic Design	Barbara Stevenson	Quick Print	362 Grand Ave.	CA
TrueType	Graphic Design		True Type Typeset	1254 Euclid Ave.	CA
Vargas	Graphic Design	Carmen Vargas		242 Stockton St.	CA
ActiveAdventure	Travel	Vera	Active Adventures	940 Solano Ave.	CA
RedRock	Travel	Jim McKenna	Red Rock Tours	420 S. Main St.	UT

FIGURE 6.3 ▸ *You can use a filter to sort a table by one or more fields.*

The simplest selection criteria specify a single value for a field. For example, to select only people in California:

1. If the Filter Design window isn't already visible, click the Edit Filter/Sort button in the toolbar.
2. To add a column to the grid for the State field, click near the right side of the Field cell in the third column to display the drop-down list, and choose State.
3. In the first Criteria row of the State column, type **CA**, and then press ↑ to move out of the Criteria row.
4. Click the Apply Filter/Sort button and verify that the datasheet now shows only 17 records, still sorted by ContactType and ContactID.

NOTE

Access treats uppercase and lowercase as equivalent when it applies selection criteria. Thus, entering ca, CA, Ca, or cA in the Criteria row will select records that have any of these values in the State field.

COMBINING SELECTION CRITERIA

To define more restrictive selection criteria, enter additional values in other columns of the *same* Criteria row. For example, to display only friends in California:

1. Click the Edit Filter/Sort button to return to the Filter Design window.
2. In the ContactType column of the first Criteria row, enter **Friend**.
3. Click the Apply Filter/Sort button in the toolbar, and verify that you see only the five friends in California.

You can use as many columns as you need in the filter grid to express your selection criteria, and the order of the columns in the grid is immaterial. The key to understanding how the selections work is that each Criteria row provides a complete description of an acceptable record. Thus, the filter you just built says, "I want to see every record in which the state is CA *and* the contact type is Friend."

If there's more than one Criteria row, a given record has to satisfy *all* the conditions entered in any one *row*. If you've used the database commands in spreadsheets such as 1-2-3 or Excel, you'll recognize this strategy for entering selection criteria. Thus, to select people who live in California *or* Kansas, you enter **CA** in the State column of one Criteria row and **KS** in the State column of another row. The label *Or* next to the second Criteria row reminds you of how the rows interact: Access will select records that satisfy the criteria in the first row *or* the second row *or* the third row, and so on.

Remember that each Criteria row must provide a complete description of a valid record. Thus, to select friends in California and Kansas, you have to enter **Friend** in both rows, as shown in Figure 6.4. This filter

FIGURE 6.4

To define alternative selection criteria, enter them on multiple Criteria rows.

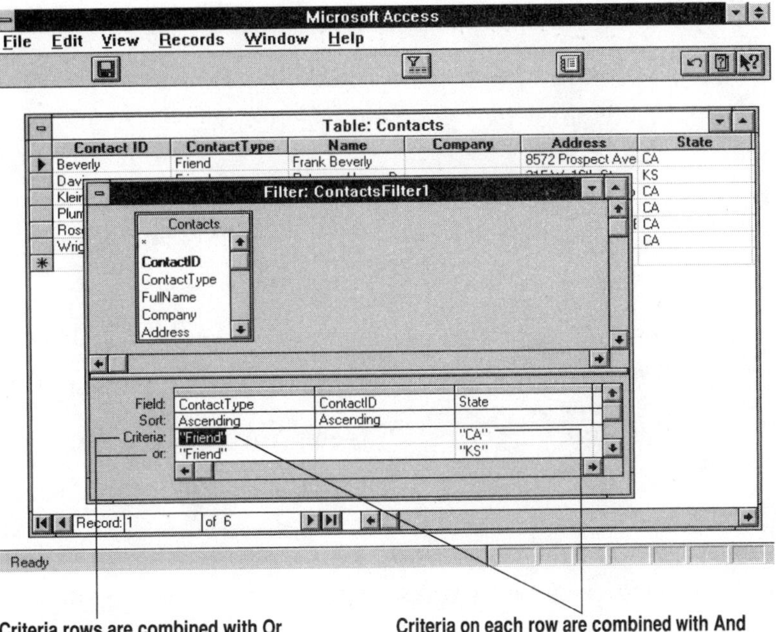

says, "I want to see every record in which the state is CA *and* the contact type is Friend, *or* in which the state is KS *and* the contact type is Friend." If you try this filter, you'll see six records. If you forget to enter **Friend** in the second Criteria row, you'll get friends in California (the condition described by the first row), together with everyone in Kansas (the condition described by the second row).

DEFINING MORE COMPLEX COMPARISONS

You wouldn't be able to do much with filters if you could only test for exact values. For example, you might want to select zip codes between 94000 and 95000 for a mailing, exclude transactions later than January 1, 1995, from your 1994 financial reports, or print only expenses greater than $100.00. To express conditions like these, you use the *comparison operators* listed in the following table. Even if you've never seen these symbols before, the meanings of most of the comparisons should be reasonably clear.

SYMBOL	MEANING
=	Equal to
<>	Not equal to
>	Greater than
<	Less than
>=	Greater than or equal to
<=	Less than or equal to
Between...And	Between two values, inclusive
In	Contained in a list of values
Is Null	Is empty (contains no data)
Like	Matches a pattern that includes wildcard symbols

WORKING WITH DATA TYPES

All the operators in the preceding table are valid for text and date/time fields, as well as number fields. Access interprets these comparisons as denoting alphabetical order for text fields, chronological order for date/time fields, and numerical order for number fields.

To experiment with data types other than text, try defining a filter for the Expenses table that selects expenses over $400 incurred on or after January 1, 1995:

1. Close the Contacts table without saving the layout changes.
2. Open the Expenses table in Datasheet view. If you wish, widen the window and adjust the coumn widths to match the field widths.
3. Click the Edit Filter/Sort button in the toolbar.

4. Add the ExpenseDate field to the grid.

5. In the first Criteria row of the ExpenseDate column, enter **>=1/1/95** to select dates on or later than January 1, 1995.

6. Add the Amount field to the grid.

7. In the first Criteria row of the Amount column, enter **>400** to select amounts greater than $400.00.

8. Click the Apply Filter/Sort button in the toolbar and verify that the datasheet displays only six records.

9. Go back to the Filter Design window and change the condition in the Amount column to **>=400**. Apply this filter and note that you now see seven expense records, including one for exactly $400.00. Figure 6.5 shows the datasheet and the filter specifications.

FIGURE 6.5

You can base selection criteria on text, date/time, number, and yes/no fields.

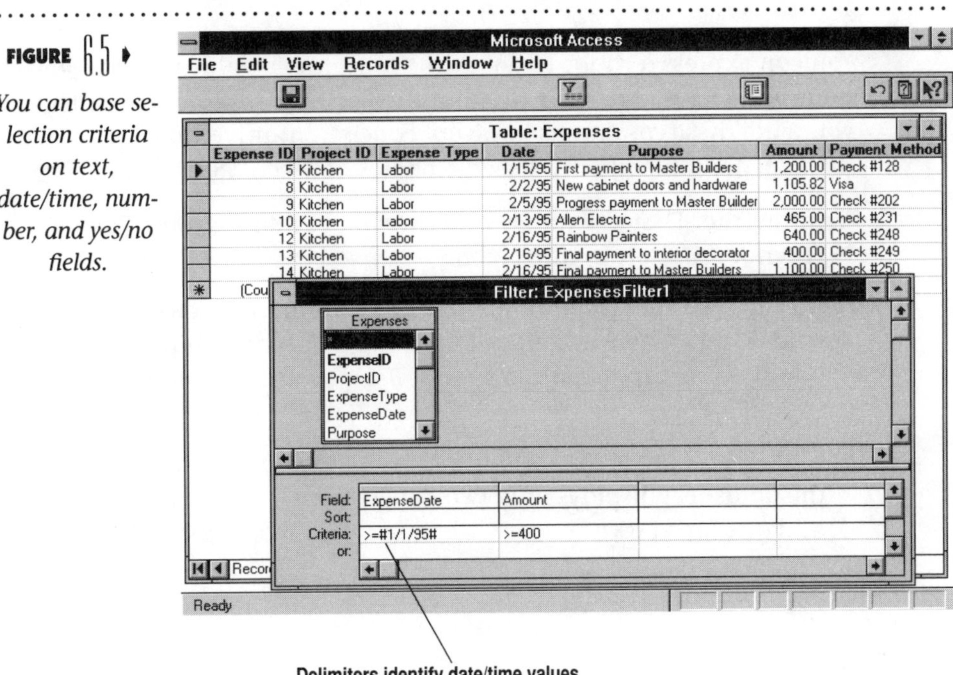

NOTE

You've probably noticed by now that Access adds quotation marks around your entries in text columns and encloses dates in pound signs (#). These special delimiters, *or punctuation marks, identify your entries as text or date/time values, respectively, and they're required in contexts in which Access can't be sure exactly what type of data you're describing. For example, all by itself on a report, the expression 1/1/95 might mean 1 divided by 1 divided by 95 instead of January 1, 1995. In filters and queries, however, Access can deduce the data types of your entries in the Criteria rows from the data types of the corresponding fields, so you don't have to type the delimiters yourself.*

You can express a range of date/time or numeric values with conditions like **>=500 And <=1100**, but the Between...And operator lets you write these conditions in a very concise, intuitive way. Try refining the Expense table filter to select expenses between $500 and $1100:

1. If the Filter Design window isn't already visible, click the Edit Filter/Sort button in the toolbar.
2. Change the condition in the Amount column to **Between 500 and 1100**. When you move out of the cell, notice that Access adjusts your capitalization so that *Between* and *And* have initial capital letters.
3. Click the Apply Filter/Sort button in the toolbar and verify that the datasheet displays only two expense records, one for $640 and one for $1100.

NOTE

The Between...And operator is inclusive—it includes values that exactly match the upper or lower boundary of the range.

To test for blank values, use the Is Null operator. For example, in a query based on the Projects table, you could select unfinished projects by entering **Is Null** in the Criteria row of the FinishedDate column.

SAVING AND RESTORING FILTERS

Access doesn't save your filter specifications with the datasheet layout; when you close the Datasheet window, Access always discards the filter. Often, this is exactly what you want—when you use filters for fast ad hoc inquiries, for editing a very specific group of records, or for "What-If" analyses (for example, figuring out how many records you'd select for a mailing according to various criteria), you may never need to repeat exactly the same inquiry.

If you do want to save a filter for future use, do one of the following:

- Click the Save button in the toolbar in Filter Design view.
- Select the File ➤ Save as Query command.
- Right-click the title bar of the Filter Design window and then choose Save as Query from the popup menu.

The wording of this menu option reminds you that filters are a special form of queries, and they're saved in the same format. You'll learn about queries in the next section.

To reuse a previously saved filter in a later work session:

1. From the Datasheet window, choose Edit Filter/Sort to move to Filter Design view.
2. Choose File ➤ Load from Query or right-click the window title bar and then choose Load from Query from the popup menu.

3. Choose the filter you want from the Filter list in the dialog box shown in Figure 6.6 to load it into the Filter Design grid.
4. Edit the filter specifications if you wish.

FIGURE 

You can reinstate a stored filter by choosing it from a list.

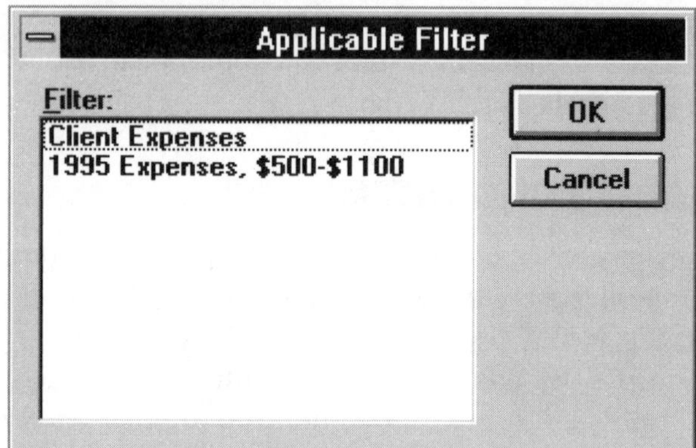

TIP

The Applicable Filter dialog box displays only filters and queries based on the table that's open, so you don't have to worry about choosing an inappropriate filter or query.

Before you move on to learning about queries, save the Expenses table filter:

1. If the Filter Design window isn't already visible, click the Edit Filter/Sort button in the toolbar.
2. Click the Save button in the toolbar.

3. In the Save As dialog box, enter the name **1995 Expenses, $500-$1100**.
4. Close the Expenses datasheet and save your layout changes.

DEFINING SIMPLE QUERIES

As suggested earlier in this chapter, a filter is actually a special case of a more versatile, powerful database object called a *query.* When you're working in Datasheet view (or with a form, as you'll see in Chapter 7), filters are very immediate and convenient, and there's no reason to abandon them after you've learned about queries, but queries do offer significantly greater power and flexibility. You can use queries to select which fields you want to see without having to hide columns each time you open the datasheet, and you can define calculated columns that look just like real fields even though they aren't stored in any table. Perhaps the greatest gain you'll realize from defining queries is the ability to work with data from two or more tables in a very intuitive way.

Access also uses several types of queries (known as *action queries*) to carry out mass updates on tables, archive and delete records, and append records from one table to another. For now, you'll concentrate on *select queries*—queries that display selected fields and records from one or more tables and, if you wish, sort the output. By learning about queries, you'll make a quantum leap in power and flexibility because in most contexts, you can use a query anywhere you can use a table—as the data source for a form, a report, or, as you'll see shortly, another query.

As you'll learn in Chapter 10, there are Query Wizards to help you define several types of complex queries, but defining simple select queries couldn't be much easier than it already is, so Access doesn't provide a Wizard for this purpose. You've already had a taste of what it's like to build a query; you define sorting instructions and selection criteria exactly as you do in a filter.

To begin defining a query:

1. Make sure the Database window displays the list of queries.
2. Click the New command button or press Alt+N. Access displays the New Query dialog box, which is shown in Figure 6.7.
3. Click New Query or press Alt+N.

FIGURE 6.7

You can use the Query Wizards or define a new query from scratch.

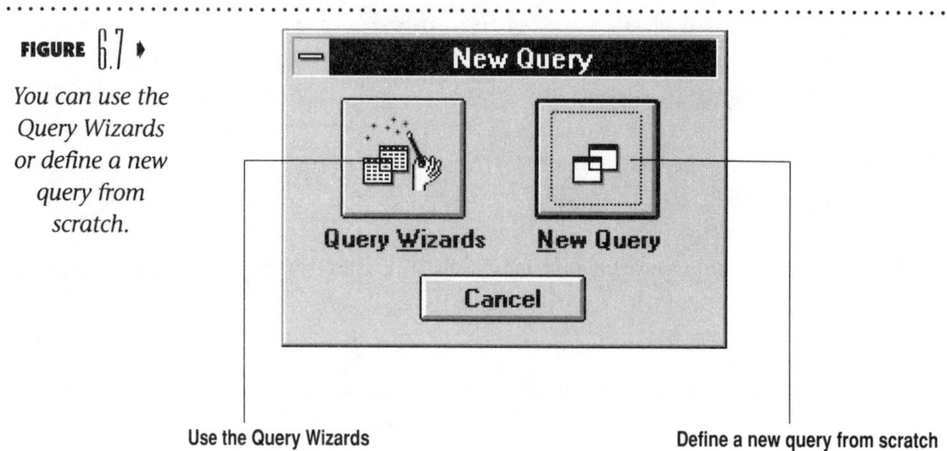

CHOOSING THE DATA SOURCE

The first step in building a query is to choose the data source, which can be one or more tables or other queries, from the Add Table dialog box shown in Figure 6.8. By default, the list in this dialog box displays only tables, but you can use the radio buttons at the bottom to see just queries or both. When you display queries, you'll also see any filters you've saved. To choose the data source, do one of the following:

- Highlight a table or query name and click the Add button or press Alt+A.

FIGURE 6.8 ➧

The data source for a query can be one or more tables or queries.

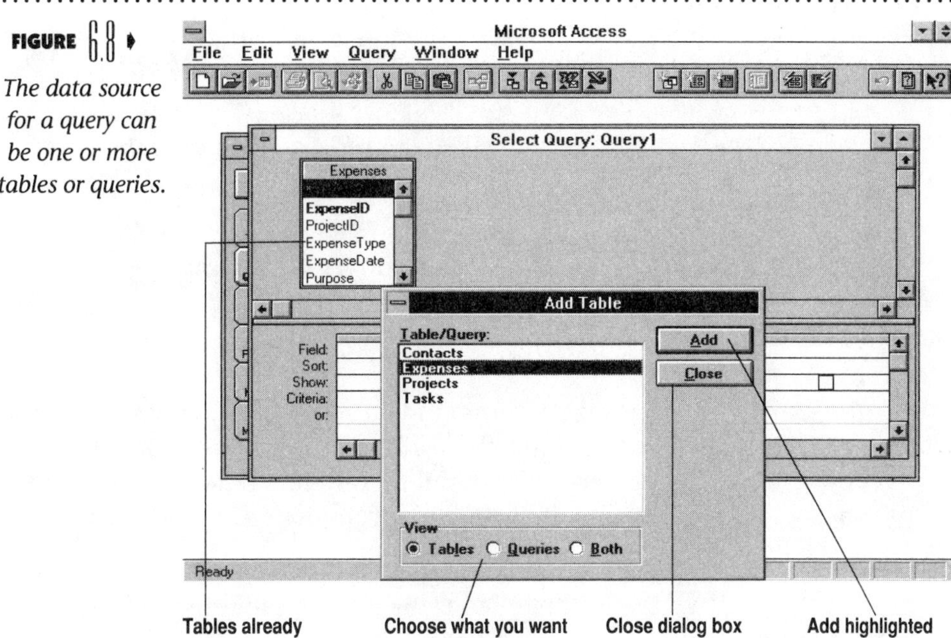

- ➧ Highlight a table or query name and press ↵.
- ➧ Double-click the name of a table or query.

When you choose a table or query, Access adds its field list to the Query Design window, which is already open and visible behind the Add Table dialog box. Choosing a table doesn't automatically close the dialog box, though; as you can see in Figure 6.8, Access leaves it open so you can pick additional tables. When you're finished, click Close or press Alt+C.

NOTE

If you later discover that you forgot a table, you can call up the Add Table dialog box by clicking the Add Table button in the toolbar, by choosing Query ➤ Add Table, or by right-clicking the Query Design window title bar and choosing Add Table from the popup menu. You can also add a table to a query by using the mouse to drag its name from the Database window to the Query Design window.

You can use the New Query command button on the toolbar to bypass the Add Table dialog box and move directly to the Query Design window. This shortcut is especially useful for building a new query based on one table or query, but it doesn't limit your options; you can always add other tables or queries later. To begin:

1. Display either the list of tables or the list of queries in the Database window.
2. Highlight a table or query name, and then click the New Query command button in the toolbar.
3. In the New Query dialog box, choose New Query.

Try using this method to begin building the query shown in Figure 6.9. (You'll add the Projects table later.)

1. Make sure the Database window displays the list of tables.
2. Highlight Expenses, and then click the New Query command button in the toolbar.
3. In the New Query dialog box, choose New Query.
4. Drag down the lower boundary of the Query Design window to enlarge the window.

FIGURE 6.9 ▸ *You can customize the Query Design window to accommodate the source tables and query specifications.*

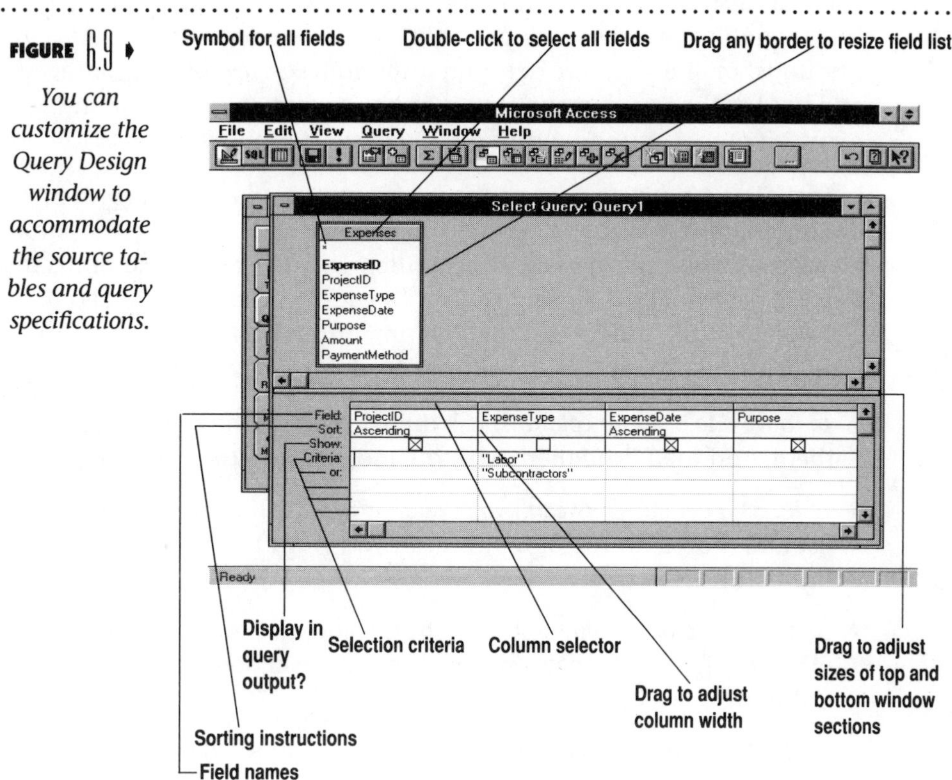

5. Drag down the heavy boundary line between the two portions of the form to make more room for the field list in the upper portion.
6. Enlarge the Expenses field list so all the field names are visible.

CHOOSING THE OUTPUT FIELDS

Unlike a filter, which stores instructions only for sorting and selecting records in the table that's already open, a query includes a complete description of the data you want to see, as well as the sorting and selection instructions. You can pick fields from one or more tables, present them in any order, and, as you'll learn in Chapter 10, include calculations. In effect, you're defining a specialized view of your data, and in fact, the result of running a query is often called a *view.* In Access, a more common term for the output of a query is *dynaset.*

To include a field in the query output, you must add it to the grid in the lower portion of the Query Design window, using exactly the same methods you use when you define a filter. The order of the columns in the grid determines their sequence in the query output datasheet. If you don't get the order right the first time (and most of the time you won't), it's easy to rearrange columns by doing one of the following:

- *To move one or more columns,* use the selectors at the top to select them, and then drag them with the mouse to a new location.
- *To insert a column between two others,* drag a field from the field list and drop it on top of the column you want to end up to the right of the new one.
- *To insert an empty column,* highlight the column you want to end up to the right of the new one and press Ins or choose Edit ➤ Insert Column.
- *To delete one or more columns,* select them and press Del or choose Edit ➤ Delete Column.

The asterisk at the top of the field list represents all the fields in a table. If you drag the asterisk to the grid instead of the individual fields, the query output includes all the fields in the table, in the order in which they occur in the table structure. Using the asterisk instead of creating a column for each field ensures that you won't have to edit the query if you later add or delete fields in the table structure.

If you do want all the fields in a table listed individually in the grid, there's an easy way to add them all at once. Try this with the Expenses table query:

1. Double-click the title bar of the field list to select all the fields.
2. Position the mouse pointer over any of the selected fields, press the left mouse button, and drag the fields to the grid.

3. Click the column selector for the ExpenseID column, and press Del to delete the column.

4. Tab over to the PaymentMethod column, and select Edit ➤ Delete Column to delete the column.

TIP

You don't have to include counter fields in the query output. Access updates counter fields whenever you add new records to a table, even if they're not visible.

DEFINING SORTING AND SELECTION INSTRUCTIONS

You already know how to define sorting instructions and selection criteria in a query; for the most part, you use exactly the same methods you use in a filter. The fact that the grid describes the appearance of the output datasheet adds a few new wrinkles, but they're all easily resolved. For example, you might need to base selection criteria on the ContactType field but not display this field in the output, or sort on State and City but display the City column to the left of the State column.

The solution to these problems lies in strategic use of the Show row, which determines whether a column in the grid is displayed in the query's datasheet. Access automatically checks this box when you add a new field to the grid. To hide a column, simply uncheck it. Here are a few of the ways you can use the Show row:

- *To base sorting or selection instructions on a column but not display it in the query output,* uncheck the Show check box.
- *To sort on two or more columns but display them in an order that does not correspond to the sort hierarchy,* add two copies of each column to the output grid. Arrange one set in the order in which you need to sort (from left to right), and uncheck the Show box for all

these columns. Place the other copies where you want them to appear in the output, and leave the Show box checked.

- *To include all the fields in a large table but keep your sorting and selection criteria readily visible in the grid,* use the asterisk symbol to represent all the fields. Then add another copy of each field you need for your sorting and selection instructions, and uncheck the Show box for these columns.

Enter the sorting and selection instructions for the Expenses query:

1. Enter **Ascending** in the Sort row for both the ProjectID and ExpenseDate columns.
2. Type **Labor** in the first Criteria row in the ExpenseType column.
3. Type **Subcontractors** in the second Criteria row in the ExpenseType column.
4. Uncheck the Show box in the Expense Type column.

SAVING A QUERY

You can save a query at any point by clicking the Save button in the toolbar, by using the File ➤ Save command, or by pressing Ctrl+S. These commands don't save the data described by the query; they save the *instructions* for extracting this data. When you're looking at the query output, the Save and Save As commands usually found on the File menu are replaced by Save Query and Save Query As, and these options also save the query specifications, not the data.

When you create a query, Access automatically assigns a name (Query1 for the first query, Query2 for the second, and so on). The first time you save a new query, Access displays the Save As dialog box to give you a chance to assign a more meaningful name.

If you run a new or modified query and then try to close the datasheet, Access displays an alert box that asks whether you want to save the query.

EXECUTING A QUERY

From Query Design view, you can display the query output in Datasheet view by clicking the Run or Datasheet button in the toolbar or by choosing Query ➤ Run. To return to Query Design view, click the Design View button or choose View ➤ Query Design. You'll probably use these commands at least a few times to test preliminary versions of a new query before you're satisfied with the results. Try running the Expense query now. Figure 6.10 shows the query datasheet.

To run a query from the Database window:

1. Make sure the Database window displays the list of queries.
2. Double-click the query name, or highlight the query name and click Open or press Alt+O.

FIGURE 6.10 ▸

The query datasheet looks just like a table's datasheet.

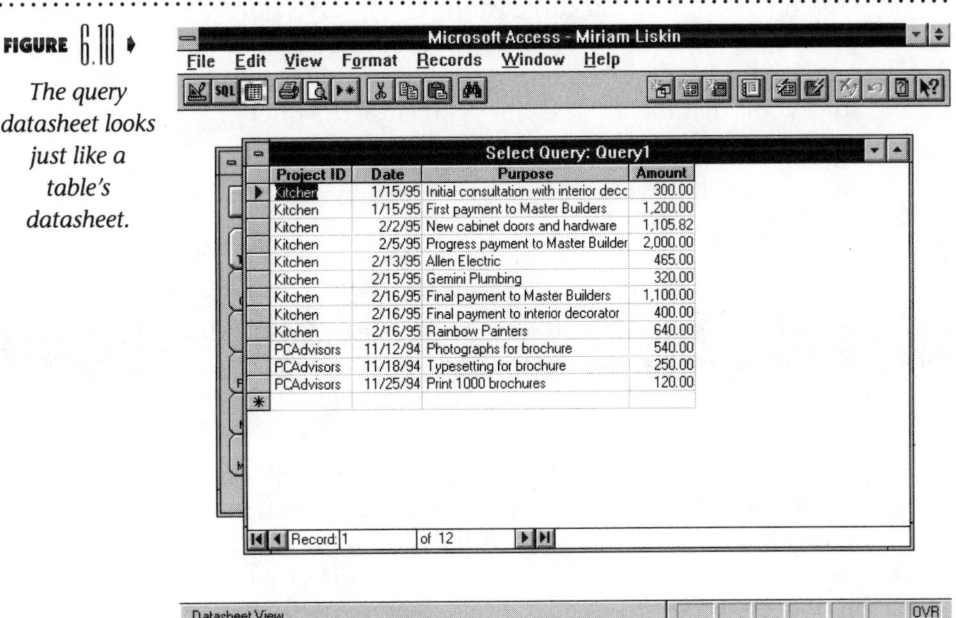

Project ID	Date	Purpose	Amount
Kitchen	1/15/95	Initial consultation with interior decc	300.00
Kitchen	1/15/95	First payment to Master Builders	1,200.00
Kitchen	2/2/95	New cabinet doors and hardware	1,105.82
Kitchen	2/5/95	Progress payment to Master Builder	2,000.00
Kitchen	2/13/95	Allen Electric	465.00
Kitchen	2/15/95	Gemini Plumbing	320.00
Kitchen	2/16/95	Final payment to Master Builders	1,100.00
Kitchen	2/16/95	Final payment to interior decorator	400.00
Kitchen	2/16/95	Rainbow Painters	640.00
PCAdvisors	11/12/94	Photographs for brochure	540.00
PCAdvisors	11/18/94	Typesetting for brochure	250.00
PCAdvisors	11/25/94	Print 1000 brochures	120.00

NOTE

When your tables are as small as the sample Organizer tables, running a query is almost as fast as opening a table, but running a complex query based on several large tables can take quite a bit longer. Access always shows you the first screenful of data almost immediately, and if you scroll through the output in sequence, Access will easily keep up with you. Be prepared to wait a while, however, if you search for a record near the end of the query dynaset (for example, WY in a mailing list sorted by state) before Access has finished processing the source table(s).

Viewing a query dynaset in Datasheet view is virtually identical to looking at a table. You can customize a query's datasheet exactly as you would a table's—by moving or hiding columns, changing the font, and adjusting the column widths or row height—and you can save your layout changes when you close the query.

NOTE

When you display a query datasheet, the Quick Sort and filter buttons are missing from the toolbar. You don't need them, because you can obtain the same effects by editing and rerunning the query.

Although a query's datasheet may not display all the data in the underlying tables, all the data you see comes from these tables. Always remember that you're viewing and editing the source table(s), not a copy. Any changes you make are applied directly to these tables, and in a single-table query, you're free to add, delete, and edit records exactly as you would in the table's datasheet. (As you'll see shortly, Access places some restrictions on what updates are permitted in a multitable query.)

If you add new records through a query, any fields that aren't displayed in the query output will remain blank (except counter fields, which Access always fills in for you). This isn't always a bad thing, however. For example, if you store customers and prospects in the same table, entering prospects through a query that doesn't include the fields required only for customers guarantees that you don't inadvertently fill in these fields, which *should* be left blank in prospect records.

TIP

If you add a record that doesn't satisfy the selection criteria in a query, the record will remain visible. However, it will disappear if you choose Records ➤ Show All Records, and you won't see it the next time you execute the query.

PRINTING A QUERY DEFINITION

To print a query definition (not the data selected by the query), highlight the name in the Database window, and then choose File ➤ Print Definition. Access displays the dialog box shown in Figure 6.11 to let you decide how much detail you want. If you were expecting to see options for printing the sorting instructions and selection criteria, you'd be disappointed; there's no easy way to do this. If you know SQL (Structured Query Language), you can check SQL to print the SQL statement that executes the query behind the scenes. If you don't know SQL, the printout won't give you a complete description of the query specifications.

FIGURE 6.11 ▸

Access lets you choose how much detail you want in the printed query definition.

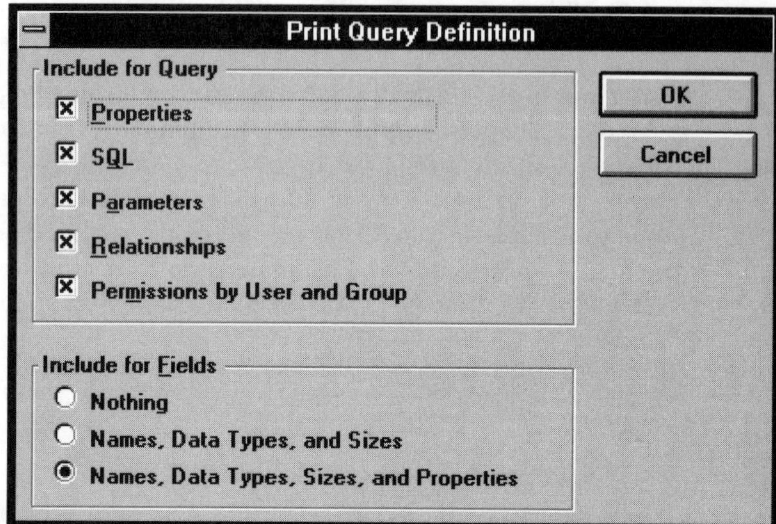

DEFINING MULTITABLE QUERIES

Defining queries based on more than one table isn't much harder than building single-table queries, especially if you've predefined the relationships between the tables. The single essential prerequisite is that you understand how to *join* the tables in your query—that is, indicate how Access should identify the matching records.

You can build a multitable query from scratch by choosing more than one table initially from the Add Table dialog box, or you can add tables later to a single-table query. You've already seen the Add Table dialog box. Try using the click-and-drag method to add the Projects table to the Expenses query:

1. If you're looking at the query datasheet, click the Design View button in the toolbar.

2. Click anywhere in the Database window. (If you can't see the Database window, click the Database Window button in the toolbar.)
3. Click the Tables "tab" so the Database window displays the list of tables.
4. Click Projects in the list of tables, drag the table over to the Query Design window, and drop it anywhere in the upper portion of the window.
5. Move the Projects table field list closer to the Expenses table list, and enlarge it until all the field names are visible.

JOINING TABLES

If you've predefined the relationships between the tables in your query, Access automatically joins the tables. Even if you haven't formally defined a relationship, Access can join tables if one has a field with the same name and data type as the primary key in the other. In the Organizer application you've defined the relationship between the Projects and Expenses tables as one-to-many, so Access joins the tables for you.

If Access doesn't join your tables automatically, or if you don't like the proposed joins, you can join the tables yourself, exactly the same way you do in the Relationships window:

1. Point to the linking field in one of the tables.
2. Press and hold the left mouse button.
3. Drag the mouse to the linking field in the other table.
4. Release the mouse button.

To define a join based on more than one field, repeat these steps for each pair of linking fields.

TIP

Because Access allows a join based on more than one field, it doesn't delete any existing joins when you define another.

To remove a join, click the join line to select it, and then press Del or choose Edit ➤ Del, or right-click the join line and then choose Delete from the popup menu.

To delete a table from a query, click anywhere in the field list for that table and then press Del or choose Edit ➤ Del, or right-click the field list and then choose Remove Table from the popup menu. Even if the table is participating in one or more joins, you don't have to delete the joins before you delete the table from the query.

If your tables have some field names in common, it's helpful to see a reminder of which table is the source for each field in the grid. To display the table names, click the Table Names button in the toolbar or select View ➤ Table Names.

To add the ProjectName field to the query:

1. Drag the ProjectName field to the grid and drop it on the Expense Type column. (Access will move this and the remaining columns to the right to make room.)
2. Click the Table Names button in the toolbar.
3. Click the Run button to execute the query. The screen in Figure 6.12 illustrates the output.

Access assumes that when you join two tables, you want to see all possible pairs of matching records—and no nonmatching records. Thus, a parent record with no matching records in the child table won't appear in the output. That's why the PetCare project doesn't appear in the screen in Figure 6.13; you haven't yet entered any expenses for this project. This linking strategy is called an *inner join.*

FIGURE 6.12 ▸

By default, the output of a query includes only the matching records from both tables.

Select Query: Query1

Project ID	Project Name	Date	Purpose	Amount
Kitchen	Remodel kitchen	1/15/95	Initial consultation with interior decc	300.00
Kitchen	Remodel kitchen	1/15/95	First payment to Master Builders	1,200.00
Kitchen	Remodel kitchen	2/2/95	New cabinet doors and hardware	1,105.82
Kitchen	Remodel kitchen	2/5/95	Progress payment to Master Builder	2,000.00
Kitchen	Remodel kitchen	2/13/95	Allen Electric	465.00
Kitchen	Remodel kitchen	2/15/95	Gemini Plumbing	320.00
Kitchen	Remodel kitchen	2/16/95	Final payment to Master Builders	1,100.00
Kitchen	Remodel kitchen	2/16/95	Final payment to interior decorator	400.00
Kitchen	Remodel kitchen	2/16/95	Rainbow Painters	640.00
PCAdvisors	Brochure for PC Advisors	11/12/94	Photographs for brochure	540.00
PCAdvisors	Brochure for PC Advisors	11/18/94	Typesetting for brochure	250.00
PCAdvisors	Brochure for PC Advisors	11/25/94	Print 1000 brochures	120.00

Record: 1 of 12

The output of a two-table query looks like a single table with one row for each record in the child table. The fields from the parent table appear to be part of the child record. For example, in Figure 6.13, it looks as if the project name is included in each expense record.

UPDATING A QUERY DYNASET

Access allows you to add or delete records in the query dynaset. It applies these changes to the child table—Expenses in the query you're building—because each row in the datasheet represents a record in this table.

You can update almost any field in either table. Of course, you can't make any changes that would violate referential integrity rules, so you can't edit the join field from the parent table unless you've enabled cascading updates. With cascading updates turned on, editing the ProjectID field in the Projects table changes this field in all the related expense records. Otherwise, changing this field would *orphan* the expense records (leave them with no matching record in the parent table).

Remember that even though a given value in a field from the parent table may appear many times in the datasheet, there's only one copy of the data—in the single matching parent record. If you edit a field in the parent table, you'll see your changes ripple through all the child rows linked to that parent. This is usually exactly what you want. For example, if you see a typographical error in the ProjectName field, you'll want to fix it once and see the correction immediately in all the matching expense rows.

Suppose, however, that you see an expense that you've assigned to the wrong project. Don't try to correct this problem by editing the ProjectName field. Changing *Brochure for PC Advisors* to *PetCare Package* does *not* move the expense from the PCAdvisors project to the PetCare project; it changes the name of the PCAdvisors project in the Projects table. You're not likely to make this mistake in a query like the one in Figure 6.12, with the ProjectID clearly visible, but if you don't include the join field in the query output, it's easy to do.

DEFINING OUTER JOINS

When you're working from the "point of view" of the child table, the default table join strategy (the inner join) is exactly what you want; you're really interested in seeing the child table data, with the parent table fields just "along for the ride."

When you switch to the "point of view" of the parent table, you'd probably rather see all the records in this table, together with the child records, if any, that match each parent. In one-to-many relationships in which you're not enforcing referential integrity, you might ask for the opposite—child records with no matching parents. In fact, you might run such a query if you decide to start enforcing referential integrity, to find any existing mismatches beforehand. Both of these joins, which might include records from one table that have no match in another, are called *outer joins*.

To define an outer join, you create the join as usual and then modify its properties:

1. Double-click the join line, click the join line to select it, and then select View ➤ Join Properties, or right-click the join line and then select Join Properties from the popup menu.

2. Select a join option from the dialog box shown in Figure 6.13.

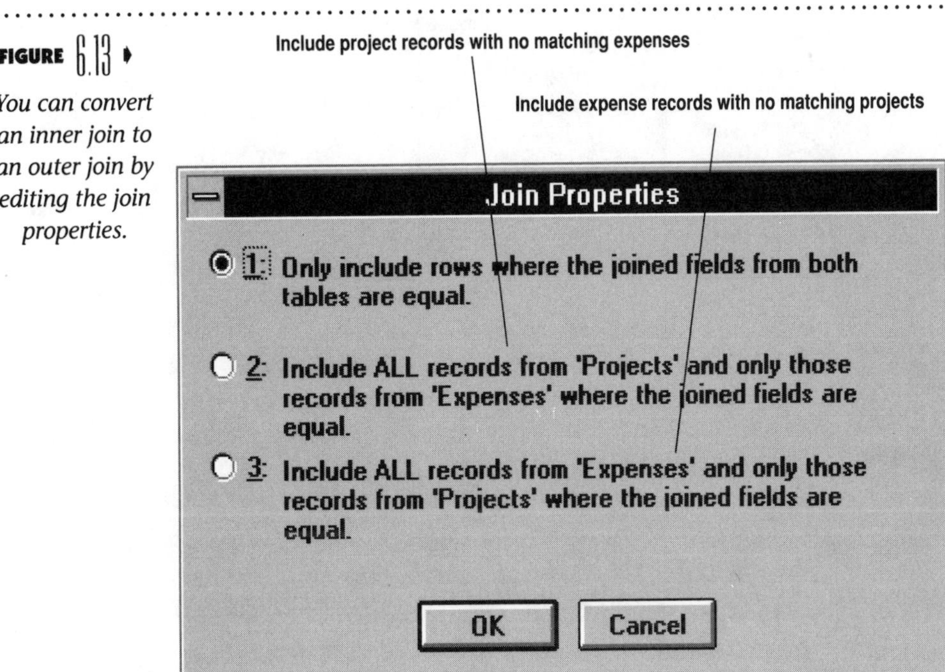
Include project records with no matching expenses
Include expense records with no matching projects
Join Properties
1: Only include rows where the joined fields from both tables are equal.
2: Include ALL records from 'Projects' and only those records from 'Expenses' where the joined fields are equal.
3: Include ALL records from 'Expenses' and only those records from 'Projects' where the joined fields are equal.
OK
Cancel

FIGURE 6.13 *You can convert an inner join to an outer join by editing the join properties.*

TIP

If you're having trouble accurately double-clicking the join line, click it once and then select View ➤ Join Properties. You can tell when you've succeeded in selecting the join line because Access displays it darker.

The join line always identifies the type of join. An outer join is displayed with an arrowhead pointing from the table you always want to see toward the one that might or might not have matching records, like this:

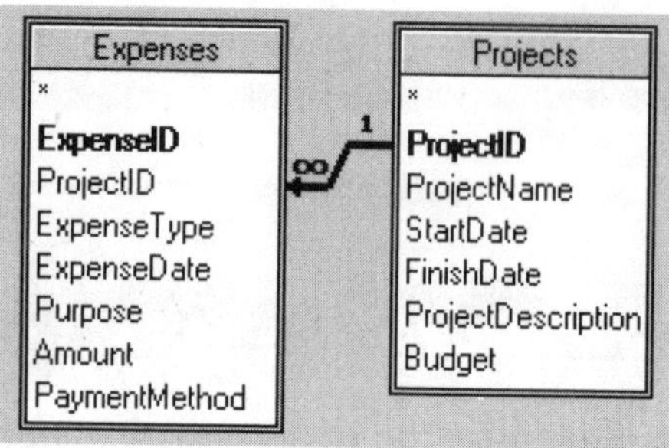

NOTE

The Join Properties dialog box always offers you three options, the standard inner join and both theoretically possible outer joins, even if you're enforcing referential integrity and couldn't possibly have mismatched records in the two tables.

The screen in Figure 6.14 shows the result of removing the selection criteria based on the expense type, checking the Show box for this field, and converting the Expenses query to an outer join that displays all the records from the Projects table. In the row for the PetCare project, which has no expenses, the expense columns in the datasheet are blank. Try making these modifications yourself (choose the second join option in the dialog box shown earlier in Figure 6.13), and confirm that your output looks like the screen in Figure 6.14.

FIGURE 6.14 ▸

You can use an outer join to display all the records from one table, even if there are no matches in the other.

Project with no expenses

Select Query: Query1

ProjectID	Project Name	Expense Type	Date	Purpose	Amount
	PetCare package				
Kitchen	Remodel kitchen	Labor	1/15/95	Initial consultation with inerior decora	300.00
Kitchen	Remodel kitchen	Labor	1/15/95	First payment to Master Builders	1,200.00
Kitchen	Remodel kitchen	Materials	1/21/95	Fabric for new curtains	95.49
Kitchen	Remodel kitchen	Labor	2/2/95	New cabinet doors and hardware	1,105.82
Kitchen	Remodel kitchen	Labor	2/5/95	Progress payment to Master Builders	2,000.00
Kitchen	Remodel kitchen	Labor	2/13/95	Allen Electric	465.00
Kitchen	Remodel kitchen	Labor	2/15/95	Rainbow Painters	640.00
Kitchen	Remodel kitchen	Labor	2/15/95	Gemini Plumbing	320.00
Kitchen	Remodel kitchen	Labor	2/16/95	Final payment to Master Builders	1,100.00
Kitchen	Remodel kitchen	Labor	2/16/95	Final payment to interior decorator	400.00
PCAdvisors	Brochure for PC Advisors	Subcontractors	11/12/94	Photographs for brochure	540.00
PCAdvisors	Brochure for PC Advisors	Subcontractors	11/18/94	Typesetting for brochure	250.00
PCAdvisors	Brochure for PC Advisors	Shipping	11/19/94	Messenger to bring proofs to client	20.00
PCAdvisors	Brochure for PC Advisors	Subcontractors	11/25/94	Print 1000 brochures	120.00

Record: 1 of 15

NOTE

If a query includes selection criteria that would exclude blank child table fields, you won't see any parent records with no matching child records because in these rows, all the child fields are blank. This is the reason you had to remove the selection criteria based on Expense Type from the query you've been building.

Access places some restrictions on how you can update the tables in an outer join, most of which are based on the referential integrity rules.

- You can't edit the join field in the parent record (in your query, the ProjectID field in the Projects table) unless you've enabled cascading updates so that the change is propagated throughout the set of matching child records. (Otherwise, you could orphan any existing child records.)

- To be able to add child records, the query output must include the join field from the child table (in your query, the ProjectID field in the Expenses table) because Access needs to know which parent record the new child record belongs to.
- If you've changed data in the parent record (for example, the ProjectName field), you have to save the record before you can edit the join field (ProjectID) from the child record. The reason is that changing the join field causes Access to immediately look up the matching parent and display its data in all the parent columns, thus eradicating your edits. This limitation can be confusing, but it's easily overcome; just press Shift+↵ or choose File ➤ Save Record.

TIP

If you're not sure which table the join field comes from, click the Table Names button in Query Design view to display the table names. If you've chosen the linking field from the "wrong" table, just delete its column and replace it with the corresponding field from the other table.

NOTE

Entering data into the blank child table fields in a row for a parent that initially has no matching child records results in adding a record to the child table.

You might want to try some of these updates with the query you built in this chapter. When you're finished, change the join back to the standard inner join and save the query under the name Project Expenses.

WHAT'S NEXT

The techniques described in this chapter give you the tools you need to view data from one or more tables selectively. Now that you've learned how to specify what data you want to see in a given context, you're ready to turn your attention to the way data is presented. Chapter 7 introduces custom forms, and Chapters 8 and 9 describe printed reports and labels.

Designing Data Entry Forms

As you've seen in the last two chapters, you can get a lot of useful work done without designing forms. Eventually, though, you'll want to use custom forms for at least some of your data entry and editing. The Datasheet view is ideal for getting the big picture, but when you need to focus on one record at a time, you'll want a custom form. Data entry forms are almost a necessity for tables with more than 15 or 20 fields, and for tables with long text and memo fields; in most cases you'll be able to fit a whole record on the screen, including a few lines of each memo.

But custom forms have a value that goes far beyond the convenience of not having to repeatedly scroll the datasheet back and forth. By designing screen forms that look just like your paper input forms, you can make data entry easier, faster, and more accurate. You can also customize forms to the differing needs of the people who use them or, if you're the only user, to the varying requirements of different tasks. Finally, you can design forms for updating tables that have a one-to-many relationship that parallel the way you visualize the data—forms that display one parent record at a time, together with all the matching child records.

Access makes it very easy to get started by providing Form Wizards for designing several very common and useful form layouts. As you'll see, most of these forms could do with some improvements, at least from an esthetic standpoint, but they're perfectly usable as is. Chapters 11 and 12 describe how to modify the forms built by the Wizards and how to create forms from scratch.

USING THE AUTOFORM WIZARD

The easiest way to build a form is to use the AutoForm button on the toolbar, which automatically builds a very simple form for any table or query. The AutoForm button calls up one of the Access Form Wizards, but unlike the other Wizards, this one doesn't ask you any questions. Instead, it makes some basic assumptions about what constitutes an acceptable form, builds the form, and opens it immediately so you can begin editing data.

You may recall that one of the options in the last Table Wizard dialog box was Enter data into the table using a form the Wizard creates for me. This option invokes the AutoForm Wizard.

Try using the AutoForm Wizard to build a form for the Tasks table:

1. Make sure the Database window displays the list of tables.
2. Highlight Tasks in the list of tables.
3. Click the AutoForm button in the toolbar.

TIP

You can also click the AutoForm button from Datasheet view.

Figure 7.1 shows the form created for the Tasks table by the AutoForm Wizard. All of this Wizard's forms share certain layout features. The fields are lined up in one column, with the field names or captions to the left as prompts. If there are too many fields to fit on the screen at once, you can use the vertical scroll bar in the form window to bring any field into view. Yes/no fields are represented by check boxes, all other fields are displayed in text boxes, and all the data entry regions appear recessed behind the surface of the screen. There's always a *form header,* which displays the name of the table or query in white letters with a dropped shadow.

Access assigns a default name to each new form, including those created by the AutoForm Wizard—Form1 for the first form you create,

FIGURE 7.1

The AutoForm button creates a simple form that includes all the fields in a table or query.

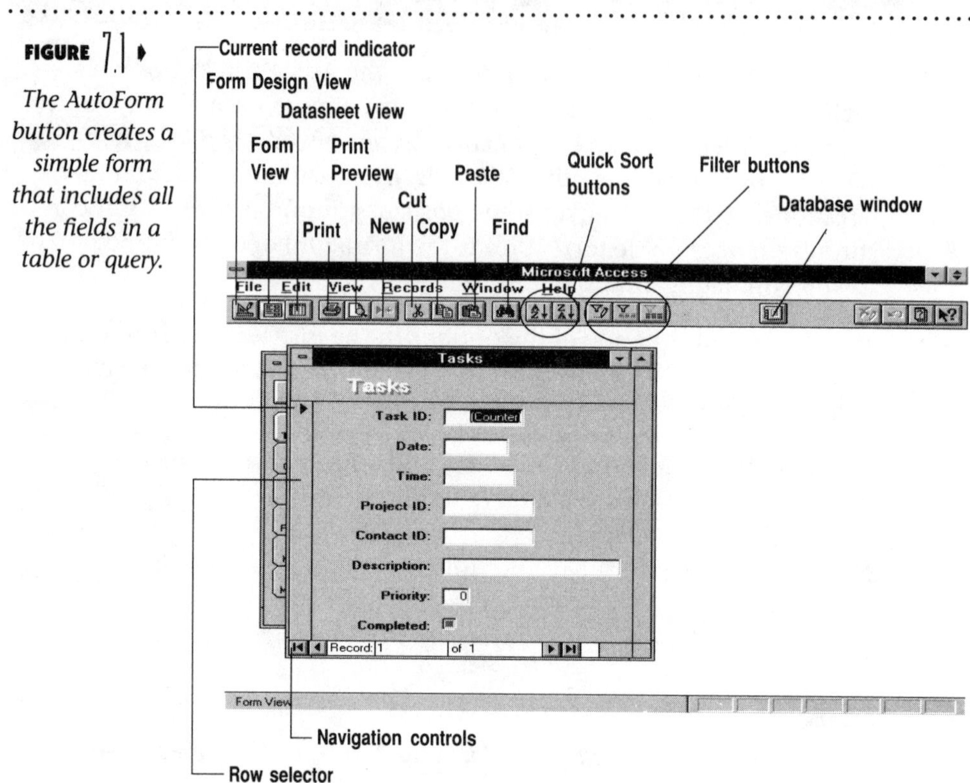

Form2 for the second, and so on. When you close the form for the first time, Access displays a Save As dialog box to give you a chance to assign a more meaningful name.

For small tables like the Tasks table, the AutoForm Wizard gives you a usable and reasonably attractive form. The most serious problem you'll encounter is that some of the text boxes are too wide and others aren't wide enough to display the full contents of the fields. Chapter 11 describes how to edit a form to modify these and many other aspects of a form's layout. In the meantime, you can view the inappropriate text box widths as little more than a minor nuisance. Access always lets you type as many characters as the field size permits and scroll through the whole field to view or edit the data.

USING FORMS TO UPDATE TABLES

If you look at the Tasks form you just created, you'll see that apart from the layout of the fields, Form view has a great deal in common with the Datasheet view introduced in Chapter 5. You're probably better equipped to understand now the statement made in that chapter that the datasheet is simply one of many possible form layouts, one that is always available for any table.

In keeping with this parallel, you can switch at will between a custom form and the built-in Datasheet view by using the Form View and Datasheet View buttons on the toolbar.

TIP

Access doesn't change the window size when you switch views, and in Datasheet view you'll probably want a larger window. Rather than adjusting the window size manually, it's usually easier to maximize the window when you switch to the Datasheet window and restore it to its former size when you return to Form view.

The Datasheet and Form view windows have all the same window control and navigation tools, which are labeled in Figure 7.1. You can use exactly the same methods in Form view and in Datasheet view to add records, delete records, and edit data. When you tab past the last field in the current record, Access saves the current record and displays the next one. You can use the Quick Sort buttons for simple sorts and define filters for more complex sorting and selection instructions.

NOTE

Don't overlook the record selector on the left side of the window, which extends the full height of the record. If the current record indicator seems superfluous, note that some form styles display more than one record at a time, and remember that the symbol changes shape (from a triangle to a pencil) when you've edited the current record since you last saved it. As in Datasheet view, the easiest way to delete a record is to click the selector and then press Del.

Now you're ready to enter some data into the Tasks table, using the AutoForm you just created.

NOTE

Remember that you can check or uncheck the Completed check box by clicking it or by tabbing into the check box and pressing the spacebar.

1. Enter the first eight records:

Date	**2/16/95**
Time	**10:00 am**
Project ID	**Kitchen**
Contact ID	**MasterBuilders**
Description	**Meet for final project review**
Priority	**1**
Completed	**Yes**

Date	**2/24/95**
Time	**1:30 pm**
Description	**Dentist appointment**
Priority	**1**
Completed	**Yes**

Date	**2/24/95**
Project ID	**Kitchen**
Description	**Buy new curtain rods**
Priority	**2**
Completed	**Yes**

Date	**2/24/95**
Project ID	**Kitchen**
Description	**Hang curtains**
Priority	**2**
Completed	**No**

Date	**2/28/95**
Time	**12:00**
Contact ID	**Vargas**
Description	**Lunch with Carmen to discuss PetCare project**
Priority	**1**
Completed	**Yes**

Date	**3/1/95**
Time	**10:00 am**
Project ID	**PetCare**
Contact ID	**PetCare**

Description	**Meet with Melanie to review brochure design**
Priority	**1**
Completed	**Yes**
Date	**3/1/95**
Time	**7:30 pm**
Contact ID	**Plummer**
Description	**Dinner with Fern**
Priority	**1**
Completed	**Yes**
Date	**3/2/95**
Description	**Buy anniversary gift for Don and Janet**
Priority	**2**
Completed	**No**

2. Click the Datasheet View button in the toolbar to switch to Datasheet view.
3. Maximize the Datasheet window.
4. Narrow the Task ID, Date, Time, and Priority columns until you can see the check box in the Completed column.
5. Click the Form view button in the toolbar to return to the form.
6. Click the Restore control in the upper-right corner of the form window to return it to its original size.
7. Close the form, and type the name **Tasks AutoForm** in the Save As dialog box.

PRINTING A FORM

To produce a printed replica of a form, do one of the following:

- In Form view or in the Database window, click the Print button in the toolbar.
- In Form view or in the Database window, use the File ➤ Print command.
- Right-click the form name in the Database window and then choose Print from the popup menu.

If you'd rather preview the printout first, click the Print Preview button in the toolbar or choose File ➤ Print Preview. Figure 7.2 shows a portion of the Print Preview produced from the Tasks table AutoForm. Printing from Form View is useful for producing a quick hard copy of a few records, but you'll usually want to design better-looking reports for most of your tables. You'll learn how in Chapters 8, 9, 11, and 12.

FIGURE 7.2 ➧

You can print a nearly exact replica of a form.

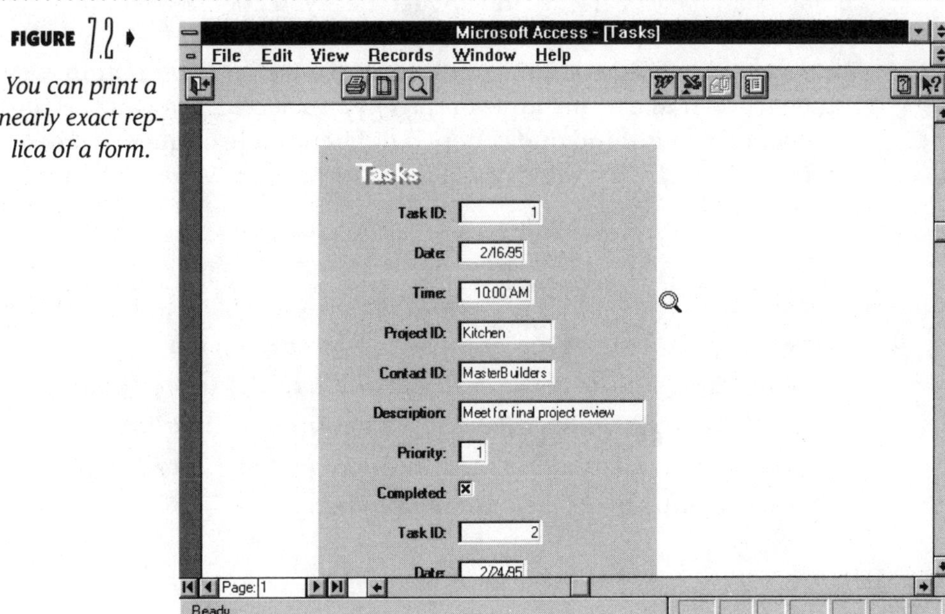

TIP

To print just one or two records, select them (using the record selectors), and then choose Selection for the Print Range in the Print dialog box.

USING THE FORM WIZARDS

If you're willing to put a little more time into the effort, you can create several different form styles very easily by using the Form Wizards. To begin creating a new form, do one of the following:

- Highlight a table or query name in the Database window and click the New Form button in the toolbar.
- Make sure the Database window displays the list of forms, and then click the New command button or press Alt+N.

Access displays the New Form dialog box shown in Figure 7.3. The combo box labeled Select A Table/Query lets you choose the data source for the form. If you called up the New Form dialog box by highlighting a table or query name and clicking the New Form button, you'll see the name of the table or query you selected, but you can always change your mind and choose a different table or query from the list. After picking a table or query, click the Form Wizards button or press Alt+W.

NOTE

The combo box at the top of the New Form dialog box doesn't differentiate between tables and queries. If you think you might forget which table or query you want, highlight the name in the Database window and click the New Form button to initiate the form design process.

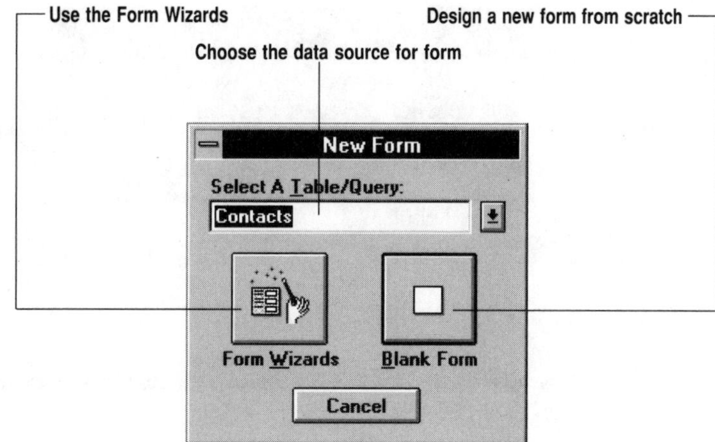

FIGURE 7.3 ▸ *The New Form dialog box lets you call up the Form Wizards or create a new form from scratch.*

To practice using the Form Wizards, begin defining a custom form for the Contacts table:

1. Make sure the Database window displays the list of forms, and click the New command button or press Alt+N.
2. Display the drop-down list for the combo box at the top of the New Form dialog box, and choose Contacts from the list of tables and queries.
3. Click Form Wizards or press Alt+W.

CHOOSING THE FORM LAYOUT

The first Form Wizard dialog box, which is shown in Figure 7.4, lets you choose the overall form layout. The message at the bottom of this dialog box displays a brief description of the selected layout. If you choose AutoForm, the Wizard bypasses all the remaining dialog boxes and builds the same form you'd get by clicking the AutoForm button on the toolbar. Later in this chapter you'll create forms that use the

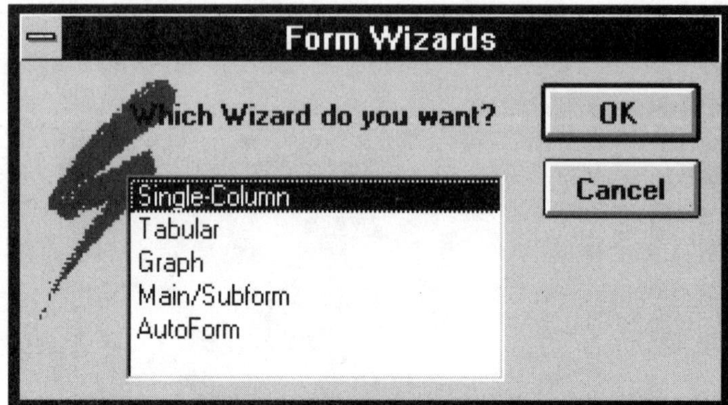

FIGURE 7.4 ▸ *The Form Wizard asks you to choose the basic form layout.*

Tabular, Main/Subform, and Graph layouts. (If you want to see these layouts right now, look ahead at Figures 7.10, 7.11, and 7.14.)

The Single-Column layout, which resembles the AutoForm, is a good choice for many tables. Don't rule out this layout for tables that have too many fields to fit on the screen at once, because it's easy to rearrange the form later. (You'll learn how to do this in Chapter 11.)

4. For the Contacts table form, choose the Single-Column form layout, and click OK to move to the next step.

CHOOSING THE FIELDS

The next Form Wizard dialog box, which is shown in Figure 7.5, lets you select the fields you want on your form. On the left side of the dialog box is a diagram of the form layout you've chosen, with lines representing the fields and heavier bars representing the labels (the field names or captions). Don't assume that every data entry form should

FIGURE 7.5

You can choose which fields you want to include on your form.

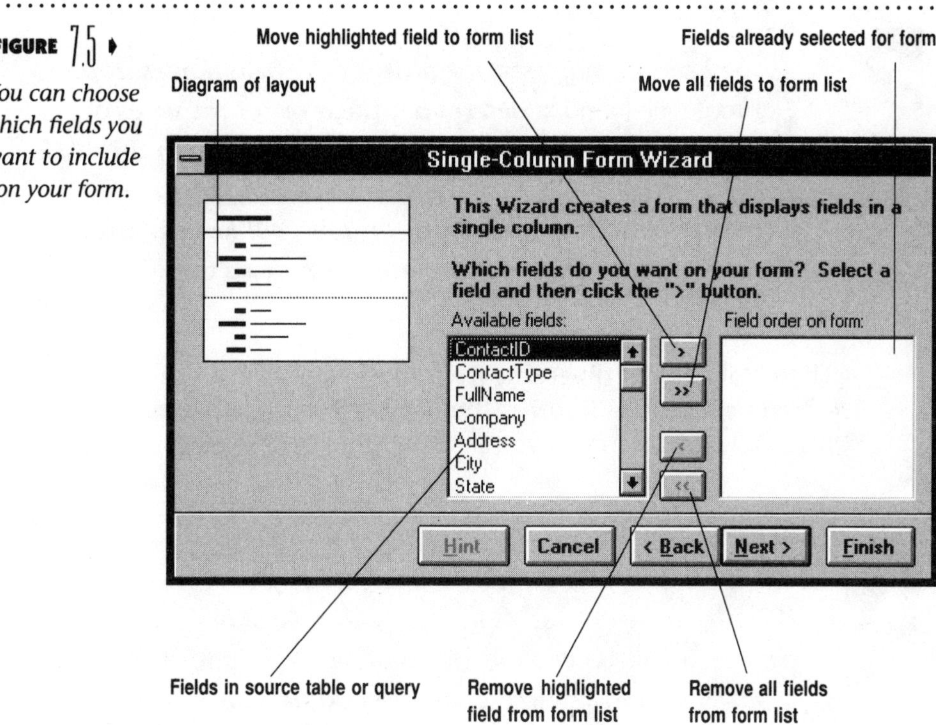

include all the fields from the source table. For example, if you store customers and prospects in the same table, entering prospects would be a lot easier using a form that doesn't display the fields that are required only for customers.

You'll recognize the method used to choose fields from your experience with the Table Wizard: the **Available fields** list box displays the fields in the source table or query, and the **Field order on form** list box displays the fields you've already selected for your form. You can use the buttons between the two lists to add or remove fields, one at a time or all at once, from the form list.

NOTE

As the heading suggests, the order of the field names in the Field order on form ***list determines the order of the fields on the resulting form. You can't rearrange the fields in this list except by removing fields and then reselecting them in a different order. Choose carefully for now, but keep in mind that you can modify the form later if you need to.***

There's one major difference from the Table Wizard—choosing a field from one list *moves* it rather than *copies* it to the other, because the Form Wizard doesn't let you put the same field on a form twice.

NOTE

The limitation just described is imposed by the Form Wizard, not by Access. When you edit a form or create one from scratch, you can put two copies of the same field on the form. Chapter 12 describes how to add fields to a form.

For the Contacts table form, choose all the fields except the Photograph field:

5. Click the >> button to select all the fields in the Contacts table for the form.
6. Highlight Photograph in the Field order on form list and click < to remove this field from the list.
7. Click Next to move to the next dialog box.

CHOOSING THE FORM LOOK

The next Form Wizard dialog box, which is shown in Figure 7.6, lets you choose the overall form style. Figure 7.7 shows an example of

FIGURE 7.6

The Wizard lets you choose one of five form styles.

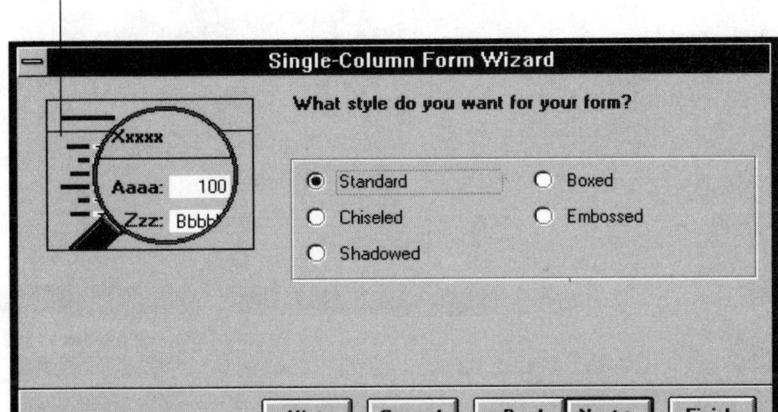

each. If you need a more immediate reminder of each style, click any of the five radio buttons in turn and watch the diagram on the left side of the dialog box, which shows you a small sample of the selected style.

TIP

The plain vanilla Standard style is less visually exciting than the others, but it's vastly easier to modify. If you anticipate editing the form created by the Wizard, it's a good idea to stick with this style until you've had some experience with the Form Designer.

For the Contacts table form, choose the Standard style:

8. Click the Standard radio button.

9. Click Next to move on to the next step.

FIGURE 7.7 ▸ *The Form Wizard's five styles are called Standard, Embossed, Chiseled, Boxed, and Shadowed.*

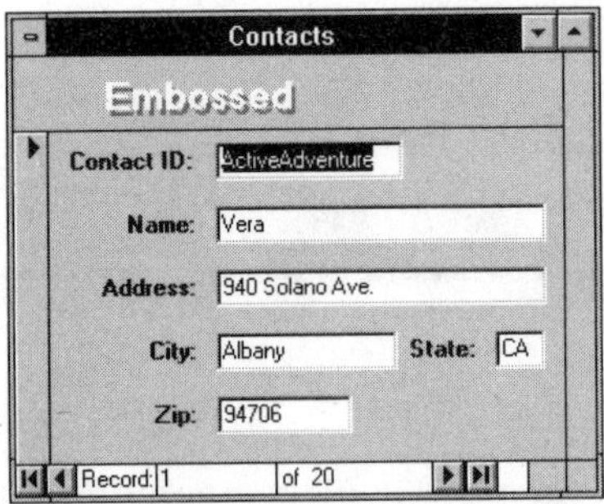

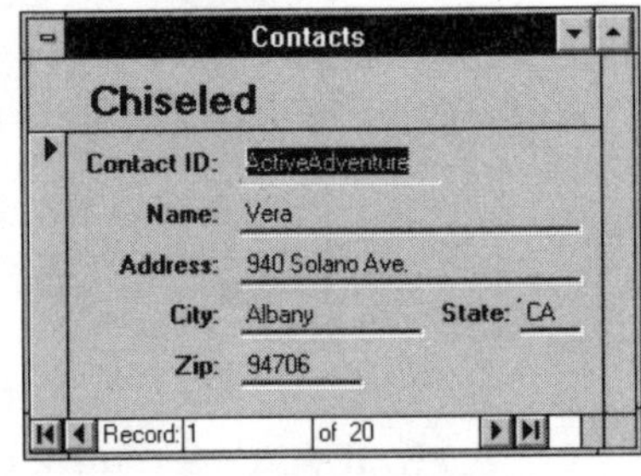

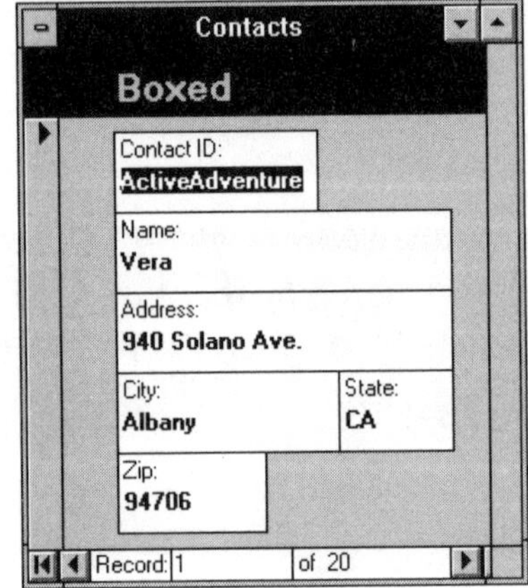

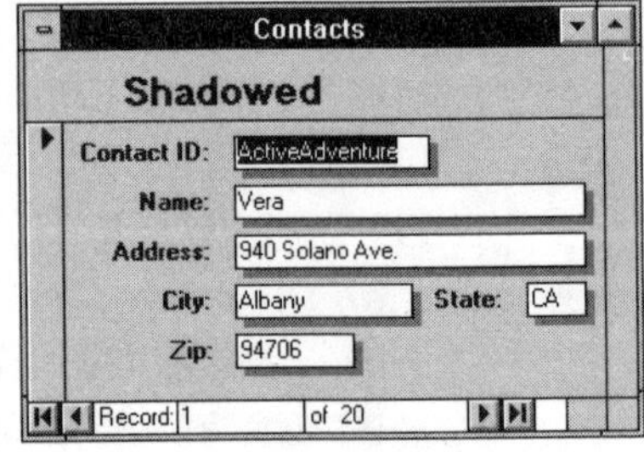

TITLING AND SAVING THE FORM

The last Form Wizard dialog box, which is shown in Figure 7.8, lets you assign a form title and decide what you want to do next. If you're sure you'll need to modify the form created by the Wizard, you can choose Modify the form's design to move immediately to Form Design view, but it's usually a good idea to try using the form first. Displaying or entering a few records is an easy way to verify that you've arranged the fields in the right order, and it will show you which text boxes are too long or too short for typical entries.

For the Contacts table form:

10. Edit the form title to change it to Contact Names and Addresses.

11. Leave Open the form with data in it selected, and click Finish.

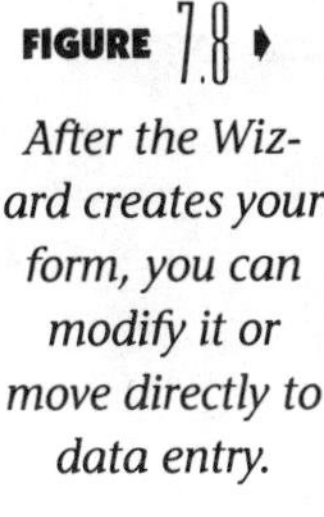

FIGURE 7.8

After the Wizard creates your form, you can modify it or move directly to data entry.

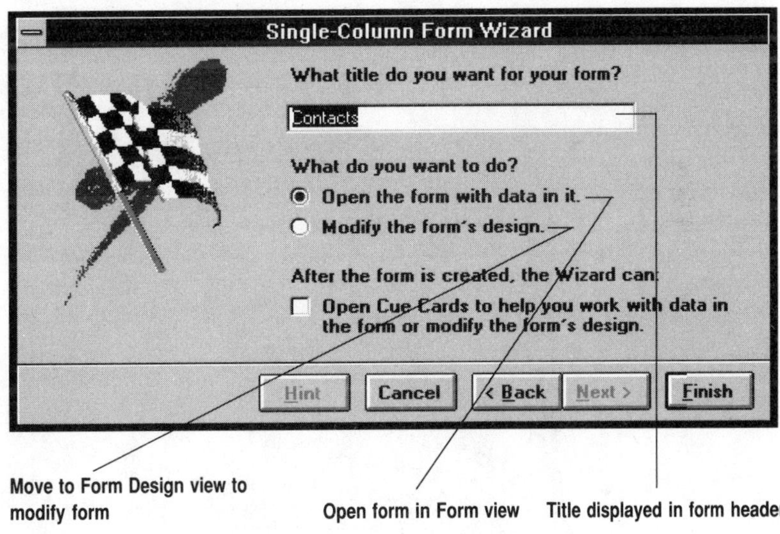

Creating most forms takes just a moment, but Access displays a progress indicator in the status bar to reassure you as the Wizard builds the form and opens it. Figure 7.9 shows the Contacts table form generated by the Form Wizard.

Try looking at a few Contacts table records, and then close and save the form:

12. Move the window up slightly, and then choose Window ➤ Size to Fit Form to adjust the window size so the vertical scroll bar disappears.
13. Try using the navigation controls to move through the first few records in the Contacts table.
14. Close the form, and save it under the name Contact Names and Addresses.

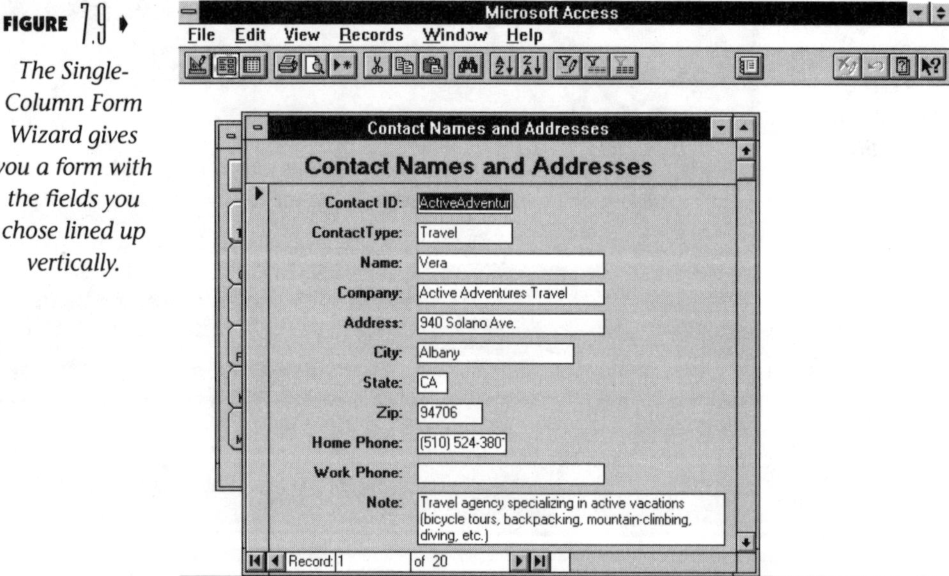

FIGURE 7.9 ➧ *The Single-Column Form Wizard gives you a form with the fields you chose lined up vertically.*

NOTE

Don't confuse the form name and the form title, although in this form they are the same. The title is simply text displayed in the form header, whereas the name is the identifier for the form itself. The form name, not the title, is displayed in the Database window.

CREATING A TABULAR FORM

For some tables you'll want a form that shows more than one record at a time but allows for more customization than the datasheet. The Tabular form layout, which arranges the fields in a single horizontal row with labels above, is ideal for this purpose. Figure 7.10 illustrates a Tabular form based on the Project Expenses query. For tables with just a few fields, you'll probably be able to use the tabular forms produced by the Wizard with few, if any, modifications. If you can't see all the fields at once, you can modify the form to correct the spacing or create two rows of fields.

FIGURE 7.10 *In a Tabular form, the fields are arranged in a row, with the labels above the data.*

Project Expenses

Project Expenses

ProjectID	Project Name	Expense Type	Date	Purpose
Kitchen	Remodel kitchen	Labor	1/15/95	Initial consultation w
Kitchen	Remodel kitchen	Labor	1/15/95	First payment to Ma
Kitchen	Remodel kitchen	Materials	1/21/95	Fabric for new curta
Kitchen	Remodel kitchen	Labor	2/2/95	New cabinet doors
Kitchen	Remodel kitchen	Labor	2/5/95	Progress payment t
Kitchen	Remodel kitchen	Labor	2/13/95	Allen Electric
Kitchen	Remodel kitchen	Labor	2/15/95	Rainbow Painters
Kitchen	Remodel kitchen	Labor	2/15/95	Gemini Plumbing

Record: 1 of 14

To build the Tabular form for the Project Expenses query:

1. Make sure the Database window displays the list of queries.
2. Highlight Project Expenses and click the New Form button in the toolbar.
3. In the New Form dialog box, make sure you see Project Expenses in the combo box, and then click the Form Wizards button or press Alt+W.
4. In the first Form Wizards dialog box, choose Tabular, and click OK to move to the next step.
5. Click >> to select all the fields in the Project Expenses query, and click Next to go on to the next step.
6. Choose the Shadowed style, and click Next to go on to the next step.
7. In the last Form Wizard dialog box, retain the default form title, Project Expenses, leave Open the form with data in it selected, and click the Finish button.
8. When Access displays the form, move it to the upper-left corner of the Access program window and make it as large as you can without maximizing it. Your form should look like the one in Figure 7.10.
9. When you save the form, give it the name Project Expenses Tabular.

The Tabular form created by the Wizard isn't perfect. The Purpose text box isn't nearly wide enough, the Project Name and Amount text boxes are too wide, and you can't see all the columns at once. It's easy to fix these problems in Form Design view, as you'll see in Chapter 11.

USING FORMS TO UPDATE TWO TABLES

Using a form based on a query is just one way to update two tables that have a one-to-many relationship. This strategy is ideal when you're working from the point of view of the child table and you just want to see some fields from the parent table for reference. In most cases, though, you'll also want a form that takes the point of view of the parent table and shows you one record from this table, together with all the matching records from the child table. Figure 7.11 shows an example based on the Projects and Expenses tables. Access calls this a Main/Subform layout because it consists of a main form (which displays the fields from the parent table) with another form displayed as a datasheet (the subform) embedded in it. This layout looks complicated, but it's easy to create using a Form Wizard.

Try using the Form Wizards to create a form similar to the one shown in Figure 7.11:

1. Make sure the Database window displays the list of forms, and click the New command button or press Alt+N.

FIGURE 7.11

In a Main/Subform layout, the main form displays one record from the parent table, and the subform displays all the matching child records.

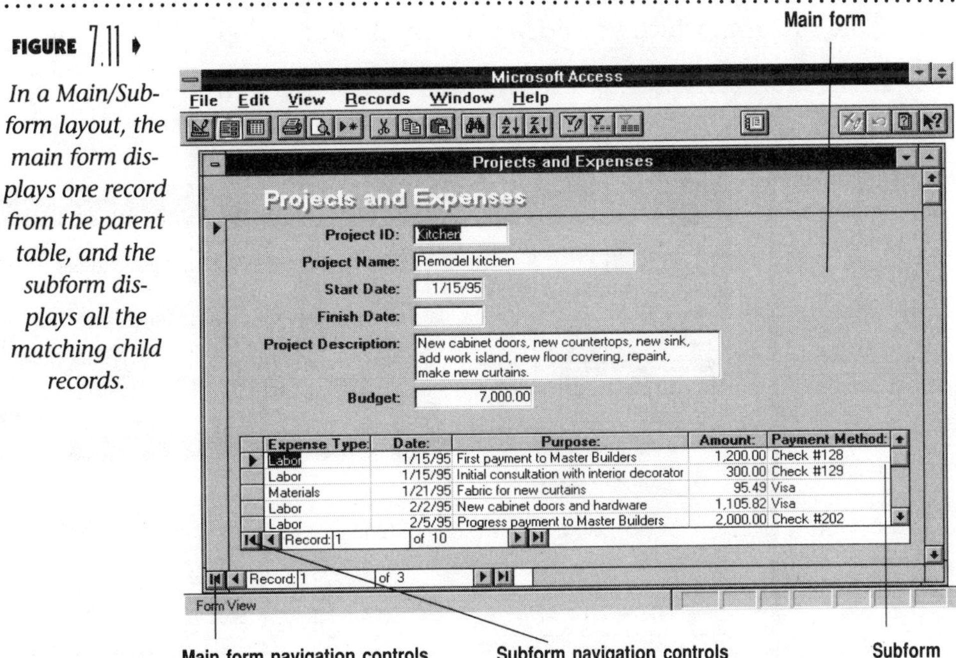

2. In the New Form dialog box, choose Projects (the table you'll display in the main form) from the list of tables, and then click the Form Wizards button or press Alt+W.
3. In the first Form Wizards dialog box, choose Main/Subform, and click OK to move on to the next step.

When you chose the name of the parent table (the Projects table) in the New Table dialog box, you hadn't yet selected the Main/Subform Wizard (or any Wizard, for that matter). Once the Wizard knows you want to use the Main/Subform layout, it displays the dialog box shown in Figure 7.12 to let you choose the table or query you want to display in the subform.

4. Select Expenses from the list of tables, and then click Next to go on to the next step.

The next step is choosing the fields you want in the main form and the subform, which you do in two very similar dialog boxes. The first,

FIGURE 7.12 ♦

The Form Wizard asks you to choose the data source for the subform.

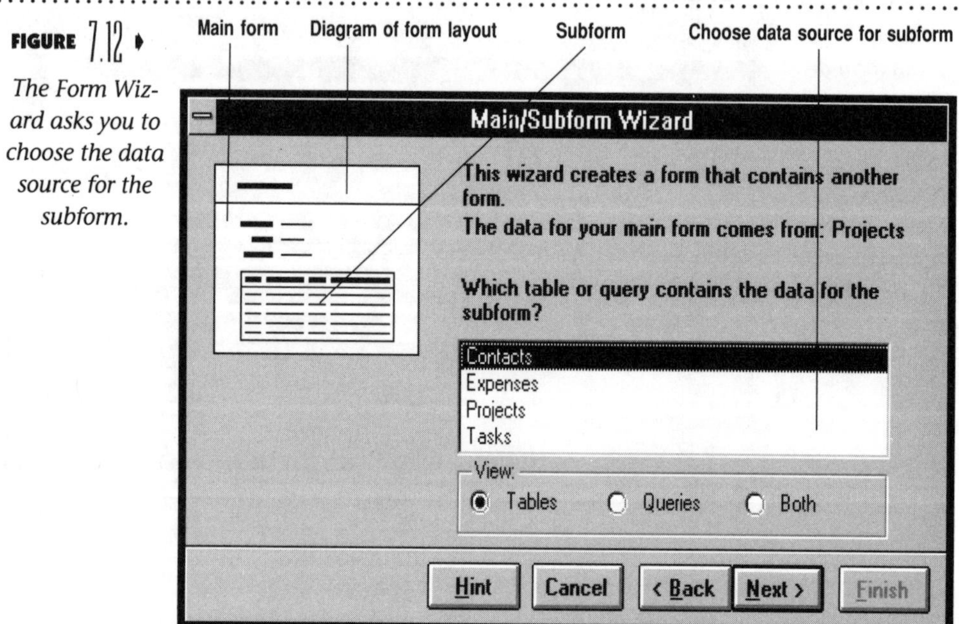

which you use to select the fields in the main form, is shown in Figure 7.13. In the second dialog box, the arrow in the diagram on the left points down toward the subform, and the Available fields list shows you the fields in the subform's data source.

NOTE

When you choose the fields for the subform, you can generally omit the field that links the two tables. It's better to display it once on the main form rather than in all the child records.

To choose the fields for the Projects and Expenses form:

5. Click >> to select all the fields in the Projects table, and then click Next to go on to the next step.

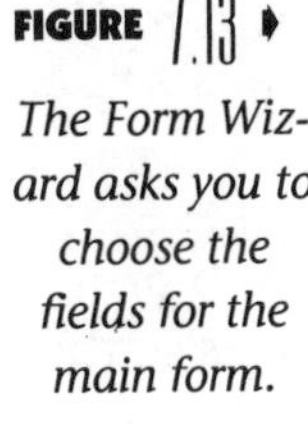

FIGURE 7.13 ▸

The Form Wizard asks you to choose the fields for the main form.

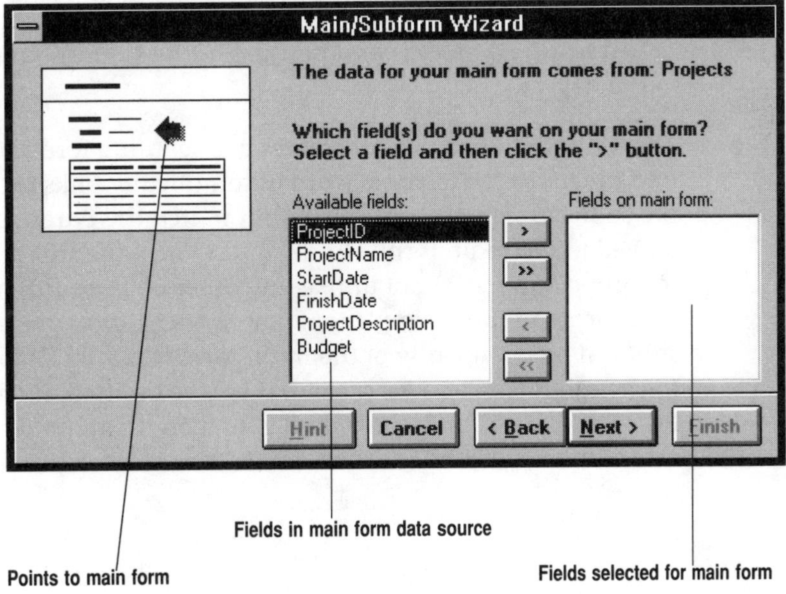

6. Click >> to select all the fields in the Expenses table, and remove ExpenseID and ProjectID from the field list. (The value in the ExpenseID field isn't meaningful to you, and you'll see the ProjectID field in the main portion of the form.) Click Next to go on to the next step.
7. Choose the Embossed form style, and then click Next to go on to the next step.
8. In the last Form Wizard dialog box, type the name **Projects and Expenses** for the form title, leave Open the form with data in it selected, and click the Finish button.
9. The Form Wizard displays an alert box with the message You must save the subform before the Main/Subform can proceed to notify you that it (not you) must save the subform. When you click OK in this dialog box, it displays the Save As dialog box to prompt you for a name. Type the name **Expenses Subform**.
10. When Access displays the form, maximize the window. Your screen will look approximately like the one shown earlier in Figure 7.11, so you can see the whole subform. (That form was modified to adjust the size and position of the subform and some of the fields.)

The Main/Subform Wizard creates two separate forms: the subform and the main form. The Wizard automatically links the forms so that the subform shows only records that match the parent record displayed in the main form. On the main form, the subform is an object (a form component) not unlike any other objects, although it's more complicated than a simple text box or check box. You can open the subform independently of the main form from the Database window (although it won't be very useful if you've omitted the field that identifies the parent record), but when you open the main form, you can't move, resize, or close the subform.

NOTE

The restrictions on what you can do to a subform are exactly the same as the rules that govern the other objects on the form: While you're using a form to enter data, you can't move, resize, or delete text boxes or any other objects.

Both the main form and subform windows have all the standard record navigation controls. The controls in the main form window move you through the parent table, and the controls in the subform window move you through the set of matching child records. When you use the Find command, Access searches the parent table if you initiated the search from the main form or the child table if you started from the subform.

Try using the Projects and Expenses form to add the first three expenses for the PetCare project:

1. Click the Next Record button in the main form window to move from the first project (Kitchen) to the next (PCAdvisors). Note that the subform shows the PC Advisors project expenses.
2. Click the ProjectID field in the main form.
3. Click the Find button in the toolbar and search the ProjectID field for *PetCare*. When Access finds the record, close the Find dialog box. You haven't entered any expenses yet for this project, so the subform will be empty.
4. Click the subform and enter the first three expense records:

Expense Type	**Subcontractors**
Date	**2/8/95**
Purpose	**Design logo for business (Carmen Vargas)**
Amount	**450.00**
Payment Method	**Check #218**

Expense Type	**Subcontractors**
Date	**2/18/95**
Purpose	**Typesetting, initial letterhead, and business card**
Amount	**80.00**
Payment Method	**Check #262**

Expense Type	**Shipping**
Date	**2/19/95**
Purpose	**Send proofs to client**
Amount	**8.95**
Payment Method	**Cash**

5. Click anywhere in the main portion of the form, and then click the New button on the toolbar to add a new record to the Projects table. When you get to the Project Description field, press Shift+F2 to open the Zoom box, type the description, and then press ↵ to return to the form. Here is the complete record:

Project ID	**Vacation**
Project Name	**Vacation, spring 1995**
Start Date	**4/8/95**
Project Descrip-tion	**Three-week vacation in Utah and Arizona, including Grand Canyon, Zion, Bryce, Arches National Parks and five-day mountain bike trip in Canyonlands.**
Budget	**3500.00**

6. Enter two expense records:

Expense Type	**Travel**
Date	**3/1/95**

Purpose	**Camping equipment**
Amount	**240.00**
Payment Method	**Visa**
Expense Type	**Travel**
Date	**3/1/95**
Purpose	**New camera bag**
Amount	**42.00**
Payment Method	**Visa**

7. Close the form, and give it the name Projects and Expenses.
8. Click the Restore button so the Database window is not maximized.
9. Open the Expenses table in Datasheet view, and verify that the new records you added using the Project Expenses form have the right Project IDs and the correct sequential Expense IDs.
10. Close the datasheet window.

BUILDING A GRAPH FORM

Access provides a Wizard for building simple forms that contain a single graph based on any table or query. You can also add a graph to a form that contains other data, and you'll learn how to do this in Chapter 12. In either case, Access doesn't consider a graph to be a special type of database component; a graph is just one of many types of objects that a form can contain. Like a subform, it's more or less equivalent to a text box or check box, although its appearance is a lot more complicated. In this chapter you'll build the simple graph shown in Figure 7.14, which plots the number of expense records by month.

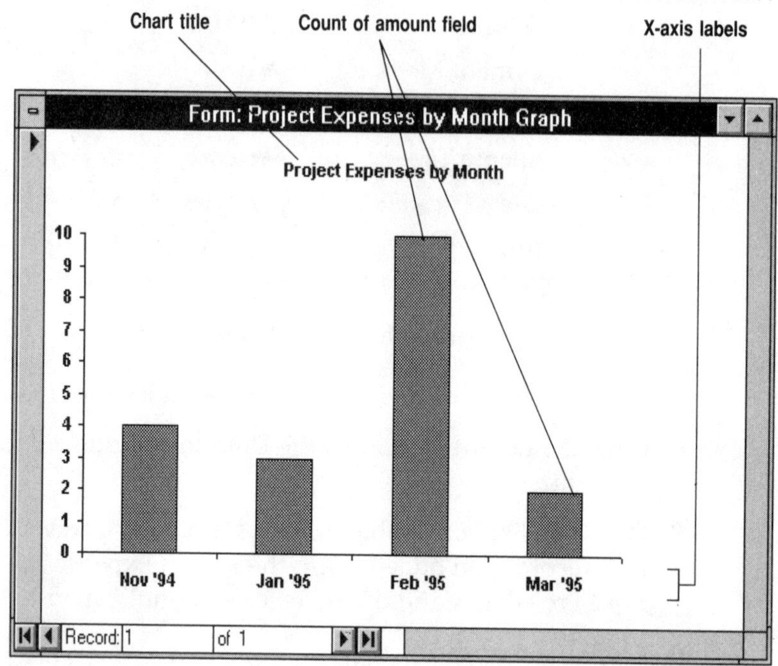

FIGURE 7.14 *The Graph Wizard builds a simple form containing a graph based on any table or query.*

Actually, it isn't Access that builds the graph. It's a separate program called Microsoft Graph, which is bundled with Access (and other Microsoft applications) and is installed in the MSAPPS\MSGRAPH5 subdirectory under your Windows program directory. If you've used other Microsoft applications, such as Excel, you may already be familiar with Graph. When you invoke the Graph Wizard, this Wizard initiates the form design process, lets you choose the data and specify a few simple graph layout options, and then turns the job over to Graph, which builds your graph "behind the scenes."

To begin building the Expenses table graph:

1. Make sure the Database window displays the list of tables.
2. Highlight Expenses and click the New Form button in the toolbar.

3. In the New Form dialog box, make sure you see Expenses in the combo box, and then click the Form Wizards button or press Alt+W.

4. In the first Form Wizard dialog box, choose Graph, and click OK to move to the next step.

The Graph Wizard displays the dialog box shown in Figure 7.15 to let you select the fields that will supply the data (the ExpenseDate and Amount fields in the graph in Figure 7.14).

FIGURE 7.15

You can choose one field for the X axis and one or more fields for the data points in the graph.

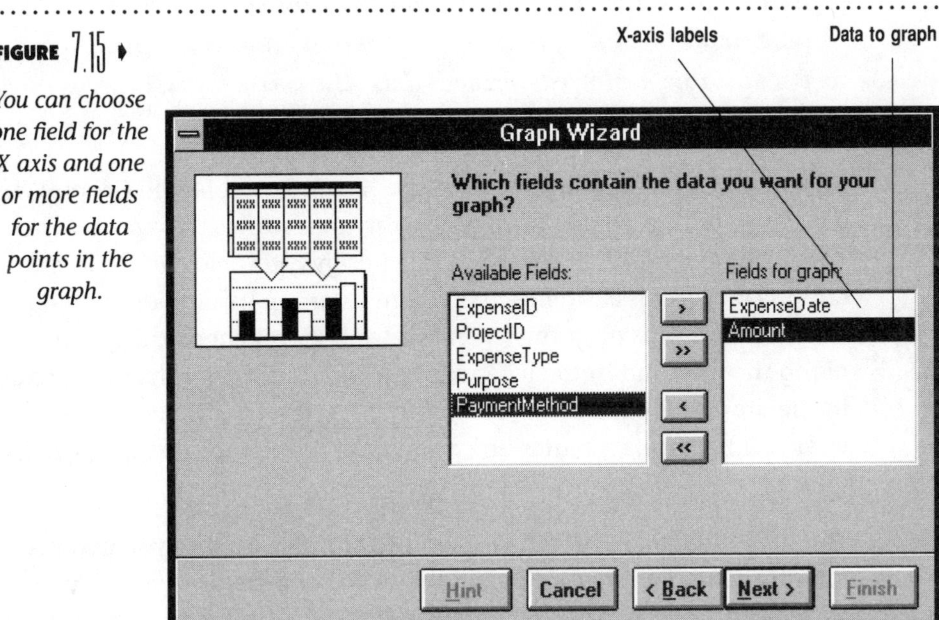

NOTE

If you don't have much experience with graphs, keep in mind that a graph plots the relationship between one independent variable*—in Access, a field that can take on any value—and one or more* dependent variables, *which depend on the independent variable. For example, in the graph in Figure 7.14, the expense date is the independent variable. The dependent variable is the number of expenses in a given month. Usually, the independent variable is plotted on the X axis (the horizontal axis) and the dependent variable is plotted on the Y axis (the vertical axis).*

When you use a date/time field as the X-axis variable, the Graph Wizard assumes that you want to group the data rather than graph each date or time separately. After you've chosen your fields, it displays a dialog box that asks whether you want to group by date only along the graph's X axis or in the legend as well. If you choose to group along the axis and in the legend, Access creates a separate data series in the graph for each major grouping interval (a year, month, or week). Otherwise, it creates one data series with a data point for each group.

The next dialog box, which is shown in Figure 7.16, lets you choose the grouping interval and define the range of date/time values you want to include in the graph. Using the combo box at the top of this dialog box, you can graph by year, quarter, month, week, day, hour, or minute. The selection criteria in Figure 7.16 select dates between January 1, 1995, and March 31, 1995.

FIGURE 7.16

In a date/time graph, you can choose the grouping interval and specify selection criteria.

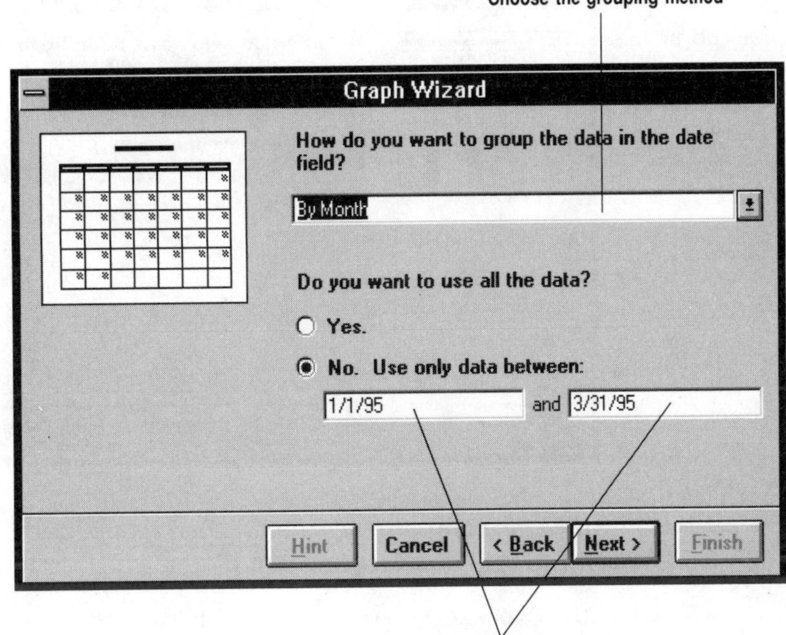

Access never plots the actual values in the source table or query; it always computes a sum, average, or count based on the fields you've selected for the data points and graphs the results. If you're thinking this operation is a lot like building a totals query with groups, you're right, and that's exactly what Access does—it runs the equivalent of a query behind the scenes to produce the data for the graph.

If you chose just one field in the first Graph Wizard dialog box, Access assumes you want to graph the number of records with each distinct value in that field. Otherwise, it lets you choose which calculation you want in the dialog box shown in Figure 7.17. For example, if you chose Sum for the graph you're building, Access would group records

FIGURE 7.17 ▸

You can graph the sum, average, or count of the records in each group.

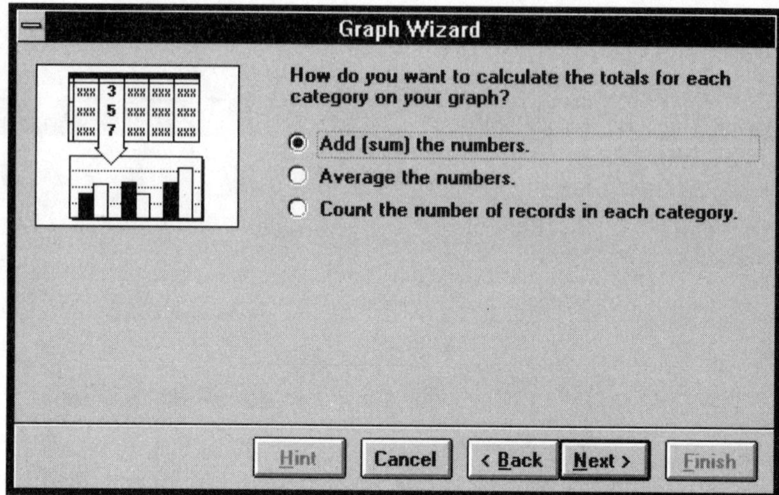

by ExpenseDate, compute the sum for each group, and display the sums in the graph. To select the data for the Expenses table graph:

5. Select the ExpenseDate and Amount fields, and then click Next to go on to the next step.
6. Select Only along the graph's axis in the dialog box that lets you specify where you want to group data, and then click Next to go on to the next step.
7. Select By Month for the grouping interval, leave the Yes button selected to include all the data in your graph and then click Next to go on the next step.
8. Choose Count the number of records in each category (the sums vary too much to produce a good-looking graph), and then click Next to move on to the next step.

The next dialog box, which is shown in Figure 7.18, lets you choose the graph type and tell the Wizard where to find the data. To choose a graph type, click one of the large buttons on the right side of the dialog box. To see what your own data would look like in any available graph style, click its button and watch the sample graph on the left side of the dialog box.

FIGURE 7.18 ▸

The Graph Wizard lets you choose the overall graph type.

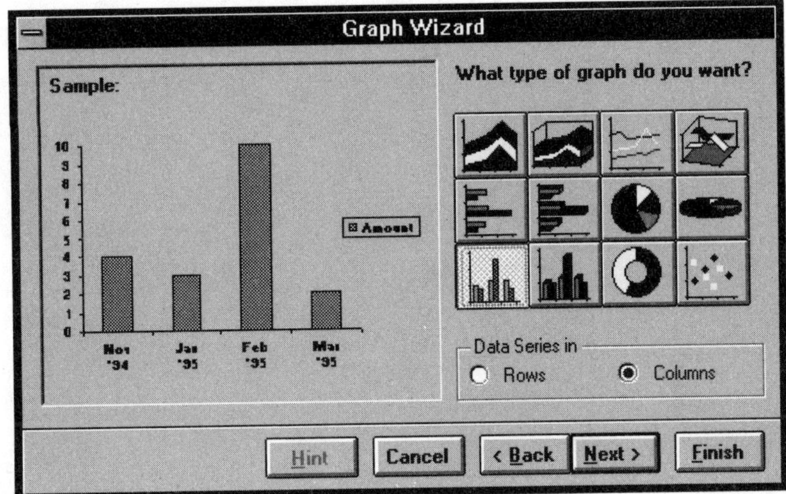

When you graph data from a table or query, select the Columns radio button to identify the data series. If this seems unnecessary, remember that Graph can handle data from a variety of sources, not just Access, and it doesn't make any assumptions about the organization of the data. If you visualize the data source for the graph in Datasheet view, you'll understand that each data series comes from a column.

The next dialog box, which is shown in Figure 7.19, lets you choose a few overall formatting options for your graph. Make these selections to complete the Expenses table graph:

9. Leave the default graph type selected. (It's the button in the lower-left corner.)
10. Leave the default, Columns, selected for the Data Series option, and click Next to move on to the next step.
11. Enter the title **Project Expenses by Month**.

FIGURE 7.19

The Graph Wizard lets you set a few overall formatting options.

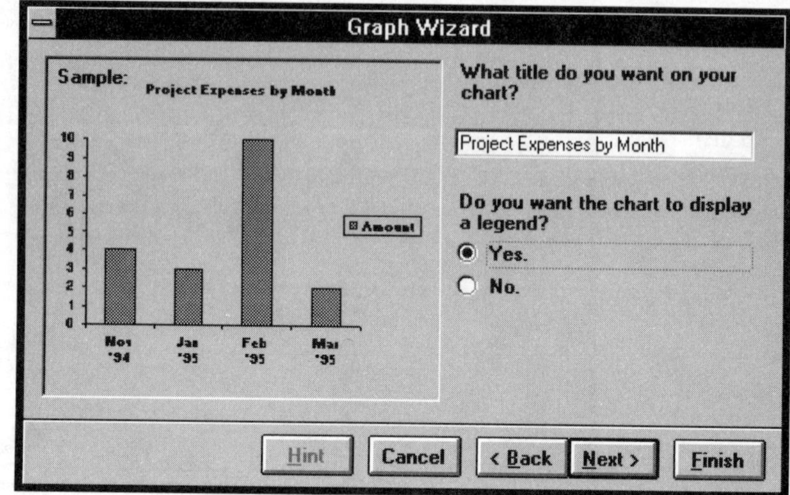

12. Select No to omit the legend (with only one data series, you don't need one), and click Next to move on to the next step.
13. In the last Graph Wizard dialog box, select **Open the form with the graph displayed on it**, and click Finish to display the completed graph. Your form should look approximately like the one in Figure 7.14.
14. Close the form and save it under the name Project Expenses by Month Graph.

Like the other forms produced by the Wizards, the graph forms leave something to be desired. In the graph in Figure 7.14, you might want a Y-axis title to identify the quantity you're graphing. You can call up the Graph program while you're modifying a form to make these and other modifications to the graph.

WHAT'S NEXT

By using the Form Wizards, you can build custom forms that let you display data on the screen in a variety of specialized layouts. To interact with the outside world, you'll also need to define reports to print your data on paper. Chapter 8 introduces the Access Report Wizards and shows you how to produce several basic report layouts, and Chapter 9 describes how to print labels.

Designing Reports

Despite all the talk about the "paperless office," printed reports remain the dominant medium for sharing data with your coworkers. There's still no better way to compare several sections of a lengthy report than to spread them out side by side on the conference table. After all, you still can't view more than a page or two of text at a time even on a large screen, and not everyone owns a laptop, much less one small enough to use on a crowded bus. And if not all your colleagues have Access, know how to use it, or care to learn, what better way to share the fruits of your labor than to print a clear, readable, attractively formatted report?

Access makes it easy to get started by providing report Wizards for designing several very common and useful report styles, including single-column lists, tabular layouts, and reports with subtotal groups and summary statistics. As you'll see, most of these reports could do with some esthetic improvements, but using the Wizards and modifying the resulting reports is often much easier and is certainly less intimidating than starting from scratch. This chapter concentrates on learning to use the Wizards and describing the data you want on your reports. Chapters 11 and 12 will teach you to modify the appearance and contents of the reports built by the Wizards and to create reports from scratch.

USING THE AUTOREPORT WIZARD

The easiest way to build a report is to highlight a table or query name in the Database window and then click the AutoReport button on the toolbar. Like the AutoForm button described in Chapter 7, the AutoReport button invokes a Wizard that doesn't ask you any questions; it simply builds a simple report that includes all the fields in the source table or query and then immediately previews this report on the screen. Figure 8.1 illustrates the AutoReport for the Expenses table.

FIGURE 8.1

The AutoReport button creates a simple columnar report that includes all the fields in a table or query.

Expenses

14-Mar-95

Expense ID:	1
ProjectID:	PCAdvisors
Expense Type:	Subcontractors
Date:	11/12/94
Purpose:	Photographs for brochure
Amount:	540.00
Payment Method:	Check #32
Expense ID:	2
ProjectID:	PCAdvisors
Expense Type:	Subcontractors
Date:	11/18/94
Purpose:	Typesetting for brochure
Amount:	250.00
Payment Method:	Check #58
Expense ID:	3
ProjectID:	PCAdvisors
Expense Type:	Shipping
Date:	11/19/94
Purpose:	Messenger to bring proofs to clie
Amount:	20.00
Payment Method:	Cash

NOTE

You can also produce a report by clicking the AutoReport button while working with a table or query in Datasheet view. Even if you've hidden some columns, the AutoReport will include all the fields in the source table or query.

It's easy to use the AutoReport Wizard, but you won't be satisfied with the results unless the source table or query has only a few fields and most of these are numeric, date/time, or short text fields. No matter how many fields there are, the AutoReport Wizard squeezes all of them onto one row, and many of the columns will be so narrow that the data is meaningless.

Try using the AutoReport button to reproduce this report:

1. Make sure the Database window displays the list of tables.
2. Highlight Expenses in the list of tables.
3. Click the AutoReport button in the toolbar.

The AutoReport Wizard prints the name of the source table or query and the current date once, at the very beginning of the report (*not* at the top of each page), and it prints the page number in the lower-right corner of each page. The report lists records in the order in which you entered them (which is rarely the order you'd prefer).

Access assigns a default name to each new report, including those created by the AutoReport Wizard—Report1 for the first report you create, Report2 for the second, and so on. When you close the report for the first time, Access displays a Save As dialog box to give you a chance to assign a more meaningful name.

The most obvious layout problem is the fact that many of the text boxes are the wrong width. The inappropriate field widths are harder to live with on a report than on a form because there's no way to scroll through a long text field in a report. Fortunately, it's easy to correct this problem, as you'll learn in Chapter 11.

USING THE REPORT WIZARDS

If you're willing to put in just a little more effort, you can very easily create several different report styles, some of them quite complex, by using the Report Wizards. Even if you're defining a layout not much different from the AutoReport, the other Wizards offer several significant advantages—first and foremost, the ability to choose the fields you want on the report and specify their order, and the ability to choose portrait or landscape mode on a laser printer. To begin creating a new report, do one of the following:

- Highlight a table or query name in the Database window and click the New Report button in the toolbar.
- Make sure the Database window displays the list of reports, and then click the New command button or press Alt+N.

Access displays the New Report dialog box shown in Figure 8.2. The combo box labeled Select A Table/Query lets you choose the data

FIGURE 8.2

The New Report dialog box lets you call up the Report Wizards or create a new report from scratch.

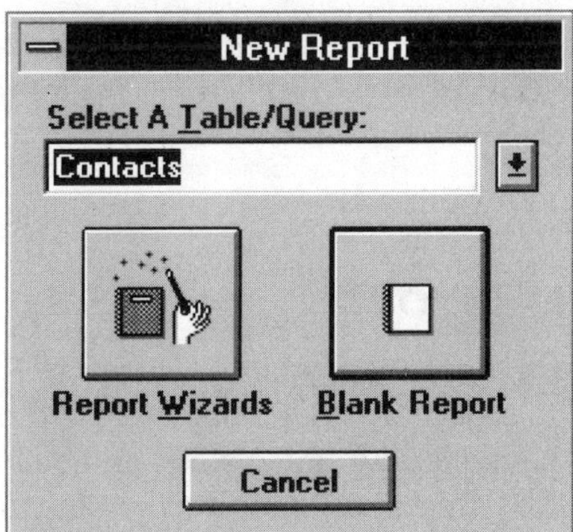

source for the report. If you called up the New Report dialog box by highlighting a table or query name and clicking the New Report button, you'll see its name in the combo box, but you can always change your mind and choose a different table or query. After you pick the data source, click the Report Wizards button or press Alt+W.

TIP

The combo box at the top of the New Report dialog box doesn't differentiate between tables and queries. If you think you might forget which table or query you want, highlight the name in the Database window and click the New Report button to initiate the report design process.

To begin exploring the Report Wizards, define a report that prints all the records in the Contacts table:

1. Make sure the Database window displays the list of reports, and click the New command button or press Alt+N.
2. Display the drop-down list for the combo box at the top of the New Report dialog box, and choose Contacts from the list of tables and queries.
3. Click Report Wizards or press Alt+W.

CHOOSING THE REPORT LAYOUT

The first Report Wizard dialog box, which is shown in Figure 8.3, lets you choose the overall report layout. If you choose AutoReport, the Wizard bypasses all the remaining dialog boxes and builds the same report you'd get by clicking the AutoReport button on the toolbar. Later in this chapter you'll create reports that use the Tabular, Group/Totals, and Summary layouts. (If you want to see these layouts right now, look ahead at Figures 8.12, 8.14, and 8.20.) Chapter 9 shows you how to use the Mailing Label Wizard and the MS Word Mail Merge Wizard for mailings. The Single-Column layout, which resembles the AutoReport and

FIGURE 8.3

The Report Wizard asks you to choose the basic report layout.

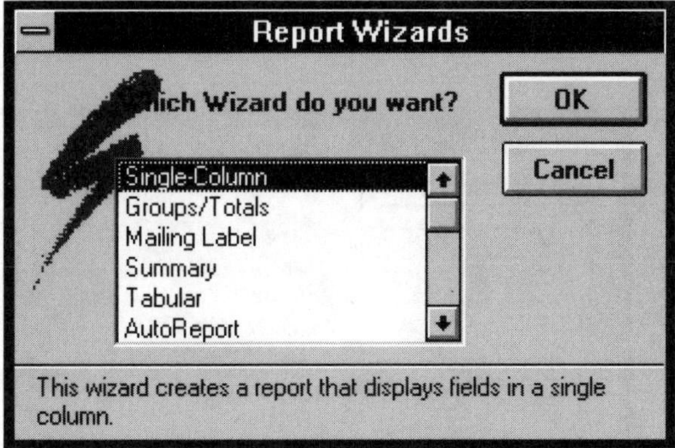

the Single-Column forms you created in Chapter 7, is a good choice for tables with a lot of long text or memo fields, and you'll use this layout for the Contacts table:

4. Highlight Single-Column, and click OK to move to the next step.

NOTE

You may have been hoping to see a layout equivalent to the Main/Subform form layout, but there is no equivalent Report Wizard. In Chapter 12 you'll learn how to embed one report in another to create a very similar layout.

CHOOSING THE FIELDS

The next Report Wizard dialog box, which is shown in Figure 8.4, lets you select the fields you want on your report. On the left side of the dialog box is a diagram of the report layout you've chosen, with thin lines representing the data and heavier lines representing the report

FIGURE 8.4 ▸

You can choose the fields you want on your report and specify their order.

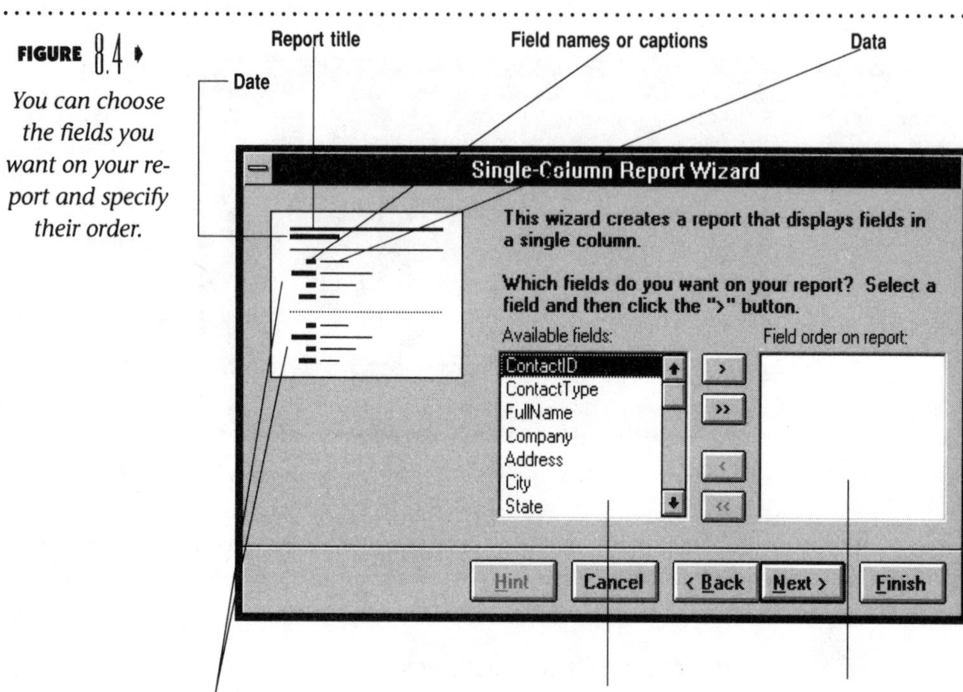

title, current date, and field names (or captions). From your experience with the Form Wizards, you should feel comfortable using the buttons between the Available fields list and the Field order on report list to add or remove fields, one at a time or all at once.

NOTE

As the heading suggests, the order of the field names in the Field order on report ***list determines the sequence of the fields on the report. You can't rearrange the fields in this list except by removing fields and then reselecting them in a different order. Choose carefully for now, but keep in mind that you can modify the report later if you need to.***

For the Contacts table report, choose all the fields except Photograph:

5. Click the >> button to add all the fields in the Contacts table to the report.
6. Highlight Photograph in the **Field order on report** list and click < to remove this field from the report.
7. Click Next to move on to the next step.

CHOOSING THE SORT ORDER

After you've chosen the fields for your report, the Report Wizard displays the dialog box shown in Figure 8.5 to let you choose the sort order for your report. You can sort by up to ten fields, but you'll rarely need to choose more than two or three. The order in which the fields are listed in the **Sort order** list determines the sort hierarchy: Access arranges records in order by the first sort field and then, within this group, in order by the second, and so on.

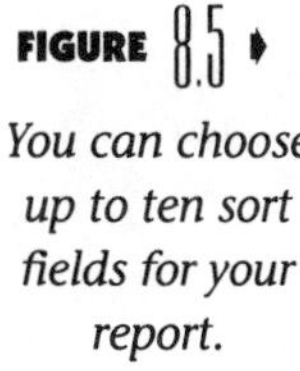

FIGURE 8.5

You can choose up to ten sort fields for your report.

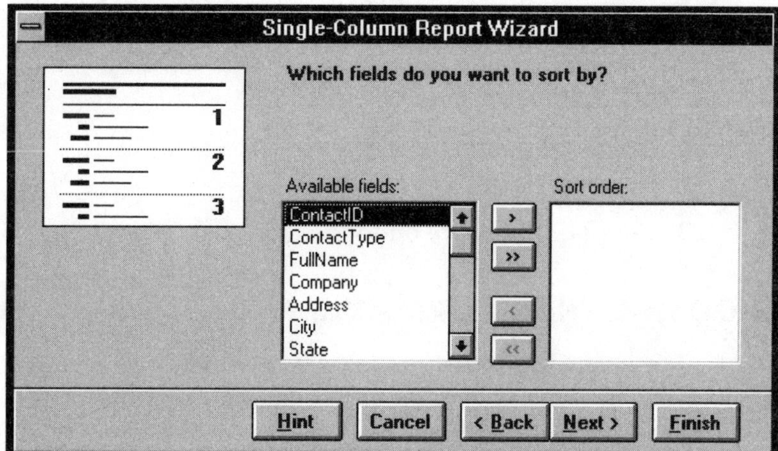

WARNING

The Report Wizards don't let you sort in descending order or sort on a field that doesn't appear on your report. For example, you can't sort on ContactID but omit this field from the report and print the FullName field instead. Both of these limitations are imposed by the Report Wizards, not Access. You can overcome both by modifying the report later.

NOTE

The Report Wizard doesn't show you memo or OLE object fields in the Available fields ***list because you can't sort on these data types.***

To print the Contacts report sorted by contact type, and within contact type in alphabetical order:

8. Highlight ContactType in the **Available fields** list, and click the > button to select it.
9. Highlight ContactID in the **Available fields** list, and click the > button to select it.
10. Click Next to move on to the next step.

CHOOSING THE REPORT STYLE

The next Report Wizard dialog box, which is shown in Figure 8.6, lets you choose the overall report style, page orientation, and line spacing. Figure 8.7 shows an example of each of the three styles. If you need a more immediate reminder, click any of the three radio buttons in turn and watch the diagram on the left side of the dialog box, which shows you a small sample of the selected style.

FIGURE 8.6 ▸

The Report Wizard lets you choose the overall report style.

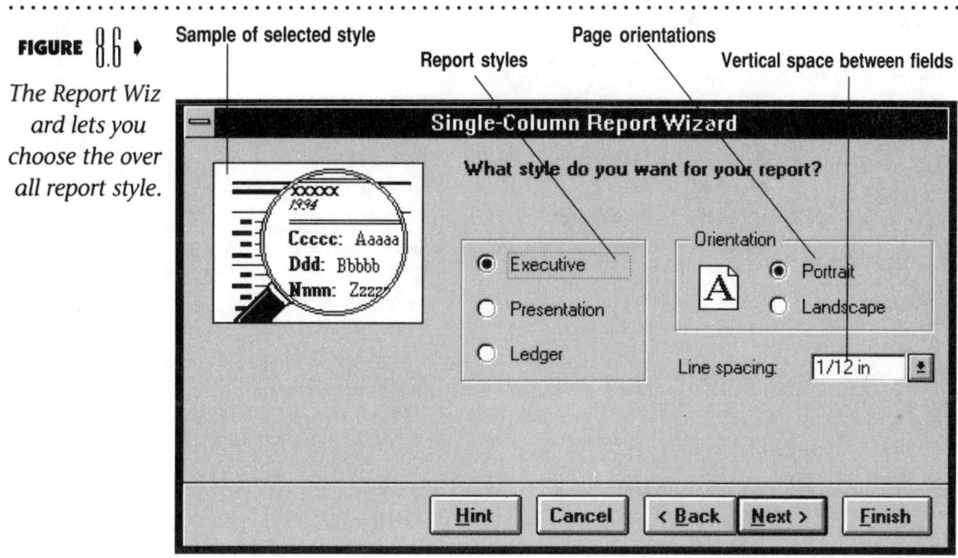

If you have a laser printer, you can choose either Portrait (vertical) or Landscape (horizontal) orientation. Landscape is often a better choice for columnar reports that include long text fields, because you can fit more data on one line. Unfortunately, choosing Landscape orientation doesn't cause the Report Wizard to choose a larger default width for text fields, so you may end up with a report that doesn't fill the page and still doesn't show enough of each field. You'll have to edit the report later to adjust the field widths.

The Line spacing option governs the vertical spacing *between* fields, not *within* the group of lines that make up a field. The default spacing for the Executive and Presentation styles, 1/12 in., gives you a little extra space between fields compared to the spacing between the lines that make up a text or memo field. If you want completely uniform vertical spacing, choose 0 (the default for the Ledger style).

FIGURE 8.7

The three report styles are called Executive, Presentation, and Ledger.

Expenses by Date

14-Mar-95

Project ID	Expense Type	Date	Purpose	Amount	Payment Method
PCAdvisors	Subcontractors	11/12/94	Photographs for brochure	540.00	Check #32
PCAdvisors	Subcontractors	11/18/94	Typesetting for brochure	250.00	Check #58
PCAdvisors	Shipping	11/19/94	Messenger to bring proofs to client	20.00	Cash
PCAdvisors	Subcontractors	11/25/94	Print 1000 brochures	120.00	Check #77
Kitchen	Labor	1/15/95	Initial consultation with interior decorator	300.00	Check #129
Kitchen	Labor	1/15/95	First payment to Master Builders	1,200.00	Check #128
Kitchen	Materials	1/21/95	Fabric for new curtains	95.49	Visa
Kitchen	Labor	2/2/95	New cabinet doors and hardware	1,105.82	Visa
Kitchen	Labor	2/5/95	Progress payment to Master Builders	2,000.00	Check #202
PetCare	Subcontractors	2/8/95	Design logo for business (Carmen Vargas)	450.00	Check #218
Kitchen	Labor	2/13/95	Allen Electric	465.00	Check #231
Kitchen	Labor	2/15/95	Gemini Plumbing	320.00	Check #243
Kitchen	Labor	2/16/95	Final payment to Master Builders	1,100.00	Check #250
Kitchen	Labor	2/16/95	Final payment to interior decorator	400.00	Check #249
Kitchen	Labor	2/16/95	Rainbow Painters	640.00	Check #248
PetCare	Subcontractors	2/18/95	Typesetting, initial letterhead, and business card	80.00	Check #262
PetCare	Shipping	2/19/95	Send proofs to client	8.95	Cash
Vacation	Travel	3/1/95	New camera bag	42.00	Visa
Vacation	Travel	3/1/95	Camping equipment	240.00	Visa
				9,377.26	

Executive

FIGURE 8.7

The three report styles are called Executive, Presentation, and Ledger. (continued)

Expenses by Date

14-Mar-95

Project ID	Expense Type	Date	Purpose	Amount	Payment Method
PCAdvisors	Subcontractors	11/12/94	Photographs for brochure	540.00	Check #32
PCAdvisors	Subcontractors	11/18/94	Typesetting for brochure	250.00	Check #58
PCAdvisors	Shipping	11/19/94	Messenger to bring proofs to client	20.00	Cash
PCAdvisors	Subcontractors	11/25/94	Print 1000 brochures	120.00	Check #77
Kitchen	Labor	1/15/95	Initial consultation with interior decorator	300.00	Check #129
Kitchen	Labor	1/15/95	First payment to Master Builders	1,200.00	Check #128
Kitchen	Materials	1/21/95	Fabric for new curtains	95.49	Visa
Kitchen	Labor	2/2/95	New cabinet doors and hardware	1,105.82	Visa
Kitchen	Labor	2/5/95	Progress payment to Master Builders	2,000.00	Check #202
PetCare	Subcontractors	2/8/95	Design logo for business (Carmen Vargas)	450.00	Check #218
Kitchen	Labor	2/13/95	Allen Electric	465.00	Check #231
Kitchen	Labor	2/15/95	Gemini Plumbing	320.00	Check #243
Kitchen	Labor	2/16/95	Final payment to Master Builders	1,100.00	Check #250
Kitchen	Labor	2/16/95	Final payment to interior decorator	400.00	Check #249
Kitchen	Labor	2/16/95	Rainbow Painters	640.00	Check #248
PetCare	Subcontractors	2/18/95	Typesetting, initial letterhead, and business card	80.00	Check #262
PetCare	Shipping	2/19/95	Send proofs to client	8.95	Cash
Vacation	Travel	3/1/95	New camera bag	42.00	Visa
Vacation	Travel	3/1/95	Camping equipment	240.00	Visa
				9,377.26	

1

Presentation

FIGURE 8.7 ▸

The three report styles are called Executive, Presentation, and Ledger. (continued)

Expenses by Date

14-Mar-95

Project ID	Expense Type	Date	Purpose	Amount	Payment Method
PCAdvisors	Subcontractors	11/12/94	Photographs for brochure	540.00	Check #32
PCAdvisors	Subcontractors	11/18/94	Typesetting for brochure	250.00	Check #58
PCAdvisors	Shipping	11/19/94	Messenger to bring proofs to client	20.00	Cash
PCAdvisors	Subcontractors	11/25/94	Print 1000 brochures	120.00	Check #77
Kitchen	Labor	1/15/95	Initial consultation with interior decorator	300.00	Check #129
Kitchen	Labor	1/15/95	First payment to Master Builders	1,200.00	Check #128
Kitchen	Materials	1/21/95	Fabric for new curtains	95.49	Visa
Kitchen	Labor	2/2/95	New cabinet doors and hardware	1,105.82	Visa
Kitchen	Labor	2/5/95	Progress payment to Master Builders	2,000.00	Check #202
PetCare	Subcontractors	2/8/95	Design logo for business (Carmen Vargas)	450.00	Check #218
Kitchen	Labor	2/13/95	Allen Electric	465.00	Check #231
Kitchen	Labor	2/15/95	Gemini Plumbing	320.00	Check #243
Kitchen	Labor	2/16/95	Final payment to Master Builders	1,100.00	Check #250
Kitchen	Labor	2/16/95	Final payment to interior decorator	400.00	Check #249
Kitchen	Labor	2/16/95	Rainbow Painters	640.00	Check #248
PetCare	Subcontractors	2/18/95	Typesetting, initial letterhead, and business card	80.00	Check #262
PetCare	Shipping	2/19/95	Send proofs to client	8.95	Cash
Vacation	Travel	3/1/95	New camera bag	42.00	Visa
Vacation	Travel	3/1/95	Camping equipment	240.00	Visa
				9,377.26	

Ledger

For the Contacts table report:

11. Leave the default Executive style selected.
12. Leave the default Portrait orientation selected.
13. Leave the default 1/12 in. line spacing selected.
14. Click Next to move on to the next step.

TITLING AND SAVING THE REPORT

The last Report Wizard dialog box, which is shown in Figure 8.8, lets you assign a report title, select a few overall page layout options, and

FIGURE 8.8

After the Wizard creates your report, you can modify it or preview it on the screen.

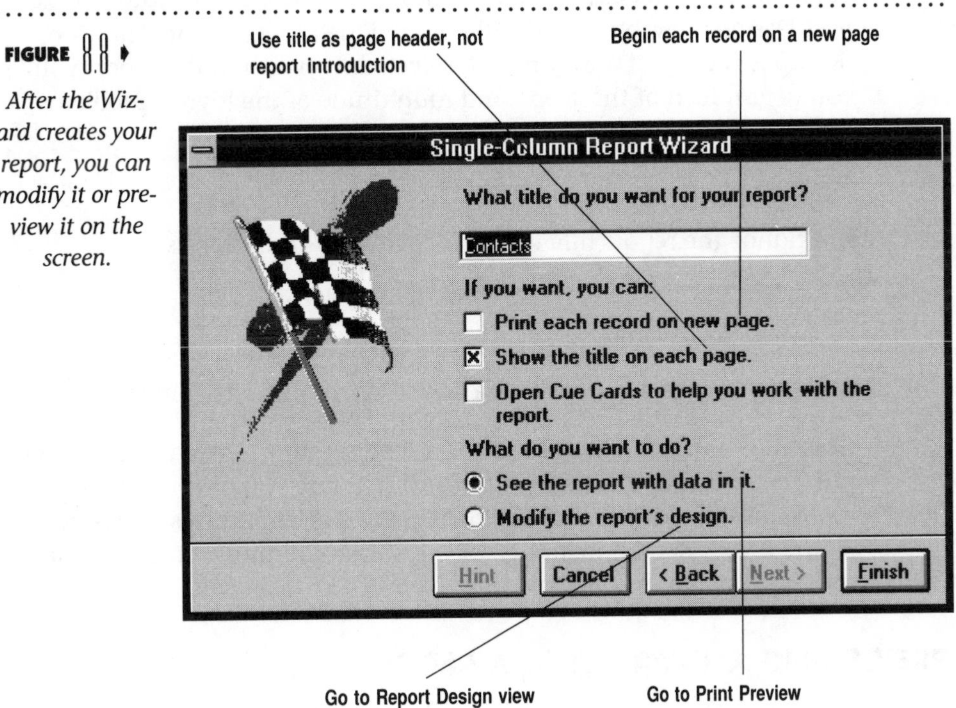

decide what you want to do next. The first two check boxes below the report title let you make important decisions about the report layout:

- Check **Print each record on new page** to guarantee that each record begins on a new page. Otherwise, Access prints as many records on each page as will fit. (Even if you don't check the **Print each record on a new page** option, Access avoids splitting any record across a page break.)
- Check **Show the title on each page** to print the report title as a page header. Otherwise, Access prints the title just once, at the very beginning of the report.

If you're sure you'll need to modify the report created by the Wizard, you can choose **Modify the report's design** to move immediately to Report Design view, but it's usually a good idea to leave the default option, **See the report with data in it**, selected. Previewing the report will let you get an idea of the scope and magnitude of the layout problems before you embark on modifications.

For the Contacts table report:

15. Change the report title to Contact Names and Addresses.
16. Leave **Print each record on new page** unchecked.
17. Leave **Show the title on each page** checked.
18. Leave **See the report with data in it** selected, and click Finish.

Creating most reports takes just a moment, but the Wizard displays a progress indicator in the status bar to reassure you as it builds the report and opens it (either in Print Preview or Report Design view). Figure 8.9 shows the first page of the Single-Column Contacts table report.

PREVIEWING AND PRINTING A REPORT

When you choose **See the report with data in it** in the last Report Wizard dialog box, Access displays the report in Print Preview rather than printing it immediately. You've already seen this window if you tried printing a datasheet in Chapter 5. If you haven't had much experience with

FIGURE 8.9 ▸ *The Single-Column Report Wizard builds a report with the fields lined up vertically on the page.*

Contact Names and Addresses

14-Mar-95

Contact ID: PCAdvisors
ContactType: Client
Name: Robert Santorelli
Company: PC Advisors
Address: 1738 Sacramento St.
City: San Francisco
State: CA
Zip: 94109
Home Phone:
Work Phone: (415) 626-3528
Note:

Contact ID: PetCare
ContactType: Client
Name: Melanie Fong
Company: PetCare Services
Address: 2819 Oak Rd.
City: Walnut Creek
State: CA
Zip: 94596
Home Phone:
Work Phone: (415) 982-3055
Note:

Windows software, it's worth spending a few more minutes exploring the Print Preview window, which is shown in Figure 8.10 with the first page of the Contact Names and Addresses report visible.

FIGURE 8.10 ▸

You can preview a report on the screen in Print Preview.

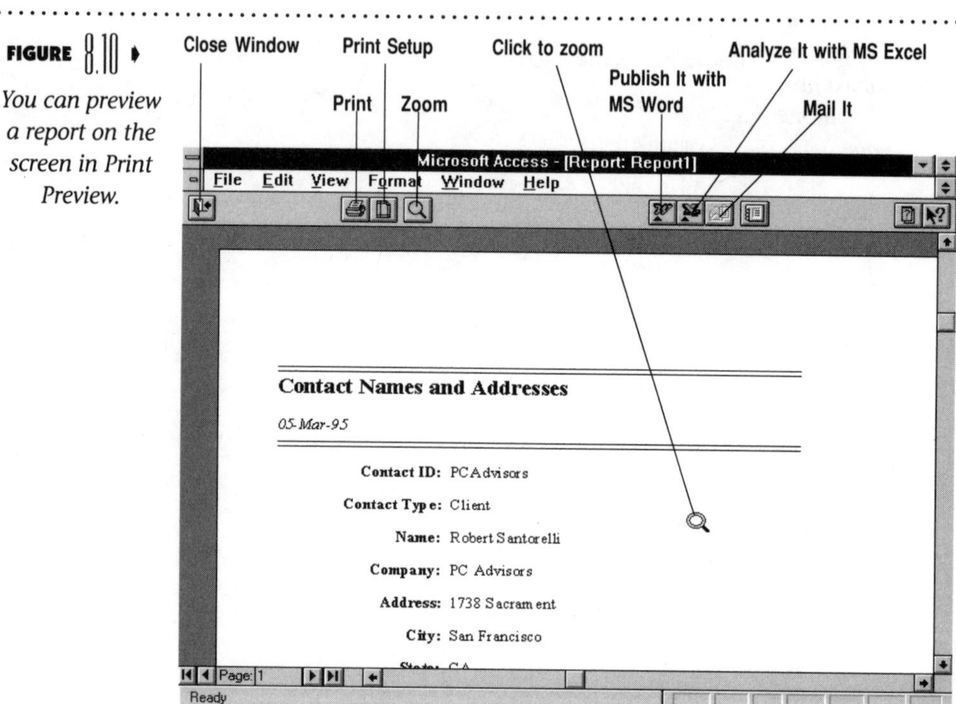

You can switch between the magnified view shown in Figure 8.10 and the full-page view shown in Figure 8.11 by clicking the Zoom button in the toolbar or by clicking anywhere on the report image. As you can see in these figures, whenever the mouse pointer is positioned over the page, it looks like a magnifying glass. The navigation controls at the bottom of the Print Preview window let you move to the first, last, next, previous, or any specific page of the report.

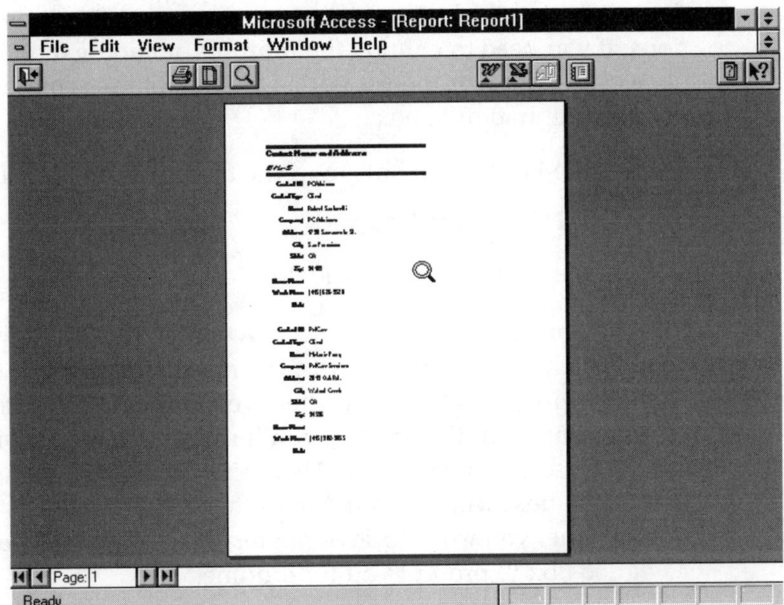

FIGURE 8.11 ▸ *The full-page view in Print Preview shows you one page at a time.*

TIP

To zoom in on a particular part of the page, position the mouse pointer over the area you want to see before you click to switch views.

To print the report from Print Preview, do one of the following:

- Click the Print button in the toolbar.
- Choose File ➤ Print.
- Press Ctrl+P.

Access displays the standard Windows Print dialog box, which allows you to choose which pages to print and to set a few overall print options. If you need to change the margins or choose a different printer, page orientation, or type of paper, use one of these methods to open the Print Setup dialog box:

- Click the Print Setup button in the toolbar from Print Preview.
- Choose File ➤ Print Setup.
- Click the Setup button in the Print dialog box.

After you print the report, Access leaves the Print Preview window open. When you're finished with the report, the method you use to close the window determines where you go next. If you click the Close Window button in the toolbar, you'll move to Report Design view. Using the close box or choosing File ➤ Close eventually takes you back to the Database window, but Access first displays an alert box that asks whether you want to save the report and then displays the Save As dialog box to prompt you for a name.

Try paging through the Contact Names and Addresses report, and then close the Print Preview window and save the report under the name Contact Names and Addresses.

To print a report from the Database window, highlight the report name and do one of the following:

- Click the Print button in the toolbar.
- Choose File ➤ Print.
- Press Ctrl+P.
- Right-click and then select Print from the popup menu.

CREATING A TABULAR REPORT

The Single-Column layout is ideal for tables with many long text or memo fields and for situations in which you need to examine one record at a time. When you want to see many records together, in a more attractive format than you can obtain by simply printing the datasheet, the Tabular layout fits the bill. Figure 8.12 illustrates a Tabular report based on the Tasks table. This report was created using the Report Wizards and then edited to adjust the column widths and correct the alignment of the headings. You'll probably want to edit nearly all the reports produced by the Tabular Report Wizard as well, but using the Wizard is the fastest, easiest way to construct the basic layout.

FIGURE 8.12 ▸

In a Tabular report, the fields are arranged in a row, with column titles above the data.

Tasks

14-Mar-95

Date	Time	Project ID	Contact ID	Description	Priority	Completed
2/16/95	10:00 AM	Kitchen	MasterBuilders	Meet for final project review	1	Yes
2/24/95		Kitchen		Hang curtains	2	No
2/24/95		Kitchen		Buy new curtain rods	2	Yes
2/24/95	1:30 PM			Dentist appointment	1	Yes
2/28/95	12:00 PM		Vargas	Lunch with Carmen to discuss PetCare project	1	Yes
3/1/95	10:00 AM	PetCare	PetCare	Meet with Melanie to review brochure design	1	Yes
3/1/95	7:30 PM		Plummer	Dinner with Fern	1	Yes
3/2/95				Buy anniversary gift for Don and Janet	2	No

1

To build a Tabular report based on the Expenses table:

1. Make sure the Database window displays the list of tables.
2. Highlight Expenses and click the New Report button in the toolbar.
3. In the New Report dialog box, make sure you see Expenses in the combo box, and then click the Report Wizards button or press Alt+W.
4. In the first Report Wizard dialog box, choose Tabular, and then click OK to move on to the next step.
5. Click >> to select all the fields in the Expenses table. Then highlight Expense ID in the Field order on report list and click < to remove this field from the report. (The unique number in this field doesn't give you any meaningful information about the records.) Click Next to move on to the next step.
6. Choose ExpenseDate as the sort field, and then click Next to move on to the next step.
7. Choose the Presentation report style.
8. Select Portrait orientation.
9. Leave the default 1/12 in. line spacing selected.
10. Click Next to move on to the next step.
11. Change the report title to Expenses by Date.
12. Check See all the fields on one page.
13. Leave See the report with data in it selected, and click the Finish button.
14. When Access displays the report in Print Preview, maximize the window. Your report should look like the one in Figure 8.13.

FIGURE 8.13

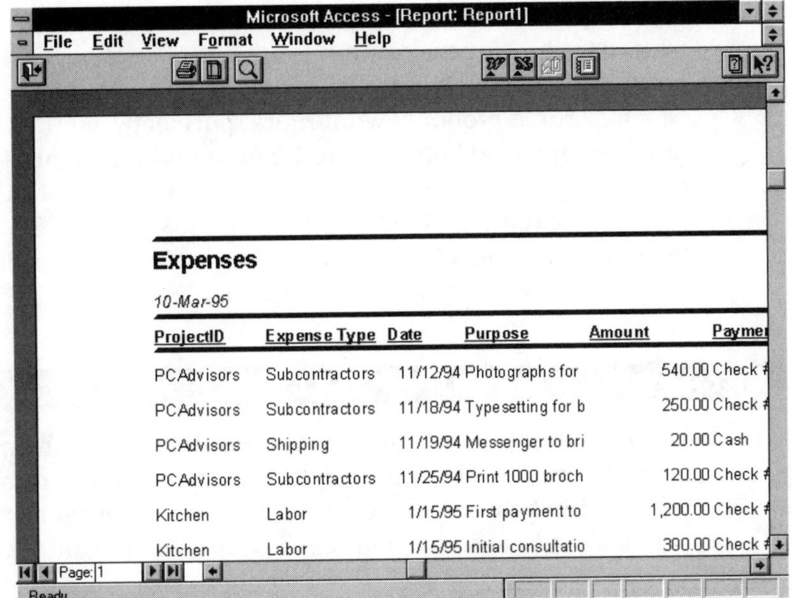

The Tabular Expense report lists records in order by date.

NOTE

When you build a Tabular report, the last Report Wizard dialog box doesn't include the option to begin each record on a new page because it wouldn't make much sense to do so when each record occupies just one line.

The report you just created demonstrates all the distinguishing features of the Tabular layout: each field has its own column, with the field names (or captions) at the top as column titles, and there's a grand total at the end of the report for each numeric column.

The Expenses by Date report also illustrates all the problems typical of reports generated by the Report Wizards. The Amount column is too wide, and the Purpose column isn't wide enough. In fact, it would be nice to stretch this field to occupy more than one line, as well as to widen it. You'd probably want more space between the Date and Purpose columns and between the Amount and Payment Method columns, and the Date and Amount column headings would look better if they were right justified over the columns of data. You'll see in Chapter 11 how easy it is to fix these problems. In the meantime, close the report and give it the name Expenses by Date.

CREATING A GROUP/TOTALS REPORT

The Tabular report layout is ideal for listings in which each record is treated as more or less equivalent, and there may or may not be any relationship between adjacent records. The Expenses by Date report you designed in the previous exercise is a good example.

Often, you'll want to create reports with a more complex structure, in which *groups* of records are clearly discernible. For example, instead of simply listing all your expenses in chronological order, you might want to group expenses by project, group the records in each project by expense type, and sort within each type by date.

In simple cases all you'll want to do is leave some extra space or draw a line between groups, but more often you'll want a format like the one in Figure 8.14, which was produced by the Group/Totals Report Wizard (and then modified to adjust the column widths). The Group/Totals layout has a heading at the top of each group and subtotals and, optionally, percentages, at the end. Below each Expense Type subtotal, you can see what percentage this group is of the total expenses for the project group, and below each project subtotal is the percentage that the project represents of the grand total.

FIGURE 8.14

The Group/Totals Report Wizard generates reports with group summary statistics.

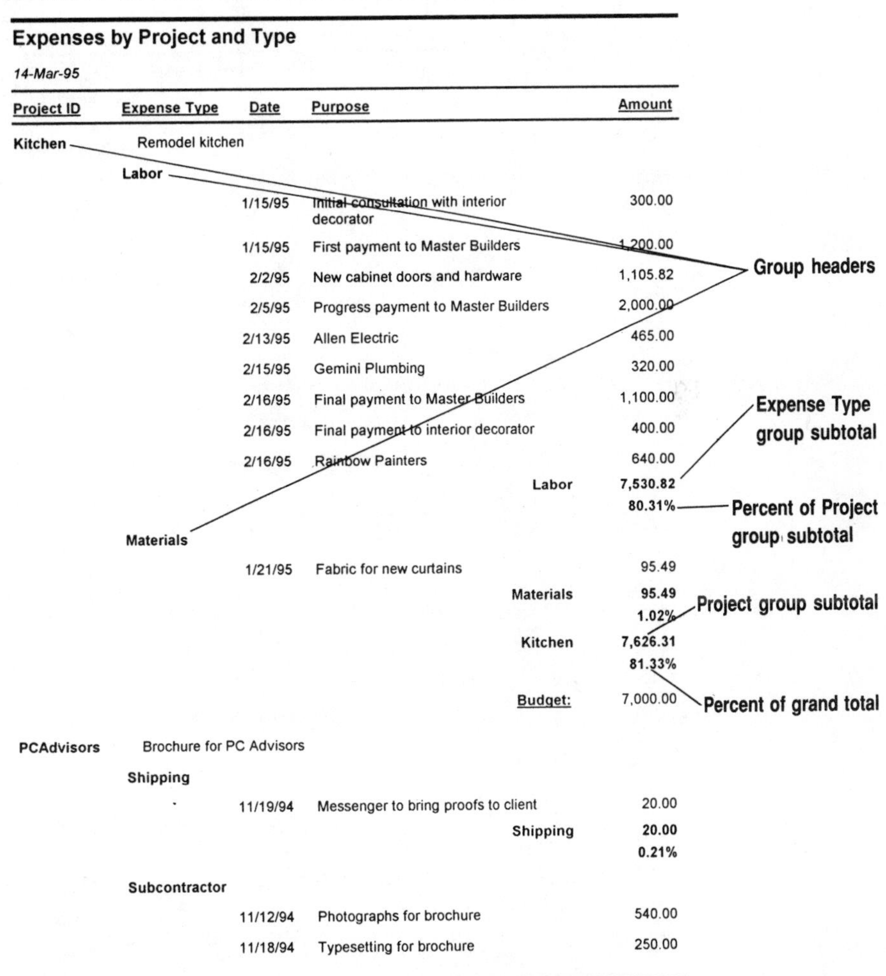

Expenses by Project and Type

14-Mar-95

Project ID	Expense Type	Date	Purpose	Amount
Kitchen	Remodel kitchen			
	Labor			
		1/15/95	Initial consultation with interior decorator	300.00
		1/15/95	First payment to Master Builders	1,200.00
		2/2/95	New cabinet doors and hardware	1,105.82
		2/5/95	Progress payment to Master Builders	2,000.00
		2/13/95	Allen Electric	465.00
		2/15/95	Gemini Plumbing	320.00
		2/16/95	Final payment to Master Builders	1,100.00
		2/16/95	Final payment to interior decorator	400.00
		2/16/95	Rainbow Painters	640.00
			Labor	**7,530.82**
				80.31%
	Materials			
		1/21/95	Fabric for new curtains	95.49
			Materials	**95.49**
				1.02%
			Kitchen	**7,626.31**
				81.33%
			Budget:	7,000.00
PCAdvisors	Brochure for PC Advisors			
	Shipping			
		11/19/94	Messenger to bring proofs to client	20.00
			Shipping	**20.00**
				0.21%
	Subcontractor			
		11/12/94	Photographs for brochure	540.00
		11/18/94	Typesetting for brochure	250.00

1

FIGURE 8.14 ▸ *The Group/Totals Report Wizard generates reports with group summary statistics. (continued)*

Project ID	Expense Type	Date	Purpose	Amount
		11/25/94	Print 1000 brochures	120.00
			Subcontractors	**910.00**
				9.70%
			PCAdvisors	**930.00**
				9.92%
			Budget:	1,800.00
PetCare	PetCare package			
	Shipping			
		2/19/95	Send proofs to client	8.95
			Shipping	**8.95**
				0.10%
	Subcontractor			
		2/8/95	Design logo for business (Carmen Vargas)	450.00
		2/18/95	Typesetting, initial letterhead, and business card	80.00
			Subcontractors	**530.00**
				5.65%
			PetCare	**538.95**
				5.75%
			Budget:	3,200.00
Vacation	Vacation, spring 1995			
	Travel			
		3/1/95	New camera bag	42.00
		3/1/95	Camping equipment	240.00
			Travel	**282.00**
				3.01%
			Vacation	**282.00**
				3.01%
			Budget:	3,500.00
			Grand Total :	
				9,377.26

2

To help delineate the groups (ProjectID and ExpenseType here), the Report Wizard separates the fields that define each group and prints them once at the beginning of each group and again at the end with the subtotals, rather than repeatedly in all the records in the group.

TIP

If you need more space for long text fields, you can modify the report later to move the detail lines to the left, underneath the group headers, without sacrificing much in readability.

Try building a simple version of the report shown in Figure 8.14. (In Chapter 11 you'll learn to adjust the field widths and fine-tune the page layout.)

1. Highlight the Expenses table in the Database window and click the New Report button in the toolbar.
2. In the New Report dialog box, make Expenses appear in the combo box, then click the Report Wizards button or press Alt+W.
3. In the first Report Wizard dialog box, choose Groups/Totals, and click OK to move on to the next step.
4. Choose the ProjectID, ExpenseType, ExpenseDate, Purpose, and Amount fields, and then click Next to move on to the next step.

CHOOSING THE GROUP FIELDS

The Report Wizard lets you define up to four groups, which you choose using the dialog box shown in Figure 8.15. The diagram on the left side of the dialog box shows the report layout, with the group headers and subtotals shown as heavy black lines. Choose your group fields in order from the largest group to the smallest.

FIGURE 8.15 ➧

You can define up to four groups in a Group/Totals report.

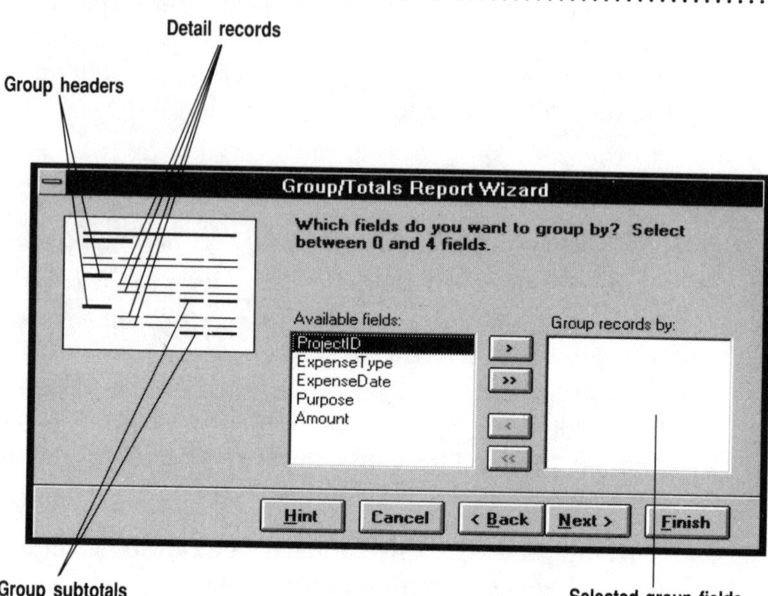

NOTE

The Report Wizard doesn't let you base a group on a field that doesn't appear on your report. For example, in a report based on the Contacts table, you can't group on ContactID but print the FullName field instead. This is a limitation of the Report Wizard, not Access, and you can overcome it by modifying the report later.

If you're thinking that this sounds a lot like choosing sort fields, there's a very good reason. The ability to print records in groups depends on the fact that you're also sorting by the same fields that define the groups. If you didn't sort by ProjectID, how could you guarantee that all the records from each project would be printed together, without records from any other project in between? When you use the Group/Totals Wizard, you don't have to explicitly request these sorts; the Wizard takes care of this essential detail.

For the Expenses report, choose two group fields:

5. Highlight ProjectID in the **Available fields** list and click > to select it as the first (largest) group field.
6. Highlight ExpenseType in the **Available fields** list and click > to select it as the second (smaller) group field.
7. Click Next to move on to the next step.

DEFINING THE GROUPING METHOD

So far you've learned to sort based only on the whole contents of a field, but the Group/Totals Report Wizard gives you a lot more flexibility in defining groups. For example, you can group on just the first letter of a last name or an ID code to print a phone book with a subheading for each letter, group a to-do list by week or by day, or group transactions on a financial report into ranges by dollar total (for example, 0–$500, $501–$1,000, $1,001–$1,500, and so on).

To accomplish the equivalent sorts in a query, you'd have to write some complex expressions, but the Report Wizard lets you choose the grouping method for each group field from the combo boxes in the dialog box shown in Figure 8.16. As explained at the top of the dialog

FIGURE 8.16 ▸

The Report Wizard lets you choose a grouping method for each group field.

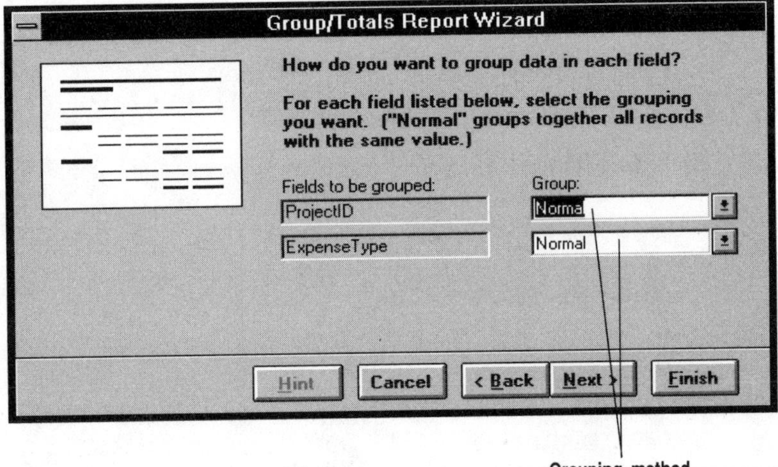

box, choosing Normal results in grouping records based on the exact value, and this choice is always available. The additional options, which depend on the data type, are listed in the following table. Figure 8.17 shows a few examples of the effects you can achieve with the various grouping methods.

DATA TYPE	GROUPING METHODS
Text	1st Character
	1st 2 Characters
	1st 3 Characters
	1st 4 Characters
	1st 5 Characters
Number (intervals)	10
	50
	100
	500
	1,000
	5,000
	10,000
	50,000
	100,000
	500,000
Date/Time	Year
	Quarter
	Month
	Week
	Day
	Hour
	Minute

FIGURE 8.17 ▸

You can choose different grouping methods for text, date/time, and number fields.

Contacts

14-Mar-95

Contact ID	Name	Company	Home Phone	Work Phone
A				
ActiveAdventure	Vera	Active Adventures Travel	(510) 524-3801	
Adams	Jeffrey Adams		(510) 845-6783	(510) 522-8950
Allen	Christopher Allen	Allen Electric		(510) 525-9225
B				
Beverly	Frank Beverly		(619) 482-3984	
D				
Davis	Peter and Laura Davis			
F				
FutureDesigns	Marilyn Williams	Future Designs		(415) 459-2939
J				
JacksonOBrien	Ann Jackson and Katherine O'Brien	Gemini Plumbing		(510) 848-2350
K				
Klein	Don and Janet Klein		(415) 861-5498	
M				
MasterBuilders	Michael A. Barton	Master Builders		(707) 452-1385
P				
PCAdvisors	Robert Santorelli	PC Advisors		(415) 626-3528
PetCare	Melanie Fong	PetCare Services		(415) 982-3055
Plummer	Fern Plummer		(510) 549-3769	
Q				
QuickPrint	Barbara Stevenson	Quick Print		(510) 654-8342
R				
Rainbow	George Roth	Rainbow Painters		(510) 601-8350
RedRock	Jim McKenna	Red Rock Tours		(801) 259-4492
Rosenberg	Norman Rosenberg		(818) 528-3899	(213) 952-3845 ext. 544
S				
Sanders	The Sanders Family		(503) 652-8938	
T				
TrueType		True Type Typesetters		(510) 821-3540
V				
Vargas	Carmen Vargas			(415) 536-0942
W				
WrightMills	Carol Wright-Mills		(510) 548-1891	

1

CHOOSING THE SORT ORDER

After you choose the group fields and select a grouping method, the Report Wizard displays the dialog box shown in Figure 8.18 to let you choose additional sort fields. As suggested by the label **Sort within groups by**, your selection governs the order of the detail records *within* the smallest group (in this case, within each Expense Type group).

FIGURE 8.17 ▶

You can choose different grouping methods for text, date/time, and number fields. (continued)

To Do List

12-Feb-95

Date	Time	Project ID	Contact ID	Description	Priority	Complete
Week of 12-Feb-95						
2/16/95	10:00 AM	Kitchen	MasterBuilders	Meet for final project review	1	Yes
Week of 19-Feb-95						
2/24/95		Kitchen		Hang curtains	2	No
2/24/95		Kitchen		Buy new curtain rods	2	Yes
2/24/95	1:30 PM			Dentist appointment	1	Yes
Week of 26-Feb-95						
2/28/95	12:00 PM		Vargas	Lunch with Carmen to discuss PetCare project	1	Yes
3/1/95	10:00 AM	PetCare	PetCare	Meet with Melanie to review brochure design	1	Yes
3/1/95	7:30 PM		Plummer	Dinner with Fern	1	Yes
3/2/95				Buy anniversary gift for Don and Janet	2	No

1

FIGURE 8.17 ▸

You can choose different grouping methods for text, date/time, and number fields. (continued)

Expenses by Amount

14-Mar-95

Project ID	Expense Type	Date	Purpose
Kitchen			
Amount from $0 to $499			
	Labor	1/15/95	Initial consultation with interior decorator
	Materials	1/21/95	Fabric for new curtains
	Labor	2/13/95	Allen Electric
	Labor	2/15/95	Gemini Plumbing
	Labor	2/16/95	Final payment to interior decorator
Amount from $500 to $999			
	Labor	2/16/95	Rainbow Painters
Amount from $1000 to $1499			
	Labor	1/15/95	First payment to Master Builders
	Labor	2/2/95	New cabinet doors and hardware
	Labor	2/16/95	Final payment to Master Builders
Amount from $2000 to $2499			
	Labor	2/5/95	Progress payment to Master Builders
PCAdvisors			
Amount from $0 to $499			
	Subcontractors	11/18/94	Typesetting for brochure
	Shipping	11/19/94	Messenger to bring proofs to client
	Subcontractors	11/25/94	Print 1000 brochures
Amount from $500 to $999			
	Subcontractors	11/12/94	Photographs for brochure
PetCare			
Amount from $0 to $499			
	Subcontractors	2/8/95	Design logo for business (Carmen Vargas)
	Subcontractors	2/18/95	Typesetting, initial letterhead, and business card

NOTE

Because Access automatically sorts records by all the group fields, these fields aren't included in the Available fields ***list, which displays only the fields that might be different for each record in the smallest group.***

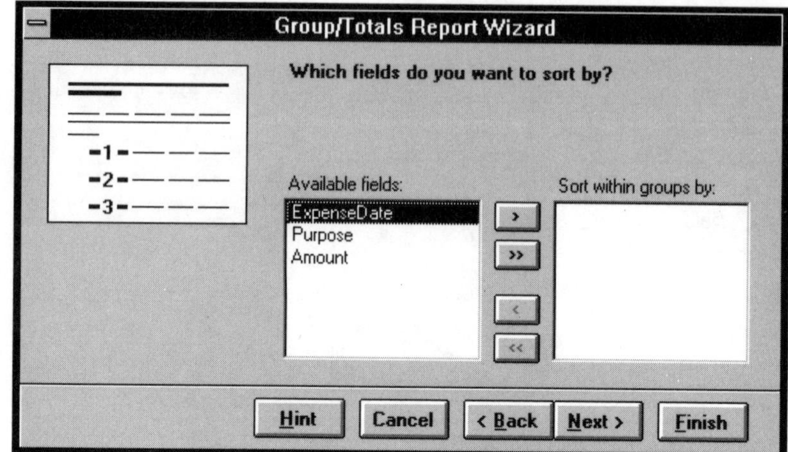

FIGURE 8.18 ▸ *The Report Wizard lets you choose the sort order within the smallest groups.*

To finish building the Expenses report:

8. From the dialog box shown in Figure 8.16, choose Normal for the grouping method for both ProjectID and ExpenseID, and click Next to move on to the next step.
9. Highlight ExpenseDate in the **Available fields** list and click > to move it to the sort list, and then click Next to move on to the next step.
10. Choose the Presentation report style.
11. Select Portrait orientation.
12. Leave the default 1/12 in. line spacing selected.
13. Click Next to move to the next dialog box.
14. In the last Report Wizard dialog box, change the report title to Expenses by Project and Type, leave **Calculate percentages of the total** selected, leave **See the report with data in it** selected, and click the Finish button. Figure 8.19 shows the report in the Print Preview window, scrolled to the right to show all the columns.

FIGURE 8.19 *The Expenses by Project and Type report includes subtotals for each type of expense within each project.*

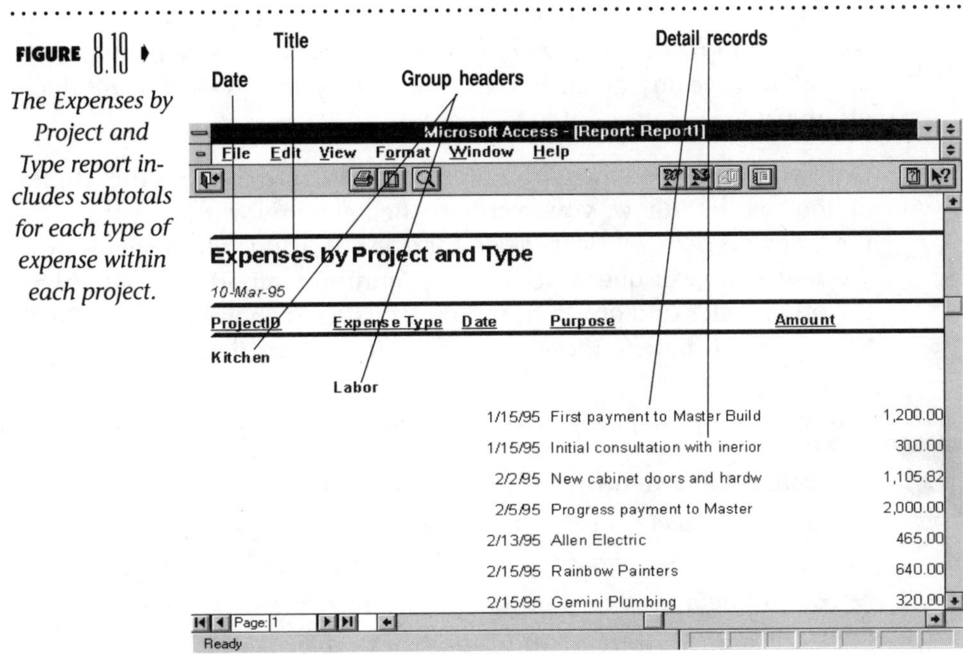

15. Close the window and save the report under the name Expenses by Project and Type.

DEFINING SUMMARY REPORTS

When you print a report like the one you designed in the previous exercise, you won't always want to see every record. Sometimes you're only interested in the group summary statistics and the grand totals. If you've already designed a Group/Totals report, you can modify it to suppress the detail data, but Access gives you a Wizard that lets you produce a better-looking summary report with less effort.

The Summary Report Wizard begins by displaying a dialog box nearly identical to the one shown earlier in Figure 8.15 to let you choose the group fields. Next, you choose the grouping method for each field, using exactly the same dialog box pictured in Figure 8.16. The Wizard doesn't prompt you for any additional sort fields, because the report doesn't include any detail records, and Access always sorts by all the group fields.

Once you've defined the report groups, the Wizard displays the usual dialog box that allows you to choose the fields you want on your report. However, the **Available fields** list doesn't include all the fields in the source table or query. Because the Summary report includes only the group fields and group summary statistics, it shows you only fields that can contribute to these statistics—the numeric fields.

NOTE

Choose the summary fields carefully, because not all the numeric fields in a table are reasonable candidates for group sums. For example, it wouldn't make sense to sum a counter field used as a unique record identifier or a code field like the Priority field in the Tasks table.

Try using the Summary Report Wizard to build a summary version of the Group/Totals report you created in the previous exercise:

1. Make sure the Database window displays the list of tables.
2. Highlight Expenses and click the New Report button in the toolbar.
3. In the New Report dialog box, make sure you see Expenses in the combo box, and then click Report Wizards or press Alt+W.
4. In the first Report Wizard dialog box, choose Summary, and click OK to move to the next step.
5. For the group fields, choose ProjectID and then ExpenseType, and then click Next to move on to the next step.

6. Choose Normal for the grouping method for both fields, and then click Next to move on to the next step.
7. Highlight Amount in the **Available fields** list and click > to move it to the **Field order on report** list, and then click Next to move on to the next step.
8. Choose the Executive report style.
9. Select Portrait orientation.
10. Click Next to move to the next dialog box.
11. In the last Report Wizard dialog box, change the report title to Expenses by Project. (The Wizard will add the word *Summary* to the title you enter.) Leave **Calculate percentages of the total** selected, leave **See the report with data in it** selected, and click the Finish button. Figure 8.20 shows the report in the Print Preview window.
12. Close the Print Preview window and save the report under the name Project Expenses Summary.

FIGURE 8.20

A Summary report includes sums and, optionally, percentages of the totals for the groups.

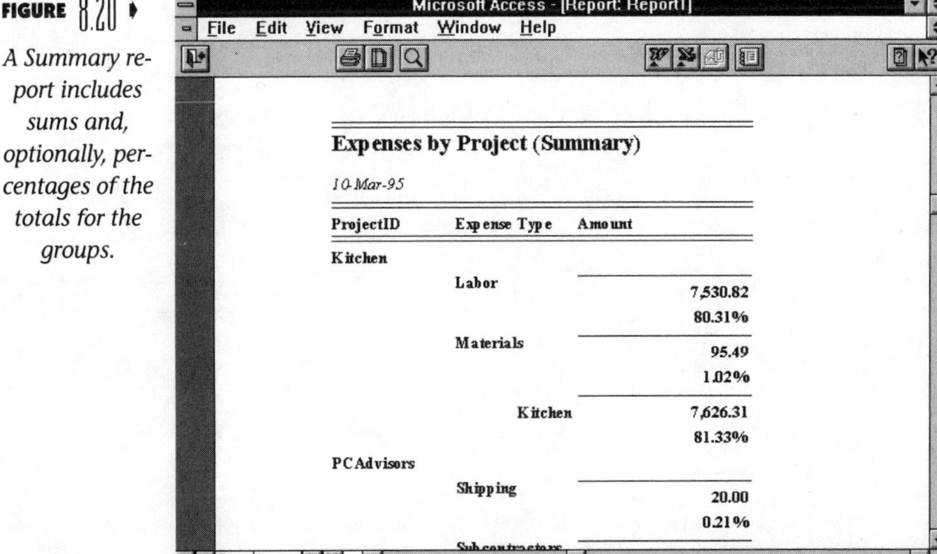

WHAT'S NEXT

You'll probably be able to use the Report Wizards to produce most of the basic report layouts you need. Most of the reports will require at least a few modifications, but the Wizards can give you a good head start. In Chapter 11 you'll learn how to edit the reports generated by the Wizards, but first, in the next chapter, you'll learn how to do mailings (labels and letters) with Access.

Mailing Labels and Mail Merge Letters

If you have a name-and-address list in your database, the odds are that you have to produce mailings of some kind—mailing labels, personalized letters, and/or envelopes. Access makes it easy to design labels, using a Report Wizard that in most cases produces perfect or nearly perfect results.

There isn't a Wizard to help you design envelopes or letters, but it's not hard to design these report styles from scratch, as you'll see in Chapter 12. Often, though, you'll produce better results, and more easily, by using your word processor. If you're using Microsoft Word for Windows version 6, mail merge is fast, easy, and intuitive, and you can initiate and direct the process either from Word or from Access. With other word processors you'll have to export your data. This chapter shows you how to use both of these methods.

USING THE MAILING LABEL WIZARDS

Strictly speaking, Access doesn't distinguish between mailing labels and reports; a mailing label is simply one of many possible report layouts. It's not hard to define labels from scratch, but Access provides a Report Wizard for the purpose, and unlike the Wizards you used in Chapter 8, the Mailing Label Wizard nearly always produces results you can use without modification.

NOTE

Despite the use of the term* mailing label*, you can use the Mailing Label Wizard to produce many other types of labels, including name tags, inventory stock labels, and disk labels, as well as forms like two- or three-across listings on plain paper.

To try the Mailing Label Wizard, begin defining mailing labels for a holiday mailing based on the Contacts table:

1. Make sure the Database window displays the list of tables, highlight Contacts, and click the New Report button in the toolbar.
2. In the New Report dialog box, choose Report Wizards.
3. In the first Report Wizard dialog box, choose Mailing Label, and click OK to go on to the next step.

DESCRIBING THE LABEL CONTENTS

There's one major difference between the Mailing Label Wizard and the other Report Wizards: all the Wizards let you choose the data you want on your report, but only the Mailing Label Wizard gives you any control over the layout. There are so many different ways you might structure a name-and-address table, and so many ways you might want to arrange the fields in that table on a label, that the Mailing Label Wizard doesn't even try to second-guess you. Instead, it lets you construct the layout line by line, using the controls in the dialog box shown in Figure 9.1 (with a typical layout visible) to place fields, punctuation marks, spaces, and text on the label. The diagram in the upper-left corner of the dialog box reminds you that on a typical label, each line might include more than one field, as well as spaces and punctuation marks.

FIGURE 9.1 ▸

The Mailing Label Wizard lets you design the layout of your mailing label.

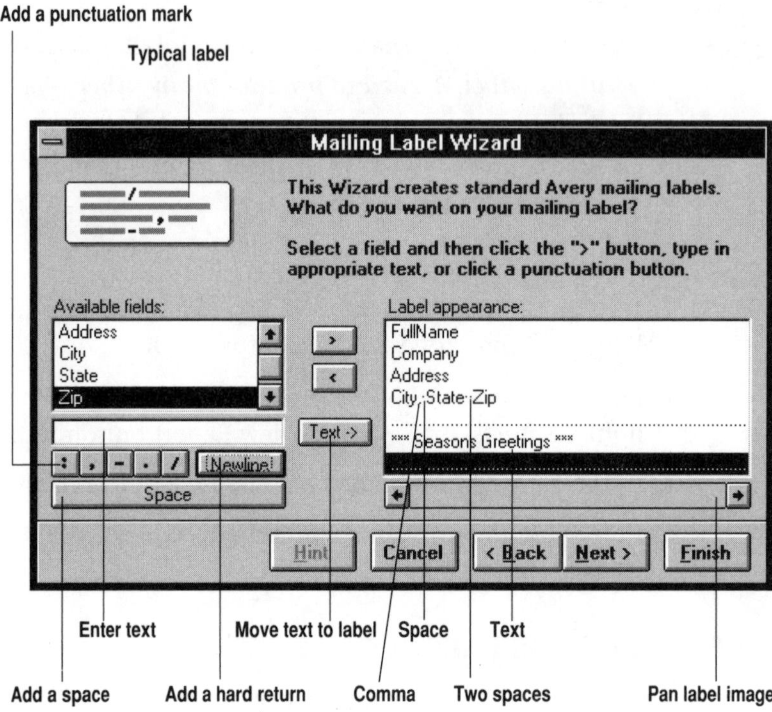

You'll recognize the familiar **Available fields** list and the buttons used to add and remove fields from the label—but probably not much else—in the first Mailing Label Wizard dialog box. Instead of a simple list of the fields you've selected for the report, there's a replica of the label layout you're building. As you can see in Figure 9.1, fields are represented by their names and spaces are displayed as dots. The scroll bar below the **Label appearance** box lets you pan left and right to view all the data on a wide label, but you probably won't need to use this control very often.

NOTE

Unlike the other Wizards, the Mailing Label Wizard doesn't give you a way to add all the fields at once to the label layout, because you can't rearrange them afterward.

You already know how to add fields to the report: highlight a field name in the **Available fields** list and click the > button, or simply double-click the field name. To enter free-form text, type your text in the box directly below the field list, and then click the Text button to place your text on the label. You can use the text option to add the prefix *Attn:* before a contact name, print a short message like *Seasons Greetings* or *Spring Class Schedule Enclosed,* or include your return address on a shipping label.

NOTE

The Mailing Label Wizard permits only ten lines on a label and only ten fields in each line, but this limitation is not built into Access. If you need to create a more complex layout, you can edit the label later.

Under the text entry box is a group of buttons that you might visualize as a mini-typewriter with five punctuation keys, a ↵ key (labeled NewLine), and a spacebar. To add a punctuation mark or space to the label, click the appropriate button. Because each line on the label might consist of any combination of fields, spaces, and punctuation marks, you have to tell the Wizard where to end one line and begin the next by clicking the NewLine button.

To experiment with the Mailing Label Wizard, try building a label for your holiday greeting card mailing:

4. Highlight FullName in the **Available fields** list, click > to move it to the label, and then click the NewLine button.

5. Highlight Company in the **Available fields** list, click > to move it to the label, and then click the NewLine button.
6. Highlight Address in the **Available fields** list, click > to move it to the label, and then click the NewLine button.
7. Highlight City in the **Available fields** list, and click > to move it to the label.
8. Click the comma button and then the Space button.
9. Highlight State in the **Available fields** list, and then click > to move it to the label.
10. Click Space twice to add two spaces to the label.
11. Highlight Zip in the **Available fields** list, click > to move it to the label, and then click the NewLine button.
12. Click the Newline button once more to add a blank line to the label.
13. Click in the text box below the **Available fields** list, type ***** Seasons Greetings *****, click the Text button to move the text to the label, and then click the NewLine button. Your label should look like the one in Figure 9.1.
14. Click the Next button to move on to the next step.

CHOOSING THE SORT ORDER

The next step is choosing the sort order for the labels, which you can do in the dialog box shown in Figure 9.2. Like the other Report Wizards, the Mailing Label Wizard lets you choose up to ten sort fields. You'll sort the Contacts labels by zip code.

15. For the Contacts mailing labels, choose Zip, and then click Next to move on to the next step.

DESCRIBING THE LABEL LAYOUT

The next dialog box, which is shown in Figure 9.3, lets you choose the size and physical layout of the labels you'll be printing on.

FIGURE 9.2

You can choose the sort order for your labels.

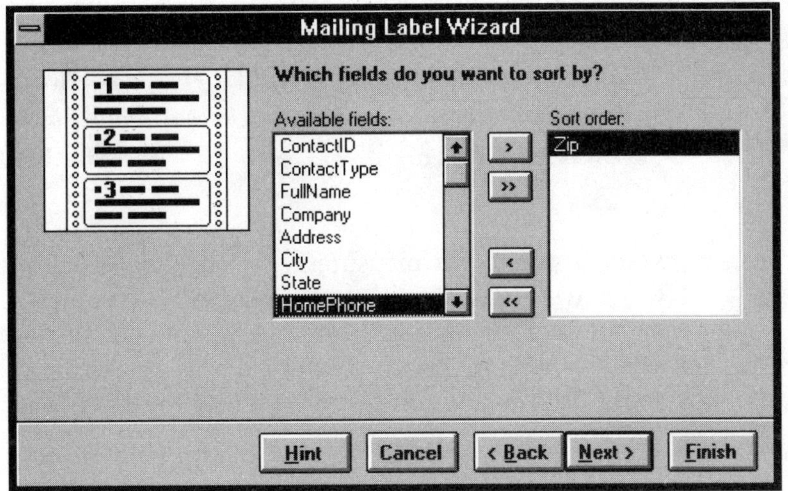

FIGURE 9.3

You can choose the label size and page layout.

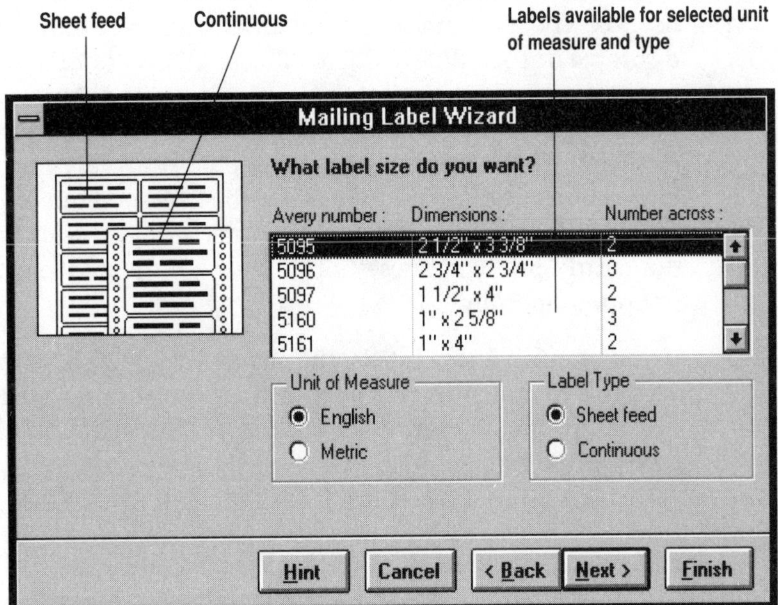

TIP

Choose the unit of measure and label type you want before you select the label size. Both of these options govern which Avery label forms are displayed in the label size list box.

If you're using metric measurements, click the Metric radio button below the Avery number. This option doesn't just convert the measurements in the Dimensions column of the list from inches to millimeters, it selects a different group of Avery labels—those commonly in use outside the United States, in countries where the metric system is the standard.

The Label Type radio buttons let you select the type of paper you're printing on. Like the Unit of Measure options, the Label Type radio buttons determine which Avery label choices appear in the label size list box. The diagram in the upper-left corner of the dialog box shows a sample of each type: a sheet of laser labels and one-across continuous tractor-feed labels. If you choose Sheet Feed, Access assumes that you have a laser printer and that you're printing on plain paper or sheets of laser printer labels. Based on the Avery number, Access knows how much space to leave at the top and bottom of each sheet of labels. If you're printing on a printer with a tractor feed, such as a dot matrix printer, choose Continuous; on these labels, there's no top or bottom margin.

If you're using Avery labels, the easiest way to choose the right label layout is to match the number in the first column of the label size list box to the one on your label package. Otherwise, you'll have to scroll through the list.

NOTE

The numbers in the Dimensions column of the label size list box represent the height (or depth) and width of the printable area on one label. Thus, 1 1/2" x 4" describes a label $1\frac{1}{2}$ inches high and 4 inches wide. In the continuous labels, heights like $\frac{15}{16}$ and $1\frac{7}{16}$ reflect the fact that there is a small gap between labels that are spaced 1 inch or $1\frac{1}{2}$ inches apart.

To choose the label layout for the Contacts table labels:

16. Leave the default unit of measure (English) selected. If you have a laser printer, leave the default label type (Sheet feed) selected; otherwise, select the Continuous radio button.
17. If you have a laser printer, choose Avery number 5163 to print labels 2 inches deep, 4 inches across, and two-across on the page. Otherwise, choose Avery number 4168 to print one-up labels $2\frac{1}{6}$ inches deep and 4 inches across.
18. Click Next to go on to the next step.

CHOOSING THE FONT CHARACTERISTICS

The next Label Wizard dialog box, which is shown in Figure 9.4, lets you pick a font and specify its size, weight, color, and other special attributes. The default font, which is visible in Figure 9.4, is 10 pt. bold Arial.

This dialog box doesn't look like the standard Access Font dialog box, which you used in Chapter 5 to customize the datasheet, but it gives you control over the same font properties. The Font name combo box displays only printer and TrueType fonts, without the symbols that distinguish between the font classes in the standard Font dialog box. The screen fonts are missing because you'll nearly always want to print labels (although you might preview them on the screen). You might also want to check out the options in the Font weight combo box, which offers

FIGURE 9.4

The Mailing Label Wizard lets you customize the font used on your labels.

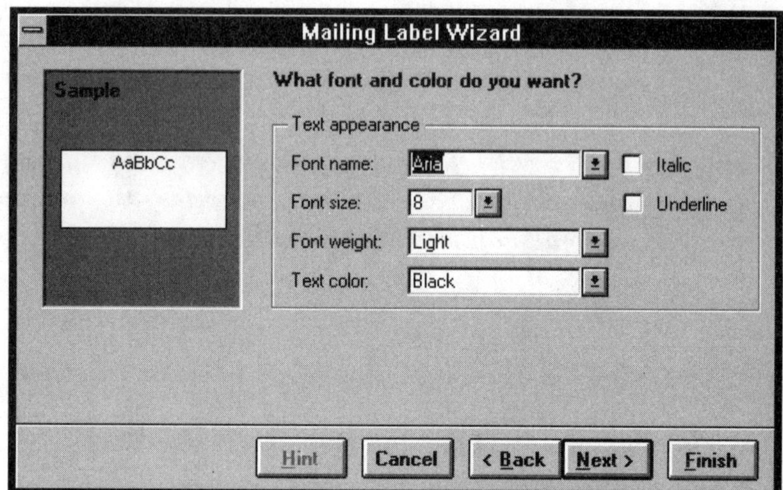

four gradations (Light, Normal, Bold, and Heavy) rather than simply letting you turn boldfacing on or off. If you're having trouble visualizing what your selections will look like on the finished label, watch the Sample area on the left side of the dialog box.

NOTE

The Wizard doesn't let you select different fonts or font attributes for individual fields on your label—the font you choose is used for the entire label. You can modify the form later if you need to customize the appearance of individual items.

You might want to spend a few minutes experimenting with various options for the mailing labels you're building for the Contacts table. Before you go on to the next step, make these selections:

18. Display the drop-down list for the Font name dialog box, and choose Courier or Courier New.

19. Set the font size to 12 points.

20. Select Normal from the Font weight combo box.

21. Click Next to move on to the next step.

SAVING THE LABELS

The last Label Wizard dialog box, which resembles the one displayed by the other Wizards, simply asks what you want to do next. If you're sure you'll need to modify the report created by the Wizard, you can choose Modify the mailing label design to move immediately to Report Design view, but it's usually a good idea to select the default option, See the mailing labels as they will look printed, and look for potential problems in the Print Preview window.

For the Contacts table labels, leave See the mailing labels as they will look printed selected, and click Finish.

WARNING

If you've defined too many lines of data or chosen a font too large for your label layout, the Mailing Label Wizard displays an alert box to notify you that There isn't enough space in the mailing label to fit all the lines you've created. Some lines won't be placed. ***You can't go back now and fix the problems, but if you don't want to start over, you can modify the report later to add the missing items.***

Creating the labels takes just a moment, but Access displays a progress indicator in the status bar to reassure you as the Wizard builds the report and opens it. Figure 9.5 shows the labels you just created in

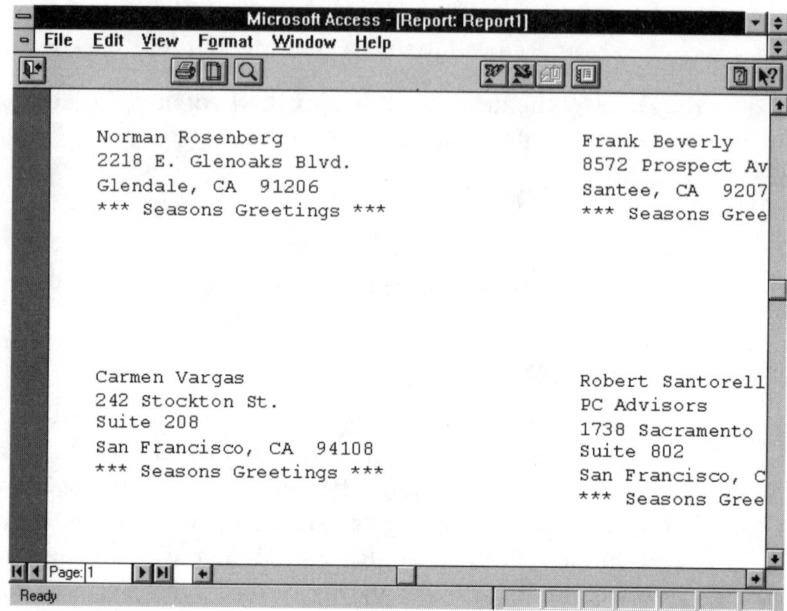

FIGURE 9.5 *You can preview labels on the screen and then print them.*

the Print Preview window. The preview is an accurate rendition of the placement of the data on the printed page, although you might have hoped to see the outlines of the individual labels as well.

When you're ready to exit from preview mode, the method you use to close the window determines where you go next. If you click the Close Window button in the toolbar, you'll move to Report Design view to modify the new labels. If you close the window using the close box, Access prompts you to save the report and displays the Save As dialog box to let you enter a name. Then it returns you to the Database window. When you're finished with the labels you just created, save the report under the name Two-Across Holiday Labels.

Unlike the documents produced by the other Report Wizards, mailing labels often look fine with no modifications. The Mailing Label Wizard makes all the fields nearly the full width of the label, so you'll rarely have to edit the report to adjust field widths. If you look at the two-line addresses (such as the one for PC Advisors), you'll see that the

Wizard allows each item on a label to expand onto as many lines as necessary to accommodate the full contents.

There's only one problem with the layout of the labels you just created: the blank line you deliberately added between the last line of the address and the "Seasons Greetings" message doesn't appear on the printout. To prevent empty fields from leaving unsightly blank lines on the label, the Mailing Label Wizard automatically suppresses *all* blank lines. For the most part, you'll appreciate this—when there's no company name, the address prints right below the name, and if there's no name, the company name prints on the first line of the label. The fact that the Wizard also suppresses blank lines that you added deliberately is an unfortunate corollary, but you can fix this problem by editing the label report later. You'll learn how to do this in Chapter 11.

PRINTING MAIL MERGE LETTERS

You'll learn in Chapter 12 how to design reports from scratch, and it's easy to create simple mail merge letters this way. If all you need is a short letter with a few paragraphs of text, there's no need to go outside Access. On the other hand, it's not easy to vary the font or character formatting within a paragraph or to insert fields into the middle of a paragraph of text. For more complex page layouts or more detailed formatting, you can accomplish a lot more (and a lot more easily) by using a word processor.

In most cases you won't want to print letters or envelopes for every record in a table, and you won't need to use all the fields. If you're sending the mailing to more than a few people, you may have to sort by zip; otherwise, you'll probably want to print in alphabetical order. If you're thinking, "This calls for a query," you're right; the best way to prepare for a mail merge is to define a query that selects the fields you need to print and the records that should be included and then sorts these records into the appropriate order.

Using a query also lets you print data derived from more than one Access table. For example, in a donor database you could print thank-you letters that include both the donor's name and address (from the donor table) and the contribution date and amount (from the contribution table).

To experiment with the Access mail merge options, build a query that selects only graphic design contacts from the Contacts table:

1. Highlight Contacts in the list of tables in the Database window, and click the New Query button in the toolbar.
2. Choose New Query to build a query from scratch.
3. Add the ContactType, FullName, Company, Address, City, State, and Zip fields to the grid.
4. Uncheck the Show box for the ContactType field.
5. In the Criteria row for the ContactType field, type **Graphic Design**.
6. Run the query and verify that the datasheet displays four records.
7. Close the query, and save it under the name Graphic Design Contacts.

MERGING DATA WITH MICROSOFT WORD

If you have Microsoft Word for Windows version 6, the easiest way to carry out a mail merge is to use the Microsoft Word Mail Merge Wizard. This method makes efficient use of both time and disk space, because you don't have to copy your data from one format to another. Word can read an Access database directly, and the Wizard helps you by establishing the linkage between your Word document and your Access database.

There are two ways to call up the Microsoft Word Mail Merge Wizard:

- Highlight a table or query name in the Database window, and then click the Merge It button on the toolbar.
- Use any of the methods outlined in Chapter 8 to begin creating a new report, choose Report Wizards, and choose MS Word Mail Merge from the list of Wizards.

The Mail Merge Wizard displays the dialog box shown in Figure 9.6, which allows you to merge your data with an existing Word document or to create a new document. If you choose Link your data to an existing Microsoft Word document, Access displays an Open File dialog box to let you pick the document.

TIP

If you don't already have a form letter set up for mail merge in Word, you may find it easier to set up the merge using the Word Mail Merge Helper than to use the Access Wizard described in this chapter.

If you choose a document that is already linked to a different data source (not necessarily an Access table), the Wizard displays an alert box that warns you, The data source of the document you selected is different from the source you selected when starting the Mail Merge wizard. Would you like the Mail Merge Wizard to change the source? Choosing No cancels the merge, and choosing Yes updates the Word document to recognize the new data source and proceeds with the merge.

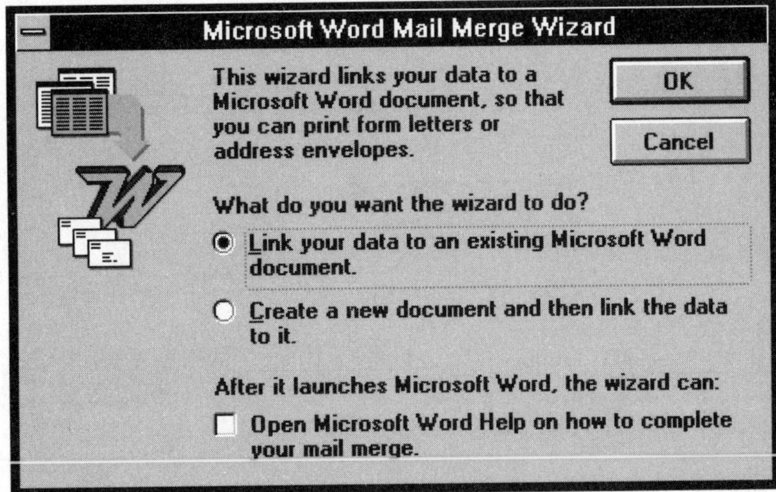

FIGURE 9.6 *You can merge Access data with an existing Word document or create a new document.*

NOTE

Neither Access nor Word can determine whether the data source you choose is appropriate for your mail merge document. If you change the data source to one with fields that don't match the merge codes in the Word document, you'll get errors when you try to execute the merge.

Whether you elect to use an existing letter or create a new one, the Wizard launches Word if it's not already running so you can edit your letter and perform the merge. The screen in Figure 9.7 shows a typical letter, with the name and address fields from the Contacts table forming the inside address.

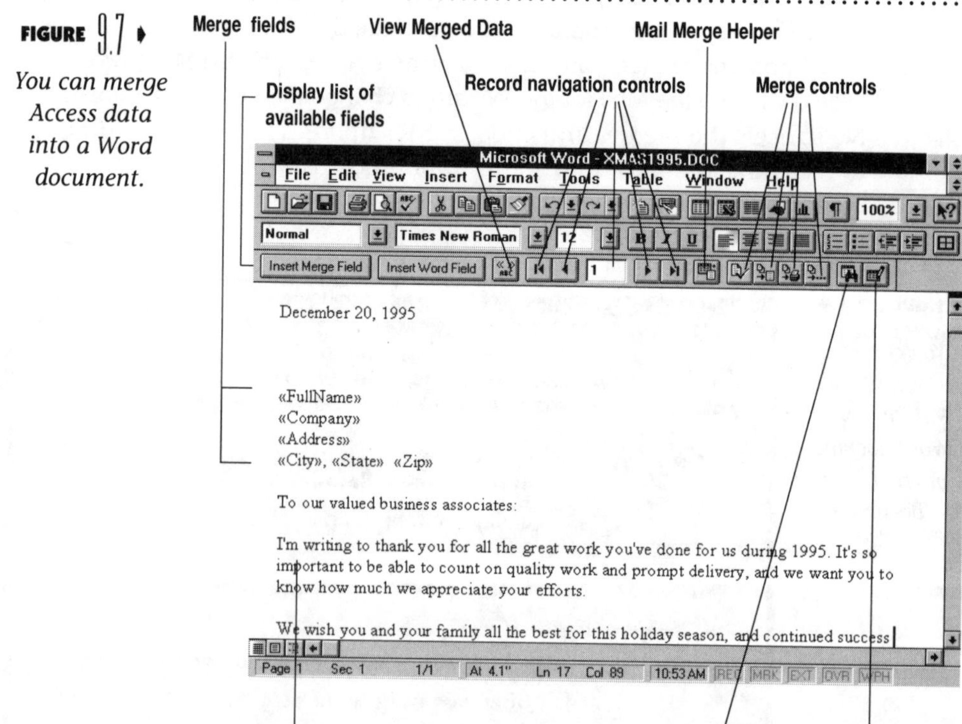

FIGURE 9.7 ▸ *You can merge Access data into a Word document.*

A complete discussion of Word's mail merge capabilities is beyond the scope of this book, but you'll find it easy to set up merge letters. Once the Mail Merge Wizard has linked your Word document to your Access database, clicking the Insert Merge Field button in the Word toolbar displays a list of fields in the source table, and choosing a field from this list inserts it into the letter. If you have Word, you might want to try creating a mail merge letter based on the Graphic Design Contacts query.

TIP

The easiest way to verify that you've set up your letter correctly before you print is to click the View Merged Data button in the Word toolbar to display the merged fields rather than the merge codes and then use the navigation controls to move through the table and display various records.

EXPORTING DATA

If you're using a word processor other than Microsoft Word, you'll have to use a slightly less direct method for producing mail merge letters based on Access data. Ideally, every word processor would be able to read an Access database directly, the way Microsoft Word can. In this less-than-ideal world, programs vary widely in the formats they use internally to store data and in the external formats they can read or import, and you'll have to export (copy) your Access data into a format your word processor *can* read.

WARNING

When you establish a link between an Access table or query and a Word 6 document, this link is dynamic—every time you open the Word document and perform a mail merge, you'll be getting the newest version of the data. In contrast, when you export data, you're creating a copy of the data as of the moment you perform the export. ***You'll have to repeat the export operation each time you want to perform the merge with up-to-date Access data.***

To begin exporting data, highlight the name of any table or query in the Database window, and then choose File ➤ Export or click the Export button in the toolbar. Access displays a dialog box with a scrolling list of the export formats it can write. If you're using Microsoft Word version 2, choose Word for Windows Merge. If you're not sure what formats your word processor can recognize, Text (Delimited) is a good guess. A great many programs, including Microsoft Word for DOS, WordPerfect, and AmiPro, can read this format directly or convert it to their own mail merge format.

After you choose the export format, Access displays another simple dialog box that lets you pick the table or query you want to export. If you chose the export option from the table list in the Database window, you'll see only tables listed at first; if you started from the list of queries, you'll see only queries. In either case you can use a set of radio buttons below the scrolling list box to display the names of tables, queries, or both.

NOTE

Even if your word processor lets you sort or select records, it's usually better to use an Access query. Access specializes in these fundamental database operations and will deliver faster performance than your word processor. Also, exporting a table copies the data to a separate disk file. If your tables are large, exporting only the fields and records you need for a mailing will save a great deal of time and disk space.

The next step is to name the file you're creating and, if you wish, specify its location on your hard disk, using a standard Windows File Save (not Save As) dialog box. The default location is your Access program directory (C:\ACCESS if you installed Access using the default settings), but you'll probably want to write the file to the drive and subdirectory where you normally store your word processor documents.

Access always proposes a name for the output file consisting of the first eight letters of the name of the table or query you're exporting and an extension based on the export format. For a text file or Word merge file, Access assigns the extension .TXT, and it's usually best to retain this default.

TIP

Because DOS file names can't include spaces, Access substitutes underscores for any spaces in your table or query name. You'll find it easier to remember (and type) the text file names if you edit the file name initially displayed in the Export dialog box to eliminate the underscores.

To export the Graphic Design Contacts query you created earlier in this chapter:

1. From the Database window, click the Export button or choose File ➤ Export.
2. In the Export dialog box, choose Text (Delimited).
3. In the list of Access objects, click Both so that the object list displays both tables and queries.
4. Highlight Graphic Design Contacts in the object list and click OK to move on to the next step.
5. In the Export to File dialog box, change the name of the output file from GRAPHIC_.TXT to GRAPHDES.TXT.

The details of the next step in the export process depend on the export format you chose earlier, because Access only asks you to provide information relevant to the particular export format you're using.

EXPORTING DATA FOR MICROSOFT WORD

When you export to a Word for Windows merge file, Access displays the dialog box shown in Figure 9.8 to let you describe the date and time formats you want in the export file. In most cases you can retain the default settings. Once you see the merge file you've produced, you'll have a better idea of whether the settings are appropriate.

EXPORTING TO A DELIMITED TEXT FILE

In a delimited text file, each record begins on a new line, the fields are separated by commas, and text fields are enclosed in quotation marks. Figure 9.9 shows the text file created by exporting the Graphic Design Contacts query. Many programs that can read this format don't care about the Access field names, either because they assign their own or because they identify the fields solely by their positions—the first field is everything up to the first comma, the second field is everything from the first comma to the second, and so on. Other programs, including Microsoft Word, can read field names stored in the first row of the text file and use them as the merge field names.

FIGURE 9.8 ▸

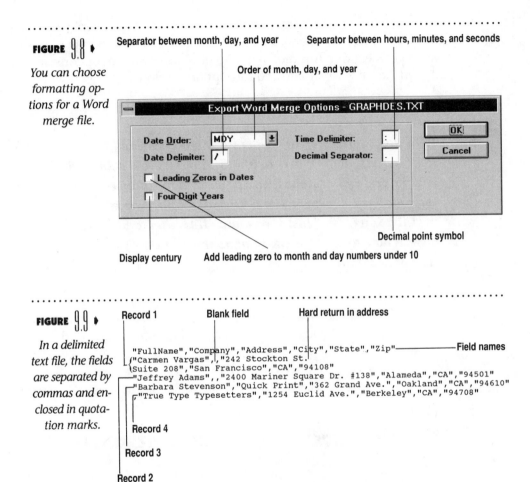

You can choose formatting options for a Word merge file.

Separator between month, day, and year

Separator between hours, minutes, and seconds

Order of month, day, and year

Export Word Merge Options - GRAPHDES.TXT

Date Order: MDY

Time Delimiter: :

Date Delimiter: /

Decimal Separator: .

OK

Cancel

Leading Zeros in Dates

Four Digit Years

Decimal point symbol

Display century

Add leading zero to month and day numbers under 10

FIGURE 9.9 ▸

In a delimited text file, the fields are separated by commas and enclosed in quotation marks.

Record 1

Blank field

Hard return in address

Field names

```
"FullName","Company","Address","City","State","Zip"
"Carmen Vargas",,"242 Stockton St.
Suite 208","San Francisco","CA","94108"
"Jeffrey Adams",,"2400 Mariner Square Dr. #138","Alameda","CA","94501"
"Barbara Stevenson","Quick Print","362 Grand Ave.","Oakland","CA","94610"
"True Type Typesetters","1254 Euclid Ave.","Berkeley","CA","94708"
```

Record 4

Record 3

Record 2

TIP

The easiest way to examine a text file you've created is to open it in Notepad. Turn off word-wrap so that each record begins on a new line and you can see clearly where the records begin and end.

When you export to a delimited text file, Access displays a very simple dialog box with just one check box, labeled Store Field Names in First Row. You can expand this dialog box to display additional options, as shown in Figure 9.10, by clicking the Options button.

NOTE

Some programs, especially older word processors and spreadsheets, don't expect to find field names in a delimited text file and will mistake them for data. If this happens to you, you'll get a merge letter addressed to "FullName" living in "City, State Zip." Just throw away this letter, and make a mental note to omit the field names the next time you export your Access data.

The options you'll use most often are the ones at the bottom of the dialog box, which let you control the display format for dates and

FIGURE 9.10

You can specify formatting options for a delimited text file.

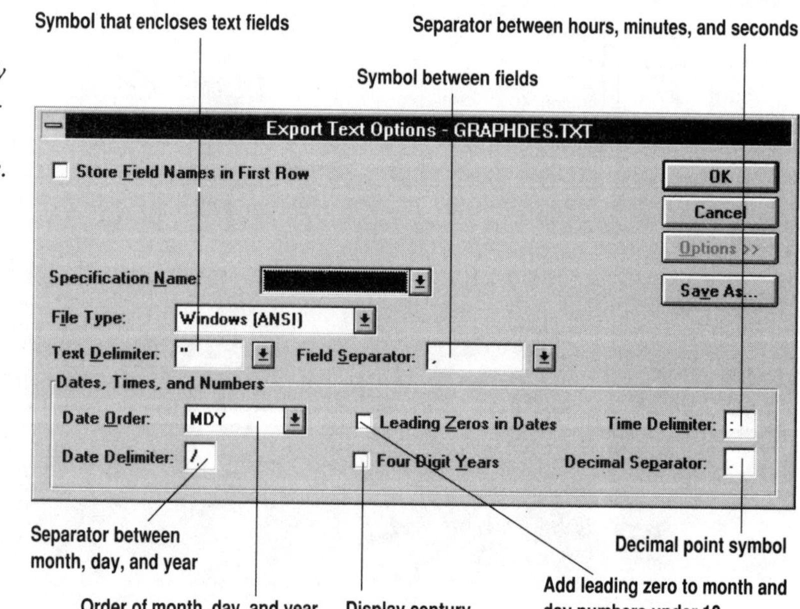

numbers. In some cases you may have to change the text delimiter character—the punctuation mark used to enclose text fields. The Text Delimiter combo box offers three options: double quotes (the default), single quotes, or {none}, which eliminates the delimiters entirely. If you wish, you can enter a different delimiter, but remember that the choice is not really up to you; you must choose the character your word processor expects to find in a delimited text file.

NOTE

Many programs don't require delimiters around text fields, but you must use them if your data includes embedded commas. Without quotation marks around the name, your word processor would interpret the comma in a name like **John Robinson, Jr.** ***as the comma that signals the end of the name field, and the*** **Jr.** ***would be read as the next field.***

The Field Separator combo box lets you choose commas, tabs, or spaces as your field separators. Most PC programs expect to find commas, but many Macintosh programs require tabs.

WARNING

Not all word processors can handle fields that include hard returns (like the hard returns in Carmen Vargas' address in Figure 9.9). Some programs will interpret a hard return in the middle of a field as the end of a record. If this happens to you, you'll have to edit the text file (using your word processor or a simple text editor like Notepad) to delete the hard returns and perhaps edit the resulting address to fit on one line.

To finish exporting the Graphic Design Contacts query:

6. Check Store Field Names in First Row, and click OK.

NOTE

When you export data to a text file, Access writes date/time and numeric fields as they are stored internally, regardless of the display format you're using within Access. Date/time fields always include both the date and time, and numeric fields will have different numbers of decimal places.

OTHER EXPORT OPTIONS

Although this chapter has concentrated on exporting data for *mailings,* Access offers a variety of other export formats. If you also have any of the other programs whose data file formats are listed in the Export dialog box, try exporting one of the Organizer tables to that format and opening the resulting data file using the other program. For example, you might export the Expenses table to the Excel or Lotus worksheet format to see what this data looks like in a spreadsheet.

WHAT'S NEXT

In this chapter you have learned a variety of techniques for producing mailings from your Access data. For the most part, these methods are easy, fast, and produce good results, even if you end up having to export your data. In the next chapter we'll return to working entirely within Access, and you'll learn how to carry out calculations and compute summary statistics.

Performing Calculations

So far you've worked with data exactly as you entered it into the tables in your database. But if you followed the advice in Chapter 3 and didn't include values that could be calculated from fields in the same or other tables, you'll eventually need to perform these computations. You've seen a few examples of calculations—in the reports produced by the Group/Totals and Summary Report Wizards. To define your own calculations, you'll have to learn to write the expressions that describe them. Access offers an Expression Builder, which can give you some assistance, but building an expression is never as automatic as using a Wizard, and for the most part you'll be on your own.

If you think the terms *calculation* and *expression* have purely mathematical connotations, this chapter will broaden your horizons. In Access, these words are used in a more general sense to describe the wide variety of manipulations and transformations you can carry out on text, dates, and times, as well as on numeric data.

You can use expressions in queries, on forms, and on reports, but when you first start experimenting with calculations, the easiest, fastest, most immediate way to test expressions is to use them in a query. For this reason, and because you'll often use queries to carry out calculations, this chapter concentrates on queries. Chapter 12 shows you how to apply some of the same techniques to include calculated values in forms and reports.

WRITING SIMPLE EXPRESSIONS

An *expression* is a combination of fields, *constants* (arbitrary values that you specify), *operators* (symbols that represent simple calculations), and *functions* (special named operators that perform complex calculations).

You can begin writing very simple expressions using just the fields in your tables and the four arithmetic operators:

+	Addition
–	Subtraction
*	Multiplication
/	Division

You refer to fields in expressions by their names, and if you've chosen your field names judiciously, your expressions will be easy to read and understand. For example, if you had fields called Subtotal, SalesTax, and Discount in a sales transaction table, you could calculate the net sale amount with the expression

```
Subtotal – Discount + SalesTax
```

There's one special proviso: If a field name contains spaces, you must enclose it in brackets. (The brackets are optional otherwise.) For example, if your sales tax field was named Sales Tax rather than SalesTax, you would have to write the previous expression this way:

```
Subtotal – Discount + [Sales Tax]
```

NOTE

Don't confuse the field captions with their names. Even though you're probably more accustomed to seeing the captions, remember that you have to use the field names in expressions.

You can also use constants in expressions. For example, if your sales tax rate is 8 percent, you could calculate the sales tax by multiplying the Subtotal field by the constant 0.08:

```
Subtotal * .08
```

You've already used constants to specify values in the Criteria rows in queries. In that context, Access can always recognize a constant for what it is, and it always knows what type of data (text, numeric, date/time, and so on) the constant represents. You may recall that Access automatically adds quotation marks around text constants and pound signs around dates and times that you enter into query criteria. In expressions, you have to type these delimiters yourself because Access can't always guess your intentions; it could mistake a text constant for a field name or a date for an expression involving division. (*12/15/95* might mean either December 15, 1995, or 12 divided by 15 divided by 95.)

NOTE

Access proofreads your expressions and automatically adjusts your spacing and punctuation to conform to its standards. It encloses all field names in brackets, whether or not they contain spaces. Elsewhere in an expression spaces aren't significant, and if you type spaces before or after an operator, Access removes them. Most of the expressions in this book include extra spaces to make them more readable, but you don't have to type the spaces when you try the examples.

WORKING WITH DATE/TIME FIELDS

The + and – operators behave exactly as you'd expect when you use them with numeric fields. You can also use these operators with date/time fields to carry out *date arithmetic:*

- *When you subtract one date/time value from another,* the result is the elapsed time, expressed in days.
- *When you add a number to a date/time value,* the result is a date or time the specified number of days in the future.

- *When you subtract a number from a date/time value,* the result is a date or time the specified number of days in the past.

As a simple example you could calculate an invoice due date by adding 30 days to the date stored in your invoice date field:

```
InvoiceDate + 30
```

All date/time fields store both a date and a time, even if you've formatted them to display only one or the other. The date portion is represented by a number, and the time is expressed as a fraction. To display the result of a date/time calculation in hours, multiply it by 24 (the number of hours in a day). For example, when you subtract 1:30 P.M. from 4:30 P.M., the result is .125 (1/8 of a day). Multiplying by 24 yields 3, the number of hours. Thus, with fields called StartTime and EndTime, you could calculate the elapsed time between the two with the expression

```
(EndTime – StartTime) * 24
```

NOTE

The parentheses in this expression are required to force Access to perform the subtraction first and then multiply the result by 24. Normally, multiplication and division take precedence over addition and subtraction. Without the parentheses, Access would try to multiply StartTime by 24 and then subtract the result from EndTime.

WORKING WITH TEXT FIELDS

There's a very important operator used only with text and memos: the & operator, which *concatenates* (adds together) text and/or memo data. For example, if you had separate fields for a person's first name and last name, you could write the full name as

```
FirstName & LastName
```

This is a legitimate expression, but it won't give you exactly the results you want: if the first name is *Jeffrey* and the last name is *Adams,* the result will be *JeffreyAdams*. You can solve this problem by adding a space between the first name and last name, expressed as a constant text string enclosed in quotation marks:

```
FirstName & " " & LastName
```

When you look at the label reports generated by the Mailing Label Wizard, you'll see that the Wizard uses the & operator to combine the fields, spaces, and punctuation marks that you place on each line on a label. For example, the city/state/zip line on the mailing labels you defined in Chapter 9 is printed using the expression

```
City & ", " & State & "  " & Zip
```

This expression concatenates five text strings: the City field, a constant consisting of a comma and a space, the State field, a constant consisting of two spaces, and the Zip field.

USING FUNCTIONS

A *function* is a named operator that lets you carry out specialized calculations and data manipulations that would otherwise be impossible without programming. Each function is designed to operate on specific types of input and transform this input into a predictable type of output. You might think of a function as a kind of machine, perhaps a pasta machine or bread-maker—if you supply the right ingredients, you'll get the product you expect.

For most people, the term *function,* like *calculation,* has mathematical connotations, and Access does indeed offer quite a few mathematical and financial functions. But in most business and personal applications, you probably won't need many mathematical functions. The Access functions that manipulate text and operate on date/time data will prove far more useful.

To use a function in an expression, you write the name of the function, followed by a pair of parentheses that enclose the inputs, or *arguments,* if any. For example, the Month function takes a date as input and gives you back as output a number between 1 and 12, which represents the month. To find the month portion of the ExpenseDate field, you'd use the expression

```
Month(ExpenseDate)
```

There's one function you'll need to recognize if you modify label reports created by the Mailing Label Wizard: the Trim function, which takes a text expression as input and removes any trailing spaces (spaces at the end). The Mailing Label Wizard uses this function to remove trailing spaces from each line of the label.

Not every function requires input from you. The very useful Date, Time, and Now functions read the system clock and tell you the current date, current time, and current date and time, respectively. All the reports generated by the Wizards use the Now function to print the current date in the Report Header or Page Header section. When you use these functions in expressions, include the parentheses after the function names, but don't type anything between the parentheses. For example, to calculate the elapsed time between the current date and an expense date, you could use the expression

```
Date() – ExpenseDate
```

USING EXPRESSIONS IN QUERIES

You can use expressions in queries to create *calculated fields* or, more accurately, *calculated columns*—columns that appear in the datasheet along with real fields but aren't stored in any table. To define a calculated column, type an expression in the Field row of the query grid instead of entering a field name. The screen in Figure 10.1 shows a query designed to test different ways of calculating the markup on work done by subcontractors. The first calculated column adds $50 to the Amount field, and the second multiplies it by 1.15 (to mark up the amount by 15 percent).

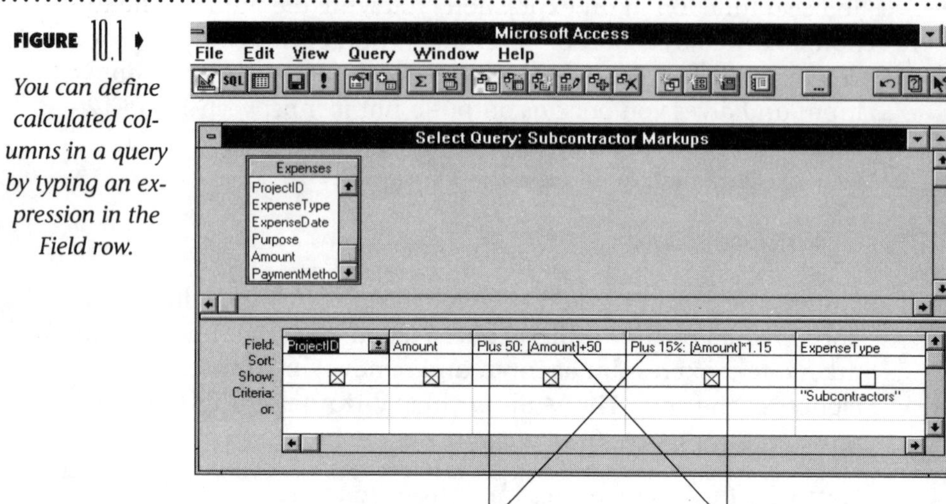

FIGURE 10.1 ▸ *You can define calculated columns in a query by typing an expression in the Field row.*

When you display the query's datasheet, you can't edit calculated values, since they aren't stored anywhere in your database. If you try to edit a calculated column, Access displays a message in the status bar that identifies the field and explains the problem: Field "Expr1" is based on an expression and can't be edited.

NAMING CALCULATED COLUMNS

When you finish entering the expression that defines a calculated column, Access automatically gives it a name: Expr1 for the first expression in a query, Expr2 for the second, and so on. To assign a more descriptive name, like the ones in Figure 10.1, simply type it, followed by a colon, before you begin typing your expression.

TIP

You can use calculated columns in the expressions that define other calculated columns, exactly as you would fields: simply refer to them by name.

To experiment with calculated columns, modify the Project Expenses query you created in Chapter 6 to display each expense amount as a percentage of the overall project budget:

1. Make sure the Database window displays the list of queries, highlight Expenses with Project Data, and click the Design button to open the query in Query Design view.
2. Drag the Budget field to the grid and drop it to the right of the Amount column.
3. Scroll the grid to the right so that at least one empty column is visible.
4. Enter **Percent:Amount/Budget** in the Field row of this empty column. Widen the colum so you can see the whole expression.
5. Run the query and adjust the column widths in the datasheet so you can see all the columns. Your screen should look something like the one in Figure 10.2.

FORMATTING CALCULATED VALUES

You're probably not happy with the way Access displays the calculated percentage in the query you just defined. By default, Access displays calculated values in General Number format—that is, exactly the way it stores and manipulates them internally. When you divide one number by another, the number of decimal places you see will vary widely, and you'll rarely need as many decimal places as you see in Figure 10.2.

FIGURE 10.2 *Calculations can be based on fields from any table in a query.*

Select Query: Project Expenses

ProjectID	Project Name	Expense Typ	Date	Purpose	Amount	Budget	Percent
Kitchen	Remodel kitchen	Labor	1/15/95	First payment to Master	1,200.00	7,000.00	0.1714285714286
Kitchen	Remodel kitchen	Labor	1/15/95	Initial consultation with i	300.00	7,000.00	0.0428571428571
Kitchen	Remodel kitchen	Materials	1/21/95	Fabric for new curtains	95.49	7,000.00	0.0136414285714
Kitchen	Remodel kitchen	Labor	2/2/95	New cabinet doors and	1,105.82	7,000.00	0.1579742857143
Kitchen	Remodel kitchen	Labor	2/5/95	Progress payment to Ma	2,000.00	7,000.00	0.2857142857143
Kitchen	Remodel kitchen	Labor	2/13/95	Allen Electric	465.00	7,000.00	0.0664285714286
Kitchen	Remodel kitchen	Labor	2/15/95	Rainbow Painters	640.00	7,000.00	0.0914285714286
Kitchen	Remodel kitchen	Labor	2/15/95	Gemini Plumbing	320.00	7,000.00	0.0457142857143
Kitchen	Remodel kitchen	Labor	2/16/95	Final payment to Master	1,100.00	7,000.00	0.1571428571429
Kitchen	Remodel kitchen	Labor	2/16/95	Final payment to interior	400.00	7,000.00	0.0571428571429
PCAdvisors	Brochure for PC Ac	Subcontractors	11/12/94	Photographs for brochu	540.00	1,800.00	0.3
PCAdvisors	Brochure for PC Ac	Subcontractors	11/18/94	Typesetting for brochure	250.00	1,800.00	0.1388888888889
PCAdvisors	Brochure for PC Ac	Shipping	11/19/94	Messenger to bring proc	20.00	1,800.00	0.0111111111111
PCAdvisors	Brochure for PC Ac	Subcontractors	11/25/94	Print 1000 brochures	120.00	1,800.00	0.0666666666667
PetCare	PetCare package	Subcontractors	2/8/95	Design logo for busines	450.00	3,200.00	0.140625
PetCare	PetCare package	Subcontractors	2/18/95	Typesetting, initial letterl	80.00	3,200.00	0.025
PetCare	PetCare package	Shipping	2/19/95	Send proofs to client	8.95	3,200.00	0.002796875
Vacation	Vacation, spring 19	Travel	3/1/95	New camera bag	42.00	3,500.00	0.012
Vacation	Vacation, spring 19	Travel	3/1/95	Camping equipment	240.00	3,500.00	0.0685714285714

Record: 1 of 19

NOTE

This behavior isn't unique to calculated values. If you didn't choose a display format for your table fields, they would also appear exactly the way they are stored (for example, dollar amounts might appear as 12.5, 7.49, and 124).

To help you make your query output more presentable, Access lets you assign a display format for calculated columns exactly as you do for table fields—by choosing a value for the Format property. The only difference is that the properties of query columns aren't always visible in Query Design view, the way the field properties are in Table Design view. If you want to see them, you have to display the *property sheet* for the query by using one of these methods:

- Click the Properties button in the toolbar.
- Choose View ➤ Properties.
- Right-click anywhere in the Query Design window and choose Properties from the popup menu.

The screen in Figure 10.3 shows the property sheet with the properties of the calculated Percent column visible.

FIGURE 10.3

You can edit the properties of fields and calculated columns in the query property sheet.

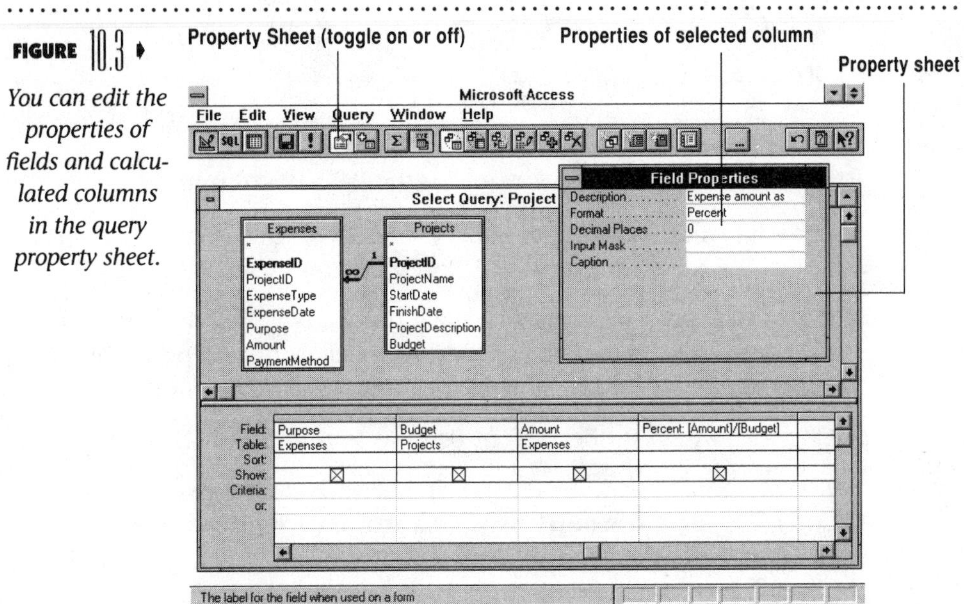

NOTE

The Properties button is a toggle button. Pressing it displays the property sheet if it is not visible or removes it from the screen if it is.

When you work in Query Design view with the property sheet visible, the list of properties changes to reflect the currently selected object. When you're working in a particular column, you'll see the field properties, which mirror the properties you can enter for a table field. Try clicking a field list to see the field list properties or anywhere else in the Query Design window to see the overall query properties.

NOTE

When you edit the Format property or other properties of a field, the properties you set apply only in the query; the properties defined in the table remain the defaults in all other contexts.

To choose a better display format for the Percent column:

1. If you're still looking at the query datasheet, click the Design button in the toolbar to return to Query Design view.
2. Click the Properties button in the toolbar to display the query property sheet. If necessary, adjust the size and position of the property sheet window so it doesn't obscure the query grid.
3. Click anywhere in the Percent column to display the field properties for this column.
4. Enter **Expense amount as percentage of project total** for the Description property.
5. In the Format combo box, choose Percent.
6. Enter **0** for the Decimals property (the default is 2).
7. Run the query and adjust the column widths so you can see all the columns at once. Now you'll see the Percent column formatted like this:

Percent
4%
17%
1%
16%

NOTE

When you close a query, Access remembers whether the property sheet was displayed. The next time you open any query, you'll see the property sheet if it was displayed the last time you worked in Query Design view.

CALCULATING SUMMARY STATISTICS

In addition to carrying out a calculation for each record in a table (or, more broadly speaking, for each row in the output of a query), you can compute summary statistics based on some or all of the records in a table. For example, you could calculate the total amount of money owed to you by your customers, find the earliest or latest order date, or figure out the average dollar total on your orders.

In Chapter 12 you'll learn to add these summary statistics to forms and reports. To compute statistics in a query, you must create a *totals query* instead of the select queries you've been working with so far. To identify a query as a totals query, do one of the following:

- Select View ➤ Totals.
- Click the Totals button in the toolbar.

NOTE

The Totals button is a toggle button—it turns the totals feature on if it is not already on, or off if it is. The symbol on the button face is the Greek letter sigma, which is commonly used in mathematics to represent sums.

When you create a totals query, Access adds a row to the query grid labeled Total. To define a summary calculation, you enter the *aggregate operator* that describes the statistic you want in the Total row and enter the field on which you want to base the calculation in the Field row. Thus, to compute the total of the Amount field in the Expense table, you would create a column with Amount in the Field row and Sum in the Total row. The cells in the Total row are combo boxes, and you can either type the aggregate operator or choose it from the drop-down list. The available aggregate operators are listed in the following table:

AGGREGATE OPERATOR	MEANING	DATA TYPES
Count	Number of nonblank values	All
Sum	Sum (total)	Numeric, date/time, yes/no
Avg	Average	Numeric, date/time, yes/no
Min	Minimum value	Text, numeric, date/time, yes/no
Max	Maximum value	Text, numeric, date/time, yes/no
StDev	Standard deviation	Numeric, date/time, yes/no
Var	Variance	Numeric, date/time, yes/no
First	Value from first row	All
Last	Value from last row	All

NOTE

When you use the Count aggregate operator, you're counting the number of records with nonblank values in the field in the Field row. If you want to count all the records in the table, be sure to choose a field that can't be blank, such as the primary key field.

The screen in Figure 10.4 shows a query that calculates statistics for payments to subcontractors. The query includes columns for the total amount, the earliest and latest expense dates, and the number of expense records. The screen in Figure 10.5 illustrates the output.

FIGURE 10.4

You can compute summary statistics based on all or some of the records in a query.

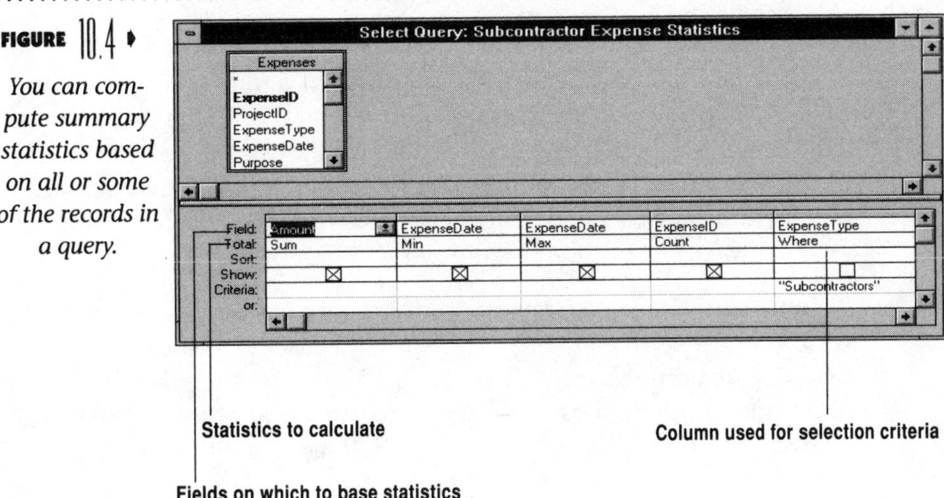

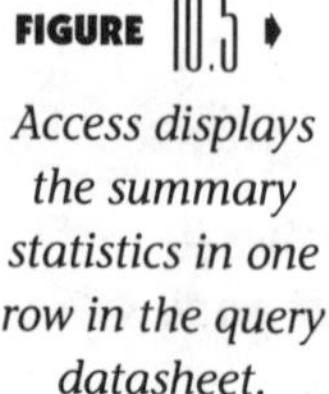

FIGURE 10.5 ▸ *Access displays the summary statistics in one row in the query datasheet.*

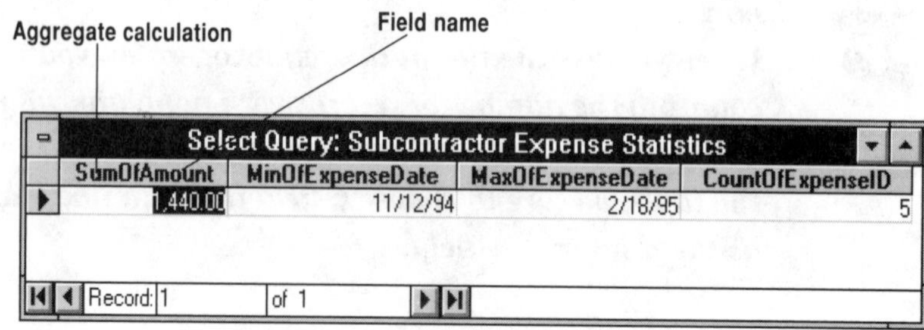

You can define the name of an aggregate column the same way you do any other calculated column, by typing the name at the beginning of the expression in the Field row. If you don't assign your own name, Access creates one by combining the type of statistic with the field name. These names are reasonably descriptive, but as you can see in Figure 10.5, they're often longer than you'd like.

All the columns displayed in the datasheet of a totals query are calculated, so you can't edit any of the data. If you try, Access displays an even more drastic message than it does for individual calculated columns in a normal select query: This Recordset is not updateable. (*Recordset* is a generic term that refers to either the records in a table or the rows in the output of a query.)

Because statistics in one row in a totals query are derived from many records in the source table(s), it doesn't make sense to include any fields in the output except the calculated statistics themselves. If you place additional fields in the query grid, Access interprets these fields as instructions for grouping records. You'll learn about calculating group statistics a little later in this chapter.

To build a query that calculates statistics based on all the records in the Expenses table:

1. Highlight the Expenses table in the Database window and click the New Query button in the toolbar.
2. In the New Query dialog box, choose New Query.

3. Click the Totals button in the toolbar.
4. Drag the Amount field to the grid, and drop it in the first column.
5. Click the Field row, and enter the column name **Total:** in front of the word *Amount*.
6. Display the drop-down list for the combo box in the Total row, and choose Sum from the list.
7. Enter **Earliest: ExpenseDate** in the Field row of the second column.
8. In the Total row of this column, start typing **Min**. Note that Access fills in the correct aggregate operator name as soon as you've typed the *M*.
9. In the Field row of the third column, enter **Latest: ExpenseDate**.
10. In the Total row of this column, start typing **Max**. When you type the *M,* Access fills in *Min*. When you type the *A*, you'll see *Max*.
11. Enter **Number: ExpenseID** in the Field row of the fourth column.
12. In the Total row of this column, enter **Count**.
13. Run the query. Your output should look like the screen in Figure 10.6.

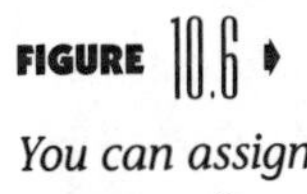

You can assign names for columns that compute aggregate statistics.

Select Query: Query1

Total	Earliest	Latest	Number
9377.26	11/12/94	3/1/95	19

Record: 1 of 1

DEFINING SELECTION CRITERIA

You won't always want to see statistics based on every record in a table. For example, you might want to include only payments to subcontractors, not all the records in the Expenses table.

You define selection criteria in a totals query exactly as you do in a select query, by adding fields to the grid and entering the criteria in one or more Criteria rows—with one important difference. To distinguish these columns from columns that describe summary statistics or grouping instructions (which you'll learn about in the next section), you must enter the **Where** in the Total row. If this seems strange, imagine describing your selection criteria like this: "I want to calculate the sum of the expense amount in records *where* the expense type is 'Subcontractors.'"

NOTE

The word* where *comes from SQL, a query language used behind the scenes to execute Access queries.

Although you might want to display the columns on which you're basing selection criteria (to remind you what the selections are), Access doesn't allow you to include fields from individual records in the output. The output row in the datasheet of a totals query is derived from many records in the source table(s), and Access can't guarantee in advance that all the records that contribute to this row will have the same value in a particular field. Thus, even if you enter criteria that select one value in a column, Access unchecks the Show box when you enter **Where** in the Total row. If you insist on checking it again, Access displays an alert box that warns you, Can't display the field in which Total cell is "Where". Turn off the Show option for that field when you try to run the query.

TIP

The best way to display a visible reminder of the selection criteria in a query is by including a brief description in the query name (for example,* Purchases by California Customers *or* Orders Over $500*).

To add the selection criteria to the Expenses query:

14. Drag the ExpenseType field to the grid.
15. Choose Where from the combo box in the Total row, and enter **Subcontractors** in the Criteria row.
16. Run the query. The Number column should now show 5, the number of payments to subcontractors in the Expenses table.
17. Close the query and save it under the name Subcontractor Expense Statistics.

CALCULATING GROUP STATISTICS

Access doesn't limit you to computing a single set of statistics for a table. You can also group the rows in the output and compute statistics *for each group*. You can visualize a query like this as being very similar to the reports generated by the Summary Report Wizard, which also groups records based on the contents of one or more fields and displays only the group totals, not the individual detail records.

To define the groups in a query, add a column to the grid for each group field, and enter **Group By** in the Total row. Just as when you sort, you have to arrange the columns in order from the largest group (on the left) to the smallest (on the right). The query shown in Figure 10.7 groups expense records by project and within each project by expense type. For each group, it computes the number of expenses, the dollar total, and the average amount. The screen in Figure 10.8 shows the output.

FIGURE 10.7

You can compute summary statistics for one or more groups in a totals query.

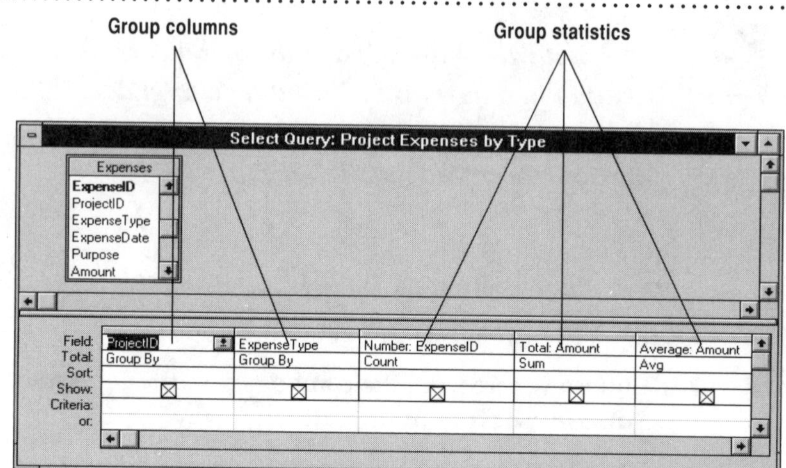

FIGURE 10.8

Access displays one row for each group in the query datasheet.

Select Query: Project Expenses by Type

Project ID	Expense Type	Number	Total	Average
Kitchen	Labor	9	7,530.82	836.76
Kitchen	Materials	1	95.49	95.49
PCAdvisors	Shipping	1	20.00	20.00
PCAdvisors	Subcontractors	3	910.00	303.33
PetCare	Shipping	1	8.95	8.95
PetCare	Subcontractors	2	530.00	265.00
Vacation	Travel	2	282.00	141.00

Record: 1 of 7

Access automatically sorts the output of the query by the group fields. If you prefer to see the rows in descending order, you can enter **Descending** in the Sort row for any group field. You can also sort by other columns in the query. For example, the screen in Figure 10.9 shows the project expenses sorted in descending order based on the total amount.

FIGURE 10.9 ▸

You can sort the query output based on a calculated summary statistic.

Select Query: Project Expenses by Type

Project ID	Expense Type	Number	Total	Average
Kitchen	Labor	9	7,530.82	836.76
PCAdvisors	Subcontractors	3	910.00	303.33
PetCare	Subcontractors	2	530.00	265.00
Vacation	Travel	2	282.00	141.00
Kitchen	Materials	1	95.49	95.49
PCAdvisors	Shipping	1	20.00	20.00
PetCare	Shipping	1	8.95	8.95

Record: 1 of 7

NOTE

If you select a descending sort for any group field, Access arranges all the groups in descending order. Thus, you can't sort the projects in ascending order but sort the expense types within each project in descending order.

Remember that each row in the output of a totals query with groups represents one unique combination of the group fields (ProjectID and ExpenseType in the query in Figure 10.8), and the statistics in each row are derived from one or more records in the underlying table.

As in any other query, you're not limited to working with one table at a time. The screen in Figure 10.10 shows a version of the Project Expenses by Type query shown earlier in Figure 10.7 that includes the ProjectName field from the Projects table. Be careful how you define the groups in a query like this one. Because you can't add a field that is displayed just for information, you have to call ProjectName a group field, so the query in Figure 10.10 has three groups—based on ProjectID, ProjectName, and ExpenseType. In fact, there can't be more than one value in the ProjectName field for any given value of ProjectID, but that doesn't violate any rules for grouping records.

FIGURE 10.10

You can display fields from more than one table in a totals query with groups.

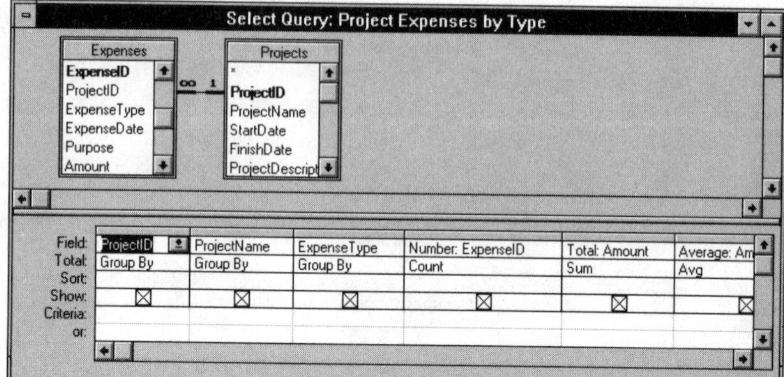

TIP

If you want to see only a long description field (ProjectName in the query in Figure 10.10) but sort the query output by the shorter code field (ProjectID), uncheck the Show box for the code field. If you remove ProjectID from the query and group rows by ProjectName, Access will display the query output sorted by ProjectName.

DEFINING GROUP SELECTION CRITERIA

You can use the same kind of selection criteria described earlier in this chapter to limit the records that contribute to the statistics in a totals query with groups. For example, you could modify the query shown in Figure 10.10 to include only expenses incurred after January 1, 1995, by adding the ExpenseDate field to the grid, entering **Where** in the Total row, and entering **>= 1/1/95** in the Criteria row.

But that's not all you can do. You can also define selection criteria that determine whether or not an entire group appears in the query output. You distinguish between the two types of criteria by where you put them:

- *To define criteria based on a group calculation,* enter them in the Criteria rows of the column that describes the calculation.
- *To define criteria based on a field in one of the source tables,* add the field to the grid, enter **Where** in the Total row, and enter the condition in the Criteria rows.

It's perfectly legitimate to have both types of criteria in the same query. Try building a query that displays group statistics for expenses in February, 1995, and includes only groups based on more than one expense record:

1. Highlight the Expenses table in the Database window and click the New Query button in the toolbar.
2. In the New Query dialog box, choose New Query.
3. Click the Totals button in the toolbar.
4. Drag ProjectID and ExpenseType to the grid, and make sure that Group By is visible in the Total row for both columns.
5. In the third column, enter **Number: ExpenseID** in the Field row and **Count** in the Total row.
6. In the fourth column, enter **Total: Amount** in the Field row and **Sum** in the Total row.
7. In the fifth column, enter **Average: Amount** in the Field row and **Average** in the Total row.
8. Drag the ExpenseDate field to the next empty column, enter **Where** in the Total row, and enter **2/*/95** in the Criteria row.
9. Enter **>1** in the Criteria row for the Number column to select groups with more than one expense record.
10. If the property sheet is not visible, click the Properties button in the toolbar to display it.
11. Click the Total column, and then select Standard for the Format property and enter **2** in the Decimals property.

12. Click the Average column, and then select Standard for the Format property and enter **2** for the Decimals property.
13. Run the query. Your results should look like the screen in Figure 10.11.
14. Close the query and save it under the name February 1995 Expense Statistics.

FIGURE 10.11 ▸

Select Query: February 1995 Expense Statistics

Project ID	Expense Type	Number	Total	Average
Kitchen	Labor	7	6,030.82	861.55
PetCare	Subcontractors	2	530.00	265.00

Record: 1 of 2

A totals query based on group selection criteria.

DISPLAYING A TOP TEN LIST

Sometimes when you rank groups in a totals query by sorting the output by a field other than the group field, you're not really interested in seeing all the groups. For example, you might want to use a query that lists your customers in descending order by total sales to find out who your best customers are. If you define *best* in terms of a specific dollar amount, you can enter selection criteria in the column that computes the sales total to exclude groups below that amount, but sometimes what you want is the top 10 (or top 5, or top 100) groups, regardless of the actual values of the calculated statistics.

To "cut off" the query output after a specific number of rows, simply display the query property sheet and set the Top Values property to the number of rows you want to see. If you'd rather see a percentage of the total number of rows, enter the percent (for example, **25%**) instead of a number. In either case, Access shows you the rows that come *first* in the query output. Depending on the sort order, that might mean either the *highest* or the *lowest* values in the sort fields.

TIP

You can use the Top Values property in any query, not just a totals query, to display the top values in any column, based on the sort order.

To modify the query you created in the last section so it displays the top three project expense categories:

1. Open the February 1995 Expense Statistics query in Design view.
2. Delete the selection criteria in the Number column.
3. Select the ExpenseDate column and press Del to delete it.
4. Enter **Descending** in the Sort row of the Total column to sort the query output so it displays the *top* values first, not the lowest.
5. Display the property sheet if it is not already visible, and click in the top half of the window to display the query properties.
6. Enter **3** in the Top Values property so the query displays the top three project expense categories.
7. Run the query. Your results should look like the screen in Figure 10.12.
8. Close the query and save it under the name Top 3 Project Expense Categories.

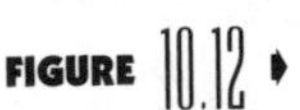

FIGURE 10.12

You can restrict a query's output to the top few values in a column.

Select Query: Top 3 Project Expense Categories

Project ID	Expense Type	Number	Total	Average
Kitchen	Labor	9	7,530.82	836.76
PCAdvisors	Subcontractors	3	910.00	303.33
PetCare	Subcontractors	2	530.00	265.00

Record: 1 of 3

DEFINING VARIABLE SELECTION CRITERIA

Often, you'll want to reuse a query with the same *type* of selection criteria but not exactly the same criteria. For example, you might use a query to display incomplete tasks entered during various ranges of dates. So far, the only way you know to do this is to edit the query each time and enter different date selection criteria, but you can easily automate the process by defining a *parameter query*.

A *parameter* is a placeholder for a specific value, which you'll enter in a dialog box when you run the query. To set up a parameter query, enter the prompt you want Access to display in the dialog box in the Criteria row instead of a specific value or condition. You have to enclose the prompt in square brackets so Access doesn't mistake it for a text string. For example, to prompt for the type of expense to include in a query based on the Expenses table, enter **[Type of Expense:]** in the Criteria row of the ExpenseType column.

If you're using a condition based on one of the comparison operators rather than testing for a single value, just put the dialog box prompt where you'd normally type the value: right after the operator. For example, you could prompt for the earliest expense date by entering **>= [Earliest expense date to include:]** in the ExpenseDate column. The query shown in Figure 10.13 uses two parameters with the Between operator in the Date column to select incomplete tasks between two arbitrary dates. This figure illustrates the dialog box displayed to collect the first parameter when you run the query from the Query Design window.

NOTE

Access displays a separate dialog box to collect each prompt you enter in a parameter query, not a single dialog box that collects all the variables.

FIGURE 10.13

A parameter query prompts you to enter your selection criteria.

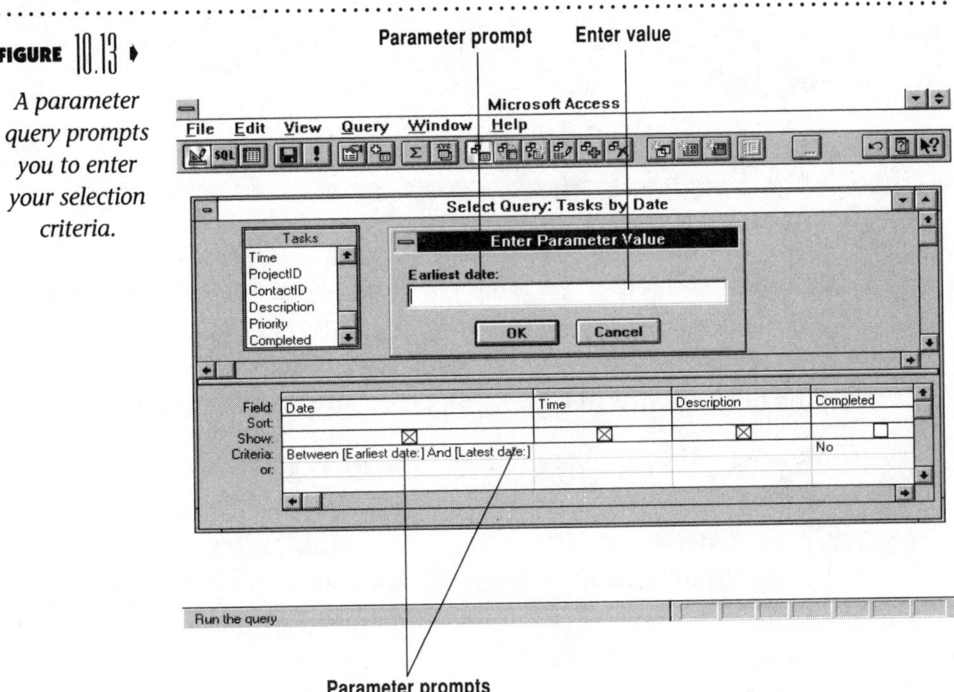

DEFINING CROSSTAB QUERIES

Access doesn't offer any help in constructing totals queries like the ones described thus far, but there is a Query Wizard for building *cross-tab queries.* A *crosstab* (short for *cross-tabulation*) is a statistical chart that computes the same statistic (such as a count or sum) for every possible combination of two different variables. For example, in a mail order business you might want a crosstab of products against states that shows how many of each product you've sold in each state. The screen in Figure 10.14 shows the result of running a query that displays a crosstab of projects against expense types.

Despite its simple appearance, producing a crosstab can be complicated, and Access gives you a special type of query for this purpose. You can create a crosstab query from scratch, by clicking the Crosstab

FIGURE 10.14 ▸

A crosstab query displays one statistic for every possible combination of two variables.

Crosstab Query: Expenses by Project

Project ID	RowTotal	Labor	Materials	Shipping	Subcontractors	Travel
Kitchen	7626.31	7,530.82	95.49			
PCAdvisors	930.00			20.00	910.00	
PetCare	538.95			8.95	530.00	
Vacation	282.00					282.00

Record: 1 of 4

Query button in the toolbar and then filling in your instructions in the query grid, but it's much easier to use the Wizard. To begin building the query shown in Figure 10.14:

1. Make sure the Database window displays the list of queries and click the New button.
2. Choose Query Wizards or press Alt+W in the New Query dialog box to display the list of Query Wizards shown in Figure 10.15.
3. Highlight Crosstab Query and click OK to move on to the next step.

FIGURE 10.15 ▸

You can use a Query Wizard to define a crosstab query.

Like all the other Wizards, the Crosstab Query Wizard first displays a dialog box that lets you choose the table or query you'll use as the data source for your crosstab. At the bottom of this dialog box is a diagram of the structure of a crosstab, which also appears in subsequent dialog boxes with more and more details filled in.

4. Choose Expenses and then click Next to move on to the next step.

The next dialog box, which is shown in Figure 10.16 with the specifications for the crosstab you're building filled in, lets you choose up to three columns that will appear at the left side of the crosstab chart as row titles. If you choose more than one column, you'll get one row for each unique combination of the values in these columns, just as you would in a totals query with two groups.

After you choose a field, Access fills in some sample values in the diagram at the bottom of the dialog box, as you can see in Figure 10.16, to show you what data the rows in your crosstab will contain. The

FIGURE 10.16

You can choose one or more columns for the crosstab row titles.

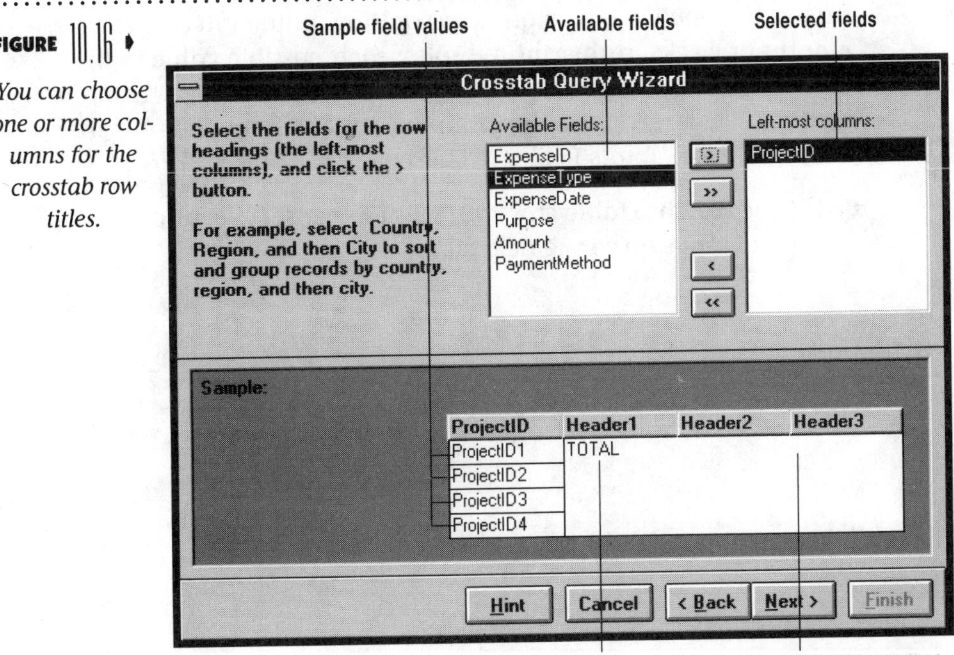

word *TOTAL* in the second column reminds you that Access can add a column to the crosstab to display overall row totals. (The row totals are optional, as you'll see shortly.) Thus, in the query in Figure 10.14, the column labeled Row Total displays the project totals.

5. For the Expense table crosstab, select ProjectID, and then click Next to move on to the next step.

NOTE

Despite the wording of the prompt, remember that when you choose columns to appear on the left side of the crosstab, you're determining what values will appear in the rows in the crosstab table.

The next dialog box, which is very similar to the one in Figure 10.16, lets you choose one (and only one) field to supply the column headings in the crosstab. If you choose a date/time field, the Wizard assumes that you'll want to group records by a time interval (such as months or weeks) rather than display each possible value in the crosstab, and it displays another dialog box to let you choose the grouping method. You'll recognize the grouping options from your experience with the Group/Totals Report Wizard.

6. For the Expense table crosstab, select ExpenseType, and then click Next to move on to the next step.

TIP

Usually it's best to choose the variable that can take on a greater number of different values (ProjectID in the crosstab you're building) for the row titles and use the variable with fewer different values (ExpenseType) as the column titles. However, you can choose more than one field for row titles but only one for column titles, and this constraint may force you to choose a field for the column titles that results in a very wide crosstab table.

Next, the Crosstab Query Wizard displays the dialog box shown in Figure 10.17 to let you choose the value that will appear in the individual cells in the crosstab chart. You choose a field first and then pick the aggregate calculation you want. When you run the crosstab query, Access calculates the statistic you chose for each possible combination of values in the field(s) displayed in the rows of the crosstab and the field displayed in the columns. The query you're building will display the sum of the Amount field for each combination of project and expense type.

7. For the Expense table crosstab, highlight Amount in the Available fields list, and then highlight Sum in the Functions list. The Wizard displays Sum(Amount) in the crosstab diagram.
8. Click Next to move on to the next step.

NOTE

If you don't want row totals in your crosstab, uncheck the box labeled Calculate Summary for Each Row.

FIGURE 10.17

You can choose the calculated statistic you want in the cells of the crosstab.

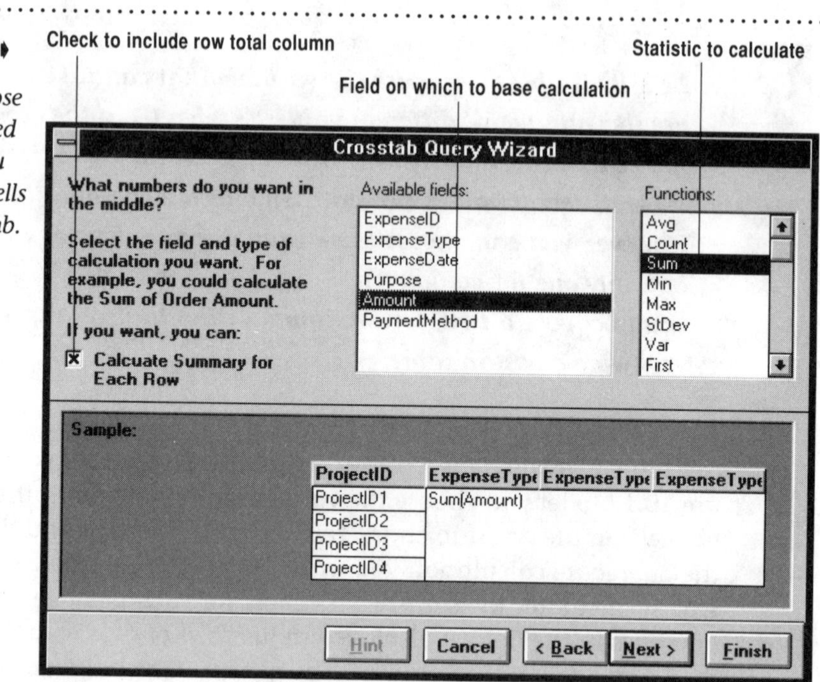

The last Crosstab Query Wizard dialog box lets you name your query and decide what to do next. Of course, you'll probably want to take a look at the query output, but usually you'll want to open the query in Query Design view to format the numeric values displayed in the cells.

9. In the last Crosstab Query Wizard dialog box, enter the name **Projects and Expenses Crosstab**.

10. Click Modify the query's design and then click Finish to complete the query.

The screen in Figure 10.18 shows the Projects and Expenses crosstab query in Query Design view. A crosstab query is defined by three types of components: row headings, column headings, and the value displayed in the cells of the crosstab. When you define a crosstab query from scratch, you identify these elements by your selections in the Crosstab row.

FIGURE 10.18 ▸

To define a crosstab query, you specify the row headings, the column headings, and the value you want to calculate.

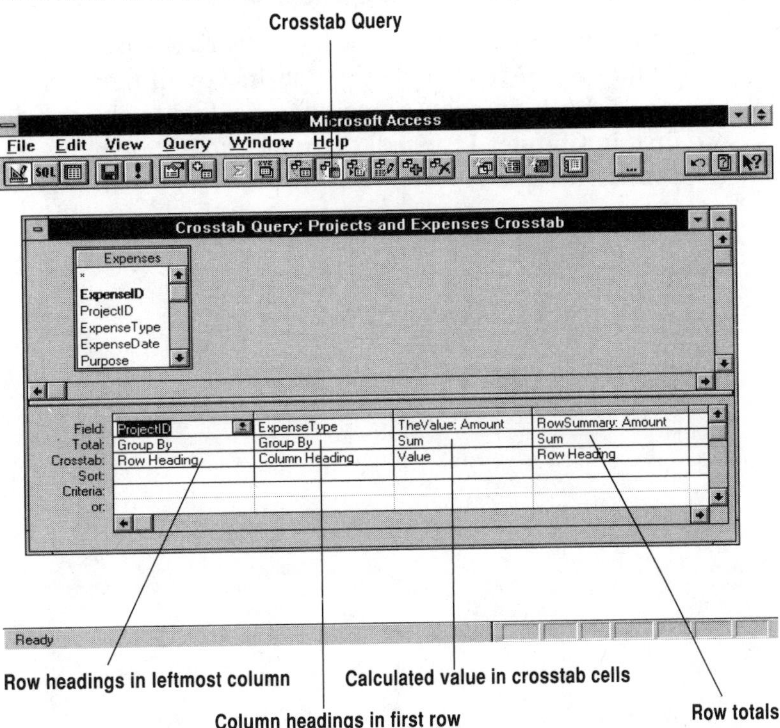

NOTE

You can define selection criteria in a crosstab query the same way you do in a totals query: for each field that contributes to the selections, add a column to the grid, enter Where in the Totals row, and enter the criteria in one or more Criteria rows.

WHAT'S NEXT

This chapter has introduced a variety of techniques for performing calculations in Access and demonstrated all of them with queries. Chapter 12 shows you how to include calculated values in documents. But first, in Chapter 11, you'll learn how to improve the appearance of your forms and reports.

Modifying the Appearance of Forms and Reports

By now you probably feel you've been asked to put up with a lot of problems—some esthetic and some more substantive—in your work with the forms and reports you generated with the aid of the Access Wizards. This chapter shows you how to rectify many of these problems and make your forms and reports more useful and presentable. You'll learn to move and resize objects, change fonts, select colors, draw lines and boxes, and add graphics. All of these modifications are easy to make, but in combination they can have a tremendous impact.

Most of the techniques you'll learn in this chapter apply equally to forms and reports. To avoid confusion, this book uses the generic term *document* to refer to either a form or report in contexts in which they are interchangeable. Where there are significant differences, the more specific terms *form* and *report* will call your attention to the distinction.

Before you get started, there's one caveat. It's possible to be seduced into spending an inordinate amount of time tinkering with the appearance of a form or report to get it "just right." Try to restrain yourself, except in those few crucial reports that present important data to your colleagues and coworkers.

WORKING IN DESIGN VIEW

To create a new document from scratch or modify a document generated by one of the Access Wizards, you'll work in *Design view,* where you'll see the layout and structure of the document itself rather than the data in your tables. You can move to Design view from almost any stage in the life cycle of a form or report.

If you want to create a new document from scratch:

- Choose Blank Form or Blank Report rather than Form Wizards or Report Wizards from the New Form or New Report dialog box.

To modify a document that already exists do one of the following:

- *From the last Form Wizard or Report Wizard dialog box,* choose Modify the form's design or Modify the report's design.
- *After previewing a report you just created using a Report Wizard,* exit from Print Preview by clicking the Close Window button in the toolbar. (This option isn't available for forms.)
- *In the Database window,* highlight the name of a form or report and click the Design button.
- *From Form view,* click the Design View button in the toolbar. (This option isn't available for reports.)

The screen in Figure 11.1 shows the Contact Names and Addresses form you created using the Single-Column Form Wizard in Chapter 7, with the Form Design window maximized and all the essential elements labeled. If you want to try the examples in this chapter, take a moment to open this form in Design view.

You've already seen the term *object* used to describe major database components, such as forms and reports. The smaller components that make up these documents can also be referred to as objects, but another word that's becoming popular in Windows to describe objects on forms and reports is *controls.* It seems reasonable to use this term for combo boxes, radio buttons, and command buttons, which you manipulate with the mouse as if they were mechanical controls. For the sake of consistency, Access uses the same term for simple text boxes and for objects you can't manipulate at all, such as lines, boxes, labels, and data displayed on reports.

You'll recognize many of the controls in the Contact Names and Addresses form—the text boxes that display and collect the fields, the associated labels that identify the fields, and the independent label that serves as the form title. Every object has a border, which is always visible in Design view to indicate the object's size. Whether you see the border on the finished form or report is up to you, as you'll learn later in this chapter.

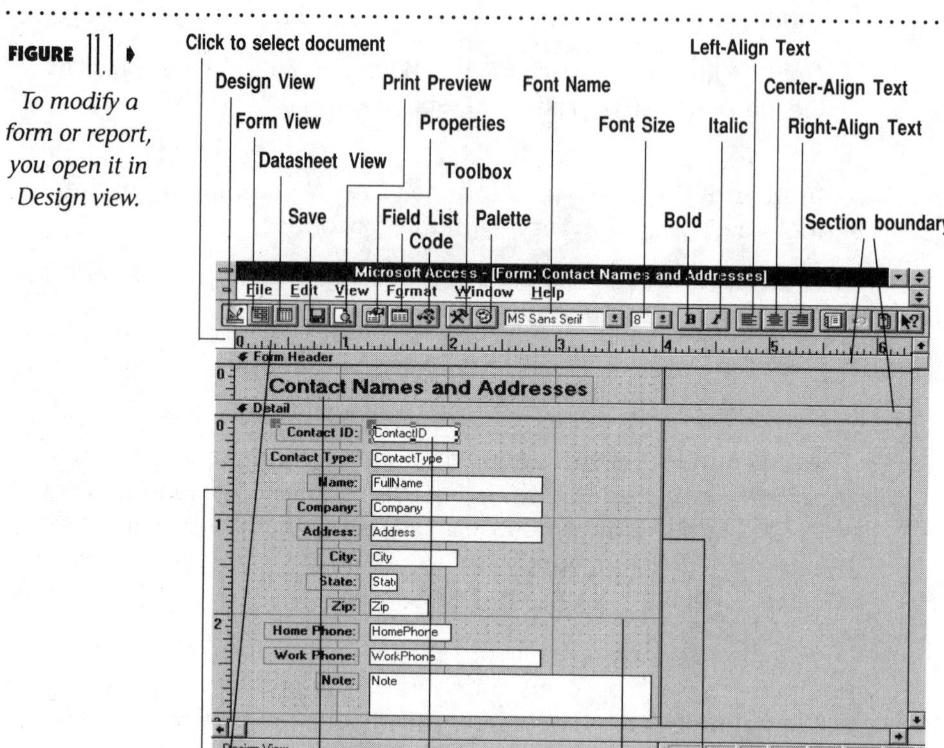

FIGURE 11.1 *To modify a form or report, you open it in Design view.*

NOTE

Many controls consist of two linked but independent objects: a data entry region and a label. This book uses the term **control** ***to describe the combination and refers to the individual components as*** **objects.**

Access gives you a variety of tools to help you construct and modify documents; you'll get an introduction to most of them in this and the next chapter. To display or hide these aids, you can use buttons in the toolbar or options on the View menu. All of these are toggles—they turn a feature on if it is off or off if it is on. When a tool is visible, its command button appears depressed, and you'll see a check next to the corresponding option on the View menu.

Access normally displays rulers along the top and left edges of the Design View window to help you judge the size and position of objects. To display or hide the rulers, use the View ➤ Ruler command.

NOTE

In both forms and reports, the scale in the ruler measures inches on the printed page, not on the screen. The actual size of a printer inch on the screen depends on the size of your monitor and your video mode.

In the background of the form, Access displays an alignment grid consisting of lines spaced 1 inch apart and a network of dots in between. To display or hide the grid, use the View ➤ Grid command.

NOTE

If you still can't see the grid after you've turned it on, it's because the grid density is set too fine. You'll encounter this problem in some of the documents generated by the Wizards, and you'll learn how to correct it later in this chapter.

THE STRUCTURE OF A DOCUMENT

Every Access document is made up of sections, which are defined in terms of the place they occupy in the data display or printing sequence:

SECTION	LOCATION
Form or report header	Once at the very beginning
Page header	At the top of each page when printed
Group header	At the beginning of each group
Detail	Once for each record in the source table
Group footer	At the end of each group
Page footer	At the bottom of each page when printed
Form or report footer	Once at the very end

In Design view each section is identified by a thick bar across the top, with a label and an arrow pointing down toward the objects in the section. You can see the form header and detail sections in Figure 11.1, and if you scroll down you'll see that there's also a form footer section (which is empty). You'll find examples of all the possible section types in the Expenses by Project and Type report report you created in Chapter 8 using the Group/Totals Report Wizard. The screen in Figure 11.2 shows a version of this report created using a slightly smaller font so you can see all the sections at once.

NOTE

Forms can't have record groups, so they can't have group header or footer sections. When you use forms to view and update data, you probably won't need a page header or footer section either, because you'll see the form name in the window title bar. If you print a form often, you might want the page header section to serve as a title.

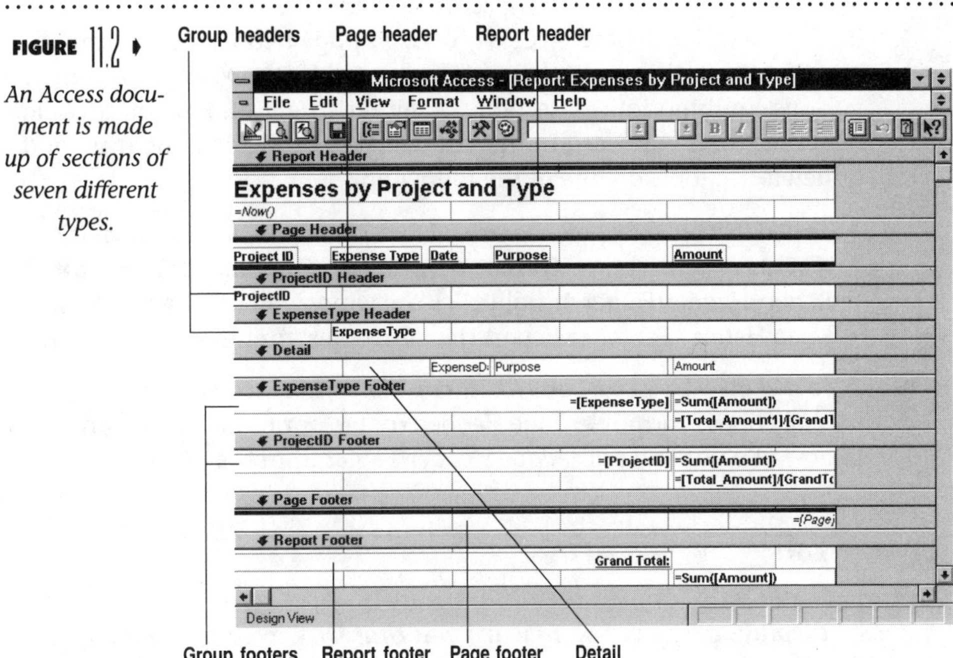

FIGURE 11.2 ▸ *An Access document is made up of sections of seven different types.*

You can resize any section by using the mouse to drag the lower boundary up or down. To change the width of the document, drag the dark vertical line that marks the right boundary.

TIP

If the width of a report plus the page margins specified in the Print setup dialog box exceed the physical width of the paper you're printing on, Access prints multiple pages for each record, just as it does when you print a wide datasheet. To ensure that a report fits within the page width, change the width and/or margins so that the total is less than or equal to the page width. For example, if the width of the report in Design view is 7 inches, you could change the left and right margins from the default 1 inch to ¾ inch.

When you create a form from scratch, you'll see only a detail section at first. In a new report, Access gives you page header, detail, and page footer sections. The documents created by the Wizards will have various combinations of sections. In either case it's up to you to decide which sections you want in the final version of the document. To add or delete sections, do one of the following:

- *To add the form or report header and footer or remove these sections if they are present,* choose Format ➤ Form Header/Footer or Format ➤ Report Header/Footer or right-click the window title bar and select Form Header/Footer or Report Header/Footer from the popup menu.
- *To add the page header and footer or remove these sections if they are present,* choose Format ➤ Page Header/Footer, or right-click the window title bar and select Page Header/Footer from the popup menu.

NOTE

If you try to remove a section that isn't empty, Access displays an alert box to warn you that Deleting these sections will also delete all controls in them ***and ask whether you want to proceed.***

TIP

To remove any header or footer section, but not both, delete any objects in the section, and then drag up the lower section boundary to shrink the height to zero.

WORKING WITH PROPERTIES

You've already had some experience with modifying the properties of various types of objects. You know how to edit field properties in Table Design view and customize the properties of a query or individual columns in the query datasheet in Query Design view. When you modify forms and reports, nearly all your activities will involve modifying object properties, either by manipulating the objects directly with the mouse or by making entries in the property sheet.

To display the property sheet or close it if it is already visible, click the Properties button in the toolbar, select View ➤ Properties, or right-click anywhere in the window and select Properties from the popup menu. The screen in Figure 11.3 shows the property sheet with the properties of the Contact Names and Addresses form visible. As you've seen in other design environments (Table Design view in Chapter 4 and Query Design view in Chapter 10), the property sheet always shows you the properties of the currently selected object.

The property sheet displays the properties of a document or any document component.

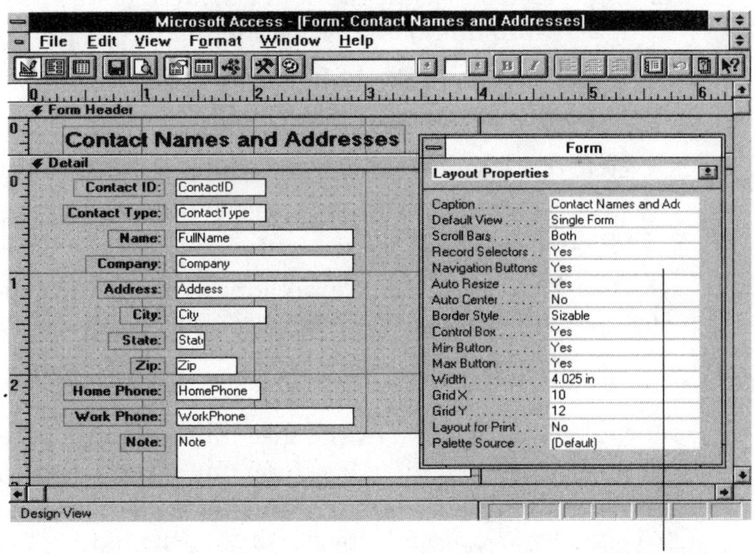

- *To display the form or report properties,* do one of the following:
  - Click the white box in the upper-left corner of the document (between the two rulers).
  - Click anywhere to the right of the document boundary but within the document window.

- Choose Edit ➤ Select Form.

- *To display section properties,* click anywhere in the section except within an object.
- *To display object properties,* click the object.

Go ahead and display the property sheet now and browse through the properties of the various objects on the Contact Names and Addresses form.

Because there are so many properties, Access lets you limit the list in the property sheet to one general class of properties, chosen from the combo box at the top of the property sheet:

- *Data properties* define the data displayed on the document and specify formatting and validation rules.
- *Layout properties* govern the appearance and position of a control section, or document.
- *Event properties* determine what happens when certain events occur (for example, when you move into a control or click a control on a form).
- *Other properties* include miscellaneous properties, such as a control's name and the message displayed in the status bar.
- *All properties* include all of the object properties.

If you're overwhelmed by the sheer number of properties, take heart. First of all, the default values for many properties should serve your needs adequately in most of your documents. Second, although you *can* modify any property by making entries in the property sheet, there are more direct methods for moving and resizing objects and for changing colors and border styles. When you do have to use the property sheet, many of the entries are combo boxes, so you won't have to memorize the options. For now you'll probably want to stick with the Layout properties.

NOTE

It doesn't matter whether you change a property by direct manipulation with the mouse or by making entries in the property sheet. All the changes you make using any methods will be reflected in the appropriate property settings, as you'll see if you work with the property sheet visible.

SETTING OVERALL DOCUMENT PROPERTIES

You'll learn about more of the overall form and report properties later in this chapter and in Chapter 12, but there are a few that you'll find useful immediately. As you might expect, the list of available properties is quite different for forms and reports.

THE FORM PROPERTIES

In an Access form the Caption property determines the title Access displays in the Form window title bar. The Form Wizards set this property to match the title you enter in the last Wizard dialog box. To change it later, simply edit the Caption property.

The Default View property governs the overall form display style. Access gives you three choices:

SETTING	DESCRIPTION
Single Form	Displays one record at a time (like the forms produced by the Single-Column Form Wizard)
Continuous Forms	Displays as many records as will fit on the screen at once (like the forms produced by the Tabular Form Wizard)
Datasheet	Displays the form in Datasheet view (like the subforms in the forms produced by the Main/Subform Wizard)

NOTE

As the name suggests, the Default View property determines the initial display mode for a form. If you choose Single Form or Continuous Forms, you can still switch to Datasheet view while using the form.

THE REPORT PROPERTIES

The report properties you'll probably want to change most often have to do with pagination. For example, in a Group/Totals report you might want to begin each group on a new page. If you use the report header section to print a cover page, you might not want this section to include the page header or page footer.

The Page Header and Page Footer properties determine when Access prints these sections:

SETTING	DESCRIPTION
All Pages	Prints on every page of the report
Not with Rpt Hdr	Omits from the report header pages
Not with Rpt Ftr	Omits from the report footer pages
Not with Rpt Hdr/Ftr	Omits from the report header and footer pages

The Force New Page property, which is available for all report sections except the page header and page footer, determines when Access begins a new page:

SETTING	DESCRIPTION
None	Begins a new page only when the page is filled
Before Section	Always begins a new page before printing the section

SETTING	DESCRIPTION
After Section	Always begins a new page after printing the section
Before & After	Always begins a new page before and after printing the section

SELECTING OBJECTS

To display or modify object properties, you'll usually have to select the object(s). Here's how:

- *To select one object,* click the object.
- *To select another object with one or more already selected,* hold down the Shift key and click the object.
- *To select a group of objects,* click outside any of them and drag to enclose the group.
- *To select all the objects at a given distance from the left or top edge of the document,* click-and-drag in the horizontal or vertical ruler.
- *To select all the objects in a document,* choose Edit ➤ Select All or press Ctrl+A.
- *To deselect the selected objects without selecting any other object,* click anywhere in the document window *except* within an object.

When an object is selected, Access displays *handles* in the border, as shown in Figure 11.4. To move or resize the object, grab the appropriate handle with the mouse and drag.

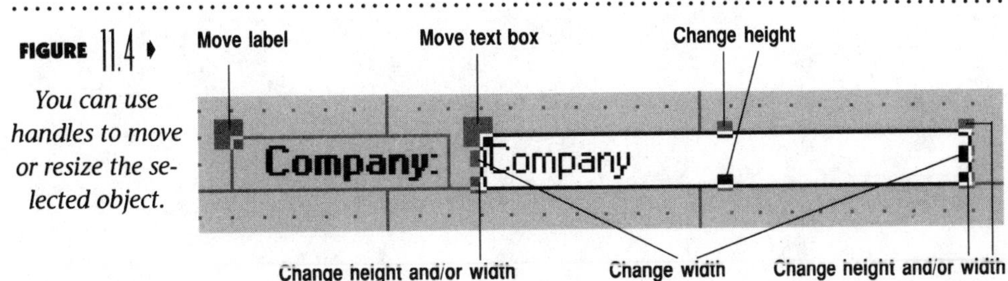

FIGURE 11.4 ➧ *You can use handles to move or resize the selected object.*

NOTE

When you select a control made up of two objects (a label and a data entry region), Access displays a full set of handles in the object you clicked, and any property changes you make are applied to this object. The linked object will have only a move handle.

TIP

You can cycle through all the objects in a document in turn by selecting any object and then pressing Tab (to move forward) or Shift+Tab (to move backward). If you're having trouble selecting small objects like lines or box borders, just select any nearby object and press Tab or Shift+Tab until the object you want is selected.

MOVING AND RESIZING OBJECTS

The first modification you'll want to make in any document created by the Access Wizards is to move and resize some of the controls. You can select and move a control using a simple click-and-drag technique: position the mouse pointer over the object, press and hold the left mouse button, and drag the object to its new position.

NOTE

To limit movement to one axis (either vertical or horizontal), hold down the Shift key before you click the control you want to move. If you begin by moving the object left or right, Access lets you move it only horizontally; if you begin by moving it up or down, Access lets you move it only vertically. This technique gives you an easy way to adjust the position of an object without disrupting its alignment with other objects.

To move two or more controls together, select them all; then click any selected control again and drag the objects where you want them. If you're not sure where to click, watch the mouse pointer, which looks like an open hand when you're over a spot suitable for dragging:

NOTE

You can use the same technique to move one control that's already selected, but watch the mouse pointer carefully while you decide where to click to begin the drag operation. If you click inside the object rather than near one of the borders, Access deselects the object and displays an insertion point to let you edit the contents.

When you use this method to drag a control made up of two objects (such as a text box or check box), both objects move together. To move either object independently, grab the large move handle in the upper-left corner. When the mouse pointer is over the right spot, it looks like a hand with a pointing finger:

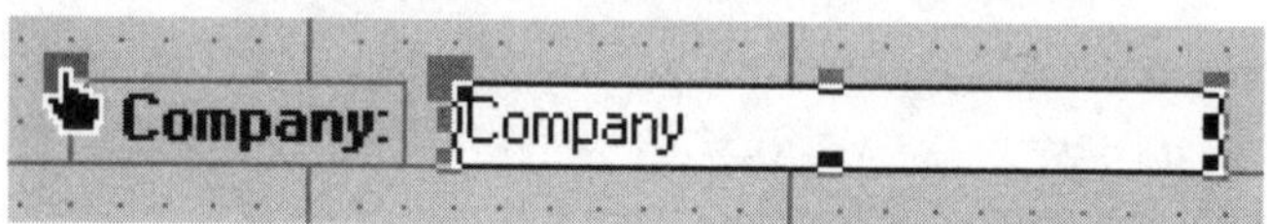

To resize one or more objects, use any of the handles *except* the move handle. When the mouse is positioned over a resizing handle, the pointer changes to a double-headed arrow that reminds you which directions the object border can move when you drag that handle.

TIP

It's a good idea to hold down the Shift key while you resize a line to avoid inadvertently creating a diagonal line. If you're having trouble using the mouse, you might find it easier to resize a line by editing the Width property in the property sheet.

To delete one or more objects, select them and press Del or choose Edit ➤ Delete. If you change your mind *before you make any other changes,* you can get back the objects by using the Undo button or the Edit ➤ Undo Delete command.

To practice these techniques, begin modifying the Contact Names and Addresses form. Don't worry about the precise size or alignment of the objects at this point; you'll learn a variety of alignment techniques in the next few sections. Use the following steps to arrange the form approximately as shown in Figure 11.5:

1. Close the property sheet or drag it most of the way off the screen to get it out of your way.

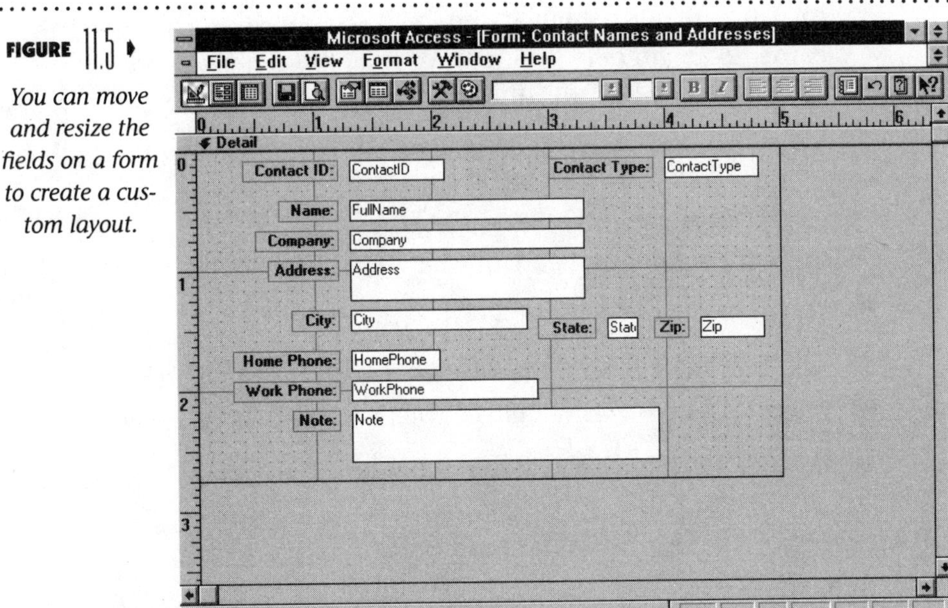

FIGURE 11.5 *You can move and resize the fields on a form to create a custom layout.*

2. Drag the form boundary to the right, to line up with the 5-inch mark on the horizontal ruler.
3. Drag up the Contact Type text box to the right of the Contact ID text box.
4. Click the City text box to select it, and use the handle in the right border to widen it to about 1½ inches.
5. Click above the FullName text box label, and drag to select the FullName and Company text boxes. (You should see only move handles in the labels.) Use the handle in the right border of either object to widen both to about 2 inches.
6. Hold down the Shift key and click the Address text box to select it along with the other two. Drag up the three text boxes to reduce the space between the ContactID and FullName controls, and then click elsewhere on the form to deselect them.

7. Click the Address text box, and use the handle in the lower-right corner to expand the field to twice its original height and the same width as the FullName and Company text boxes.
8. Move the State and Zip text boxes so they almost line up with the City text box. (You'll correct the alignment later.)
9. Select the HomePhone, WorkPhone, and Note text boxes and move them up to close the gap between HomePhone and City.
10. Widen the HomePhone text box slightly.
11. Select the label in the form header and press Del to delete it.
12. Select Format ➤ Form Header/Footer to remove these sections.
13. Drag up the lower form boundary to just below the Note field.

CHANGING THE TAB ORDER IN A FORM

When you move objects around in Design view, you're changing only the appearance of the form. When you return to using the form for data entry, you'll see that pressing Tab still moves you through the fields in their original order—the order in which you (or the Form Wizard) placed them on the form in the first place. Needless to say, this can be rather disconcerting.

You rearrange the tab order using the dialog box shown in Figure 11.6. To call up this dialog box, choose Edit ➤ Tab Order, or right-click the white box in the upper-left corner of the document or to the right of the document border, and then select Tab Order from the popup menu. You have to work with one form section at a time, which you choose using the radio buttons on the left side of the dialog box; usually it's the detail section you'll be reordering. You can use the selector buttons in the Custom Order list box to select controls and drag them where you want them in the tab order.

The Auto Order button gives you an easy way to restore what Access considers to be the "normal" tab order, in which pressing Tab moves you across each row of controls in turn, from the top of the form to the bottom. In a Single-Column form or a Tabular form (which might be described as "single-row"), the Auto Order is exactly what you want. If

FIGURE 11.6

You can specify the tab order in any section of a form.

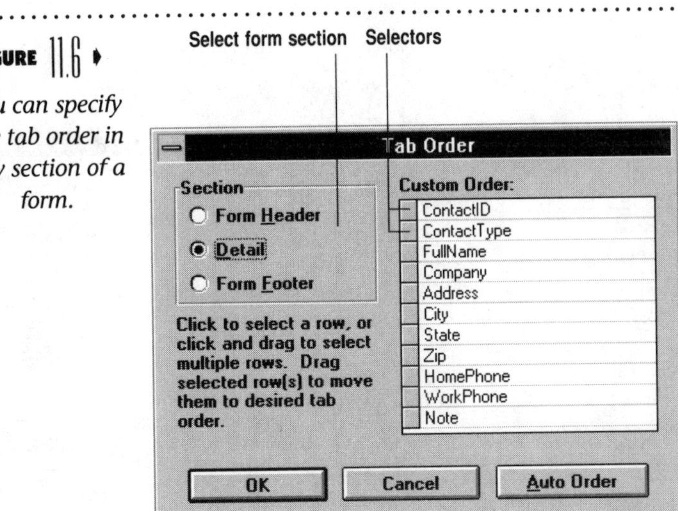

you want to create a layout in which the Tab key moves you down one column of fields and then up to the top of an adjacent column, you'll have to rearrange the controls manually in the Custom Order list box. Figure 11.7 shows an example, with the controls numbered to indicate the tab order.

ALIGNING OBJECTS

Access gives you a variety of methods for aligning objects on a form. You've already used the rulers to judge the size and position of some of the objects in the Contact Names and Addresses form, but the rulers aren't precise enough for fine adjustments. As you may already have discovered, you'll find the alignment grid to be your most useful tool for aligning objects while you're moving and resizing them. The options on the Format menu let you adjust or correct the spacing or alignment of objects after the fact.

FIGURE 11.7 ▸

You have to customize the tab order to create a form in which the cursor moves down two or more columns of controls in turn.

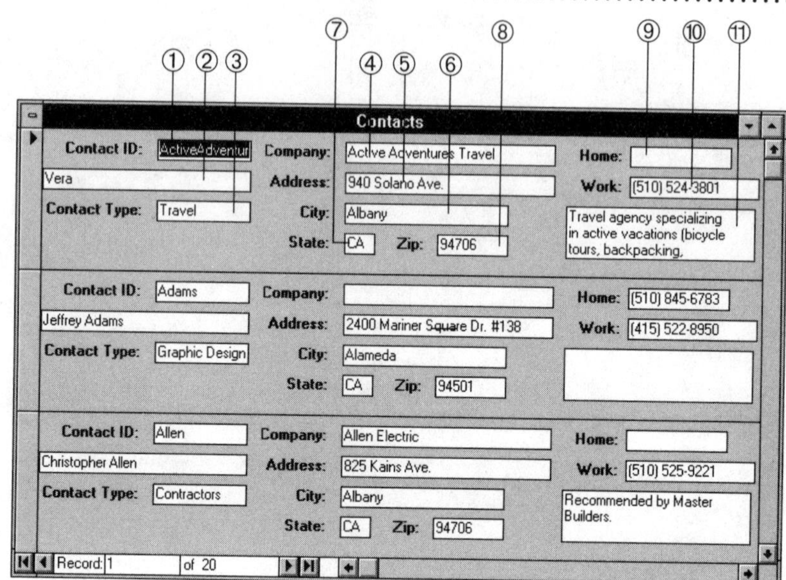

USING THE GRID

As you can see in Figure 11.5, the alignment grid consists of marker lines at 1-inch intervals and a network of evenly spaced dots in between. You can set the horizontal and vertical grid spacing independently, to any density from 2 to 64 dots per inch, but you'll see the dots only if both settings are 16 dots per inch or coarser. The default grid spacing is 10 dots per inch horizontally by 12 dots per inch vertically, but some of the Report Wizards set it finer, so you won't see the grid dots initially when you modify these reports.

To customize the grid settings:

1. Make sure the property sheet is visible and that it displays the form properties.
2. Choose Layout Properties (or All Properties) from the combo box at the top of the property sheet.
3. Set the horizontal grid spacing in the Grid X property.

4. Set the vertical grid spacing in the Grid Y property.

Although the grid is useful enough as a visual alignment tool, it can play a more active role as well if you enable the Snap to Grid option. Whenever you move or resize an object with Snap to Grid turned on, Access makes a fine adjustment to its size or position to line up the edge you moved with the nearest grid point. To turn this option on or off, select Format ➤ Snap to Grid.

TIP

The Snap to Grid option works even if the grid is too fine to see. At the finest grid density it's not very useful, but with the grid set to 20 to 30 dots per inch, it helps you keep the objects on your document lined up without detracting from your ability to fine-tune the layout.

The Snap to Grid setting is on by default, so you've probably already seen what it can do for you. Now, turn it off and make a few changes to the Contact Names and Addresses form:

1. Pull down the Format menu. If Snap to Grid is checked, click it to turn off this option.
2. Resize the Name and Address text boxes so they're both slightly narrower than the Company field.

USING THE ALIGNMENT COMMANDS

Moving and resizing objects with the mouse (either individually or in groups) is easy and intuitive, but lining up more than a few objects in a complex form using only these methods would be quite tedious. Access gives you a variety of alignment commands to help with this task. To align a group of objects:

1. Select the objects.
2. Choose Format ➤ Align.

3. Choose an alignment option from the submenu:

   - *To align the left sides of the objects with the leftmost selected object,* choose Left.
   - *To align the right sides of the objects with the rightmost selected object,* choose Right.
   - *To align the top sides of the objects with the highest selected object,* choose Top.
   - *To align the bottom sides of the objects with the lowest selected object,* choose Bottom.
   - *To align the upper-left corner of each object with the nearest grid dot,* choose To Grid.

NOTE

When you use the alignment options to line up a horizontal row of text boxes, be sure to select the labels explicitly (by holding down the Shift key and clicking each label) if you want Access to adjust the alignment of the labels as well as the text boxes. You can be sure a label is selected if it has a full set of handles, not just a move handle.

To resize a group of objects:

1. Select the objects.
2. Choose Format ➤ Size.
3. Choose an alignment option from the submenu:

   - *To adjust the size of labels or buttons to match the label text,* choose To Fit.
   - *To move all object borders to the nearest grid lines,* choose To Grid.
   - *To adjust the height of the objects to match the tallest selected object,* choose To Tallest.

- *To adjust the height of the objects to match the shortest selected object,* choose To Shortest.
- *To adjust the width of the objects to match the widest selected object,* choose To Widest.
- *To adjust the width of the objects to match the narrowest selected object,* choose To Narrowest.

To adjust the spacing within a group of objects:

1. Select the objects.
2. Choose Format ➤ Horizontal Spacing or Format ➤ Vertical Spacing.
3. Choose a spacing option from the submenu:
   - *To equalize the spacing between the objects,* choose Make Equal.
   - *To increase the spacing by one grid dot and, if you selected more than two objects, to equalize the spacing,* choose Increase.
   - *To decrease the spacing by one grid dot and, if you selected more than two objects, equalize the spacing,* choose Decrease.

Use the alignment options to correct the spacing problems on the Contact Names and Addresses form:

1. Select the FullName, Company, and Address text boxes (not the labels), and then choose Format ➤ Size ➤ To Widest to resize them all to match the Company text box.
2. Select the City, State, and Zip text boxes *and the associated labels,* and then choose Format ➤ Align ➤ Top to align them all with the City text box.
3. Switch to Form view. If the window is maximized, click the Restore control. Choose Window ➤ Size to Fit Form to adjust the window size.
4. Return to Form Design view.

CUSTOMIZING TEXT

You can customize the font and font style for text boxes, labels, and any other controls that display text by using the buttons in the toolbar or by making selections in the property sheet. The screen in Figure 11.8 shows the correspondence between the controls and the property settings they govern. In general, the property sheet gives you more choices, but the ones you'll use most often are available in the toolbar.

FIGURE 11.8

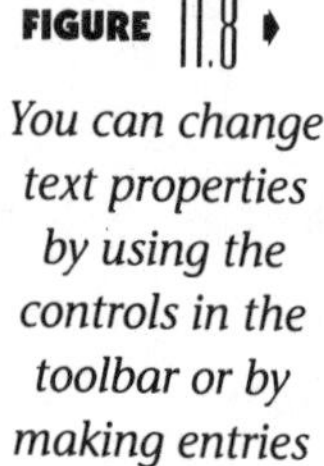

You can change text properties by using the controls in the toolbar or by making entries in the property sheet.

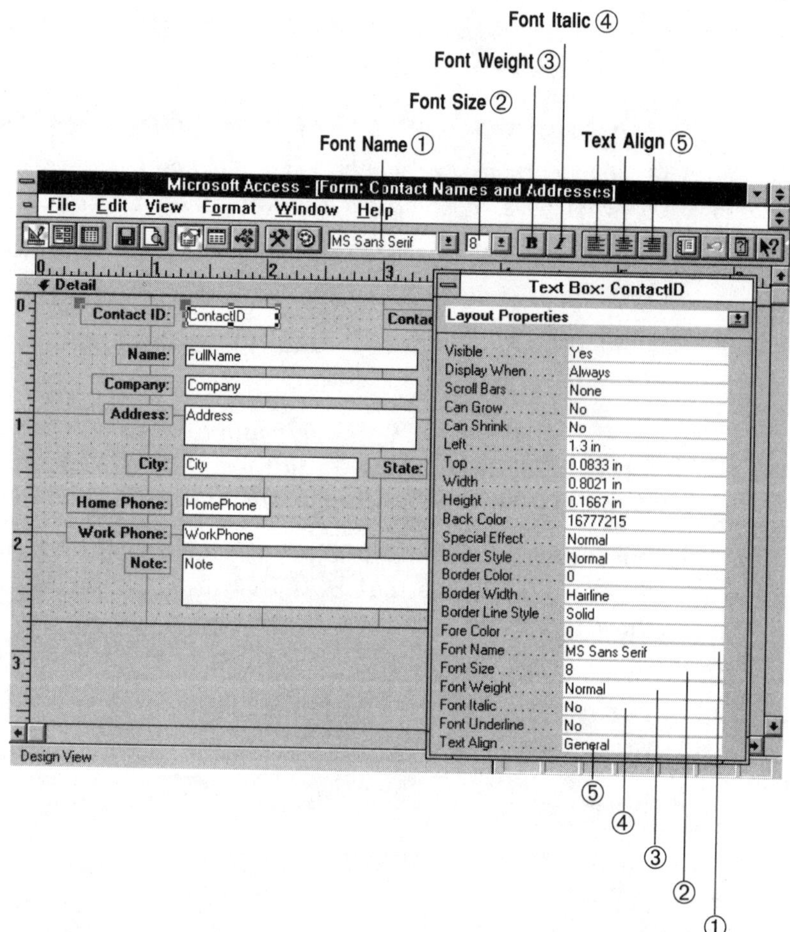

Some of the examples in this section are based on the Expenses by Project and Type report you defined using the Group/Totals Wizard in Chapter 8. Go ahead and open this report in Design view (without closing the Contacts form) so you can follow along. To begin:

1. Maximize the Design View window and make sure the property sheet is visible. Make sure Snap to Grid is turned on.
2. Display the overall report properties, and set the Grid X and Grid Y properties to 10 and 12, respectively, so you can see the grid.
3. Select all the labels in the page header section, and set the Font Underline property to No.
4. Select the text box that prints the current date below the report title. Click the Italic button in the toolbar to turn off italics, and then click the Bold button to turn on bold.

EDITING LABELS

You've seen two types of labels on the documents produced by the Access Wizards—independent label objects like the ones in the form header, report header, and group header sections and the labels associated with compound controls like text boxes and check boxes. To edit the text displayed in *any* label:

1. Click the label to select it.
2. Press F2 or click the label again to display an insertion point.
3. Use any of the standard editing techniques to edit the text.
4. Press ↵ to get out of edit mode and leave the label selected, or click elsewhere on the screen to get out of edit mode and deselect the label.

Access automatically expands a label to accommodate any additional characters you insert, and it's smart enough to preserve the alignment; if the label is right justified, for example, the label expands to the left.

TIP

If you delete characters, Access doesn't automatically shrink a label object. This usually doesn't present any problems, but if spacing is tight on your document, you can use the Format ➤ Size ➤ To Fit command to resize the label object frame to match its contents.

ALLOWING TEXT BOXES TO GROW AND SHRINK

If a text box on a form is too small to display the full contents of a field, you can still scroll through all the data. On a report, the dimensions of the text boxes are far more crucial; if they're too small to let you read your whole entry in a text or memo field, the report might not be very useful. Now that you know how to adjust the height and width of the text boxes the Report Wizards create, you can solve some of these problems.

Eventually, though, you'll build a table with a memo field in which some of the entries are considerably longer than the ones in the Contacts table. If some entries are just a few words long while others occupy more than a page, you can use the Can Grow and Can Shrink properties to overcome the limitations imposed by fixed-size text boxes:

- *To allow a field to expand onto as many lines as necessary to display the full contents,* set the Can Grow property to Yes.
- *To allow a field to shrink to occupy no space at all if it's empty,* set the Can Shrink property to Yes.

If you examine the Layout properties for the two-across holiday labels you created in Chapter 9, you'll see that Access sets both Can Grow and Can Shrink to Yes for all the text boxes on the report. For the name and address fields, this strategy is perfect; it prevents a blank FullName or Company field from generating an unsightly blank line and allows the Address field to expand onto two or more lines if necessary. Unfortunately, the text box that forms the blank line you added between the address and the message below also has Can Shrink set to Yes. To restore the blank space, you can either set Can Shrink to No or, better yet, delete this text box.

On the Expenses report:

1. Select the Amount text box and all the subtotals below it in the group footer sections, and resize these objects so the left borders line up with the 5½-inch mark in the ruler.
2. Move the Purpose text box and the corresponding label in the page header section to line up with the 3-inch mark in the ruler, and then widen the Purpose text box to about 2¼ inches.
3. Select the Date label in the page header section and click the Right-Align Text button in the toolbar to right-justify the text within the label object. Hold down the Shift key and click the ExpenseDate text box. Then select Format ➤ Align ➤ Right to align the label object with the text box.
4. Repeat these steps to right-justify the Amount label over the Amount column.
5. Make sure the property sheet is visible and that it displays the layout properties.
6. Click the Purpose text box, and set the Can Grow property to Yes.
7. Preview the report, and verify that the Purpose field expands onto two lines when the contents won't fit on one.
8. Click the Close Window button in the toolbar to return to Design view.

CUSTOMIZING THE COLOR AND STYLE OF OBJECTS

Once you've learned how to modify the essential properties of the objects on your documents—their size, position, and alignment—you're ready to turn your attention to esthetic considerations, such as fonts, colors, and border styles. If you want some examples of typical effects you can produce by combining these properties, take a look at the samples of the Form and Report Wizard styles in Figures 7.7 and 8.7.

CHANGING OBJECT COLORS AND STYLES

The easiest way to change the colors, borders, and other visual attributes of objects is to use the palette. Unless you have a color printer, you'll use color only sparingly in reports—for example, to produce a gray shadow or box background—but all the options in the palette apply in theory to both forms and reports. To display the palette or remove it from the screen if it is already visible, click the Palette button in the toolbar or use the View ➤ Palette command. You can also close the palette by clicking (*not* double-clicking) the close box in the upper-left corner of the window.

Figure 11.9 shows the correspondence between the palette controls and the corresponding object properties, on a form that illustrates some typical examples of the various selections. You'll definitely want to use the palette to choose colors (which are identified by numbers in the property sheet), but it's just as easy to set the other object attributes by making selections directly in the property sheet.

NOTE

The property sheet gives you seven choices for the Border Width and Border Line Style properties, compared with four and three, respectively, in the palette. To display an object without a visible border, click the Clear button in the palette or set the Border Style property to Clear.

To customize any of the properties available in the palette, select the objects you want to modify and then click one of the buttons or color samples in the palette. For most controls you can set the foreground, background, and border colors. For a document section, which has no foreground text or border, only the background color is enabled.

Go back to the Contact Names and Addresses form and customize several object styles:

1. Make sure the palette is displayed.

FIGURE 11.9

You can change object properties by using the controls in the palette or by making entries in the property sheet.

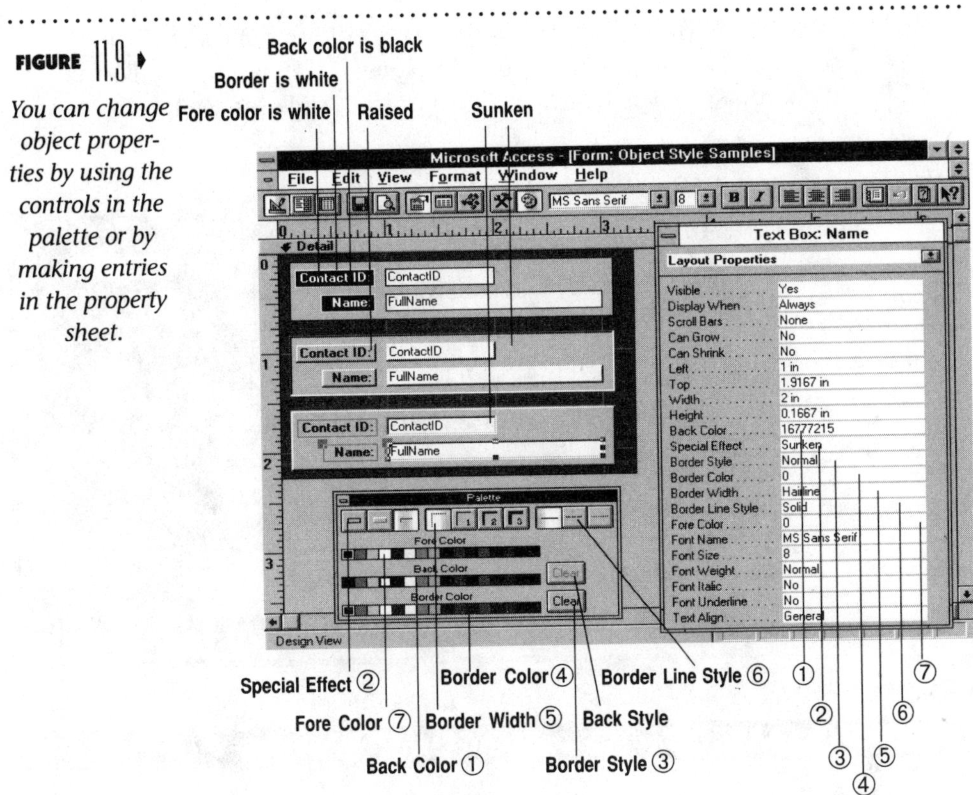

2. Select all the text boxes (not the labels), and then click the Sunken Appearance button in the palette.
3. Click the background of the form, and then click one of the dark colors in the palette (dark blue, green, or gray).
4. Click the ContactID text box. Choose 10 in the Font Size combo box in the toolbar, and click the Bold button. Widen the field to about 1¼ inches.

5. Switch to Form view to verify the effects of your changes. Your screen should look like the one in Figure 11.10. Return to Form Design view. If the window is maximized, click the Restore button.

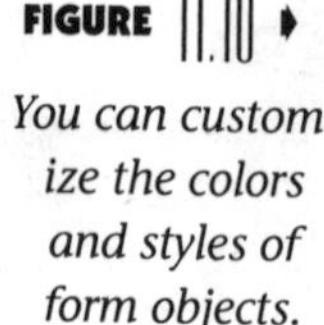

FIGURE 11.10

You can customize the colors and styles of form objects.

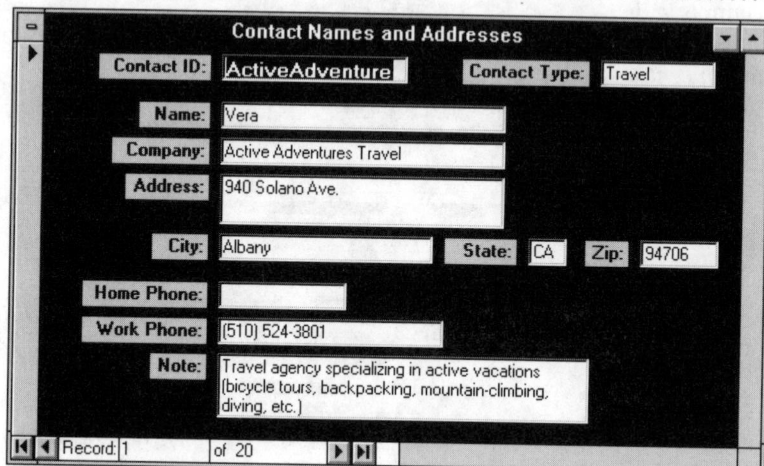

ADDING OBJECTS TO A DOCUMENT

So far you've learned how to modify the properties of existing objects, but even if you always start with a Wizard rather than defining a form or report from scratch, you'll have occasion to add new objects. You might want to add your logo or a scanned photograph to a report or use lines and boxes to set off groups of controls. To add these and other objects to a document, you use the *toolbox,* which is shown in Figure 11.11. The toolbox has 16 command buttons, one for each type of control, as well as three buttons that govern the behavior of the tools and the mouse. In this chapter you'll concentrate on the controls that enhance the appearance of your documents. In Chapter 12 you'll learn to add controls that display or collect data.

To display the toolbox or remove it from the screen if it is already visible, click the Toolbox button in the toolbar or choose View ➤ Toolbox. You can also close the toolbox by clicking (*not* double-clicking) the close box in the upper-left corner of the window.

FIGURE 11.11

The toolbox lets you create 16 types of controls.

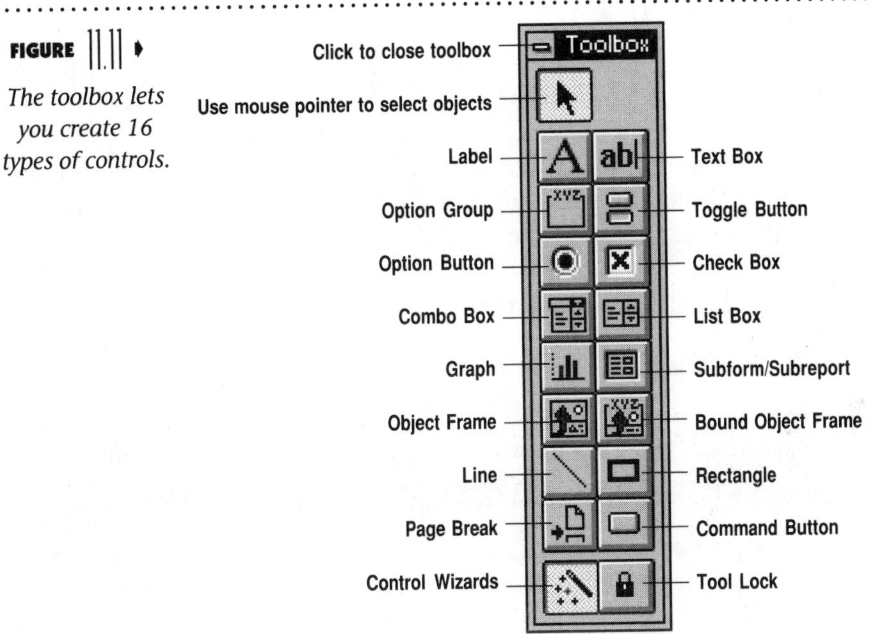

ADDING LABELS TO A DOCUMENT

When you add fields to a report defined by one of the Report Wizards or define a report from scratch, you'll often want to add your own labels. To create a label:

1. Click the Label tool in the toolbox.
2. Click in your document where you want the upper-left corner of the label or click-and-drag to define the size of the label.
3. Type the label text.

If you want to type just a few words, the first method is easiest, but labels aren't confined to just a few words. You could use a long label in the report header or footer section to describe the purpose or contents of the report or in the detail section to define a paragraph of text on a report that prints a personalized letter. For these long labels, it's better to draw the approximate size of the label with the mouse, let Access word-wrap the text as you type it, and adjust the size afterwards if necessary.

DRAWING LINES AND RECTANGLES

As you can see if you study the forms and reports you created with the Wizards, judicious use of lines and rectangles (boxes) can dress up a document and call attention to important elements. If you look at a form for which you've chosen the Shadowed look (such as the Tabular form you created in Chapter 7), you'll see that the "shadows" are actually rectangles the same size as the text boxes, offset slightly, like this:

Drawing lines and rectangles with the mouse is easy and intuitive:

1. Click the Line or Rectangle tool in the toolbox.
2. Position the cross hair in the mouse pointer where you want one end of the line or one corner of the rectangle on the form.
3. Click-and-drag to the opposite end of the line or the diagonally opposite corner of the rectangle.

NOTE

You're not limited to horizontal and vertical lines, although these are the most common; you can also draw diagonal lines.

Normally, both lines and rectangles are opaque. If you draw a new rectangle intended to enclose a group of existing objects, the rectangle will cover the objects completely. The solution to this problem depends on whether you want to see the rectangle as a solid block of color or as a simple border:

- *If you want an opaque rectangle,* select the rectangle and choose Format ➤ Send to Back to move it "behind" the other objects.
- *To display only the border,* select the rectangle and set the Back Style property to Clear in the property sheet or click the Clear button next to the Back Color samples in the palette.

To practice these techniques in the Contact Names and Addresses form:

1. Maximize the Form Design window. Make sure both the palette and toolbox are visible. Close the property sheet or move it most of the way off the screen.
2. Click the Line button in the toolbox and then draw a horizontal line the full width of the form below the ContactID and ContactType fields.
3. Click the white border color sample in the palette to change the color of the line you just drew. Click the button labeled *2* in the palette to change the line width to 2 points.
4. Move down the Note field slightly to make room for a box around the telephone numbers.
5. Click the Rectangle button in the toolbox and then draw a box around the two telephone numbers.
6. Click the Clear button next to the background color samples in the palette to make the box clear. Click the white border color sample to change the color of the rectangle border to white.
7. Switch to Form view and click the Restore button. Your screen should look like the one in Figure 11.12.
8. Close and save the form.

ADDING UNBOUND GRAPHICS TO A DOCUMENT

You can add a variety of graphics to your Access documents as *unbound OLE objects*—graphics objects not bound, or connected, to any field in a table. These objects can be drawings, scanned documents or pictures, spreadsheets, word processor documents, sound recordings, or video clips, to name just a few. The examples in this chapter use bitmap files supplied with Windows or simple drawings done with Paintbrush, so you can reproduce them (or more likely, surpass them artistically) if you're so inclined.

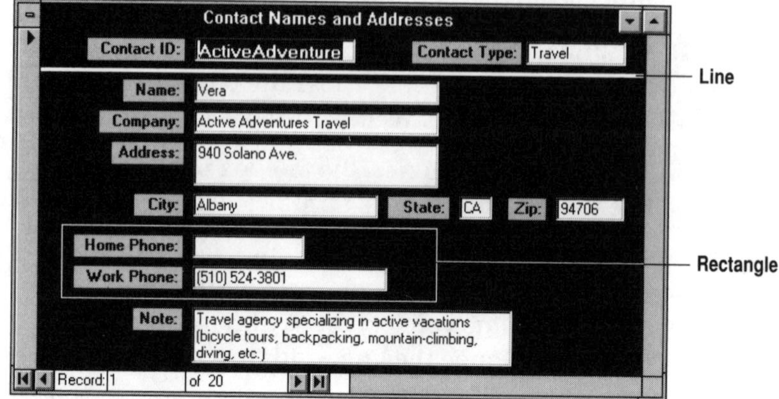

FIGURE 11.12 *You can use lines and boxes to separate and group fields.*

NOTE

The acronym OLE stands for object linking and embedding, the standard Windows method for accessing objects created by other applications by calling up those applications.

To experiment with unbound objects, open Paintbrush and draw a simple graphic to add to the Expenses report as your "company logo," and save it under the name LOGO.BMP. (If you've never used Paintbrush and don't want to tackle learning a new program, you can use another bitmap file.) To add the graphic you just created to the expenses report:

1. Maximize the Report Design View window.
2. Drag down the lower boundary of the report header section to make this section about 2 inches deep.

3. Select the three objects in this section (the line and two text boxes) and move them down as far as possible to make room for the graphic.
4. Click the Object Frame button in the toolbox.
5. Click-and-drag in the upper-left corner of the report header to draw a frame about 1¼ inches deep and 4 inches wide. Access displays the dialog box shown in Figure 11.13 to let you create a new OLE object or load in an existing file.

If you select one of the object types displayed in the scrolling list box, Access calls up the associated application to let you create a new object of that type. When you try this yourself, the list of object types you see probably won't exactly match the one in Figure 11.13; you'll see only object types supported by Windows programs installed on your computer. If you select Create from File, the dialog box changes as shown in Figure 11.14. If you know the name of your object file, you can enter it. Otherwise, click the Browse button to call up an Open File dialog box that lets you search for the file on your hard disk.

NOTE

As the term* object linking and embedding *implies, you can either create a* link *to the external object you're placing in your form or* embed *a copy of the object. If you check* Link *in the dialog box in Figure 11.14, you'll get a link to the object, which is stored outside your Access database. If you modify the object outside Access, you'll always see those changes in your document because there's just one copy of the object. If you* embed *the object, Access makes a copy and leaves the original object intact on disk. Any changes you make to the object from within Access affect only the copy stored in the .MDB file, not the original.

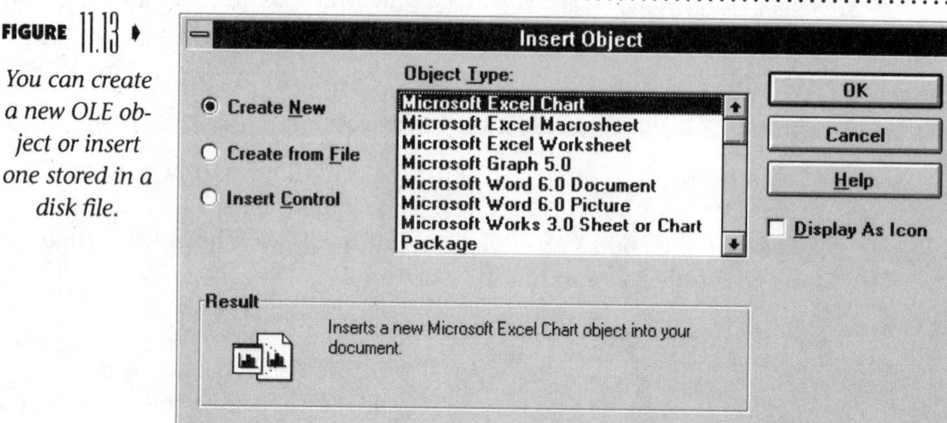

FIGURE 11.13 ▸ *You can create a new OLE object or insert one stored in a disk file.*

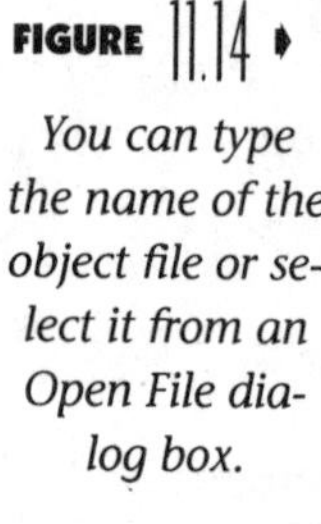

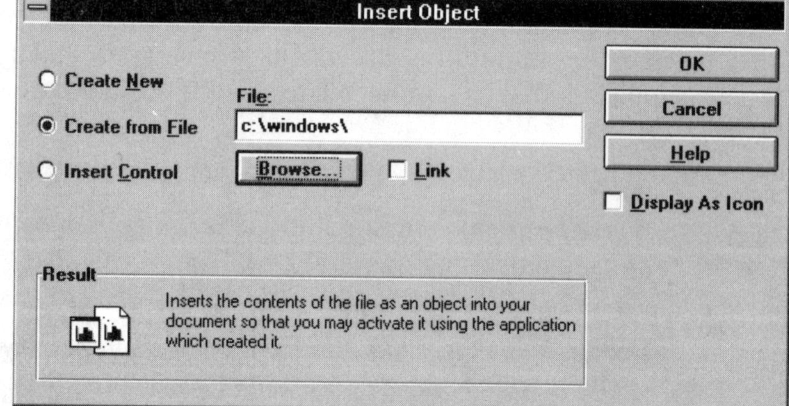

FIGURE 11.14 ▸ *You can type the name of the object file or select it from an Open File dialog box.*

To add the logo (or another bitmap file) to your report:

6. Click Create from File, and type or search for the name of your graphics file. If you didn't create a graphic, try using one of the .BMP files in your Windows program directory.
7. Click OK to insert the object into the frame on your form.

The relationship between the object and its frame is governed by the Size Mode property, which you'll find in the layout properties. You can choose any of the following options:

SETTING	DESCRIPTION
Clip	Crops the object to fit within the frame
Stretch	Adjusts the height and width of the object to match the size and proportions of the frame
Zoom	Adjusts the height and width of the object while retaining its original proportions so the whole object fits within the frame

The screen in Figure 11.15 illustrates the logo with the Size Mode property set to the default Clip and the object frame adjusted to match the size of the picture.

FIGURE 11.15

Access displays a graphic as it appears in the application that created it.

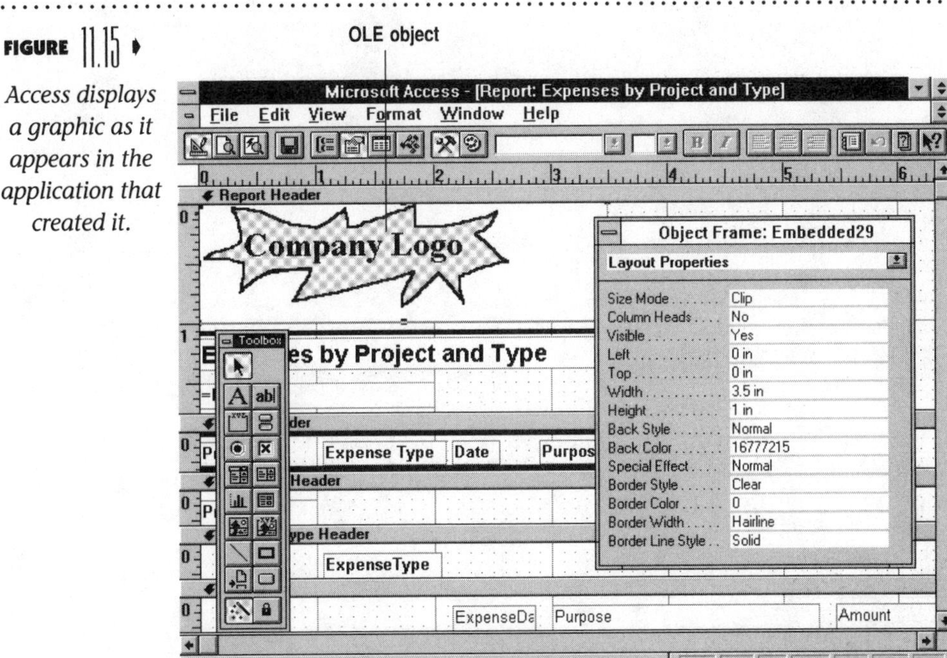

The only way to modify an OLE object is to call up the application that originally created it, which you do by double-clicking the object in Design view. While you're working in this program, the title bar will display a reminder of the source of the document you're editing, and there will be an option on the File menu for returning to Access. When you're finished making your changes, use this option to exit. You'll see an alert box that reminds you that you've changed the document and asks whether you want to update the object in your Access document.

WHAT'S NEXT

This chapter has described a variety of techniques you can use to modify the appearance of your Access forms and reports. Before you go on, you might want to spend some time polishing the forms and reports you've created using the Wizards. Chapter 12 explains how to modify the data displayed on a form or report.

Customizing the Data on Forms and Reports

Without minimizing the importance of esthetics, it's safe to say that we've saved the best for last. In this chapter you'll learn to make major changes in the data displayed on your forms and reports. Once you know how to add controls that display data, you can build new documents from scratch. This doesn't necessarily mean that you'll abandon the convenience and security of the Wizards, but it does give you the assurance that one way or another you'll be able to customize any form or report to satisfy all your evolving requirements.

CHANGING THE DATA SOURCE

Perhaps the most basic property of a form or report is the *data source*—the table or query that supplies the data for the document. The name of the data source is stored in the Record Source property, and you can switch to another data source by entering its name in the property sheet. To make it easy, Access gives you a combo box. The ability to switch data sources lets you use one form or report with several similar tables (for example, to print the same type of mailing labels from several different lists).

WARNING

Even if your document already contains controls that display data, Access won't stop you from choosing a table or query that doesn't contain all the fields on the document. When you try to run the form or report, Access will mistake the nonexistent fields for query parameters and will display dialog boxes to prompt you to enter these "parameters."

One very common reason for switching data sources is to use a report originally based on a table to print the data described by a query. For example, you could use the mailing label report you designed in Chapter 9 to print labels for various subsets of the Contacts table by choosing different queries as the data source. If you've already defined the query, so much the better, but you can create a query on the fly by clicking the Builder button to the right of the Record Source combo box. To experiment with the Query Builder, open the Expenses by Project and Type report in Design view and change the data source:

1. Make sure the property sheet is visible and that it displays the data properties for the report.
2. Display the drop-down list for the Record Source property, and choose Project Expenses from the list.
3. Click the Builder button to display the query, and then close the query and return to the property sheet.

WARNING

If you use this method to edit an existing query, Access applies your changes to the original query. If you want a new version of the query just for a specific document, use the File ➤ Save As command to save the modified query under a different name.

NOTE

If the data source is a table when you click the Builder button, Access displays an alert box that states, You have invoked the query builder on a table. Open a new query based on the table? ***Choose OK to go ahead and create a new query.***

ADDING CONTROLS TO A DOCUMENT

When you define a form or report from scratch, you'll obviously have to build the layout by adding controls to it one by one, but you'll also end up adding controls to the forms and reports generated by the Wizards. Even with the most thorough advance planning, there's nothing like using a form to enter data or showing a report to your coworkers to draw attention to what you've left out. If your initial data entry sessions bring to light the need to add fields to a table after you've already defined some forms and reports, you'll have to edit these documents to add the new fields.

If you're willing to go to a little extra trouble, you can build forms that would be impossible using only the Wizards. For example, you can add graphs to forms that already contain other objects or place fields in the forms generated by the Graph Wizard (which contain only a single graph object), and you can use controls such as combo boxes, list boxes, and command buttons, which are not supported by any of the Form Wizards.

Finally, when you use the Wizards to design forms and reports, you'll often intentionally omit fields that you know you'll need. For example, the Main/Subform Wizard uses a single-column layout for the fields on the main form, and if you choose too many fields, you'll have to scroll down to see the subform when you use the form to enter data. It's better to choose just a few fields for the main form and then modify the form later to add the rest and arrange them in an appropriate layout. You might also decide to stick with the Wizards to build the first version of a report simply because they make it so easy to pick fields and define sorting and grouping instructions.

CREATING TEXT BOXES

In Chapter 11 you learned to use the toolbox to add lines, boxes, and OLE objects to a document, and you can also use the toolbox by itself to create controls that display or collect data. However, it's much easier to use the field list, either alone or in combination with the toolbox. The *field list* displays a list of the fields in the source table or the columns in the source query for your document.

To display the field list or remove it from the screen if it is already visible, click the Field List button in the toolbar or choose View ➤ Field List. You can also close the Field List window by double-clicking the close box in the upper-left corner of the window.

You can use the field list alone to add a text box to a document: simply use the mouse to drag a field name from the list and drop it where you want it. To add more than one text box at a time to a document, select multiple fields in the field list and drag them as a group. When you drop the fields on your document, they'll end up in a single vertical column.

NOTE

When you build a new form or report from scratch, you'll get a label along with your text box. If you use the field list to add fields to a document created by a Wizard, you may not. Whether controls such as text boxes and combo boxes have labels depends on the Auto Label property; some of the Wizards leave this property set to Yes (the default), while others set it to No. In general, you'll want your new control to share the properties of similar controls on the form, so you won't have to change this setting.

Try using the field list to add the ProjectName and Budget fields to the Expenses by Project and Type report:

1. If the field list isn't already visible, click the Field List button in the toolbar.
2. Drag the ProjectName field from the field list and drop it close to the ProjectID text box in the ProjectID header section.
3. Widen the ProjectName text box to about 2 inches, and then click the Bold button in the toolbar.
4. Scroll down so you can see the whole ProjectID footer section and the section boundary below it.

5. Drag down the page footer section boundary about 1/4 inch.
6. Drag the Budget field from the field list and drop it under the two summary fields in the ProjectID footer section, a little bit to the left of these text boxes. Select the Budget text box and either of the other two objects and choose Format ➤ Align ➤ Right to align the new text box with the other two. Resize the Budget text box so all three are the same width.
7. Click the Label button in the toolbox and then click the form about an inch to the left of the Budget text box. Type the text of the new label, **Budget:**, and press ↵. Click the Right-Align Text button in the toolbar to right-justify the label.
8. Select the other three labels in the group footer and report footer sections without deselecting the Budget label, and choose Format ➤ Align ➤ Right. At this point your screen will look like the one in Figure 12.1.
9. Click the Print Preview button to preview the appearance of the report.
10. When you're satisfied with the report, close and save it.

CREATING CHECK BOXES, OPTION BUTTONS, AND TOGGLE BUTTONS

Access gives you three different visual metaphors for yes/no data: check boxes, option buttons (often called radio buttons), and toggle buttons. You've already seen numerous examples of these controls in the dialog boxes displayed by Access and the Wizards (and other Windows programs as well). In fact, many of the toolbar buttons you've been using in Design view are independent toggle buttons, including the Properties, Field List, Toolbox, Palette, Bold, and Italic buttons. Although Access lets you place any control on any document, you'll probably find the check box more suitable for reports than the other two. (Most people are accustomed to seeing check boxes on printed forms, whereas toggle buttons and option buttons seem out of place in a context in which you can't operate these controls.)

FIGURE 12.1

You can use the field list to add controls to a document.

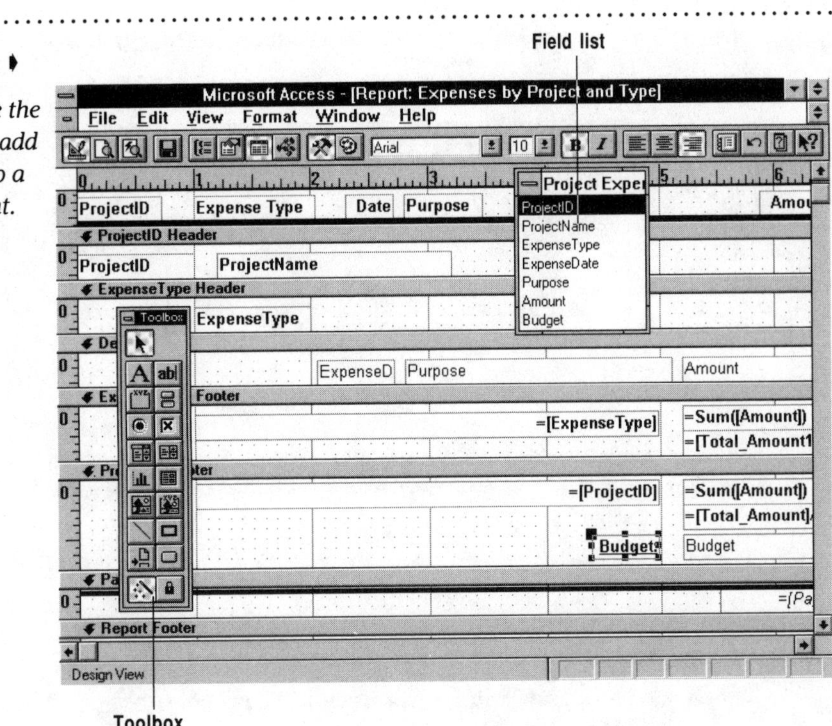

Like the yes/no data they represent, these controls can exist in two states. Figure 12.2 shows you two examples of each control so you can see what they look like when displaying the values Yes and No.

The easiest way to create a check box, option button, or toggle button is to use the toolbox and field list together:

1. Click the appropriate button in the toolbox.
2. Drag the field you want from the field list onto the document.

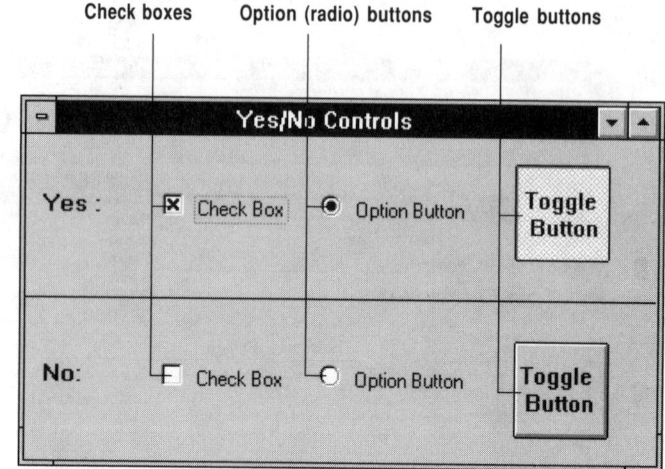

FIGURE 12.2 *You can use a check box, an option button, or a toggle button to display yes/no data.*

WARNING

Don't click the field in the field list and then release the mouse button; clicking does not associate the toolbox control with the field. You have to press and hold the left mouse button and drag the field onto the document before you release the mouse button.

NOTE

You can use this method to create a text box, but there's little advantage over simply dragging the field from the field list.

CREATING CALCULATED CONTROLS

You've already seen how to define calculated columns in a query, and you can use exactly the same expressions to display calculated values on a form or report. Since you're not displaying a field from any table, you can't use the field list to help you. Instead, you have to use the toolbox to create an *unbound* control—one not associated with any field in any table—and then write the expression that defines the value you want the control to display.

Here are the steps for creating an unbound text box:

1. Click the Text Box button in the toolbox.
2. Position the cross hair in the mouse pointer where you want the upper-left corner of the text box (not the associated label).
3. Click to create a standard-size text box or click-and-drag to create a text box and define its size at the same time.
4. To define the value you want to display in the text box, use either of these methods:
   - Click anywhere within the text box and type the expression that defines the calculation.
   - Enter the expression in the Control Source property in the property sheet.

NOTE

There's one important difference between entering an expression in a query and on a document: you must precede the expression with an equal sign to distinguish it from a field name.

If you looked closely at the expenses report you've been modifying, you've already seen several examples of calculated text boxes: the simple expression based on the Now function that displays the current date in the report header section, and the totals and percentages in the group footer and report footer sections.

The totals in the reports constructed by the Group/Totals and Summary Report Wizards are computed using *aggregate functions* that work much like the aggregate operators you learned to use in totals queries in Chapter 10. The aggregate functions have the same names as the corresponding query operators—Count, Sum, Avg, Min, Max, StdDev, and Var—and they accept the same types of input. (If you've forgotten the details, refer back to the list in Chapter 10.) For example, the sum of the Amount field in the Project Expenses report is computed with the expression

```
Sum([Amount])
```

NOTE

You don't have to enclose control names in brackets unless they include embedded spaces, but Access automatically adds the brackets for the sake of consistency if you do not.

When you use the aggregate functions on a form or report, Access figures out which records should contribute to the calculation, based on where you place the expression. The expression Sum(Amount) in the ExpenseType group header or group footer section calculates the total for the records in one group—one type of expense within one project. Exactly the same expression in the ProjectID group header or group footer section calculates the sum for the entire project. In the report header or footer section, you'll get the grand total for all the records printed on the report.

NOTE

Access has no problem printing group statistics before the group (in the group header section). If necessary, it makes two passes through the source table or query to make sure it has processed a given group of records and computed the necessary totals by the time it has to print them.

If you want to use a calculated field in the expression that defines another calculated field, you have to refer to it by its name. Up to this point you probably haven't paid much attention to the names of the controls in your documents—you probably view the controls and the underlying fields as interchangeable. Nevertheless, every object has a name, which you'll see if you choose Other Properties or All Properties from the combo box at the top of the property sheet.

NOTE

If you examine the documents generated by the Wizards, you'll see that the control names match the field names. When you add a control to a document yourself, Access assigns a name that combines the type of control with the next available sequential object number (for example, Field19). There's no need to change this default name unless you plan to refer to the field in a calculation.

The Wizards use names like Total_Amount (for the sum of the Amount field) and GrandTotal_Amount (for the grand total of the Amount field) for the calculated controls it creates. With these names, the expression that computes the percentage each project group represents of the grand total is

```
[Total_Amount]/[GrandTotal_Amount]
```

USING THE CONTROL WIZARDS

Access provides special help in creating controls that might otherwise present formidable barriers for beginners—list boxes, combo boxes, option groups, and command buttons. Like the other Wizards you've used, the Control Wizards ask you questions in a series of dialog boxes and then construct an object for you. The main difference lies in the way they're invoked. You don't call up the Control Wizards explicitly. If the Control Wizards button in the lower-left corner of the toolbox is selected (depressed), Access invokes these Wizards automatically whenever you begin defining a control for which a Wizard is available.

NOTE

If someone else set up your copy of Access or if other people use it, make sure the Control Wizards button is selected before you proceed with the examples in this chapter.

CREATING LIST BOXES AND COMBO BOXES

List boxes and combo boxes have a great deal in common: both let you choose a value from a list rather than type it. These controls are a boon to poor typists and a convenience for everyone, and they can greatly improve the accuracy and consistency of the information in your tables by preventing you from entering any value not found on the list. There are several important differences between these very similar controls:

- A combo box fits in about the same amount of space as a text box, whereas a list box almost always takes up more space vertically (although you don't need enough space to display all the list values at once).
- You can type an entry in a combo box rather than use the drop-down list, whereas you must select a list box item.
- You can specify whether a combo box should accept values that aren't on the list. This option gives you more flexibility but lets you enter incorrect data.

To begin creating a list box or combo box, you click the List Box or Combo Box button in the toolbox. Then position the crosshair in the mouse pointer where you want the upper-left corner of the control on the form, and click to create a standard-size control or click-and-drag to define the size of the list.

The sequence of Control Wizard dialog boxes is very similar for list boxes and combo boxes. To begin, you'll replace the Contact Type text box on the Contact Names and Addresses form with a list box:

1. Open the Contact Names and Addresses form in Design view, and maximize the window. Make sure the toolbox is visible and the Control Wizards button is selected.
2. Delete the Contact Type text box from the form.
3. Click the List Box button in the toolbox, and then click-and-drag to the right of the name and address fields to draw the list frame.

The first List Box Wizard dialog box lets you choose the source of the values displayed in the list, which can come from an existing table or query or from an explicit list of values that you type in yourself. The latter strategy, which you'll use for the Contact Type list, is appropriate for a short list that never (or, more realistically, rarely) changes. Otherwise, it's better to look up the list values in a table or query, even if you have to create a new table for this purpose, because the resulting list is dynamic—when you add records to the table that supplies the list values, they'll appear in the list the next time you open the form. You'll learn how to use this alternative later in this chapter.

If you elect to type in the list values, the Wizard displays the dialog box shown in Figure 12.3. First, you enter the number of columns you need in your list, and then you fill in the values themselves in the mini-datasheet in the dialog box. You can add as many items as you wish, and you can adjust the column widths by dragging the column selectors, just as you would in a table's datasheet. You can't edit the column headers, but they won't show in the finished list.

FIGURE 12.3 ▸

You can type in the values you want in a list box.

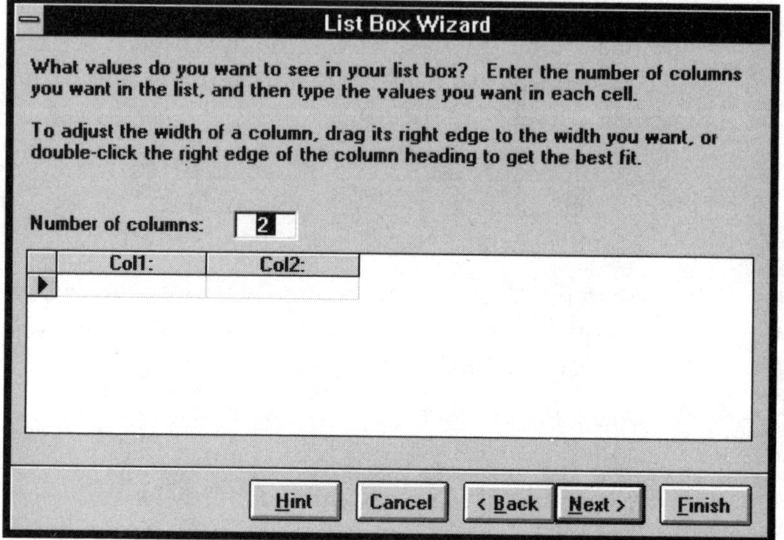

TIP

To automatically adjust the column width to just barely accommodate the contents, double-click the right column title border, where the mouse pointer looks like an arrow.

For the Contact Type list box:

4. Select I will type in the values that I want from the first List Box Wizard dialog box, and then click Next to move on to the next step.
5. Enter **1** for the number of columns.
6. Type the following list items: **Friend**, **Client**, **Graphic Design**, **Contractors**, **Travel**.
7. Click Next to move on to the next step.

The next dialog box, which is shown in Figure 12.4, lets you decide what you want Access to do with the value you choose from the list when you're using your form. You'd choose the first option, Remember the value for later use, if you wanted to use the list to choose an option and then make a decision or perform a calculation based on this choice. If you can't think of a likely example, don't worry; this option is more useful to programmers. If you want to use the list to select a value for a field rather than type it, choose Store that value in this field and then pick the field from the adjacent combo box. The field names in the drop-down list, which is visible in Figure 12.4, are drawn from the source table or query for your form.

The last dialog box asks for the text you want to display in the label that appears next to the list box or combo box on your form. The Wizard proposes a default control name (such as Field24 if there are already 23 objects on the form), but you'll want to enter a more descriptive label unless you're planning to delete it altogether.

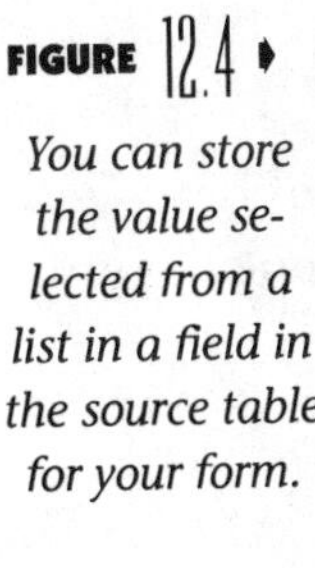

FIGURE 12.4

You can store the value selected from a list in a field in the source table for your form.

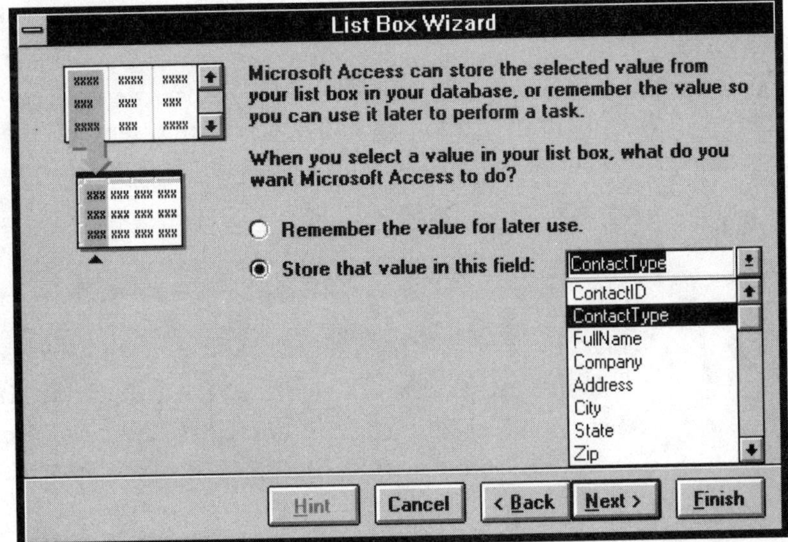

When you choose Finish in this dialog box, the Wizard places the finished list on your form. You'll probably need to resize the list frame, and it may take a few tries, switching back and forth between Form view and Form Design view, to get it right.

NOTE

If your list contains just a few items, you'll want to make the frame large enough to accommodate all of them. If the list is too long to see all at once, Access automatically adds a vertical scroll bar inside the frame. (You may have to widen the frame to accommodate it.)

To finish the Contact Type list box:

8. Choose Store that value in this field, pick ContactType from the combo box, and then click Next to move on to the next step.
9. Change the label text to **Type:**, and click Finish to place the list box on the form.
10. Adjust the size and/or position of the list and its label so that when you switch to Form view, the form resembles the one in Figure 12.5.
11. Close the form and save it.

NOTE

When you view existing records, Access highlights the list box item that matches the value of the underlying field in the current record. If the contents of the field don't match any list item, none will be highlighted.

FIGURE 12.5 ▸

You can use a list box to display a list of allowable values in a field.

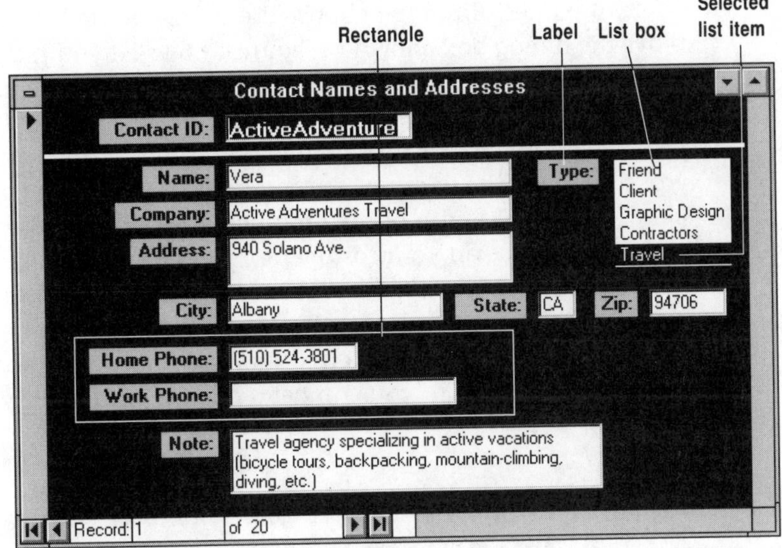

If you were creating a combo box based on a list of explicit values, the sequence of Control Wizard dialog boxes would be very similar. When you derive your list items from a table or query, there are a few extra steps. To explore this option, you'll create a combo box to replace the ContactID text box on the AutoForm you created for the Tasks table in Chapter 7. To begin:

1. Open the Tasks AutoForm form in Design view, and maximize the window.
2. Delete the ContactID text box.
3. Click the Combo Box button in the toolbox, and then click in the form where the ContactID text box used to be.
4. In the first Combo Box Wizard dialog box, choose I want the combo box to look up the values in a table or query, and click Next to move on to the next step.

The next dialog box lets you choose the table or query that will supply your list values. After you choose the source of the list items, it displays the dialog box shown in Figure 12.6 to let you pick the field(s) you want in the list. In most cases it's best to stick with just two or three fields, but feel free to choose more columns if you need them, especially if you're creating a combo box rather than a list box. Because you can adjust the width of the combo box control on the form independently of the width of the drop-down list, the list doesn't have to occupy extra space on your form when you're not actively using it. The next dialog box, which is shown in Figure 12.7 with three columns derived from the Contacts table, lets you adjust the column widths in the list. The Wizard shows you real data from the source table or query in the mini-datasheet, so you can get a good idea of what your list will look like.

FIGURE 12.6

You can choose the fields you want displayed in your combo box or list box.

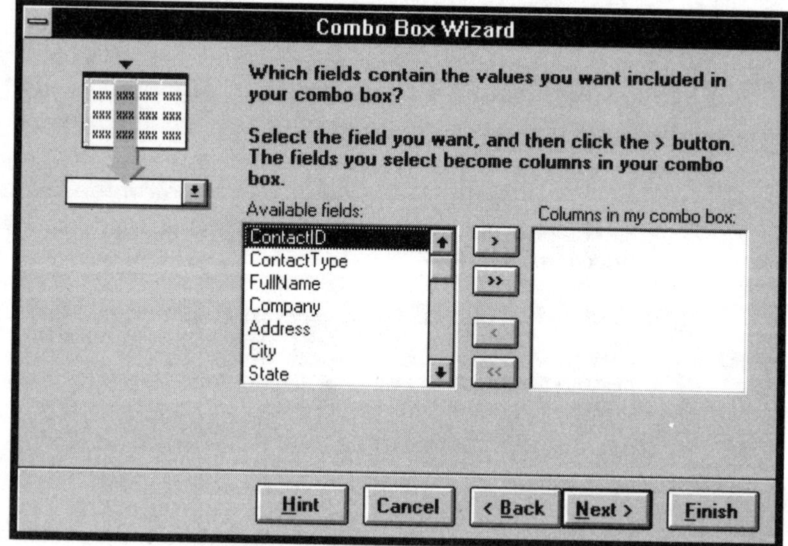

FIGURE 12.7 *You can adjust the widths of the columns in your combo box or list box.*

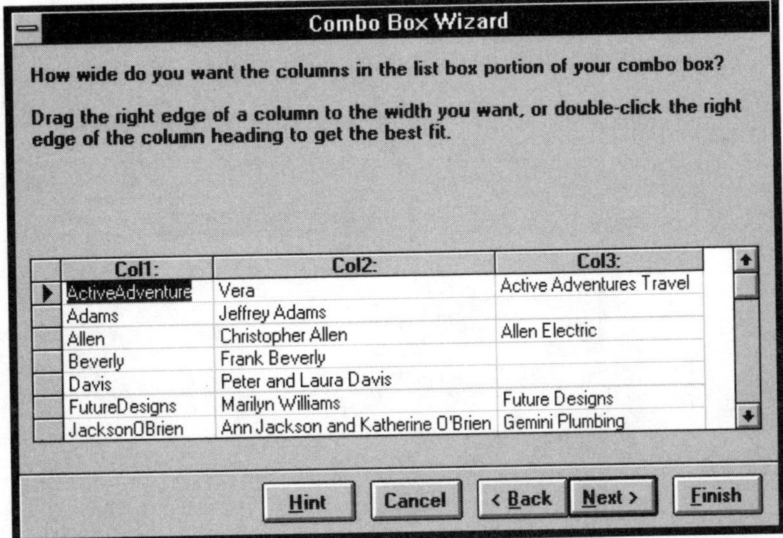

If you chose more than one field to display in the list, the Wizard displays the dialog box shown in Figure 12.8 to let you choose which list column you want associated with the field you're collecting with the combo box (which you'll choose in the next step, in a dialog box like the one shown in Figure 12.4). For example, in the combo box you're building to collect the ContactID field in the Tasks table, you'd choose the ContactID column in the dialog box in Figure 12.8.

To finish the Contact ID combo box:

5. Choose Contacts from the list of tables and queries, and click Next to move on to the next step.
6. Select the ContactID, FullName, and Company fields, and click Next to move on to the next step.
7. Adjust the column widths to approximately match those in Figure 12.7, and click Next to move on to the next step.

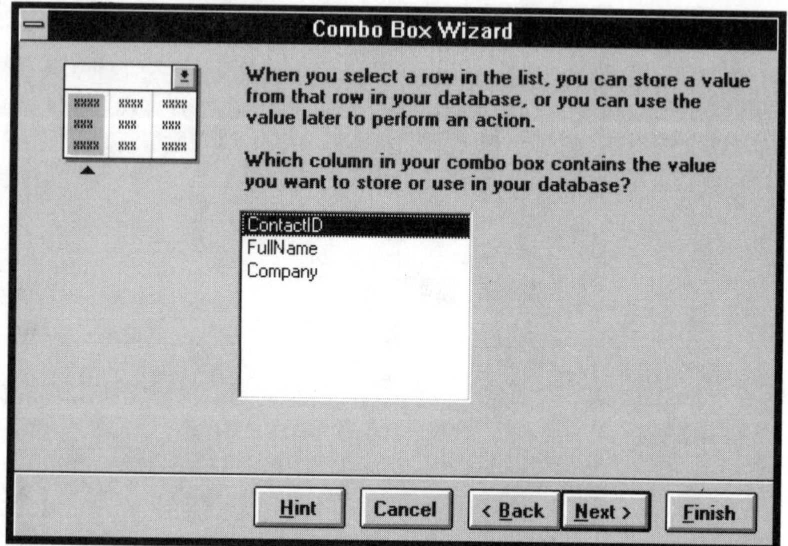

FIGURE 12.8 ▸ *You can specify which list field corresponds to the field on your form.*

8. Choose ContactID from the list of combo box list fields, and click Next to move on to the next step.
9. Choose Store that value in this field, pick ContactID from the combo box, and then click Next to move on to the next step.
10. Change the label text to **Contact ID:**, and click Finish to place the combo box on the form.
11. Adjust the size and/or position of the list and its label if necessary.
12. Switch to Form view and click the Restore control in the upper-right corner of the window so it isn't maximized. Display the drop-down list for your combo box. Your screen should look like the one in Figure 12.9.
13. Return to Form Design view and maximize the window again.

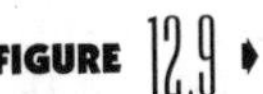

FIGURE 12.9

You can make a combo box drop-down list very wide without wasting space on your form.

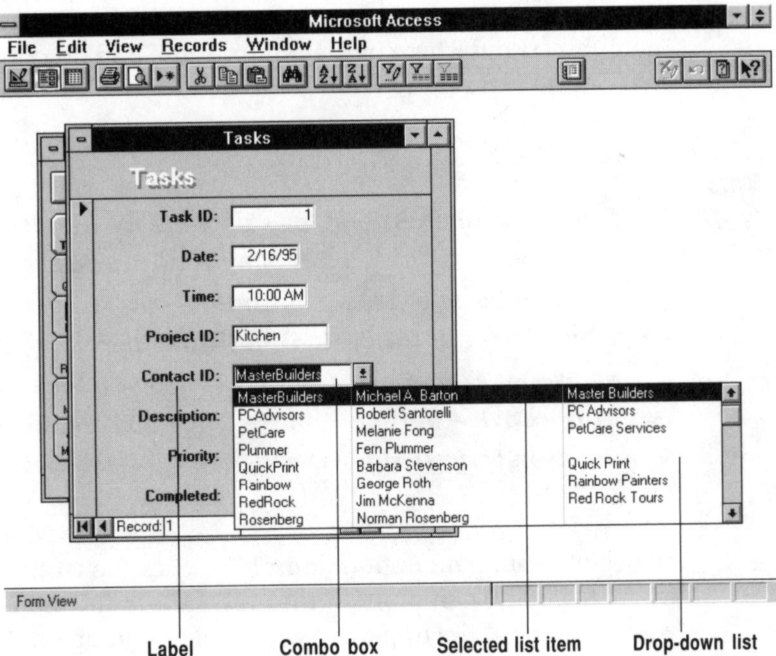

NOTE

If you derive your combo box list items from a table, Access displays them in primary key order. If you prefer a different order, define a query and base the combo box on the query, not the original table.

CREATING OPTION GROUPS

You learned earlier in this chapter how to use individual check boxes, toggle buttons, or option buttons (also known as *radio buttons*) to represent yes/no data. You can also use these controls in *option groups* to display sets of mutually exclusive options. The field you collect with an option group must be numeric, although you don't have to display the numbers anywhere in the group. You'll add an option group to the Tasks AutoForm for the Priority field.

NOTE

It's more common in Windows software to use option buttons on forms for groups of mutually exclusive options and check boxes or toggle buttons for single options. However, some of the buttons in the toolbar are option groups—for example, the Design View, Form View, and Datasheet View buttons and the three text alignment buttons in Form Design view.

To begin creating an option group, you click the Option Group button in the toolbox. Then position the cross hair in the mouse pointer where you want the upper-left corner of the group on the form, and click to create a standard-size option group frame or click-and-drag to create the group and define its size at the same time.

To create the Priority option group:

1. Delete the Priority text box from the form.
2. Click the Option Group button in the toolbox, and then click-and-drag in the lower-right corner of the form to define the size of the option group.

The first Option Group Wizard dialog box, which is shown in Figure 12.10, prompts you to enter the labels you want displayed next to the option controls in the group. You can adjust the width of the column of labels, but there's really no need to do so; it's easier to resize the option group object on the form when you're finished.

FIGURE 12.10 ▸

To define the options in a group, you enter their labels.

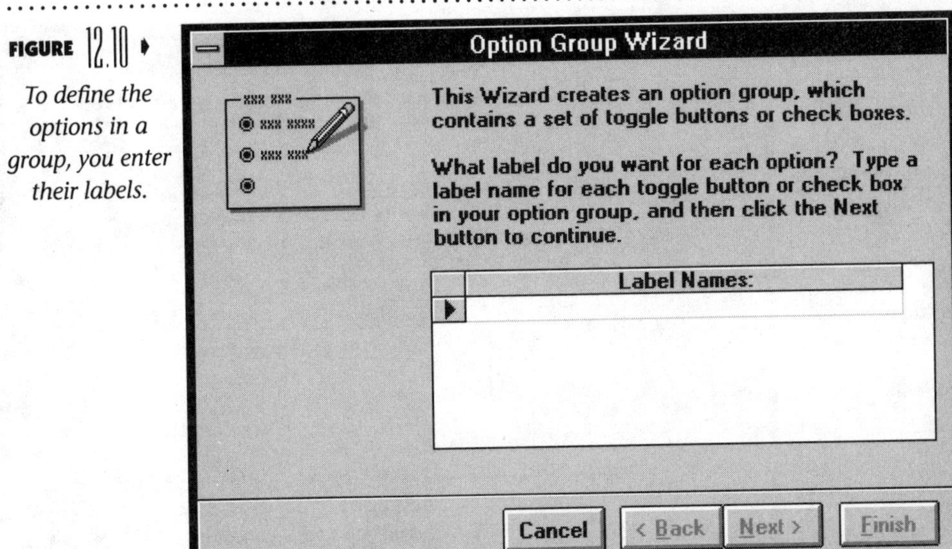

The next dialog box lets you choose a default value for new records from a combo box that displays the labels you entered in the previous step. You don't have to pick a default value. If you do, Access uses it only when you add new records to the table you're updating, *not* when you edit existing records, even if the field you're collecting is blank.

The next dialog box, shown in Figure 12.11, establishes the all-important correspondence between the option group labels and the values they represent. The defaults are sequential numbers starting with 1, but you can enter any values you wish. Next, like the other Control Wizards, the Option Group Wizard lets you choose which field you want to receive the value you select from the option group when you use the form.

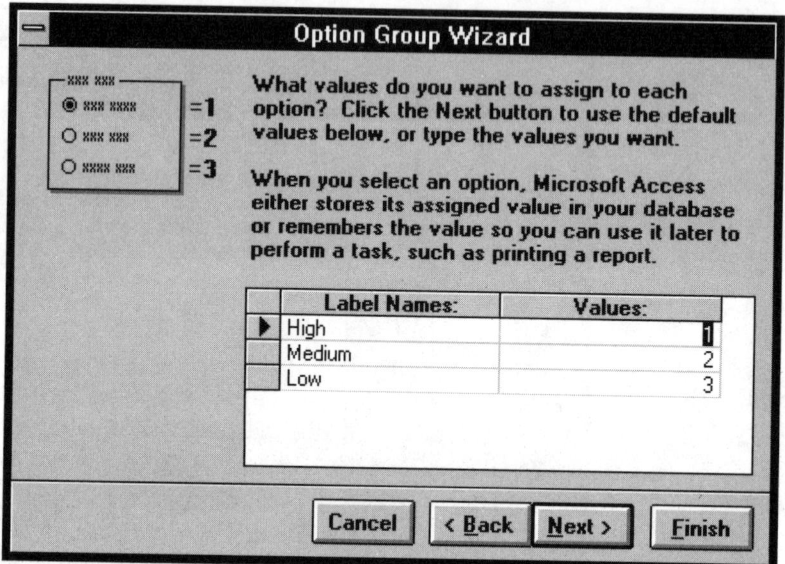
Option Group Wizard

What values do you want to assign to each option? Click the Next button to use the default values below, or type the values you want.

When you select an option, Microsoft Access either stores its assigned value in your database or remembers the value so you can use it later to perform a task, such as printing a report.

Label Names:	Values:
High	1
Medium	2
Low	3

FIGURE 12.11 *You specify the numeric values that correspond to the options in the group.*

Next, the Wizard displays the dialog box shown in Figure 12.12 to let you describe the overall appearance of the option group. To get an accurate picture of what your option group will look like, watch the Sample box on the left side of the dialog box.

NOTE

If you choose the Normal style (the default), the buttons and the frame around the option group appear flat. If you choose Raised or Sunken (as in Figure 12.12), the buttons or check boxes are displayed sunken, and the group frame is displayed using the style you selected.

To define the Priority option group:

3. Enter the labels **High**, **Medium**, and **Low**, as shown earlier in Figure 12.10, and then click Next to move on to the next step.

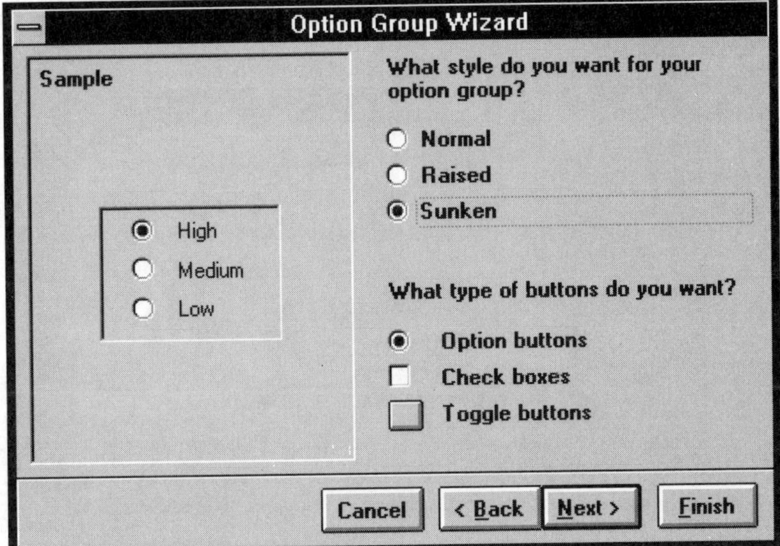

FIGURE 12.12 ▸ *You can select the type of option control and its appearance.*

4. Select High for the default value, and then click Next to move on to the next step.
5. Retain the default values—1, 2, and 3—for the High, Medium, and Low options, and then click Next to move on to the next step.
6. Select Priority as the field updated by the option group, and then click Next to move on to the next step.
7. Choose the Sunken style, and retain the default control type, option buttons. Click Next to move on to the next step.
8. Enter **Priority:** as the option group label (title), and click Finish.
9. Adjust the size and/or position of the group and the overall height and width of the form if necessary. Figure 12.13 shows what the option group looks like in Form view.
10. Close and save the form.

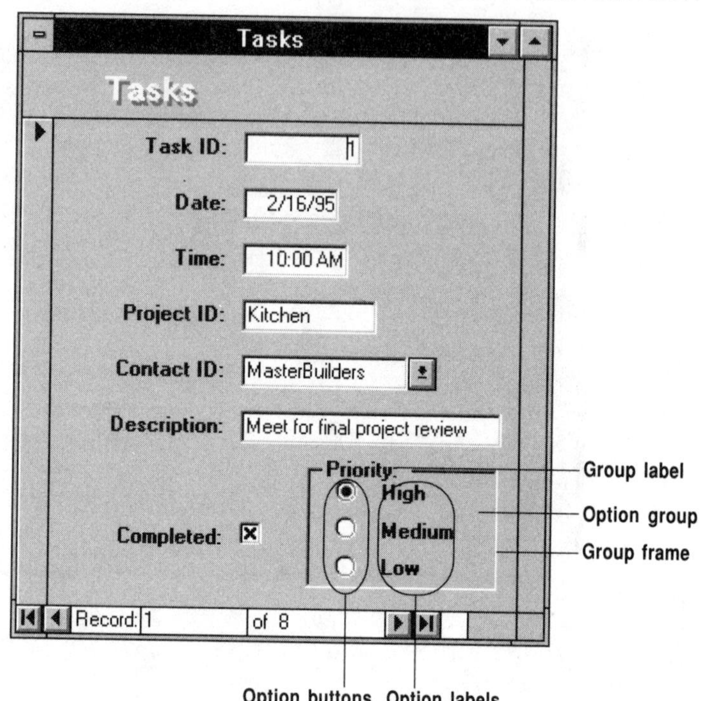

FIGURE 12.13 ▸ *You can create an option group consisting of option buttons, toggle buttons, or check boxes.*

If you dissect the option group you just created, you'll see that it consists of several objects: the individual button controls that display the options; the group frame, which represents the whole group; and a label superimposed on the upper frame border. If you want to select the group as a whole (for example, to move it), click the frame. To modify an individual component of the group, click the object you want to operate on.

CREATING COMMAND BUTTONS

If you didn't have the Control Wizards to help you, defining list and option group controls would be difficult and confusing but not impossible—it's all done with properties. If you're interested, take a look at the data properties of the list boxes, combo boxes, and option groups you define using the Wizards. Defining command buttons is more difficult; without the Control Wizards you'd have to build macros or write Access Basic code, but the Control Wizards make it easy.

You already know from your experience with *using* command buttons that clicking a button always carries out an action. When you use the Command Button Wizard, your most important task is defining this action. You can use a command button on a form to open another form, place a filter in effect, print a report or carry out a mail merge, open another Windows application, or substitute your own custom record navigation and editing controls for the standard Access controls and menu options.

As a simple example, you'll add a command button to the Projects and Expenses form to open the Tasks AutoForm form. To begin:

1. Open the Projects and Expenses form in Design view.
2. Click the Command Button button in the toolbox.
3. Position the crosshair in the upper-right portion of the form and click to place the button and invoke the Control Wizard. (You'll move and/or resize the button later if necessary.)

The central Command Button Wizard dialog box, which is shown in Figure 12.14, lets you pick the action you want your button to trigger. The structure of this dialog box is reminiscent of the one used by the Table Wizard to let you pick fields; it displays two scrolling lists, and your selection in the first governs the options displayed in the other. Scroll through the general action categories in the Categories list on the left, and watch the list of specific actions change in the list labeled When button is pressed.

The next series of dialog boxes collects any additional information the Control Wizard needs to finish defining your button, and the details depend on the action you selected in the previous step. Many of the actions, including the record navigation, editing, and filter actions, require no further information; they simply emulate the corresponding toolbar buttons or menu options.

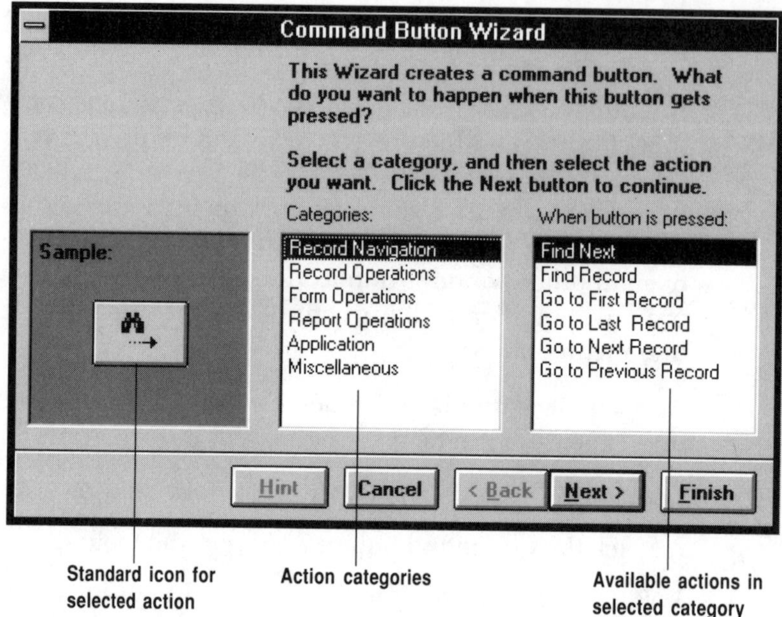

FIGURE 12.14 *To define a command button, you choose an action from the Control Wizard's list.*

If you chose the Open Form option or the options that print or preview reports, the Wizard shows you a list of available documents. After you choose the one you want to open, it displays a dialog box that asks, in effect, whether this document is linked to the one you're calling it from. When you're opening a form, you answer this question by choosing either Open the form and find specific data to display in it or Open the form and show all the records.

The latter is the default option, but when you're opening one form from another, it's almost never what you want; usually you'll want the form you're opening to display data that matches the current record in the form that's already open. For example, when you open the Tasks AutoForm form from the Projects and Expenses form, you'll want to see only tasks for the current project. To let you define the link between the two forms, the Wizard displays the dialog box shown in Figure 12.15.

FIGURE 12.15

When you open one document from another, you can define the link between the two.

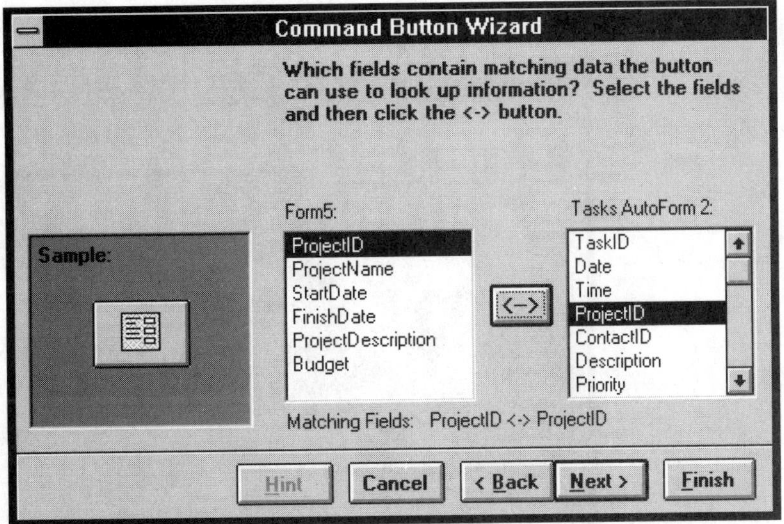

For the command button you're defining:

4. Highlight Form Operations in the Categories list, highlight Open Form in the **When button is pressed** list, and then click Next to move on to the next step.
5. Choose the Tasks AutoForm as the form you're opening, and click Next to move on to the next step.
6. Choose **Open the form and find specific data to display in it**, and click Next to move on to the next step.
7. Highlight ProjectID in both form lists and then click the button between the two lists to establish the link between the two forms. Click Next to move on to the next step.

Once you've filled in the details about the action you want your button to carry out, the Wizard displays the dialog box shown in Figure 12.16 to let you customize its appearance. You can display either an icon or text on the button:

- *To display text,* click the Text radio button and enter your text in the adjacent text box.

FIGURE 12.16 ➧

You can display a picture or text on a command button.

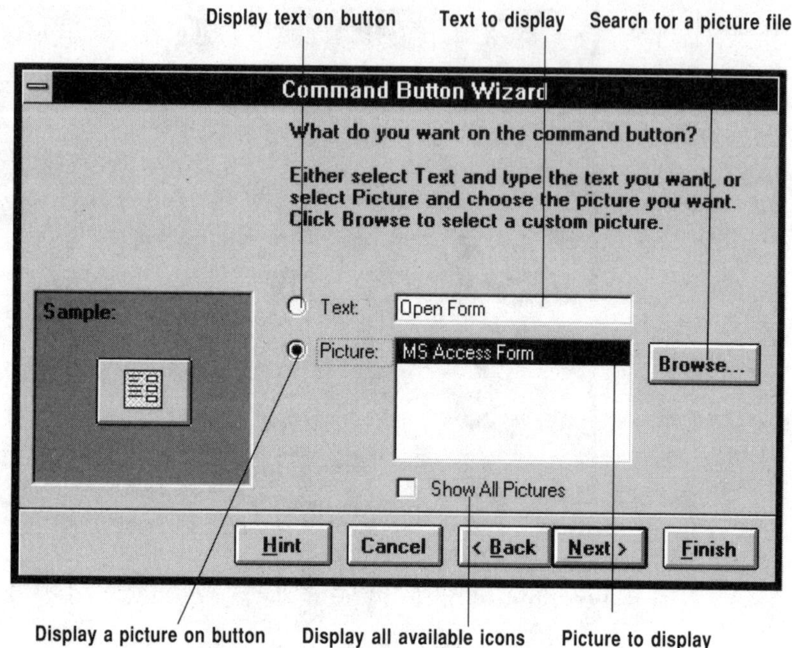

- *To display the standard icon for the action you selected,* click Picture.
- *To choose an icon from all available Access icons,* check Show All Pictures and then select an icon from the Picture list.
- *To display a picture stored in a .BMP (bitmap) or .ICO (icon) file outside Access (such as an image you've drawn using a paint program),* click Browse to invoke an Open File dialog box and search for the bitmap file.

If you don't recognize the icon you want from the names in the Picture list, scroll through the list and watch the Sample area on the left side of the dialog box, which shows you what your button will look like with the highlighted picture on its face.

TIP

If you elect to display text on the button face, don't worry if your text doesn't fit on the standard-size button displayed in the Sample area. Access resizes the button automatically to accommodate its label when the Wizard places it on your form, and you can adjust the size yourself if necessary once the Wizard has finished its job.

The last Command Button Wizard dialog box prompts you to enter a name for your button. Unlike the analogous entry for the various list box controls, which also serves as a visible label, the name of a command button isn't displayed anywhere on the form, so there's no need to change the default name (Button15 or something similar).

To finish your command button:

8. Click Show All Pictures and scroll through some of the icons to get an idea of what's available.
9. Click Text and enter **Display Tasks** in the adjacent text box. Click Next to move on to the next step.
10. Retain the default button name and click Finish to complete your command button.
11. Switch to Form view and make the window as large as you can without maximizing it. (If you maximize the Form View window, the Tasks AutoForm will also be maximized when you display it using your new command button.)
12. Click the command button to display the tasks for the first project. Move the Tasks AutoForm window to the right so your screen looks something like the one in Figure 12.17.

FIGURE 12.17 ▸ *When you use a command button to open a form, you get an independent form, not a subform.*

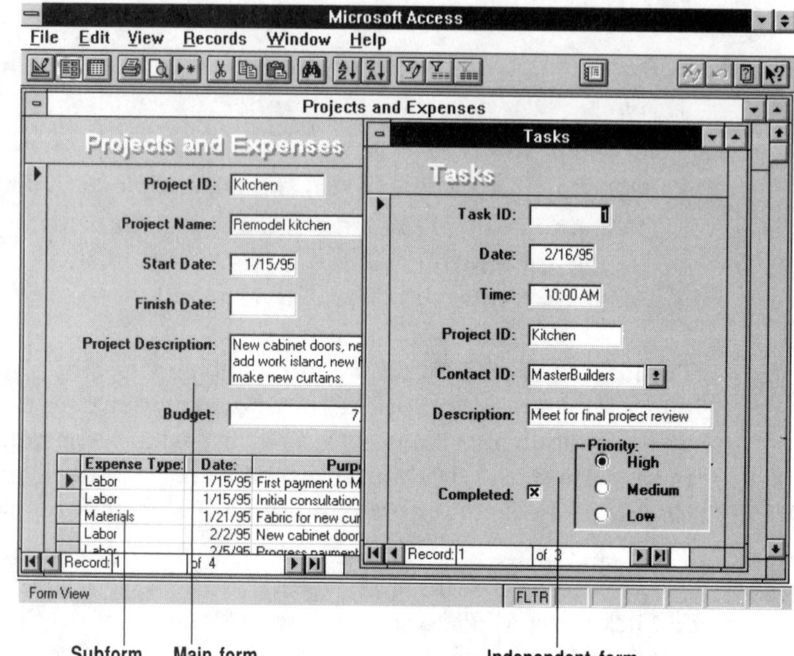

13. Close the Tasks AutoForm, move to another project record, and redisplay the tasks to confirm that you see only tasks related to the current project record.

14. Close both forms, and save your changes to the Projects and Expenses form.

NOTE

When you open one form from another, you'll initially see only matching records in the called form. However, the called form is an independent form open on the Access desktop, not a subform. If you move to another record in the main form without closing the called form, the two forms do not stay in synch.

WORKING WITH GRAPHICS

In Chapters 7 and 11 you learned to use graphics as essentially independent objects on Access documents—you used the Graph Wizard to create a form that consists entirely of a single graph, and you learned to place graphics (or other OLE objects) on documents. In this section you'll learn how to create graphs that are linked to the data on a form or report and how to store OLE objects in fields in your tables.

USING BOUND OLE OBJECTS

When you add an unbound OLE object, such as a graphics image stored in a bitmap file, to an Access document, the object becomes part of the form or report itself, not part of the data in the table you're displaying on the document. To store an OLE object such as a photograph, sound recording, or video clip in a table, you have to create an OLE object field (like the Photograph field in the Contacts table) and use a *bound OLE object* to display it on your documents.

NOTE

The word* bound *in this description reminds you that the object is connected to a field in the table you're using as the data source for the form or report, not that the object comes from outside Access.

The easiest way to add a bound OLE object to a document is to use the field list and toolbox together, exactly as you do to create any other type of bound control:

1. Click the Bound Object Frame button in the toolbox.
2. Drag the OLE object field from the field list onto the document.
3. If necessary, resize the object frame.
4. If necessary, change the Size Mode property from the default Clip to Stretch or Zoom.

These steps take care of displaying the OLE object on the document. To make sure you have something to display, there are two easy methods for getting OLE data into a field in your table, which you can use in Datasheet view as well as in Form view. The first method is the most convenient if you already have the OLE object stored in a file on disk:

1. Click the column (in Datasheet view) or object frame (in Form view).
2. Choose Edit ➤ Insert Object. Access displays the same dialog box shown in Figure 11.14 in Chapter 11 to allow you to identify or create the file that contains your OLE object.
3. Check Link to create a link to the original object, or leave it unchecked to embed a copy of the object in your database.
4. Click OK.

NOTE

There's no place to enter a global description of the type of OLE object a field is supposed to contain, and that's because Access doesn't restrict you to a single type of OLE object. Nothing will prevent you from putting a resume typed into a word processor document into the Photograph field in one record in the Contacts table, a sound recording in another, and a scanned photograph in a third.

If you still have open the application you used to create an object, you can use a simple cut-and-paste method involving the Windows clipboard to embed a copy of the OLE object into your Access table:

1. Use the application's selection and copy commands to select the data and copy it to the clipboard.
2. Switch back to Access using any standard Windows method.
3. If you don't already have a table open in Datasheet view or Form view, open one.

4. Click the column (in Datasheet view) or object frame (in Form view).
5. To paste in the data on the clipboard as a standard OLE object, select Edit ➤ Paste, press Ctrl+V, or right-click and then select Paste from the popup menu.

NOTE

You can't use this method to create a link to an OLE object file because Access can't be sure that the data you copied to the clipboard was ever saved as a file. In fact, once you've pasted the data into your Access database, there's no need to save it.

To edit an OLE object later, double-click the field, either in Datasheet view or in a custom form. Access itself can't edit an OLE object. Instead, it calls up the application that created the object. If that application isn't available, you'll get an error message.

Try a simple experiment with the Photograph field:

1. Open the Contact Names and Addresses form in Design view and maximize the Design View window.
2. Make sure the toolbox and field list are visible.
3. Click the Bound Object Frame button in the toolbox, and then drag the Photograph field from the field list onto the lower-right region on the form.
4. Resize the object frame to about 2 inches square, and then resize the form so it ends up about 6 inches wide and 3¾ inches high. Delete the label.
5. Switch to Form view and move to the third record (the one for Christopher Allen).
6. Press Alt+Tab (more than once if necessary) to return to the Program Manager.

7. Open Paintbrush, and draw a sketch of a face (or, if you're even less artistic than this author, a scribble).

8. Use the selection tool to enclose the face, and then select Edit ➤ Copy to copy the image to the clipboard.

9. Press Alt+Tab to return to Access.

10. Click the Photograph frame and select Edit ➤ Paste or press Ctrl+V.

11. Move to another record and then return to record 3 to verify that the image you pasted in is displayed. Your form will look something like the one in Figure 12.18.

12. Double-click the Photograph column to open the picture in Paintbrush.

13. Edit the image in some small way, and then choose File ➤ Exit and Return to Contact Names and Addresses. Paintbrush displays an alert box warning you that The command you have chosen will close the connection between this open embedded object and Contact Names and Addresses. Do you want to update the open embedded object before proceeding?

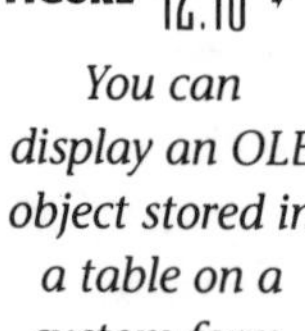

FIGURE 12.18 ➧

You can display an OLE object stored in a table on a custom form.

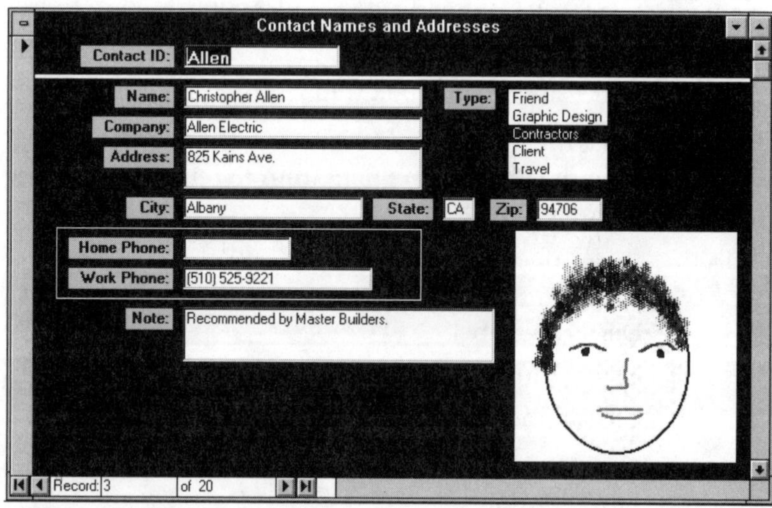

14. Choose Yes to update the image in the Access table.
15. Close and save your form.

NOTE

When you display a table that contains OLE objects in Datasheet view, you'll see only the source of the object (for example,* Paintbrush Picture*) in the OLE object columns, but that's the only difference between Datasheet view and Form view. You can use exactly the same commands to insert an OLE object into a field and to call up the original application to edit it.

ADDING A GRAPH TO A FORM

In Chapter 7 you learned to create a simple graph using the Graph Form Wizard. If you open the resulting form in Design view, you'll see that it has just one object on it—the graph. You can also add a graph to an existing form and link the graph to the form so that the data changes to match the other fields in the form. For example, you could display a graph of expenses by type on a form based on the Projects table so that the graph shows only expenses for the current project record. This type of form, which is shown in Figure 12.19, is similar to the Main/Subform layout, with the graph substituting for the subform.

To build this form:

1. Create a new form (without using a Wizard) with the Projects table as the data source.
2. Maximize the Form Design View window and expand the detail section to about 3 inches high.
3. Display the field list and toolbox if they are not already visible.
4. Drag the ProjectID and ProjectName fields from the field list and place them near the top of the form. If you wish, move and resize the labels and text boxes to match Figure 12.19.

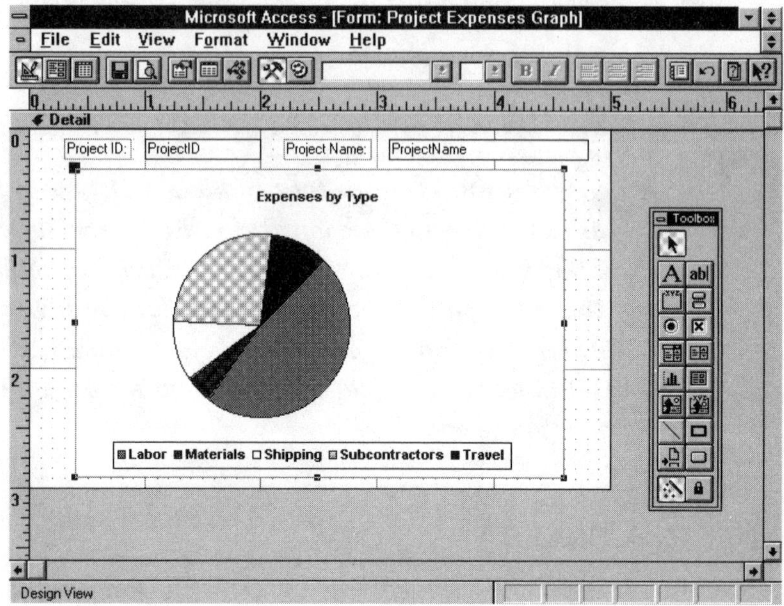

FIGURE 12.19 *You can add a linked graph to a form that contains other objects.*

5. To add the graph to the form, click the Graph button in the toolbox, and then click-and-drag in the form to draw a frame that fills most of the remaining space.

When you add a graph to an existing form, Access calls up the same Graph Wizard you used in Chapter 7, with a few small but significant differences in the sequence of dialog boxes to let you link the graph to the form. After you choose the data source and the fields you want on your graph, the Wizard displays an alert box that asks, Do you want to link the data in your graph to a field on the form? If you select Yes, the Wizard displays the dialog box shown in Figure 12.20 to allow you to define the links. Like the Main/Subform Wizard, the Graph Wizard shows you a diagram of the relationship between the main form and the graph and lets you define the link much the same way.

To define the graph in your new form:

6. In the first Graph Wizard dialog box, choose the Expenses table as the data source for the graph, and then click Next to move on to the next step.

7. Choose the ExpenseType and Amount fields for the graph, and then click Next to move on to the next step.
8. Choose Count the number of records in each category, and then click Next to move on to the next step.
9. Choose Yes from the alert box that asks if you want to link the graph to the form.
10. Highlight ProjectID in the Fields on the form list and the Fields in the graph list and click the button between the two lists to establish the link shown in Figure 12.20. Click Next to move on to the next step.
11. Choose pie chart as the graph style, make sure the Data Series in option is set to Columns, and then click Next to move on to the next step.
12. Enter the title **Expenses by Type** for the graph, and leave the Yes radio button selected to include a legend. Click Finish to complete the graph.
13. In Form Design view, Access displays a replica of the completed graph like the one in Figure 10.19; this image reflects the data in the whole Expenses table.

FIGURE 12.20

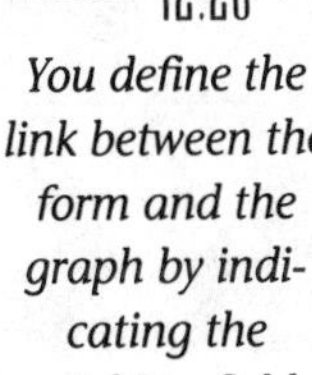

You define the link between the form and the graph by indicating the matching fields.

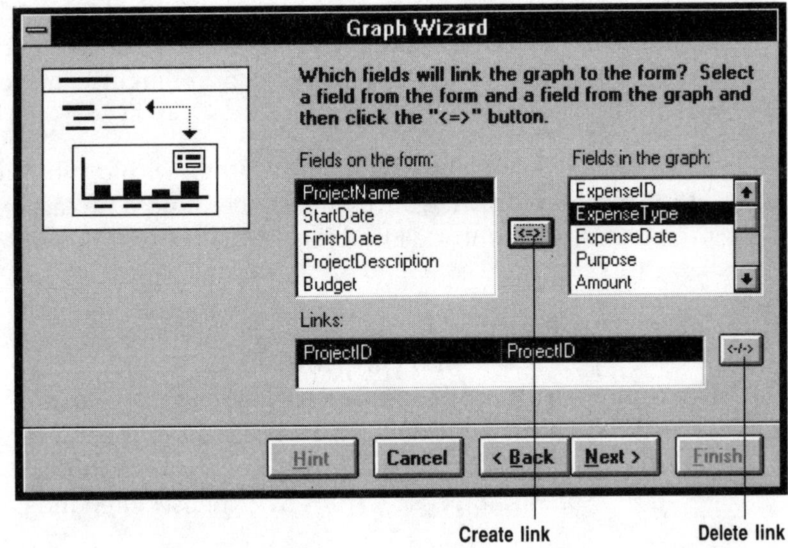

14. Switch to Form view to display the finished form, and verify that the graph changes when you move from one record to the next to show only expenses connected to the current project record.

15. Close the form and save it under the name Project Expenses Graph.

WORKING WITH SUBFORMS AND SUBREPORTS

You've already seen how easy it is to use the Main/Subform Wizard to build a form with a subform, because the Wizard takes care of placing and linking the two forms. If you've predefined the relationships in your database, though, it's almost as easy to construct this form style yourself. One reason you might want to do this is to add a second subform to a main form. There's no rule in Access that prohibits this; it's just not possible using the Wizard. Another reason is the lack of a comparable "Main/Subreport" Wizard for *reports*. This too is a limitation of the Wizards, not Access itself.

DEFINING A SUBFORM OR SUBREPORT

The easiest way to add a subform or subreport to another document is to build the subform or subreport first and then drag it from the Database window onto the main document. Remember that the subform doesn't have to be displayed in Datasheet view. The screen in Figure 12.21 shows a version of the Projects and Expenses form that also includes tasks in a second subform.

You already know one way to build a *form* with a subform (by using the Main/Subform Wizard). Now try defining a project *report* that lists expenses in an embedded subreport like the one shown in Figure 12.22:

1. To build the subreport, use the Report Wizard to construct a Tabular report based on the Expenses table. Include all the fields except ProjectID and ExpenseID (the ProjectID field, along with the other Projects table data, will be printed in the main report, and the ExpenseID field doesn't provide any meaningful information). Sort the expense records by ExpenseDate, and choose the

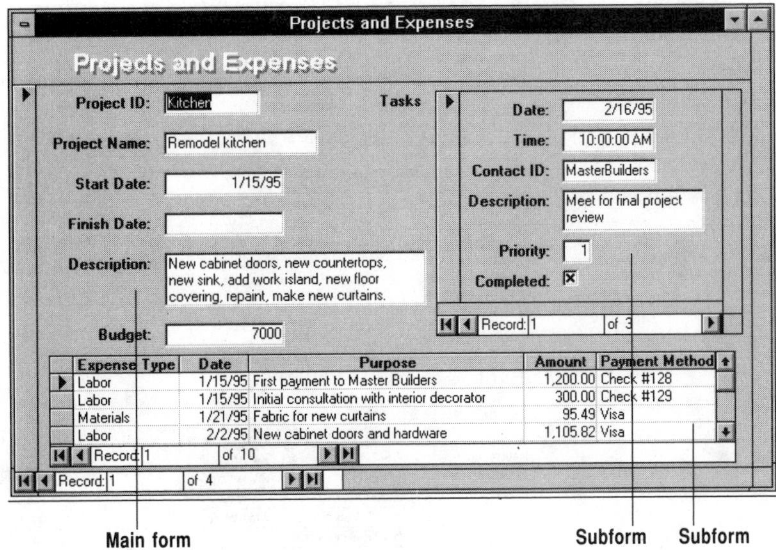

FIGURE 12.21 *A form can include more than one subform.*

Ledger style and portrait orientation. Retain the default title, Expenses. Preview the report and save it under the name Expenses Subreport.

2. To build the main report, use the Report Wizard to construct a Single-Column report based on the Projects table. Include all the fields, sort the records by ProjectID, and choose the Presentation style and portrait orientation. Retain the default title, Projects, and check **Print each record on a new page** and **Show the title on each page** in the last Report Wizard dialog box. Preview the report and save it under the name Projects and Expenses.
3. Open the Projects and Expenses report in Design view. Enlarge the window but don't maximize it. Make sure you can see part of the Database window behind the Report Design window.
4. Drag down the lower boundary of the detail section until the section is about 3½ inches high.
5. Click the Database window to bring it in front of the Report Design window.

FIGURE 12.22

You can embed one report in another and link the two based on a common field.

Projects

14-Mar-95

Project ID: Kitchen

Project Name: Remodel kitchen

Start Date: 1/15/95

Finish Date:

Project Description: New cabinet doors, new countertops, new sink, add work island, new floor covering, repaint, make new curtains.

Budget: 7,000.00

Main report

Expenses

14-Mar-95

Labor	1/15/95	Initial consultation with inerior de	300.00	Check #129
Labor	1/15/95	First payment to Master Builders	1,200.00	Check #128
Materials	1/21/95	Fabric for new curtains	95.49	Visa
Labor	2/2/95	New cabinet doors and hardware	1,105.82	Visa
Labor	2/5/95	Progress payment to Master Buil	2,000.00	Check #202
Labor	2/13/95	Allen Electric	465.00	Check #231
Labor	2/15/95	Rainbow Painters	640.00	Check #248
Labor	2/15/95	Gemini Plumbing	320.00	Check #243
Labor	2/16/95	Final payment to Master Builders	1,100.00	Check #250
Labor	2/16/95	Final payment to interior decorat	400.00	Check #249

7,626.31

Subreport

6. Click the Expenses Subreport, drag it onto the main report, and drop it below the Budget field.
7. Move the subreport all the way to the left and widen it slightly. Delete the label object.
8. Drag the right form boundary to line up with the 6½-inch mark on the ruler. If necessary, readjust the height of the detail section so it's just big enough for the subreport.
9. Move the page number in the page footer to the right, to line up with the right side of the subreport object.
10. Preview the report, and then return to Design view. Your report should look like the one in Figure 12.22.

When you use the drag-and-drop method to create a subform or subreport, Access automatically links the two documents based on the relationships saved in the database so that the subform or subreport displays only data that matches the current record in the main document. Even if you haven't formally defined any relationships, Access can link the forms if there's a common field. If you want to see how the forms are linked, look at the data properties of the subform or subreport; the Link Child Fields and Link Master Fields properties identify the matching fields in the source tables (or queries).

There are a few minor problems with the subreport you just created: the date isn't really necessary, the column widths aren't perfect, and the column titles are missing. You can correct these problems easily by editing the subreport.

EDITING A SUBFORM OR SUBREPORT

When you examine a document that contains a subform or subreport, you'll see that the subform is displayed as a simple frame, with no indication of how it will look in the finished document. To edit the subform or subreport, double-click anywhere within the object frame on the main document. The screen in Figure 12.23 illustrates the Expenses subform from the Projects and Expenses form you created in Chapter 7 as it appears when you open it in Form Design view from the main form.

FIGURE 12.23 ▸

You can open a subform in Design view from the main form.

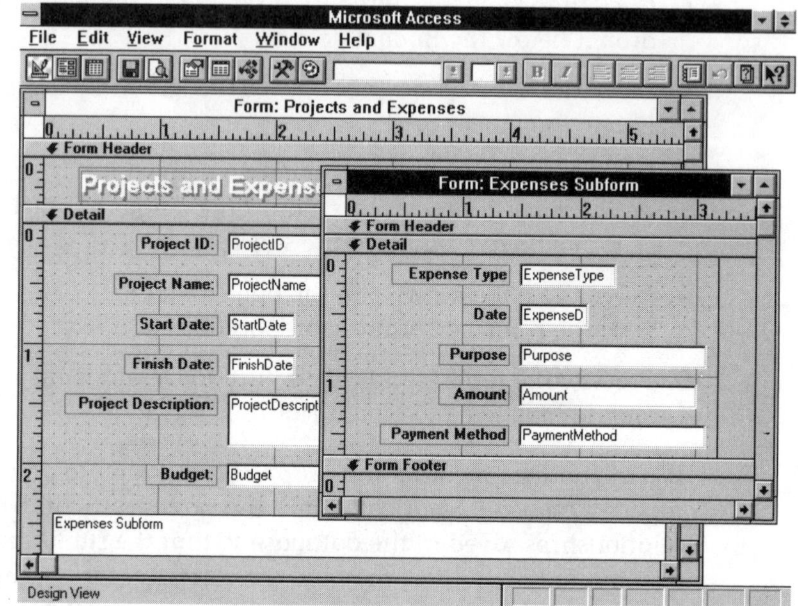

TIP

Because a subform or subreport is an independent object, stored separately in your database, you can also open it in Design view from the Database window, just as you would any other form or report.

You might be surprised to find that you still don't see the subform in Datasheet view. That's because the form is set up as a Single-Column form; Access simply displays it in Datasheet view in the main form because the Main/Subform Wizard sets the Default View property to Datasheet. You can make some modifications to the subform in Form Design view:

- *To change the column titles in the subform Datasheet view,* edit the labels associated with the text boxes.
- *To rearrange the columns,* change the tab order.

If you want to customize the layout of the datasheet, you have to switch to Datasheet view (by clicking the Datasheet View button in the toolbar). You can then use the techniques you learned in Chapter 5 to make these modifications:

- Change the column widths
- Change the row height
- Customize the font and font styles
- Freeze columns

NOTE

To adjust the overall width of the subform datasheet, resize the subform object on the main form, not the subform Datasheet View window.

TIP

Because you can't customize the datasheet directly in the subform object on the main form, it can be hard to judge the overall width of the datasheet. The best way to compare the two views of the subform is to line up the Datasheet View window with the subform object visible behind it on the main form in Form Design view, but inevitably it will take several tries to get the layout right.

Editing a subreport is very similar to editing a subform. Try it now, to repair the shortcomings of the Projects and Expenses report:

1. Double-click the subreport object on the Projects and Expenses report to open the subreport in Design view.
2. Drag down the lower boundary of the report header section about $1/2$ inch.

3. Delete the text box that prints the current date using the Now function.
4. Select all the objects in the page header section (including the two lines) and drag them up into the report header section.
5. Narrow the Amount text box to about ¾ inch, and expand the Purpose text box to fill the space. Make sure the right border of the Purpose text box is superimposed on the left border of the Amount text box so you don't disrupt the "grid" effect in the ledger-style subreport.
6. Move the Amount and Date labels in the report header to line up with the right borders of the respective text boxes.
7. Delete the page number in the page footer section, and select Format ➤ Page Header/Footer to delete these sections.
8. Close and save the subreport.

RELOADING THE SUBFORM OR SUBREPORT

If you're editing a subform or subreport from the main document, two steps are required after you've completed your modifications before you can see the effects of your changes: save the subform or subreport, and then reload the new version into the main document by clicking the subform or subreport object and then pressing ↵.

Use this method to check the effects of the modification you made in the previous section:

9. Click again in the subreport object on the Projects and Expenses report, and press ↵ to reload the subreport.
10. Preview the report, and then close and save it.

NOTE

If you're not planning to use the main document right away, this step isn't necessary. The next time you open it from the Database window, Access reloads the most recent version of the subform or subreport.

SORTING AND GROUPING INSTRUCTIONS

Most of the Report Wizards give you a chance to specify the sort order for the records, and one, the Group/Totals Wizard, lets you define groups. To modify these instructions later or to add sorting instructions or groups to a report originally created without them, you use the sorting and grouping box, which is shown in Figure 12.24 with the sorting and grouping instructions for the Expenses by Project and Type report visible. You can use this tool to add sorting instructions, to add or remove groups from a

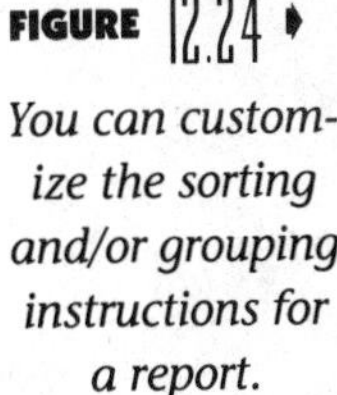

FIGURE 12.24

You can customize the sorting and/or grouping instructions for a report.

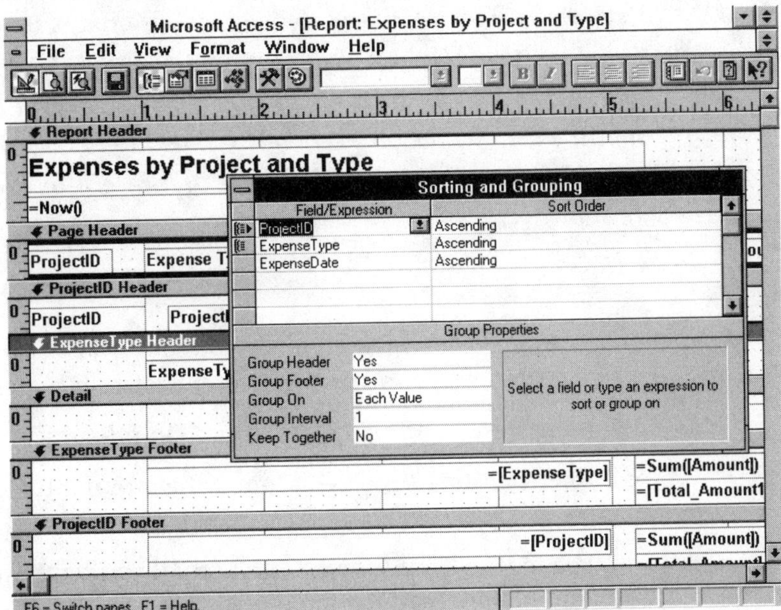

Group/Totals report, or to add groups to a report defined by the Single-Column or Tabular Report Wizard.

To display the sorting and grouping box or remove it from the screen if it is already visible, click the Sorting and Grouping button in the toolbar, choose View ➤ Sorting and Grouping, or right-click anywhere in the report background and choose Sorting and Grouping from the popup menu.

The sorting and grouping box is a lot like the Table Design view window. You enter your instructions in the upper portion of the window, and the properties of the currently selected row are displayed in the lower portion. You enter each sort field on a row in the upper portion of the window, from the largest groups (in the first row) to the smallest (in the last), and specify either ascending or descending order in the second column. Both the Field/Expression and Sort Order columns are combo boxes, so you can either type your entries or select them from the drop-down list.

TIP

A simple way to create the appearance of groups in a report if you don't need group summary statistics is to sort by a field (without defining a group based on the field) and set the Hide Duplicates property for the field to Yes, so that Access displays the field only in the first record in each "group."

To define record groups based on any sort field:

1. Enter **Yes** for the Group Header, Group Footer, or both properties.
2. Enter a grouping method in the Group On property.
3. For numeric or date/time fields, enter the group interval in the Interval property.
4. Enter **Yes** for the Keep Together property if you don't want Access to split any group across a page break.

NOTE

You have to sort on a field before you can define groups based on the field. That's the only way to guarantee that Access reads all the records in each group consecutively.

You'll recognize the choices for the Group On and Interval properties from your experience with the Group/Totals Wizard. For example, you could choose Month for the Group On property to group expenses by month or choose Interval for the Group On property and 500s for the Interval property to produce a report like the one shown in Figure 8.17, which groups records by $500 intervals in the Amount field.

NOTE

Entering grouping instructions creates the group header and/or footer sections on the report, but it does not automatically add summary statistics to the group footer or create an expression to describe the grouping method in the group header. For grouping methods other than Each Value, it's easier to use the Group/Totals Wizard and modify the resulting report than to write these expressions yourself.

WHAT'S NEXT

You've now had an introduction to all the basic database capabilities that Access offers, and you know enough to set up your own business or personal database and begin using it to do real work. Believe it or not, though, we've barely scratched the surface. Once you've had some practice with the basic methods described in this book, you'll have the tools you need to understand the more complex techniques presented in the Access manuals and more advanced books on Access. Take it slow, relax, and enjoy your work with Access.

INDEX

Page numbers in **boldface** denote definitions.

Symbols

A

B

C

D

E

G

H

I

J

K

L

M

N

O

P

Q

R

S

X

Y

Z

GET A FREE CATALOG JUST FOR EXPRESSING YOUR OPINION.

Help us improve our books and get a ***FREE*** full-color catalog in the bargain. Please complete this form, pull out this page and send it in today. The address is on the reverse side.

Name ____________________ Company ____________________

Address ____________________ City __________ State ____ Zip ________

Phone ( ) ____________________

1. How would you rate the overall quality of this book?

❑ Excellent
❑ Very Good
❑ Good
❑ Fair
❑ Below Average
❑ Poor

2. What were the things you liked most about the book? (Check all that apply)

❑ Pace
❑ Format
❑ Writing Style
❑ Examples
❑ Table of Contents
❑ Index
❑ Price
❑ Illustrations
❑ Type Style
❑ Cover
❑ Depth of Coverage
❑ Fast Track Notes

3. What were the things you liked *least* about the book? (Check all that apply)

❑ Pace
❑ Format
❑ Writing Style
❑ Examples
❑ Table of Contents
❑ Index
❑ Price
❑ Illustrations
❑ Type Style
❑ Cover
❑ Depth of Coverage
❑ Fast Track Notes

4. Where did you buy this book?

❑ Bookstore chain
❑ Small independent bookstore
❑ Computer store
❑ Wholesale club
❑ College bookstore
❑ Technical bookstore
❑ Other ____________

5. How did you decide to buy this particular book?

❑ Recommended by friend
❑ Recommended by store personnel
❑ Author's reputation
❑ Sybex's reputation
❑ Read book review in ________
❑ Other ____________

6. How did you pay for this book?

❑ Used own funds
❑ Reimbursed by company
❑ Received book as a gift

7. What is your level of experience with the subject covered in this book?

❑ Beginner
❑ Intermediate
❑ Advanced

8. How long have you been using a computer?

years ____________

months ____________

9. Where do you most often use your computer?

❑ Home
❑ Work
❑ Both
❑ Other ____________

10. What kind of computer equipment do you have? (Check all that apply)

❑ PC Compatible Desktop Computer
❑ PC Compatible Laptop Computer
❑ Apple/Mac Computer
❑ Apple/Mac Laptop Computer
❑ CD ROM
❑ Fax Modem
❑ Data Modem
❑ Scanner
❑ Sound Card
❑ Other ____________

11. What other kinds of software packages do you ordinarily use?

❑ Accounting
❑ Databases
❑ Networks
❑ Apple/Mac
❑ Desktop Publishing
❑ Spreadsheets
❑ CAD
❑ Games
❑ Word Processing
❑ Communications
❑ Money Management
❑ Other ____________

12. What operating systems do you ordinarily use?

❑ DOS
❑ OS/2
❑ Windows
❑ Apple/Mac
❑ Windows NT
❑ Other ____________

13. **On what computer-related subject(s) would you like to see more books?**

14. **Do you have any other comments about this book? (Please feel free to use a separate piece of paper if you need more room)**

PLEASE FOLD, SEAL, AND MAIL TO SYBEX

SYBEX INC.
Department M
2021 Challenger Drive
Alameda, CA
94501

Access Toolbar Buttons

New Database

Open Database

Attach Table

New Table

New Query

New Form

New Report

AutoForm

AutoReport

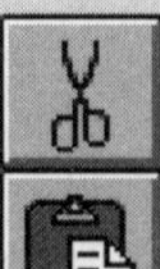

Cut

Copy

Paste

New

Find

Undo

Undo Current Field Record

F1 Help

Help

Cue Cards

Import

Export

Merge It (MS Word)

Analyze It with MS Excel

Print

Print Setup

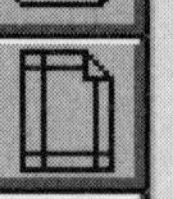

Print Preview

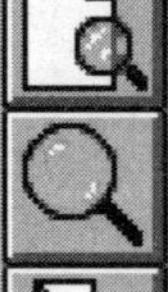

Zoom

Close Window

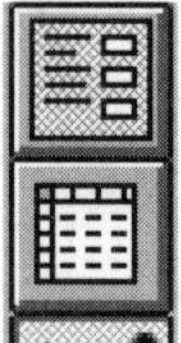

Form View

Datasheet View

Design View

Database Window

Relationships

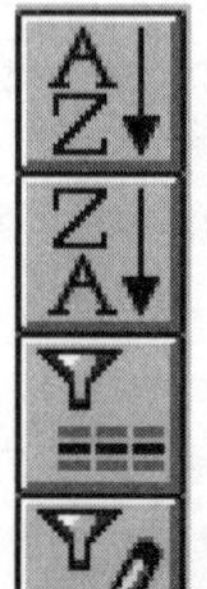

Sort Ascending

Sort Descending

Edit Filter/Sort

Apply Filter/Sort

Show All Records